CONTEMPORARY THOUGHT ON NINETEENTH CENTURY SOCIALISM

CONTEMPORARY THOUGHT ON NINETEENTH CENTURY SOCIALISM

General Editors
Peter Gurney and Kevin Morgan

Volume II
Socialism and Co-operation in Britain 1850–1918

Edited by
Peter Gurney

LONDON AND NEW YORK

First published 2021
by Routledge
2 Park Square, Milton Park, Abingdon, Oxon OX14 4RN

and by Routledge
52 Vanderbilt Avenue, New York, NY 10017

Routledge is an imprint of the Taylor & Francis Group, an informa business

© 2021 selection and editorial matter, Peter Gurney; individual owners retain copyright in their own material.

The right of Peter Gurney to be identified as the author of the editorial material, and of the authors for their individual chapters, has been asserted in accordance with sections 77 and 78 of the Copyright, Designs and Patents Act 1988.

All rights reserved. No part of this book may be reprinted or reproduced or utilised in any form or by any electronic, mechanical, or other means, now known or hereafter invented, including photocopying and recording, or in any information storage or retrieval system, without permission in writing from the publishers.

Trademark notice: Product or corporate names may be trademarks or registered trademarks, and are used only for identification and explanation without intent to infringe.

British Library Cataloguing-in-Publication Data
A catalogue record for this book is available from the British Library

Library of Congress Cataloging-in-Publication Data
A catalog record for this book has been requested

ISBN: 978-1-138-49019-2 (set)
eISBN: 978-1-351-03570-5 (set)
ISBN: 978-1-138-32100-7 (volume II)
eISBN: 978-0-429-45235-2 (volume II)

Typeset in Times New Roman
by Apex CoVantage, LLC

Publisher's Note
References within each chapter are as they appear in the original complete work

CONTENTS

Introduction: socialism and co-operation in Britain, 1850–1918   1
PETER GURNEY

PART 1
Redefining socialism   21

1   "Labour and the Poor", *Fraser's Magazine*, January 1850, 13–18.   23
    J.M. LUDLOW

2   *Report of the 2nd Co-operative Conference held at Manchester . . . 1853* (London: E. Lumley, 1853), 3–7.   28
    E.V. NEALE

3   *Life and Last days of Robert Owen, of New Lanark* (London: Holyoake & Co., 1859), 17–24.   33
    G.J. HOLYOAKE

4   "Industrial Co-operation", *Fortnightly Review*, January 1866, 479–488, 491–493, 497–499.   40
    FREDERIC HARRISON

5   "The Land! The Land!", *Co-operative News*, 5 October 1872, 505–506.   53
    WILLIAM PARE

6   "Co-operative Villages – Co-operation and Communism", *Co-operative News*, 12 February 1876; 19 February 1876, 81, 93.   58
    GEORGE DAWSON

CONTENTS

7 "Modern English Communism", *Co-operative News*, 25 August 1877, 448.   65
W.H.C.

8 "Advanced Co-operation, the Socialism of England", *English Socialism* (Manchester: Abel Heywood, 1879), 1–7.   71
HENRY TRAVIS

PART 2
Political economy   77

9 *The Economic Advantages of Co-operation Substantiated. A letter addressed to the Rev. Norman Macleod, D.D., proving the truth of the large profits from co-operative economy, as stated at the Glasgow meeting of the Association for the Promotion of Social Science* (Leeds: David Green, 1860), 12–18, 21–23, 25–26, 29–30.   79
JOHN HOLMES

10 "Land, Free Trade, and Reciprocity", *Co-operator*, 4 December 1869, 836–837.   85
JOHN PARKER

11 *The Logic of Co-operation* (Manchester: Co-op Printing Society, 1873), 6–11.   89
G.J. HOLYOAKE

12 "Suggestions for Carrying out the Proposals for the Education of Co-operators", *Co-operative News*, 4 November 1882, 743–744.   94
BEN JONES

13 *Inaugural address delivered at the twenty-first annual Co-operative Congress . . . 1889* (Manchester: Central Co-operative Board, 1889), 3–5, 7–13, 28–30.   99
ALFRED MARSHALL

14 *The Marriage of Labour and Capital* (London: The Labour Association, 1896), 1–3, 6–8.   106
HODGSON PRATT

CONTENTS

15 Resolution and Discussion on Trusts, *The 35th Annual Co-operative Congress, 1903* (Manchester: Co-op Union, 1903), 345–347.   111

PART 3
Class, democracy and the State   115

16 "Discussion at Halifax", *Notes to the People*, Vol. 2, 1852, 793–806, 823–829.   117
ERNEST JONES AND LLOYD JONES

17 *Co-operation v. Socialism: Being a Report of a Debate between Mr H. H. Champion and Mr Ben Jones* (Manchester: Central Co-op Board, 1887), 6–23.   148

18 *Trade Unionism, Co-operation, and Social Democracy* (London: Twentieth Century Press, 1892), 10–16.   158
HARRY QUELCH

19 *Co-operation is Reasonable Socialism* (Manchester: Co-op Union, 1894), 1–8.   165
W.T. CARTER

20 *The Co-operative Movement in Great Britain* (London: Swan Sonnenschein, 3rd edn, 1895), 224–241.   172
BEATRICE WEBB

21 "Trade Unionism and Co-operation", in Edward Carpenter (ed), *Forecasts of the Coming Century* (Manchester: Labour Press, 1897), 31–36, 40.   181
TOM MANN

22 *Co-operative News*, 29 April 1905, 493.   186
PHILIP SNOWDEN

23 "The Conflict of Capitalism and Democracy", *CWS Annual* (Manchester: CWS, 1910), 191–192, 196–198, 201–218.   189
PERCY REDFERN

24 *Justice*, 10 May 1913, 7.   208
JOHN MACLEAN

CONTENTS

PART 4
Utopianism and the religion of co-operation — 211

25 J.T.W. Mitchell's presidential address, *The 24th Annual Co-operative Congress, 1892* (Manchester: Co-op Union, 1892), 6–8. — 213
    J.T.W. MITCHELL

26 *Co-operative Production* (Oxford: Oxford University Press, 1894), 730–732, 809–815. — 222
    BEN JONES

27 *Co-operation as a Democratic Force: Being a Sermon Preached before the Delegates at the Co-operative Congress, Huddersfield on June 9th, 1895, in Fitzwilliam Street Unitarian Church* (London: The Labour Association, 1895), 1–7. — 229
    RAMSDEN BALMFORTH

28 "The 'Community Idea'", *Millgate Monthly*, November 1908, 87–91. — 236
    CATHERINE WEBB

29 *Co-operation for All* (Manchester: Co-op Union, 1914), 115–124. — 243
    PERCY REDFERN

PART 5
Gender and consumer organising — 251

30 "Vice President's Address", Miss Greenwood on women's position, *Report of the 17th Annual Congress of Delegates from Co-operative Societies . . . 1885* (Manchester: Co-op Union, 1885), 71–72. — 253

31 *The Marcroft Family and the Inner Circle of Human Life* (Rochdale: E. Wrigley & Sons Ltd., 1888), 50–52. — 256
    WILLIAM MARCROFT

32 *The Relations between Co-operation and Socialistic Aspirations* (Manchester: Co-op Union, 1890), 12–13. — 259
    MARGARET LLEWELYN DAVIES

CONTENTS

33 *The Women's Guild and Store Life* (London: 1892), 1–8.   266
    CATHERINE WEBB

34 *The Women's Co-operative Guild, 1883–1904*
    (Kirkby Lonsdale: WCG, 1904), 141–147, 161–163.   273
    MARGARET LLEWELYN DAVIES

35 "The Efforts of Women in the Co-operative Movement",
    Bolton Co-operative Record, January 1916, 8–9.   279
    SARAH REDDISH

PART 6
Internationalism, empire and war   283

36 *International Co-operation and the Constitution of the
    International Co-operative Alliance* (London: Co-op
    Printing Society, 1895), 1–8.   285
    EDWARD OWEN GREENING

37 *Wheatsheaf*, October 1902, 52–53.   291
    ÉDOUARD DE BOYVE

38 T.W. Allen's speech, *The 40th Annual Co-operative
    Congress, 1908* (Manchester: Co-op Union, 1908), 359–360.   295
    T.W. ALLEN

39 "Co-operation and Socialism", *Co-operative News*, 14
    January 1911, 46–47.   298
    HANS MÜLLER

40 "Mr W. Lander's Visit to West Africa", *Bolton
    Co-operative Record*, November 1914, 3–4.   302
    WILLIAM LANDER

41 W.J. Douse's presidential address, *The 47th Annual
    Co-operative Congress, 1915* (Manchester: Co-op Union,
    1915), 54–55.   306
    W.J. DOUSE

CONTENTS

PART 7
The sense of the past   309

42   "History of the Rochdale Pioneers", *Daily News*, 6 July 1857.   311
G.J. HOLYOAKE

43   *Our Story: The Co-operative Movement* (Manchester: Co-op Union, 1903), 7–28.   317
ISA NICHOLSON

44   "The Great Miners' Lock-out. £67,000 Withdrawn from the Society, 1893", in *The Coronation History of the Barnsley British Co-operative Society Limited. 1862–1902* (Manchester: Co-operative Wholesale Society, 1903), 93–99.   325

45   "Industrial Accrington: Historical Sketch of its Development", in *A History of Fifty Years of Progress of Accrington and Church Industrial Co-operative Society Ltd., 1860–1910* (Manchester: Co-op Newspaper Society, 1910), 194–205, 208.   329
JAMES HASLAM

46   *The Men who Fought for us in the "Hungry Forties": a Tale of Pioneers and Beginnings* (Manchester: Co-operative Newspaper Society, 1914), 58–74, 167–172   337
ALLEN CLARKE

47   "An Irish Utopia", in *Labour in Ireland. Labour in Irish History. The Re-conquest of Ireland* (Dublin: Maunsel & Co., 1917), 129–144.   349
JAMES CONNOLLY

Bibliography   357

INTRODUCTION
Socialism and co-operation in Britain, 1850–1918

Peter Gurney

Writing towards the end of the First World War, Charles Gide, the French economist and historian of economic thought, observed that

> The term co-operation, when it was first employed by Owen and his followers to describe a new social order, was synonymous with the term socialism, or rather (for in those days even socialism was very little known) with communism. It was the opposite of competition for followers of Owen in England just as it was for the followers of Fourier in France. Until the seventies of the last century the history of the co-operative movement and of the socialist movement were indistinguishable from one another.[1]

Gide went on to argue that the spread of Marxism had crowded out earlier forms of socialism and had encouraged the stark separation of co-operation from socialism. Like Gide, many co-operators in Britain during the late nineteenth and early twentieth centuries were well aware of these earlier affiliations and this led some of them to claim the language of socialism as their own. Interviewed in 1908, William Maxwell, ex-chairman of the Scottish Co-operative Wholesale Society and at the time President of the International Co-operative Alliance, explained how co-operation was in fact "a socialism by itself, without State interference", and concluded that "if there were to be a co-operative commonwealth, there certainly would be a vast improvement upon anything that the world had yet seen".[2] In his wider conception of co-operation it seems not unlikely that Maxwell had been influenced by his uncle, who had been an ardent Owenite.

Most existing studies of socialism pay little or no attention to the affiliations between socialism and co-operation, treating the earlier "utopian" socialism and the later nineteenth century Marxist, ethical and Fabian variants as discreet, often quite hermetically sealed phases and jumping over the development of the co-operative movement and co-operative thought entirely.[3] Those historians of popular politics who have touched on co-operation treat it mainly as a prop for liberalism, a legitimate albeit partial interpretation.[4] This volume takes a different tack, providing a bridge between these earlier and later phases, hopefully casting new light on both. The introduction which follows provides an interpretive context for the documents assembled in this reader. It considers some of the forces pulling co-operation and socialism apart as well as those pulling them closer together between the mid-nineteenth century and the end of the First World War. The relationship between co-operation and socialism comprised a complex web, for just as there were many varieties of socialism in this period, so too were there different forms of co-operation. Consequently, the ways in which these movements and their associated discourses intersected and diverged were neither straightforward nor static.

Putting aside such complexities for a moment, it is clear that Maxwell and many of his fellow co-operators believed that generalised co-operation – or a "co-operative commonwealth" – was entirely realisable, if not during the present generation then the one after perhaps. Such faith was not merely naïve but was suggested by the phenomenal success of co-operation over the preceding sixty years or so. Scores of retail co-operative ventures had been established by Owenites and Chartists between the 1820s and early 1840s but the vast majority of these collapsed and following George Jacob Holyoake's influential exercise in myth-making, most commentators have singled out the establishment in 1844 of the Rochdale Society of Equitable Pioneers as *the* foundational moment in the making of the modern movement.[5] Although G.D.H. Cole observed in his commemorative history how even the name of this society "had a very strong flavour of Owenite Socialism", the continuing importance of the earlier legacy was for a long time downplayed in subsequent historiography.[6] The dominant interpretation was that the so-called Rochdale model of co-operation, most particularly the introduction of the dividend on customers' purchases, inaugurated a shift from "community building to shopkeeping", to borrow Sidney Pollard's memorable but unfortunate phrase.[7] Workers were coming to accept the capitalist system as a kind of immovable horizon that necessarily limited popular consciousness and the co-operative store was emblematic of this shift, based as it was on the practice of working-class thrift so frequently lauded by middle-class commentators.[8] Historians now have a much more nuanced view of the co-operative movement and tend not to read it a priori as evidence of working-class "incorporation" into the capitalist system. Shopkeeping and the "divi" appealed to workers in Rochdale and elsewhere, certainly, though there was no immediate or final rejection of more transformative aspirations as many of the extracts in this volume testify.[9] One of the original objects of the Rochdale Pioneers was the establishment of "a self-supporting home colony of united interests", for instance, while Owenites in Leeds and elsewhere established "Redemption Societies" from the mid-1840s in an effort to keep the "community idea" alive.[10]

The take-off of consumer co-operation was synchronous in many localities with the fragmentation and formal dissolution of Owenism and Chartism. As these earlier initiatives were blocked, working people expended more energy on economic and social rather than political solutions to their problems and the results were quite remarkable, especially from the early 1860s onwards. By 1881, the number of distributive societies in Britain was approaching 1,000 with a total membership of well over half a million. By 1914, the number of societies had reached nearly 1,400 while membership stood at over three million. As one would expect, the heartlands of co-operation were the industrial regions of Lancashire and Yorkshire, the North-East of England and the central belt in Scotland; apart from a few exceptions such as Plymouth, co-operation made little headway in the South of England until the interwar period, with London being described as a "co-operative desert", inimical to co-operative growth owing to the structure of its labour market. Total war further convinced working people of the advantages of co-operation; while the number of societies fell slightly through amalgamation, membership had increased to more than four million by the time war ended. Established in 1863 and 1868, the English and Scottish Co-operative Wholesale Societies (CWS and SCWS) helped facilitate this expansion by supplying stores directly with myriad goods produced and processed in their own factories. These organisations were controlled by boards of directors elected from the stores and were amongst the largest businesses in the country by the turn of the century. By 1883, the CWS had annual net sales of over £4.5 million, rising to £35 million by 1914. Again, war gave a massive boost to wholesale co-operative trade, with net sales standing at well in excess of £89 million by 1919.[11] In this way, co-operators took advantage of potential economies of scale and opportunities for greater efficiency in distribution more quickly and more systematically than the majority of capitalist retailers, a fact that was not lost on observers at the time. Was it little wonder that socialists outside the movement pondered whether it might not be possible to harness co-operation to power more profound economic and social change, or that socialists inside the movement sought to steer co-operation in a more radical direction?

I

Although Gide dated the splintering of co-operation from socialism to the 1870s, the process can be traced back to mid-century in Britain, as the Chartist and Owenite movements began to disintegrate. It is a tangled story, though some key strands can be briefly unravelled. For a start, prominent leaders of late Chartism such as George Julian Harney came to identify more closely with "Social Democracy" and "socialism" in the wake of the failed European revolutions.[12] This led some, including Marx's English disciple Ernest Jones, to openly reject co-operation as merely a diversion from the political struggle that he believed was the only lasting means of securing working-class emancipation.[13] Another major Chartist figure who was dismissive of co-operation was Bronterre O'Brien. In the 1830s, he had attacked the "shopocracy" in the pages of the unstamped *Poor Man's Guardian* and had recommended "exclusive dealing" or political shopkeeping as a powerful weapon in the popular struggle for democracy.[14] With the defeat of Chartism O'Brien became disillusioned with such methods and from the late 1840s he looked increasingly to the state as the best means by which to usher in a socialist society, publishing a pamphlet entitled *State Socialism* in 1850 that detailed his plans for nationalised industries run by state-appointed managers rather than by workers directly. Although O'Brien had a loyal band of followers in London that remained faithful to his ideas after his death, such views did not find favour with the working-class majority.[15]

A most important element in this changed landscape was the emergence of Christian socialism. A group of talented clergymen and lawyers deeply concerned about the polarization of classes in the 1840s, notably Frederick Denison Maurice, Charles Kingsley, John Malcolm Ludlow and Edward Vansittart Neale, came together in the belief that the creation of a "Kingdom of God" on earth through a far-reaching Christianisation of economy and society had become an urgent necessity. Neale found the work of the French utopian socialist Charles Fourier more appealing than that of Robert Owen, because of the latter's atheism. This group became more active in the wake of the European revolutions, which reinforced the urgency of substituting social action or co-operation for individualism or competition. Profit-sharing workshops were singled out as the best means of effecting change and Christian socialists threw a great deal of energy (and Neale's money) into this cause, establishing an association of tailors in London and forming the "Society for Promoting Working Men's Associations" in 1850.[16] Christian socialists were not an homogeneous group; Maurice and Kingsley were conservatives with little faith in co-operative methods, while Neale and Ludlow came increasingly to regard co-operative stores as well as workshops as practical embodiments of their ideal.[17] Despite Marx and Engels' famous slight in the *Communist Manifesto* (1848) about Christian socialism being "but the holy water with which the priest consecrates the heart-burnings of the aristocrat", Ludlow and Neale in particular were widely revered among co-operators, most especially for the part they played in securing legal recognition for working-class associations through the Industrial and Provident Societies Acts of 1852 and 1862 – both men were trained in law.[18] Later Christian socialists such as Charles Stubbs, Bishop of Truro, continued to show a keen interest in co-operation. Stubbs wrote glowingly in the 1880s about the Owenite community at Ralahine, County Clare, regarding it as a solution to the land question, though he did misread the experiment as being primarily a profit-sharing initiative.[19] Whatever their faults, Christian socialists did not dismiss co-operation as "bastard Communism", unlike the Positivist barrister, Frederic Harrison, who regarded it as an illegitimate form precisely because of its emphasis on working-class independence and democratic control.[20]

Robert Owen and earlier utopian socialists were not simply forgotten by co-operators post-mid-century, but their legacy was reworked. Again, the role played by Holyoake, the ex-Owenite social missionary, was vital here. One vector of Owenism flowed into secularism, a budding movement that attracted a relatively small but enthusiastic network of supporters. Holyoake put himself at the head of this group, providing a focus with his long-running journal the *Reasoner*, which also covered co-operative developments.[21] After Owen's death in 1858, Holyoake attempted to appropriate his memory, presenting a sanitised rendering of Owen's thought at public meetings which he published in pamphlet form soon after.[22] This appropriation did not go uncontested. Old Owenites including William Pare and Dr Henry Travis, who acted as Owen's joint literary executors, communicated a rather different Owen through their writings, including articles in the pages of Henry Pitman's *Co-operator* in the 1860s, then later in the *Co-operative News*, the national periodical established by the movement in 1871.[23] Moreover, the legacy of utopian socialism was not only fought over and preserved at a theoretical level; some socialists embarked on renewed experiments in co-operative living long after Queenwood and the other community experiments had collapsed. It was hoped that workers as well as capitalists could take advantage of the possibilities opened up by the joint-stock form of ownership and build co-operative communities once more (or "little co-operative commonwealths" as Travis called them in 1879), but this time with funds from the stores rather than from wealthy benefactors.[24] While such ideas freely circulated within the movement, local societies proved reluctant to lend financial support and the notable example that occurred at Totley near Sheffield in 1877 when a group of workers set up a farm was financed by the social critic John Ruskin and came to grief in a relatively short time.[25]

II

The re-emergence of organised socialism in Britain in the early 1880s forced co-operators and socialists to debate their differences in public. There were major divisions between them which surfaced repeatedly over the following decades, making common understanding difficult before the First World War, prising the projects and the languages further apart. First, there was the issue of class. Although developed by working-class consumers in a period of acute conflict as a way of checking the anarchy of capitalist competition, the co-operative movement post-mid-century was closely entwined with middle-class liberal reformism. Bourgeois intellectuals such as the economists J.S. Mill, Sedley Taylor and Alfred Marshall, as well as a host of politicians and businessmen, sang the praises of co-operation in the second half of the nineteenth century. They were impressed, unsurprisingly, by the efficiency of co-operation and its ability to improve workers' lives, a lesson that co-operators were naturally keen to propagate themselves.[26] The Christian socialist connection noted already also helped to facilitate cross-class linkages. Holyoake cultured these connections and sought to speak across classes; indeed, it was precisely such opportunities for communication that made possible his successful career. He was not the only co-operator to avoid the language of class conflict whenever possible; like mainstream Owenism, co-operators hoped to effect change through persuasion and education, not revolution. Gladstone famously used the "Rochdale argument" in parliamentary debates over franchise reform in the 1860s, arguing that the thrifty habits of respectable "Rochdale man" demonstrated that he had earned the right to vote.[27] And there were many single issues which provided common ground for middle-class sympathisers and working-class co-operators. Free trade was one, though we need to be careful here because this vague term could mean different things to different people; co-operators were not doctrinaire free traders who regarded the douceur of capitalist commerce as the solution to working-class scarcity.[28] John Bright was a keen supporter early on, certainly. He appeared on co-operative platforms and his views did have some purchase – on Holyoake, for example.[29] Adherence to free trade however construed did not make co-operation any more appealing to socialists in the Social Democratic Federation (SDF) and the movement was routinely denounced for supporting the "Liberal Free Trade humbug" or "the Free Trade Fraud".[30] It would be wrong to think co-operators were totally uncritical of Bright though; his defence of adulteration as legitimate business practice was strongly condemned, as co-operative societies had from the beginning sought to provide workers with pure unadulterated food so often denied them by capitalist retailers, a cause which also garnered significant middle-class support between the 1840s and 1870s.[31]

The co-operative movement can be regarded, then, as a significant constituent part of the regime of liberal consumerism that characterised British economic and political relations in the second half of the nineteenth century.[32] During this phase, profit-sharing, or industrial co-partnership as it was sometimes called in an effort to make the idea more acceptable, provided a key focus for cross-class collaboration. Once more, this did little to build bridges between co-operators and socialists. From the 1860s onwards, capitalists keen to harmonise class antagonisms in individual enterprises and undermine trade unions backed profit-sharing initiatives, the establishment of which followed closely the tempo of industrial unrest. An early example in the mid-1860s was the Briggs Colliery in West Yorkshire, which was praised by Holyoake initially but later criticised when it became clear that this was a deliberate attempt to dissuade miners from participating in union activities.[33] Despite such examples, profit-sharing continued to attract support from other co-operative leaders besides Holyoake. The Christian socialists, particularly J.M. Ludlow and E.V. Neale, had espoused the "workshop idea" since 1848 as we have seen, and others took up this cause post-mid-century, including Lloyd Jones, the ex-Owenite convert to Christian socialism, and Edward Owen Greening, a radical liberal from a middle-class business background and an opponent of the new socialism.[34] Greening instigated the National Co-operative Festival held annually between 1888 and 1910 at the Crystal Palace at Sydenham, South London, which showcased goods produced in profit-sharing workshops, as well as helping to found a pressure group, the Labour Association for Promoting Co-operative Production, based on the Co-partnership of Workers, in 1884. Hodgson Pratt's address delivered at the National Co-operative Festival in 1896 demonstrates their belief in profit-sharing as a remedy for the "fatal war of classes" and the doctrine of state socialism.[35]

All this was hardly likely to endear co-operation to British socialists, with profit-sharing frequently described in the pages of *Justice*, the weekly organ of the

SDF, as just another "fraud".[36] Nevertheless, it would be misguided to dismiss all of those who were attracted to small-scale producer co-operatives under the banner of labour co-partnership as merely dupes of a designing bourgeoisie. Labour leader Tom Mann, for example, was a vice-president of the Labour Association and the SCWS continued to pay a bonus to its workers up until World War One.[37] We must also remember that the panacea of profit-sharing was never more than a minority cause within the co-operative movement and this became more so in the last two decades of the nineteenth century. Other voices, far more sympathetic to the "new" socialism, were frequently heard within the movement. Karl Marx's *Capital* was reviewed very favourably by the *Co-operative News*, the reviewer praising Marx for his "flashing wit and sardonic sneer" and for producing a work that "has elaborated, in a formal and scientific manner, a criticism of capitalist production, which treats it as a mere passing phase in [the] economic evolution". The main problem with the book according to the writer was that Marx was too impatient.[38] A less enthusiastic article on Thomas Kirkup's *An Inquiry into Socialism* not long afterwards concluded that the author's conception of socialism was very similar to the views expounded in the pages of the *News*, especially his emphasis on local democracy and the co-operative control of industry. Overall, Kirkup's work deserved praise because although he argued that "the present Co-operative system is only a partial realisation of the principles of Socialism, he would not sympathise for a moment with Socialistic attacks on Co-operation".[39]

III

An important turning point in the history of relations between co-operators and socialists was the decision by the CWS to abandon profit-sharing in its factories and workshops in the mid-1880s, a move that provoked a counter-attack from Neale and Holyoake and their allies which was only finally defeated in 1891.[40] After this domestic reversal, profit-sharers turned their attention to continental Europe where they played a formative role in the establishment of the International Co-operative Alliance (ICA) in 1895, which they hoped would act as a bulwark against international socialism.[41] Within Britain from this time onwards co-operation was quintessentially a consumer movement, regardless of the continued existence of a relatively small and declining number of productive enterprises outside the wholesales.[42] For sure, sloughing off the attempted tutelage of the liberal bourgeoisie made it easier to communicate with socialists in some respects, but explicitly prioritising the consumer created its own problems, as late nineteenth century socialists alternatively prioritised the producer. Interestingly, Holyoake had emphasised the potential of mobilising working-class consumers himself before siding with the profit-sharers, and co-operators were in the vanguard here, anticipating the revaluation of the consumer by the maverick economist William Stanley Jevons, whose ideas were not widely accepted by his professional peers, including by Alfred Marshall, who regarded co-operation as a middle way between capitalism and socialism.[43]

Co-operators like Ben Jones and J.T.W. Mitchell of the CWS argued for a political economy which started from the needs and well-being of all consumers rather than from the activity of workers as producers. This stress on the universality of consumption and the centrality of the sphere of distribution harks back once again to the Owenite legacy, though it generated friction with many socialists who based their critique of capitalism on different assumptions.[44] Not that Jones or Mitchell shied away from the language of class – they emphasised the importance of working-class self-activity and independence repeatedly in their speeches and writings – but for them the agency of the mass of consumers rather than labour and the class struggle was the real motor of history. Their analysis could lead to an occlusion of labour employed in co-operative enterprises and a lack of sympathy for the experience of workers *as* workers. Socialist critics pointed to strikes in factories owned by the CWS which occurred not infrequently as evidence of this insensitivity.[45] The problem was exacerbated when the CWS expanded its operations overseas in the early twentieth century, eventually buying up tea plantations in Ceylon and palm oil plantations in Sierra Leone, in order to cut out capitalist suppliers. Native labour employed on these plantations were portrayed by representatives of the CWS such as William Lander mainly as childlike, primitive people who would be civilised by co-operative development.[46] While socialists were quick to take the co-operative movement to task over the treatment of white workers employed in the metropole, they were generally silent on the conditions of black workers in the colonies, hardly surprising as many of them shared similar racist cultural assumptions.[47]

Organising around consumption depended for success on the commitment of female shoppers. While socialists occasionally tried shopkeeping themselves as a way of raising funds, they sought to mobilise men and women in their role as producers and had little to offer married women with children who played such a key role in maintaining the working-class domestic economy.[48] The co-operative movement spoke directly to the needs of such women, providing them with a means of improving their own lives as well as the lives of their families and communities. Here was a major difference between co-operation and socialism, clearly, but one that large numbers of working-class women found very positive. To better co-ordinate activity an autonomous organisation, the Women's Co-operative Guild, was established in 1883, though it faced determined opposition from chauvinistic men within the movement, which may have subsided over time though never completely disappeared.[49] Autobiographical accounts published later suggested how the class-consciousness of working-class women in this period had been formed within the sphere of consumption, a process that escaped Marxists' purview.[50] After a faltering start, the WCG grew to be the largest working-class women's organisation before World War One, with around 30,000 members of branches nationwide. Notwithstanding, women's real empowerment within the movement was heavily circumscribed; if the social space of the store was definitely female, men remained in overwhelming control of the management of local societies and no woman served as a director of the wholesales before the interwar period.[51] The Guild activist Sarah Reddish and others tried to remind co-operators of their Owenite feminist past, but the gulf between the two on questions of gender relations and the family was immense.[52]

The greatest obstacle to common understanding between socialists and co-operators before the First World War was undoubtedly their different conceptions of and attitudes towards the capitalist state. In his 1908 interview cited at the start, William Maxwell was careful to stress that the co-operative form of socialism required no "State interference" and a negative stance towards the state was common within the movement. According to the Russian anarchist Peter Kropotkin, who studied and was deeply impressed by co-operation in Britain, both leaders and "the great number of the rank-and-file" believed that their movement would lead "mankind to a higher harmonic stage of economical relations", without any aid from the state.[53] The key issue for co-operators here was independence, a concern that can also be traced back to the earlier phase. As the state was perceived to be overwhelmingly hostile towards working-class interests before mid-century, it was not surprising that radicals were convinced that they had to rely on their own efforts to bring about change. This commitment to voluntary activity did not imply a simple rejection of politics, then, but flowed instead from a deeply rooted belief in the importance of democratic control and popular agency. Robert Owen may have had "a vacant place in his mind where most men have political responses", but that was not the case for large numbers of men and women who took up his ideas and made them their own.[54] Owenism and Chartism overlapped in terms of individuals and concerns and most of the Rochdale Pioneers were themselves deeply involved in radical politics; their rule concerning political neutrality did not mean that they were apolitical but rather that they intended not to exclude radical groups that were vying for working-class support.[55] The voluntary principle continued to be vital into the late nineteenth century and beyond and led co-operators to be very distrustful of social reform imposed from above by the state.

Socialists of all kinds attacked co-operators on this score from the early 1880s, maintaining that the movement only helped the highest strata of workers leaving the poor untouched. Leaders of the SDF such as Henry Champion and Harry Quelch, but also Independent Labour Party (ILP) figures including Keir Hardie and Philip Snowden, frequently drew attention to this damaging limitation, which contained more than a grain of truth as it seems unlikely that the spectacular growth of the movement would have occurred without the increase in living standards experienced by more privileged groups of workers in the second half of the nineteenth century.[56] Nevertheless, co-operators like Ben Jones baulked at the idea of "paternal legislation", and so did the majority of the organised working class at this time.[57] The Fabian socialist Beatrice Webb served her apprenticeship researching the co-operative movement and accepted the views of Jones and Mitchell regarding the primacy of the consumer, but she parted company with them over the question of the state.[58] A younger generation of CWS ideologists proved more eager to find an accommodation, hence Percy Redfern's attempt to reconsider the relationship between democracy and what he termed "a sane and civilised Collectivism".[59] However, Tom Mann's emphasis on the need to build from the bottom up was more in harmony with the co-operative mainstream and he enjoyed reminding co-operators of their movement's utopian potential. The full development of their principles and practice, Mann remarked in a lecture to the Worcester Society in 1895, meant nothing less than the "ownership and control of the industries in the interests of every member of the community". "It was a little socialistic, certainly", he continued playfully, "but it was Co-operation".[60]

This belief in the superiority of voluntary action tended to push co-operators towards those "individualists" engaged in an increasingly heated battle of ideas with "collectivists" before World War One.[61] One of these was Archibald Primrose, Earl of Rosebery, a Gladstonian Liberal who succeeded Gladstone as Prime Minister and leader of the Liberal Party in 1894. Keen on bringing classes together and a supporter of working-class association, in 1890 the Co-operative Union honoured him with the presidency of the annual Congress at Glasgow. In his speech to Congress which received wide press coverage, Rosebery described the movement as "a State within a State", a phrase that was immediately picked up by co-operators and repeated *ad nauseum* thereafter. The description was flattering in some respects as it underlined the undeniable importance of co-operation in late Victorian Britain, but it was also deliberately confining. In his address, Rosebery cautioned that the movement's spectacular growth was not "leading them straight to the millennium" and he urged his listeners to guard against the intrusive actions of a bureaucratic state apparatus. An admission that "there was much in the socialistic movement which was good" raised a cheer from the audience, though they were soon reminded that the "objectionable" aspects of the experiments proposed by Fourier, St. Simon and Owen had thankfully been pulled down to "a reducible minimum", leaving it safe to "welcome all the rest".[62] Thus, the meaning of co-operation was continually redefined, interpreted as lending valuable support to liberalism by politicians like Lord Rosebery and as a bridge to the coming utopia by revolutionary socialists like Tom Mann. The former position probably enjoyed greater purchase within the movement before 1914, with most male co-operators identifying themselves as Liberals, though there were signs that this situation was changing.

IV

A number of developments were driving change. For one thing, leading co-operators spoke more often about the ultimate ambition of their movement in ways that made it difficult to distinguish easily between the co-operative and socialist project. At the Carlisle Congress in 1887 Mitchell declared; "Profit was made by the consumption of the people, and the consumers ought to have the profit . . . He advised co-operators never to be satisfied until they got control of the entire producing, banking, shipping, and every other interest in the country".[63] He repeated this message in his presidential address to the Rochdale Congress in 1892 and was similarly explicit when interviewed by the Royal Commission on Labour that year.[64] The seemingly inexorable rise of the wholesales convinced Mitchell and others that this was not merely an idle dream. William Openshaw of the London branch of the CWS stated in 1907 that co-operators' ultimate ambition was to become nothing less than "a practically self-supporting and self-employing community, co-extensive with the limits of the civilised world"; while the same year the vice-president of the CWS, Thomas Tweddell, explained to that august body the British Association that "when his movement succeeds in embracing the whole community then socialism will be triumphant".[65]

From the 1890s, the ultimate goal was frequently referred to as the "Co-operative Commonwealth". The precise origins of the concept remain unclear – the interwar historian of the movement, W.H. Brown, traced it back to a talk given to co-operators in London in 1866 by Dr J.J. Garth Wilkinson, the spiritualist homeopath – and we have already noted Henry Travis's usage of the plural in the late 1870s.[66] The popularity of the term was boosted by the publication of Laurence Gronlund's book, *The Co-operative Commonwealth* in 1886, though ironically the American Marxist envisaged no role for co-operatives in creating the socialists state of the future. During the next two decades the concept was employed routinely by co-operators. When everything was supplied through co-operative channels, the editor of the Burnley monthly paper stated in 1912, the movement's original ambition would be fulfilled, which was to establish "the ideals of the Co-operative Commonwealth in our midst".[67] Beyond the formal movement, experiments in communal living sprang up during the fin de siècle, such as the Bolton Co-operative Commonwealth Society set up by supporters of Gronlund and his follower Edward Bellamy (author of the utopian novel *Looking Backward*), which deeply fascinated Ben Jones and other co-operators.[68] The appeal of the term was due partly to the fact that it echoed the old Owenite language of "community", and because it signalled that there was more to co-operation than the "divi", that it had a spiritual side and could in fact constitute a kind of religion for its most zealous activists, as did socialism.[69] An elaborate culture constructed around the store instilled faith in the cause by means of ritual, social events and classes in "history from below".[70] And of course, late-nineteenth century British socialists frequently described their own ultimate ambition as the "Co-operative Commonwealth": the national and local labour press helped popularise the term; it figured as the promised land in Walter Crane's socialist cartoons for *Justice*; James Connolly and other Irish revolutionary socialists used it; and the concept figured in Robert Tressell's novel, *The Ragged-Trousered Philanthropists*.[71] The term could serve to conceal differences, admittedly, but it could also bring co-operators and socialists into closer dialogue with one another.

Besides such conceptual and linguistic shifts, the wider context of political change and industrial conflict altered relationships, generating new forces of attraction but also repulsion, which varied according to time and space. In the West Riding of Yorkshire, co-operation was stronger than trade unionism and it helped facilitate the emergence of independent labour politics there. The first ILP county councillor in the Colne Valley was George Garside, a prominent co-operator, elected at Slaithwaite in 1892.[72] The extent and intractability of working-class poverty was being rediscovered at this time by the social investigations of Charles Booth among others, generating widespread political debate and fuelling demands for old age pensions and other forms of state intervention. Socialist parties were in the vanguard here, prioritising the problems of unemployment and poverty over worker autonomy, for instance, and forcing liberalism to reinvent itself to meet the collectivist challenge.[73] Co-operators for their part were often divided over the appropriate stance to adopt, because of their hostility towards the state and because they feared that aid from above would undermine those habits of working-class thrift on which their success depended. Under the leadership of the Christian socialist, Margaret Llewelyn Davies, the WCG tried "settlement" work in poor neighbourhoods in Sunderland and elsewhere as a practical solution around the turn of the century, but the experiment smacked of "slumming" and it soon became apparent that the problem of poverty would not be solved without state intervention.[74] The movement eventually declared in favour of old age pensions at its annual Congress in 1901.[75]

The experience of workplace conflict was another vital factor encouraging co-operators and socialists to forge better understanding. From the beginning, local co-operative societies had often helped members survive periods of industrial unrest and their involvement became more pronounced towards the end of the century and on up to the outbreak of war. Like the Owenites, co-operators tended to decry class conflict, regarding their own essentially peaceful mode of social and economic transformation as preferable to the confrontational tactics favoured by some trade unionists, another reason why they were commonly praised by their social superiors. Nevertheless, they were ineluctably drawn into taking sides more openly as industrial relations deteriorated. An example of this occurred in Yorkshire in 1893 when a major lockout in the coal industry generated serious violence – including the fatal shooting by troops of two striking miners. Writing a decade later in the jubilee history of the Barnsley Society, the anonymous author provided a detailed account of the strike, though admitted that some members would no doubt be displeased.[76] Over time co-operators become far less concerned about causing offence to die-hard liberals within their ranks and the movement lent a great deal of support during the general labour unrest that shook Britain between 1910 and 1914. A study published by the WCG in 1912 documented in detail the way in which many local societies had managed to keep prices down and had provided various forms of relief, the secretary of the Walsall Society proudly claiming that "so far as we are aware, not one of our members went short of food during the strike". The CWS played a crucial role, extending credit to societies to enable them to pay "divi" and loaning the Northumberland Miners' Union money for strike pay when other bankers had refused. According to the report's author, these events had demonstrated vividly how important it was for workers to build up "financial reserves similar to those possessed by the capitalists" and for co-operators to eventually take over the nation's industry.[77] CWS involvement in the working-class struggle did not abate; in 1913 the organisation sent numerous relief ships to aid strikers and their families during the Dublin lockout.[78]

While the impact of labour unrest on individual societies could be serious, particularly in areas more dependent on single industries, transformations in the economic structure of capitalism were perceived as posing a more general threat from the late nineteenth century onwards. Co-operators became increasingly anxious about the rise of monopolies and the spread of trusts, cartels and syndicates (the terms were often used vaguely and interchangeably), was a subject frequently discussed at local meetings and in the co-operative press. The writings of radical liberal journalists and economists such as J.A. Hobson and D.H. Macgregor were widely known and it was feared that trusts might shut out the movement more effectively from particular markets and sources of supply. Co-operators had been bedevilled by boycotts organised by private traders from the outset and the wholesales were partly a response to such attacks. Capitalist amalgamations, it was understandably feared, would greatly magnify the scale of this challenge in the future. Most leading socialists did not share such misgivings, instead regarding capitalist monopoly as a sort of midwife for state socialism, so there was no simple coming together over this issue.[79] The effect on relations tended to be positive, however, as co-operators gradually reassessed their attitude towards political action. The rise of trusts led many within the movement to question the division between political and economic domains that was central to liberal consumerism and it raised serious doubts about the neutrality of the capitalist state. The decision by Congress in 1901 to back the call for railway nationalisation following the movement's victimisation by private owners was symptomatic of this shift, as was the resolution against capitalists trusts passed at the Congress held two years later.[80] In the 1908 interview, Maxwell emphasised that political representation was now a necessity because "the fight with the shopkeeper is past, and the fight with the capitalist, the syndicate, and the huge company is yet to come".[81]

V

The pressure to engage more directly in the formal political field mounted in the years immediately preceding war and evidence suggests that the rapprochement between socialists and co-operators quickened during this period. Bourgeois observers may have indignantly brushed aside Philip Snowden's remark in 1907 that "Socialism and Co-operation are twin brothers", but more people were coming to this view.[82] Some leading socialists shared co-operators' anxieties about the rise of trusts, including the Scottish revolutionary John Maclean who observed in 1912 that "distribution is a field where the class war is beginning to break out with a virulence equal to that experienced in the economic and the political fields".[83] Urging co-operators to take sides openly in this war a year later, Maclean noted how the ILP was greatly increasing its power within local co-operative societies, though he no doubt overestimated the pace of change as his perspective was coloured by his experience of the co-operative movement in Scotland, where societies were often more overtly left-wing.[84] Notwithstanding important regional variation, there was much to recommend the idea that economics and politics were collapsing together in the early twentieth century. Joseph Chamberlain's campaign for tariff reform after 1903 demonstrated such a collapse and so did government repression of trade unions during the so-called great labour unrest.[85] Most important, the drive to war that pervaded civil society and the state helped fuel an atmosphere of impending crisis that demanded a novel response. Internationally, co-operators looked to the ICA, which was no longer dominated by profit-sharers but was led instead by Dr Hans Müller who tried to bring socialists and co-operators into closer harmony by arguing for a synthesis of Marxism and what he termed "Nealeism".[86] Unsurprisingly, national barriers proved difficult to overcome. Ritualistic displays of internationalism were a marked feature of co-operative culture as they were of socialist culture before the First World War, certainly, though continental observers remarked on how patriotic British co-operators were, a fact that became only too obvious after war was declared.[87]

As the conflict dragged on and consumption issues became more explicitly politicised, the co-operative movement – seriously mistreated by the state during the war – shifted decidedly to the left. It established a Co-operative Party in 1917 and popularised an anti-profiteering discourse that made it easier than it had ever been to make common cause with socialists.[88] For a brief period it looked as if the interests of workers as consumers as well as producers might be brought together in a broad coalition against capitalist profiteers and monopolists grown fat on the suffering of the majority. In October 1917, 1,000 delegates from 500 co-operative societies attended an emergency conference at Central Hall, Westminster, at which speakers denounced the government for subjecting the movement to unjust forms of taxation and excluding co-operators from wartime committees: the only remedy was direct political representation. Significantly, the general secretary of the Labour Party, Arthur Henderson, addressed the conference and sought to placate fears that Labour wanted the upper hand in any future alliance. Admittedly no firebrand, Henderson went much further: "He would be prepared, if need be, that the Labour Party as now known should cease to exist, if by so doing they could combine the whole of the democracy in a great people's party."[89] Despite such conciliatory signs, those who hoped for the reunification of socialism and co-operation were to be disappointed, as relations between the movements and concepts remained fraught throughout the interwar years and beyond. Co-operation continued to play a key role in working-class life nevertheless, inflecting the culture of labour socialism in ways that historians have yet to fully recover.[90]

Notes

1 Charles Gide, 1917. *Les Sociétés Coopératives de consummation* (3rd edition). Quotation here is from the English translation, *Consumers' Co-operative Societies*, 1921. Manchester: Co-operative Union, 220. A classic discussion of this conceptual splitting is A.E. Bestor, 1948. "The Evolution of the Socialist Vocabulary". *Journal of the History of Ideas* 9 (3): 259–302.

2 *Millgate Monthly*, March 1908, 334.
3 See, *inter alia*, Max Beer, 1929. *A History of British Socialism*. London: G. Bell & Sons; Keith Laybourn, 1997. *The Rise of Socialism in Britain*. Stroud: Sutton; Mark Bevir, 2011. *The Making of British Socialism*. Princeton: Princeton University Press; Noel Thompson, 2015. *Social Opulence and Private Restraint: The Consumer in British Socialist Thought Since 1800*. Oxford: Oxford University Press.
4 Eugenio Biagini, 1992. *Liberty, Retrenchment and Reform: Popular Liberalism in the Age of Gladstone, 1860–1880*.Cambridge: Cambridge University Press; Marcella Sutcliffe, 2014. *Victorian Radicals and Italian Democrats*. London: Boydell Press.
5 See Part 7, Chapter 42.
6 G.D.H. Cole, 1945. *A Century of Co-operation*. Manchester: Co-operative Union, 77.
7 Sidney Pollard, 1960. "Nineteenth-Century Co-operation: From Community Building to Shopkeeping". In *Essays in Labour History*, edited by Asa Briggs and John Saville. London: Macmillan.
8 E.J. Hobsbawm, 1964. *Labouring Men: Studies in the History of Labour*. London: Weidenfeld and Nicolson.
9 For a critical assessment of the historiography, see my monograph *Co-operative Culture and the Politics of Consumption in England, 1870–1930*. Manchester: Manchester University Press, 1996, chapter 1.
10 G.J. Holyoake, 1882. *Self-Help by the People*. London: Trübner & Co., 9th ed., 11; Benjamin Jones, 1894. *Co-operative Production*. Oxford: Oxford University Press, 102.
11 Cole, *A Century of Co-operation*, 371–372; Percy Redfern, 1938. *The New History of the C.W.S.* London: J.M. Dent & Sons, 532–533; Martin Purvis, 1998. "Stocking the Store: Co-operative Retailers in North-East England and Systems of Wholesale Supply, c. 1860–77". *Business History* 44 (4): 55–78; John Wilson, Anthony Webster and Rachel Vorberg-Rugh, 2013. *Building Co-operation. A Business History of the Co-operative Group, 1863–2013*. Oxford: Oxford University Press; D.C.H. Watts, 2017. "Building an Alternative Economic Network? Consumer Cooperation in Scotland from the 1870s to the 1960s". *Economic History Review* 70 (1): 143–170.
12 See my article, 2014. "The Democratic Idiom: Languages of Democracy in the Chartist Movement". *Journal of Modern History*, 86 (3): 591–592.
13 See Part 3, Chapter 16; Miles Taylor, 2003. *Ernest Jones, Chartism, and the Romance of Politics, 1819–1869*. Oxford: Oxford University Press.
14 See my monograph, 2015. *Wanting and Having: Popular Politics and Liberal Consumerism in England, 1830–70*. Manchester: Manchester University Press, 149–150, 159, 161.
15 Alfred Plummer, 1971. *Bronterre. A Political Biography of Bronterre O'Brien 1804–1864*. London: George Allen & Unwin, 201; Stan Shipley, 1972. *Club Life and Socialism in mid-Victorian London*. Oxford: Ruskin College.
16 Charles Raven, 1920. *Christian Socialism, 1848–1854*. London: Macmillan; Torben Christensen, 1962. *Origin and History of Christian Socialism, 1848–54*. Aarhus: Brill; N.C. Masterman, 1963. *J.M. Ludlow: the Builder of Christian Socialism*. Cambridge: Cambridge University Press; Philip N. Backstrom, 1974. *Christian Socialism and Co-operation in Victorian England*. London: Croom Helm; Edward Norman, 1987. *The Victorian Christian Socialists*. Cambridge: Cambridge University Press. For the movement's later history see Peter d'Alroy Jones, 1968. *The Christian Socialist Revival, 1877–1914. Religion, Class, and Social Conscience in Late-Victorian England*. Princeton: Princeton University Press.
17 See Part 1, Chapters 1 and 2.
18 John Saville, 1954. "The Christian Socialists of 1848". In *Democracy and the Labour Movement*, edited by John Saville. London: Lawrence & Wishart.
19 Charles William Stubbs, 1884. *The Land and the Labourers*. London: Swan Sonnenschein, chapters 6 and 7; Malcolm Chase, 2018. "'True Democratic Sympathy':

INTRODUCTION

Charles Stubbs, Christian Socialism, and English Labour, 1863–1912". *Labour History Review* 83 (1): 17.

20 See Part 1, Chapter 4.
21 For this movement see the two volumes by Edward Royle: 1974. *Victorian Infidels: The Origins of the British Secularist Movement, 1791–1866*. Manchester: Manchester University Press; 1980. *Radicals, Secularists and Republicans. Popular Freethought in Britain, 1866–1915*. Manchester: Manchester University Press.
22 See Part 1, Chapter 3.
23 See Part 1, Chapter 5.
24 Donna Loftus, 2002. "Capital and Community: Limited Liability and Attempts to Democratize the Market in mid-Nineteenth Century England". *Victorian Studies* 45 (1): 93–120; Part 1, Chapter 8.
25 See Part 1, Chapters 6 and 7.
26 See Part 2, Chapter 9.
27 Michael E. Rose, 1977. "Rochdale Man and the Stalybridge Riot. The Relief and Control of the Unemployed during the Lancashire Cotton Famine". In *Social Control in Nineteenth Century Britain*, edited by A.P. Donajgrodzki. London: Croom Helm.
28 See Part 2, Chapter 10; Part 5, Chapter 34.
29 G.J. Holyoake, 1885. *Robbing a Thousand Peters to Pay One Paul*. London: Cassell & Co.
30 *Justice*, 14 November 1885, 4; 10 October 1891, 1; 7 March 1896, 5; 13 March 1909, 2. Socialist criticisms of free trade are discussed in Frank Trentmann, 1997. "Wealth versus Welfare: The British Left between Free Trade and National Political Economy before the First World War". *Historical Research* 171: 70–98. Trentmann conveniently downplayed his earlier findings in: F. Trentmann, 2008. *Free Trade Nation. Commerce, Consumption, and Civil Society in Modern Britain*. Oxford: Oxford University Press.
31 John Burnett, 1989. *Plenty and Want. A Social History of Diet in England from 1815 to the Present Day*. London: Routledge.
32 See *Wanting and Having: Popular Politics and Liberal Consumerism*, for a full discussion.
33 R.A. Church, 1971. "Profit-Sharing and Labour Relations in England in the Nineteenth Century". *International Review of Social History* 16 (1): 2–16.
34 See my article, 1994. "The Middle Class Embrace: Language, Representation and the Contest over Co-operative Forms in Britain, 1860–1914". *Victorian Studies* 37 (2): 253–286.
35 See Part 2, Chapter 14; Gurney, *Co-operative Culture*, 67–69.
36 *Justice*, 11 January 1890, 1; 10 May 1890, 1; 15 September 1906, 1.
37 See Part 3, Chapter 21; James Kinloch and John Butt, 1981. *History of the Scottish Co-operative Wholesale Society Limited*. Glasgow: Co-operative Wholesale Society, 153–161.
38 *Co-operative News*, 9 April 1887, 349. Marx was himself initially sceptical of co-operative forms but expressed a more sympathetic attitude in *The Civil War in France* (1871), following the experience of the Paris Commune.
39 *Co-operative News*, 28 January 1888, 85.
40 For the debate see Percy Redfern, 1913. *The Story of the C.W.S. Being the Jubilee History of the Co-operative Wholesale Society Limited, 1863–1913*. Manchester: Co-operative Wholesale Society, 182–187.
41 See Part 6, Chapter 36; Rita Rhodes, 1995. *The International Co-operative Alliance During War and Peace, 1910–1950*. Geneva: International Co-operative Alliance; Mary Hilson, 2018. *The International Co-operative Alliance and the Consumer Co-operative Movement in Northern Europe, c. 1860–1939*. Manchester: Manchester University Press.

42 For a positive reassessment of these ventures see Steven Toms, 2012. "Producer Co-operatives and Economic Efficiency: Evidence from the Nineteenth-Century Textile Industry". *Business History* 54 (6): 883–904.
43 See Part 2, Chapter 11; Part 2, Chapter 13; Sandra Peart, 1996. *The Economics of W. S. Jevons*. London: Routledge.
44 See Part 2, Chapter 12; Noel Thompson, 1984. *The People's Science: The Popular Political Economy of Exploitation and Crisis, 1816–34*. Cambridge: Cambridge University Press.
45 Redfern, *The Story of the C.W.S.*, 172–173, 234–235, 263–266, 281–282; *Justice*, 8 September 1888, 3; 26 April 1913, 2; 10 May 1913, 6–7.
46 See Part 6, Chapter 40; Rita Rhodes, 2012. *Empire and Co-operation: How the British Empire used Co-operatives in its Development Strategies, 1900–1970*. Edinburgh: John Donald; Tony Webster, 2019. *Co-operation and Globalisation. The British Co-operative Wholesales, the Co-operative Group and the World since 1863*. London: Routledge; Nikolay Kamenov, 2019. "Imperial Cooperative Experiments and Global Market Capitalism, c.1900–c.1960". *Journal of Global History* 14 (2): 219–237.
47 See Stephen Howe, 1993. *Anticolonialism in British Politics: The Left and the End of Empire, 1918–1964*. Oxford: Clarendon; Paul Ward, 1998. *Red Flag and Union Jack: Englishness, Patriotism and the British Left, 1881–1924*. Woodbridge: Royal Historical Society; John Callaghan, 2007. *The Labour Party and Foreign Policy: A History*. Abingdon: Routledge.
48 *Co-operative Culture*, 175–176; Henry Pelling, 1965. *The Origins of the Labour Party, 1880–1900*. Oxford: Clarendon Press, 156; Karen Hunt, 2000. "Negotiating the Boundaries of the Domestic: British Socialist Women and the Politics of Consumption". *Women's History Review* 9 (2): 389–410.
49 See Part 5, Chapters 30, 31 and 34.
50 See especially, 1931. "Memories of Seventy Years, by Mrs Layton". In *Life As We Have Known It by Co-operative Working Women*, edited by Margaret Llewelyn Davies. London: Leonard and Virginia Woolf; Peter Gurney, 2017. *The Making of Co-operative Culture in England*. London: Bloomsbury Academic, 109–110.
51 See Part 5, Chapter 34, and my article, 2020. "Redefining 'the woman with the basket': The Women's Co-operative Guild and the Politics of Consumption in Britain during World War Two". *Gender & History* 32 (1): 189–207.
52 See Part 5, Chapter 35; Part 4, Chapter 28.
53 Peter Kropotkin, 1910. *Mutual Aid; A Factor of Evolution*. London: William Heinemann, 271–272.
54 E.P. Thompson, 1963. *The Making of the English Working Class*. London: Victor Gollancz, 783.
55 Cole, *A Century of Co-operation*, 72–73; Edward Royle, 2000. "Chartists and Owenites: Many Parts but One Body". *Labour History Review* 65 (1): 2–21; Tom Scriven, 2017. *Popular Virtue. Continuity and change in Radical Moral Politics, 1820–70*. Manchester: Manchester University Press; Part 7, Chapter 46.
56 See Part 3, Chapters 17, 18, 19, and 22; Cole, *A Century of Co-operation*, 71.
57 Pat Thane, 1984. "The Working Class and State 'Welfare' in Britain, 1880–1914". *Historical Journal* 27 (4): 877–900. Marc Brodie however argues that the poor themselves were often more receptive to statist reform in, 2014."'You Could Not Get Any Person to be Trusted Except the State': Poorer Workers' Loss of Faith in Voluntarism in Late 19th Century Britain". *Journal of Social History* 47 (4): 1071–1095.
58 See Part 3, Chapter 20.
59 See Part 3, Chapter 23.
60 *The Co-operative Record of the Birmingham District*, April 1895, 15.
61 Stefan Collini, 1979. *Liberalism and Sociology: L. T. Hobhouse and Political Argument in England, 1880–1914*. Cambridge: Cambridge University Press.

62 *Newcastle Daily Chronicle*, 27 May 1890, 5; *Twenty-Second Annual Co-operative Congress, 1890.* Manchester: Co-operative Union, 7.
63 *Nineteenth Annual Co-operative Congress, 1887.* Manchester: Co-operative Union, 7.
64 See Part 4, Chapters 25 and 26.
65 *Labour Co-partnership*, September 1907, 137; *Co-operative News*, 17 August 1907, 1002.
66 W.H. Brown, 1937. *The Co-operative Manager: Being the Silver Jubilee History, 1912–1937, of the National Co-operative Manager's Association.* Manchester, 60.
67 *Burney Co-operative Record*, August 1912, 5–6.
68 See Part 4, Chapter 26.
69 See Part 4, Chapters 27, 28 and 29. The classic discussion of this phase of socialist culture remains Stephen Yeo, 1977. "A New Life: The Religion of Socialism in Britain, 1883–1896". *History Workshop Journal* 4 (1): 5–56. See also Kevin Manton, 2003. "The Fellowship of the New Life: English Ethical Socialism Reconsidered". *History of Political Thought* 24 (2): 282–304.
70 See *Co-operative Culture*, chapters 2–5; Part 7, Chapters 44 and 45.
71 See Part 7, Chapter 47.
72 E.P. Thompson, 1994. "Homage to Tom Maguire". In *Persons and Polemics*. London: Merlin Press, 26.
73 José Harris, 1972. *Unemployment and Politics: A Study in English Social Policy, 1886-1914.* Oxford: Clarendon Press; Bill Lancaster, 1987. *Radicalism, Co-operation, and Socialism: Leicester Working-Class Politics, 1860–1906.* Leicester: Leicester University Press; Rosemary O'Day and David Englander, 1993. *Mr Charles Booth's Inquiry: Life and Labour of the People in London Reconsidered.* London: Hambledon Press; Eileen Janes Yeo, 1996. *The Contest for Social Science: Relations and Representations of Gender and Class.* London: Rivers Oram Press.
74 Seth Koven, 2004. *Slumming: Sexual and Social Politics in Victorian London.* Princeton: Princeton University Press; Part 5, Chapter 32.
75 *Co-operative Culture*, 185.
76 See Part 7, Chapter 44; Quentin Outram, 2018. "The Featherstone Massacre and Its Forgotten Martyrs". In *Secular Martyrdom in Britain and Ireland*, edited by Quentin Outram and Keith Laybourn. Cham, Switzerland: Palgrave Macmillan.
77 F.M. Eddie, 1912. *Co-operation and Labour Uprisings.* Hull: Women's Co-operative Guild, 3, 6, 10–11.
78 Keith Harding, 1988. "'The Co-operative Commonwealth': Ireland, Larkin, and the *Daily Herald*". In *New Views of Co-operation*, edited by Stephen Yeo. London: Routledge; Patrick Doyle, 2019. *Civilising Rural Ireland. The Co-operative Movement, Development and the Nation-State, 1889–1939.* Manchester: Manchester University Press, 133–134.
79 *Co-operative Culture*, 202–204.
80 Ibid, 83; Part 2, Chapter 15.
81 *Millgate Monthly*, March 1908, 335.
82 *Punch, or the London Charivari*, 13 November 1907, 348.
83 "Co-operation and Trusts". *The British Socialist*, 4 April 1912, 156–162.
84 See Part 3, Chapter 24; Pelling, *The Origins of the Labour Party*, 203–204.
85 Ross McKibbin, 1984. "Why was there no Marxism in Great Britain". *English Historical Review* 99 (391): 297–331.
86 See Part 6, Chapters 38 and 39.
87 See Part 6, Chapters 37 and 41.
88 *Co-operative Culture*, 208–216; Mary Hilson, 2002. "Consumers and Politics: The Co-operative Movement in Plymouth, 1890–1920". *Labour History Review* 67 (1): 7–27; Karen Hunt, 2010. "The Politics of Food and Women's Neighbourhood Activism in First World War Britain". *International Labor and Working-Class History* 77 (1): 8–26.

89 *Justice*, 25 October 1917, 2; *Labour Leader*, 25 October 1917, 4; G.D.H. Cole, 1948. *History of the Labour Party from 1914*. London: Routledge & Kegan Paul, 53.
90 See Daniel Weinbren, 1997. *Generating Socialism: Recollections of Life in the Labour Party*. Stroud: Sutton Publishing; Nicole Robertson, 2010. *The Co-operative Movement and Communities in Britain, 1914–1960. Minding Their Own Business*. Farnham: Ashgate; Emily Mason, 2017. "'The Co-operative Commonwealth Is the Only Answer to the Fascist Empire': Support for Republican Spain Within the British Co-operative Movement, 1936–1939". *Labour History Review* 82 (3): 189–213; and my articles, 2005. "The Battle of the Consumer in Postwar Britain". *Journal of Modern History* 77 (4): 956–987; 2015. "'The Curse of the Co-ops': Co-operation, the Mass Press and the Market in Interwar Britain". *English Historical Review* 130 (547): 1479–1512; 2019. "'Co-operation and Communism Cannot Work Side by Side': Organised Consumers and the early Cold War in Britain". *Twentieth Century British History* 30 (3): 347–374.

Part 1

REDEFINING SOCIALISM

1

"LABOUR AND THE POOR", *FRASER'S MAGAZINE*, JANUARY 1850, 13–18.

J.M. Ludlow

[John Malcolm Ludlow (1821–1911), was a barrister and one of the main founders of the Christian Socialist movement. After witnessing the 1848 revolution in Paris he became convinced that "social factories" ("ateliers") that the French Socialist Louis Blanc had urged the Provisional Government to establish were the best means of harmonising relations between capital and labour. The Industrial and Provident Societies Act of 1852 that afforded co-operative societies some measure of legal protection was drafted mainly by Ludlow. [N. C. Masterman, *J.M. Ludlow: the builder of Christian Socialism* (Cambridge: Cambridge University Press, 1963); A.D. Murray ed., *John Ludlow. The autobiography of a Christian Socialist* (London: Cass, 1981)] Ludlow's essay, which he signed J.T. and from which the following extract is taken, discusses the detailed social investigations by Henry Mayhew and others which had appeared in the *Morning Chronicle*. Note the editor adds a disclaimer to the effect that he does not agree with all of the writer's opinions. Ludlow here provides vivid illumination of the "Condition of England question". Reports from rural districts demonstrate how people are living "not like men but beasts", though reports from manufacturing districts are more positive; Ludlow praises paternalistic factory masters in particular for humanising conditions. Despite this, evidence demonstrates constant capitalist pressure on workers' wages, "until the profits swallow up the wages, and vice or crime makes up the maintenance of the defrauded workman". Ludlow summarises conditions and rates of pay in the slop tailoring trade in particular to demonstrate this relentless downward trend which forces many into prostitution to make ends meet. Cut-throat competition is the root cause of the problems faced by the poor and different remedies proposed such as charity, emigration of labour and economic protectionism are discussed, Ludlow noting that advocates of the latter cause include "all the worst elements of selfishness and mammon-worship". The extract outlines Ludlow's Christian Socialist solution, which includes various practical measures such as co-operative workshops but also prioritises social over political reform, requiring a complete change of heart by all classes of society.]

And where is the remedy? It lies not in any system or theory, not in any party cry or economical machinery, but in a thorough change of spirit. 'Make me a clean heart, O God, and renew a right spirit within me!' must be the cry of this whole nation. We must feel that we are members of one society, having common profit and common loss; members of one Church, many members under One Head; members, to use that most wonderful saying of the apostle, members 'one of another.' We must learn to feel that all property, all talent, all strength, all learning, all labour, is but a trust for the benefit of all; ay, learn that of all of these gifts of God, and not of one of them only, does that startling axiom of Proudhon—'Property is a theft!'—become very truth, when each is enjoyed for self alone, without sense of duty to God or to our neighbour. When once we feel this, we shall cease to put our trust in any single panacea, we shall use every means in our power to extirpate the evil, from our hearts first, and then from our lives. But we shall see, indeed, with sorrow, that this universal civil war cannot cease at once; that competition must be attacked with its own weapons; that mere justice requires that a machinery should be set on foot to force wages up, instead of that complex one now existing to force them down.[1]

There appear to be two means by which the working man can peacefully and successfully contend against the twofold evil of the low wages which he receives for his work, and of the high prices he has to pay for his food and other articles of consumption. The latter may be met by the plan described by the correspondent of the *Morning Chronicle* for the Manufacturing Districts, in speaking of the 'People's mill' at Leeds.

> The People's mill grinds corn of all kinds, and supplies to its large circle of proprietors flour and grain, perfectly unadulterated, and as near cost price as the actual working expenses will permit. The number of members is about 5000, and the vast majority are working men. Each pays 1*l*. 1*s*. entrance money. There is no yearly subscription. The average amount annually saved by the subscribers was computed by the managing miller as about equal to each member's subscription; that is to say, the flour in the mill can be had so much cheaper than the same flour in shops, as to save an ordinary family about a pound in the year. The great advantage, however, looked to is the purity of the article.

It is obvious that this plan can be made applicable, and far more easily, to butchers' and bakers' shops, and, in fact, to every establishment of retail trade. Under the name of 'Protective Unions,' the system, it was stated some time since in the *New York Tribune,* is very prosperous in Boston, and is rapidly extending itself throughout New England. It has made less progress in New York, though even here there is a 'Protective Union Bakery,' to which a grocery and provision store has probably by this time been added.

Against low wages a remedy may be found in the operative partnerships, or 'Associations Ouvrières,' the most practical result as yet of the February revolution, and which have made such progress in France during the past year. I have before me a bundle of deeds of settlement and regulations belonging to these associations, which space alone prevents me from referring to at length. The tailors, who are sixty men on an average at work, with about 300 'adherents,' have been working for the last twelvemonth on equal wages, and have realized 6*l.* per cent profit on a business of 4000*l.* a-year. Another tailors' association at Bordeaux, thirteen men in all, netted 8000*f.* profit in four months, working by the job, but with an equal right to dividends. The armchair makers (*menuisiers en fauteuils*), seventy in number, began with a capital of 504*f.,* and have a business now worth 100,000*f.* a-year. The cabinet-makers (*ébénistes*), in the same yard—the Cour St. Joseph, in the Faubourg St. Antoine—have, like them, much more work than they can get through, and work so well that they are able to sell somewhat dearer than their capitalist rivals. The cooks, who unfortunately are divided into several rival associations (one of which has lately failed), can afford to give the working classes as good a breakfast at four sous as they can obtain elsewhere for ten. The paviours, who have two associations, have got into their hands by tender a large portion of the paving of Paris. To that extent has the movement spread, that 104 associations, by their delegates, are now engaged in forming an *Union des Associations,* the main object of which is to establish what is termed by them a 'mutuality of credit,' by means of exchange-bonds, payable in labour and produce,—a great idea, the main developement of which is owing to a gentleman well known by his abolitionist efforts, and now a resident amongst us, M. Jules Lechevalier. In America also, the working classes have their eyes open to these experiments. The *New York Tribune* advocates them. In Boston there is already a 'Tailors' Associative Union,' whilst in Pennsylvania the *Philadelphia Ledger,* speaking of a strike amongst the Boston tailors, has pointed out that

> Their emancipation is in their own hands, if they will direct their *hands* with *their own heads,* instead of allowing them to be directed by the heads of others. They must alter the system, which they can do peacefully and effectually, without infringing the rights of anybody. But how can they alter it? Merely by doing that in concert which their employers do singly—work for the public. . . . The remedy of labourers is combination, not competition; and combination to work in partnership, instead of not to work at all.

In our own country, though Mr. Babbage in his *Economy of Machinery and Manufacture,* and Mr. Mill in his great work, have both openly advocated the associating the labourer to a share in profits; although Mr. Mill has declared, that 'to this principle, in whatever form embodied, it seems to him that futurity has to look for obtaining the benefits of co-operation, without constituting the numerical majority of the co-operators an inferior caste;' and notwithstanding the examples of co-operation afforded by the miners and fishermen of Cornwall (the latter of whom are shewn to beat the Yarmouth, as well as the Irish fishermen on their own coasts) and also by the crews of whaling ships,—little seems to have been done with success towards the creation of joint-stock operative associations. The joint-stock woollen mills of the West Riding of Yorkshire, of which interesting accounts were furnished by Mr. Aldam to the Commons' Committee on Joint-stock Companies in 1844, and published by them in the Appendix to their Report, afford perhaps the nearest approach to the working out of the principle, although the achievement of co-operation, not amongst operatives properly so called, but amongst small manufacturers.

The principle of association appears to me the only effectual remedy against this fearful beating down of wages below 'living prices,' against this fearful realizing of capitalists' imaginary profits out of the starvation and degradation of the workman. Let this principle be applied, not in one shape, but in a thousand. In those trades where fair profits can yet be obtained, without trenching upon the due share of the operative, let him be simply and at once associated to the profits, that the marriage between capital and labour may be established upon a firm basis. In those trades where the profit has been annihilated by a delusive cheapness, let the operative endeavour to supply as far as possible the place of capital by combination and an exchange of labour. And let those who feel with me that the operative has need to be sustained in this effort to rescue himself from his present thraldom, and that all who, wittingly or unwittingly, have contributed to bring him into that thraldom, lie under the deepest responsibility towards him,—let all such now contribute their counsel, their funds, their custom, to further his deliverance.[2]

But let us be deaf no longer. Let every sect and creed enter into friendly competition for improving the condition of the people of England. Let the Church especially put forth all her strength to grapple with the hundred-headed evil. She has been supine far too long. As I look upon her benefices and episcopal sees, upon her deacons, her priests, and her bishops, I seem to see the skeleton of a great army, the battlefield of a holy warfare; all the strongholds are occupied—officers to command them there are plenty, but the privates are nowhere, or fighting on their own account. What are all our religious societies, but irregular partizans, guerilla bands, ill-armed and ill-disciplined, too often unscrupulous in their means of warfare? Let the parish on the one hand cease to be a mere 'geographical expression' (to adopt the Austrian's insolent language about Italy); let it become a centre of radiating life; let it be no more for the working classes a mere dispenser of legal relief, but the source and focus of all local action; let the poor be no more helped *in* their poverty but helped *out of* it,—by parochial lodging-houses, parochial baths and wash-houses, savings'-banks, friendly meetings between class and class, and every other institution which can be brought within the compass of parochial efforts and parochial control. On the other hand, let all these scattered seeds of Catholicity, which the huge landslip of the sixteenth century has buried far underground, be set free to vegetate once more by a deeper labour of the plough, and we shall see them from our lighter and richer Protestant soil, casting forth shoots far healthier and more vigorous than even the rankest growths which have yet pierced the thick clay of Romanism. Let the Protestant orders of both sexes, bound by no vows, go forth in joyful self-devotion to battle with the wretchedness and the vice of England. The Training Institution for Nurses in

Fitzroy Square, Mrs. Fry's or Miss Sellon's Sisters of Mercy, are but the merest germs of future religious Socialism. The care of the sick, the reformation of the prisoner, the government of the adult pauper, the training of the pauper child, are all works which, I am firmly convinced, can never be adequately performed either by mere mercenary labour or skill or by solitary self-devotion, but which require both a special and religious vocation in the individual, and the support and comfort of an organized fellowship. We must have Orders of nurses, Orders of prison attendants, Orders of workhouse masters, workhouse matrons, workhouse teachers, perhaps parish surgeons,—bodies of men and women that shall shew forth in its purity the essential communism of the Church, and leaven the whole of society with a spirit of self-devoted industry. Let such a spirit once go abroad, let it raise labour to the rank of a sacred duty, the holier in proportion to its very arduousness and repulsiveness, and the word 'Penitentiary' will no more be a shameful lie, nor the word 'Workhouse' a promise unfulfilled; our wastes will be cultivated, our marshes drained; the soil shall no more be robbed of its fruitfulness by wasteful cultivation, nor neglected by slothful ignorance; our polluted rivers shall no more bear away to the sea the exhaustless wealth of the sewage of our towns, nor our atmosphere grow thick with the wasted carbon of our smoke; the well-drained houses of our air streets shall no more breed fever and pestilence, sweeping away children, shattering the frames of the adult, already weakened by starvation wages; feelings of mutual sacrifice, confidence, and love, will gradually supplant those feelings of mutual encroachment, of mutual distrust and hatred, which now estrange class from class, and man from man; the very word 'Society' will seem too foreign and merchant-like to express the mutual relations of Englishmen, and in good old Saxon phrase, used of yore for kingdoms as for republics, England will be truly one Commonwealth and one Church.

Do these words seem visionary and ideal? Would it not be better anyhow to try how nearly we can realize them, than to measure how far we fall short of the promise they hold out, as an excuse for folding our arms and doing nothing?

J. T.

Notes

1 Do these appear strong expressions? A high rate of wages is acknowledged to be a good by the greatest of living political economists, Mr. Mill; as, for instance, when he says, in speaking of combinations amongst workmen, that 'if it were possible for the working classes, by combining among themselves, to raise or keep up the general rate of wages, it need hardly be said that this would be a thing not to be punished, but to be *welcomed and rejoiced at.*'

2 The formation of such operative partnerships might probably be greatly assisted by some special law, such as relate to friendly societies, savings' banks, building societies, and loan societies,—the last-named associations for the most part wholly unworthy of the privilege. But the whole law of partnership in England stands in need of enlargement and reform.

2

REPORT OF THE 2ND CO-OPERATIVE CONFERENCE HELD AT MANCHESTER . . . 1853 (LONDON: E. LUMLEY, 1853), 3–7.

E.V. Neale

[Edward Vansittart Neale (1810–1892), was a wealthy barrister and leading Christian Socialist. An early supporter of the Working Men's College, Neale encouraged the Amalgamated Society of Engineers to establish co-operative workshops during the great lock out in the trade in 1852, an initiative that soon ran into the sands causing Neale considerable financial loss. A tireless advocate of profit sharing, the same year he aided the passage of the Industrial and Provident Societies Act, often referred to by co-operators as their "Magna Charta". [Philip N. Backstrom, *Christian Socialism and Co-operation in Victorian England* (London: Croom Helm, 1974)] In an effort to focus local initiatives that were rapidly developing, the Christian Socialists established a national annual conference for co-operators in 1852. This extract is taken from their second conference in Manchester, at which Neale was appointed chair. His opening address, reproduced here, has been accurately described by one historian of Christian Socialism as Neale's "manifesto". [Torben Christensen, *Origin and History of Christian Socialism, 1848–54* (Aarhus: Brill, 1962), p. 335] In it, Neale sketches a blueprint for the better co-ordination of co-operative effort, wherein the store serves as a practical stepping-stone for a much wider transformation: the eventual emancipation of the worker through the establishment of "a system of exchange of labour, founded upon principles of strict justice". However, Neale's vision like that of Christian Socialists more generally, is resolutely apolitical, depending for its success on a universal change of heart.]

PREFATORY ADDRESS OF THE EXECUTIVE COMMITTEE APPOINTED BY THE CONFERENCE.

THE Report which follows, with its various Appendixes, exhibits the present state of the effort now being made to carry into practice the principles of Co-operation, in its weakness, and in its strength;—in the weakness, in part natural to the infant state of many Co-operative Establishments, to small resources and undeveloped business, in part arising from the influence of that spirit of selfish distrust, disunion, individualism, which it is the great object of Co-operation to overcome;—in the strength, resulting from the earnestness inspired by the consciousness of efforts directed to a worthy end.

Co-operation, rightly understood, does indeed propose to itself a most worthy end of human effort. It seeks to introduce institutions which shall promote the exercise of justice and truthfulness in the ordinary dealings of ordinary life; and thus to prepare the ground for that nobler state of society, to be anticipated from the disposition to unite for the common good, which these virtues will foster. But that end, like all other noble and great ends which man can propose to himself, has to be attained by a persevering labour in details, such as often seem to those engaged in them insignificant and worthless; and if we do not make very clear to ourselves the way in which these details will contribute towards the attainment of the end proposed, we shall be liable to grow faint-hearted; we shall seem to be making no progress, when, in fact, we are making progress, such progress as is possible; we shall be in danger of growing disgusted with the indifference, the opposition, the petty jealousies, the mean selfishness, with which we must unavoidably come in contact in the rough world of experience, till at last we draw back from the hard task of working to make a better society, and please ourselves by idly dreaming of some "Good time coming," when all men will become at once unselfish, and truthful, and happy, and society mend itself of its own accord.

That they may do what they can to guard against so great an evil, the Executive Committee have determined shortly to state how, according to their convictions, Co-operative Stores and Industrial Societies can promote the true principles of Co-operation, and thus conduce to the amendment of society; that those who are favourably disposed towards such institutions may both know what it is important to insist upon in respect to them, and feel, that in supporting them, when properly formed, they are doing what it is well worth while to do.

That men may truly work together, three things are indispensable, that they should exercise justice to each other, in the division among the producers of the proceeds of any work which many are jointly engaged in producing, and in the exchange of one kind of work for another; and that they should be ready to promote whatever conduces to the common advantage or enjoyment. These three qualities correspond to the three divisions of human action which the political economists point out as concerned with industry, Production, Distribution, and Consumption. The Co-operative Workshop or Industrial Society has, for its social object, to secure *justice in production*—to divide the results of all work done there among those who in any way, by capital, labour, or skill, contribute to produce it, according to what in justice each ought to have; not, as is the case in ordinary workshops, according to what each man's strength of body, of mind, or of position, enables him to snatch for himself. Again, the Co-operative Store or Provident Society, has for its object to secure *justice in distribution and exchange,* not carrying on this important function as society now carries it on, by placing men between the producer and consumer, with the maxim, "make the most that you can out of both;" "buy cheap and sell dear," as their "Golden Rule:" but providing for its being carried on upon its true basis, as an agency, for the mutual benefit alike, of the producer to whom it will seek to give a just price for what he produces, and of the consumer to whom it will supply these articles at only so much increase of price as is due to the capital, labour, and skill, required in the transaction.[1]

For the third function, that of consumption, or the enjoyment of the things produced, no special provision is made by the arrangements now contemplated. They leave the institutions adapted to promote this object to grow up, as we are satisfied they will grow up, of themselves, so soon as by the practice of justice in production and distribution, wealth becomes more equally diffused among the population, and self-interest less dominant, than is at present the case.

We believe that it is the absence of any proposals relating to this function of consumption, which, more than anything else, has made many zealous social reformers, look with comparative indifference on the workshops and stores to which Co-operative efforts have appeared to be limited. Their imaginations have been so accustomed to revel amongst the promised delights or advantages of a higher social condition, the gardens, the libraries, the halls, the schools, the pleasant dwellings, the varied occupations of that hoped-for world, that they do not recognize in the sterner working world of Co-operation, in its workshops and stores, the seeds of the very institutions to which they look forward. And yet is it not evident that before we can obtain the enjoyments which wealth secures, we must possess the sources from which wealth springs? And what are these, but those workshops and stores, those means of production and distribution, with which Co-operation busies itself? Have not these been, during the last century, the source of that vast accumulation of wealth in the hands of the manufacturing and trading classes in England, which has raised them to their present importance, and placed half the land of England in their hands? Let the working classes, whose limbs and whose brains are indispensable to all the operations of industry or trade, set themselves in right earnest to form centres of production and distribution for themselves, on those principles by which alone they, as a class, can benefit, the principles of mutual justice; and they may, if they will, change the wealth-producing process, from being one by which a few are made very rich by the labour of many, into one by which the whole body, through their joint exertions, gradually enrich each other. With the possession of wealth will come the means of creating the outward sources of enjoyment of which so much has been said: still more, with the possession of wealth *thus acquired* will come the spirit through which these sources of enjoyment will be able to be enjoyed. At present, if the population of England could be suddenly placed amidst such institutions as social reformers have dreamt of, we believe that they would be unable to keep them in operation. For all these institutions assume the general existence among those who are living under them, of a regard for what is due to others, a spirit of courtesy, a readiness to help each other, a trustful, unselfish disposition, of all which we see, unfortunately, but scanty traces at present, and cannot hope to see more, until we see in the dealings between man and man the general exercise of that virtue of justice, sterner and less attractive, but the indispensable condition of all social good.

Now the institutions by which justice may be secured in the production and distribution of wealth, the working classes of England have the power to found with an assurance of success, if only they have the *will!* The steps in the process are few and easy to be followed. The first step is to take the supply of their own consumption, the distribution of the articles which they require for their own use into their own hands, as they may do by means of Co-operative Stores. The second step is to combine these Stores by means of general centres of supply, one of which already exists in London in the Central Co-operative Agency, and thus make themselves important as wholesale buyers. The third step is to use their power of buying, thus organised, in setting up productive institutions, with their proper centres of supply, to make what they want to buy. The fourth step is to institute among these productive institutions a system of exchange of labour, founded upon principles of strict justice. These arrangements will doubtless, require time for their development, but they are clearly not impracticable. When these have been effected, the institutions, by which the advantages and enjoyments promised by Social Reformers may be attained, will begin to spring up on all sides; the forms of a higher social order of things will make themselves visible resting upon the solid foundation of just dealing, and gradually built up by the spirit of mutual trust and genuine goodwill—which the exercise of this humbler virtue will call forth, or foster.

Let no man then suffer himself to be discouraged when he is engaged in the task, often difficult and wearisome, of setting in motion a Co-operative Store, or a Co-operative Workshop, by the thought that what he is doing costs much exertion and seems to be of little use. Ploughing and harrowing is hard, unpromising work, but let a good seed bed be once prepared, and the good seed sown, in due time the golden harvest will reward the husbandman's toil.

Sow the good seed of justice, in those great functions of human activity—the production and distribution of the fruits of labour; prepare the good seed bed of institutions in which this seed can be properly nourished: the eternal laws of God's providence will not fail to give you in due time the glorious harvest of a true human society.

And that time may be nearer than present appearances may lead many to think. Follow out in thought the advantages of many sorts, which a well conducted and thriving manufactory situated in the country could place within the reach of those employed in it; consider how soon by such a process as has been indicated many such manufactories might be established; and you will see how speedily the wise employment of the resources now in the hands of the working classes of this country would begin to improve their outward condition.

The plans by which, in our judgment, the progress to this end may be materially accelerated, are brought before you in the Report and Appendixes to it. We ask for them your earnest consideration; and if, as we hope, you approve of them as well suited for the end they propose, your hearty support, and, as far as practicable, your influence with other Co-operative bodies whose attention has not yet been awakened to the importance of such plans of union, to lead them to consider and adopt them. Co-operative Societies in Great Britain may now be counted by hundreds, and it needs only a hearty union among them to produce results at which they would be themselves surprised. The Report will bring before you also, what we cannot but continually recur to, because they are of the first importance, the *principles* upon which your social institutions, your stores and your workshops must be founded, if they are really to promote the work for which they are intended. All errors can be amended, all shortcomings made good, except errors and shortcomings here. The construction of a true human Society is the noblest work of man; it can be accomplished only by being undertaken and carried on in the noblest spirit; in that spirit which does not ask what can *I get* for myself, but what can *I do* that shall be most just, most true, most generally useful.

Note

1 The Committee do not wish to be considered as intending by these words to cast any particular reproach on tradesmen, whether wholesale or retail, who individually, may, in their several spheres, be kind and honourable men. They refer only to the false position in which, from the want of good social arrangements for carrying on the important functions of trade, all traders are necessarily placed. The same remark applies to what has been said about production.

3

LIFE AND LAST DAYS OF ROBERT OWEN, OF NEW LANARK (LONDON: HOLYOAKE & CO., 1859), 17–24.

G.J. Holyoake

[George Jacob Holyoake (1817–1906) grew up in a respectable working-class family in Birmingham; his mother was a button maker and his father was a printer. Holyoake became a skilled whitesmith in a foundry but quit and became a "Social Missionary" for the Owenite movement in 1840. He gained early notoriety for his attacks on Christianity, for which he was sentenced to six months imprisonment on a charge of blasphemy in 1842. [Edward Royle, *Victorian infidels: the origins of the British secularist movement, 1791–1866* (Manchester: Manchester University Press, 1974)] Although he liked to cultivate an image of himself as a martyr for the cause of freethought, he is best understood as a kind of "movement entrepreneur" who made a living from publishing radical and secularist works, giving lectures and writing for the developing institutions of labour. [Peter Gurney, "Working-Class Writers and the Art of Escapology in Victorian England: the Case of Thomas Frost", *Journal of British Studies*, 45/1 (2006), 66–67] When Owen died in November 1858 Holyoake addressed various meetings in London and the provinces held to commemorate Owen's life. This pamphlet is the text of a speech originally delivered in the Public Hall, Rochdale, in January 1859. Holyoake played an important role in transmitting and re-working Owen's legacy, here at a meeting presided at by Jacob Bright, brother of John Bright, the renowned ex-leader of the Anti-Corn Law League and local mill owner. Bright was careful not to identify himself with Owen's socialist opinions but acknowledged that they had been sincerely held; while Holyoake in return was a model of politeness, a quality he carefully cultivated post-mid-century much to the annoyance of other veteran democrats such as Thomas Cooper and W.J. Linton. Unsurprisingly, Holyoake presented a somewhat sanitised version of Owen, portraying him primarily as a "publicist" of advanced views. The more revolutionary aspects of Owen's thought, particularly his attacks on the family and religion, Holyoake preferred to either excuse or else marginalise.]

Though I had the privilege of knowing Mr. Owen twenty years, and of having my attention professionally drawn to his views, I do not assume myself to be capable of giving an adequate estimate of his character or services. I pretend to express only my own conception of them. There are few men living who know the whole compass of his career—who have read all his speeches—all his writings—all his remarkable correspondence; who have perused the newspaper comments upon his proceedings, during the last fifty years of his public agitations. I know few who have done so, and without doing this no one can fully appreciate the nature or extent of the influence he has exercised. Not only England, but America, London, and the capitals and courts of every nation in Europe, have, at one time or other, resounded with his name. Emperors have been his guests, kings his listeners, princes his friends, statesmen his correspondents, philosophers his partners. The foremost men of the past age turned to him for inspiration; rulers waited upon his words, and the peoples of two worlds once believed in him as a deliverer. A man must have native force of character who achieves this. It is not a well-meaning man of mere feeble philanthropy, but a man of ability, of feeling, and of truth, to whom we pay the tribute of our respect to-night.

To Mr. Owen's memory I offer homage, but it is the homage of discrimination. That is the manliest reverence which praises within the limits of truth. I hate the flatterer. Either he is a knave who intends to impose upon me, or a patron who intends to befool me, or a coward who applauds because he has not the courage to condemn, or a weak-eyed man who can only see one thing at a time. I hate the men who, by wholesale praise, hide from me what I should be, and keep me what I am. I prefer the man who blows hot and cold to him who blows all hot, because I want to be invigorated, not to be stifled. This sentiment will rule all I say. I stand here to honour him of whom I speak, by frankness as well as praise, and not to pour hollow compliments into the 'dull cold ear of death.'

Robert Owen, like Thomas Paine, was endowed with great natural capacity for understanding public affairs. He was accustomed to give practical and notable opinions upon public questions, quite apart from his own doctrines; and his society was sought as that of a man who had the key of many State difficulties. Those know little of him who suppose that he owed his distinction wholly to his riches. A man must be wise as well as wealthy, to achieve the illustrious friendships which marked his career. He had personally an air of natural nobility about him. He had, as the *Daily News* says, 'an instinct to rule and command.' I only knew him late in life, when age had impressed measure upon his steps and deliberateness on his speech. When he had the vivacity of youth and middle age, he must have been an actor on the political stage of no mean mark. He always spoke as 'one having authority.' He had a voice of great compass, thorough self-possession, and becoming action. Like many other men, he spoke much better than he wrote. Only two or three years ago, at a private dinner, arranged that Mr. Joseph Barker might be introduced to him, there were several University men, and authors of some note, present. Mr. Owen's conversation was the most brilliant of all the company. On the last occasion on which he presided in public was when he made the presentation of a purse to his faithful attendant Mr. Rigby. The patrician manner in which he spoke of his old friend, the dignity without haughtiness, the kindness without condescension, I never saw equalled. It was a relic of the old manner, which I have seen alleged in romance, as the characteristic of the princely employer, but which I never witnessed before. The meeting was like a reception by Talleyrand.

Mr. Owen's speeches had vivacity and humour. His writings have little of either. His best book, and the one that made his reputation, his 'Essays on the Formation of Character,' Francis Place revised for him. Mr. Owen ought always to have put his manuscripts into the hands of others. He had noble thoughts, but when he took his pen in hand he fell into principle spinning, which is always duller reading than the Fifth Book of Euclid. It is very true and very important, but it bores you. However, his Life of himself—his last work and most interesting of all—contains more personal facts of interest and importance than any political biography which has appeared in our time.

The impression Mr. Owen made upon workmen of the last generation is best described by one whose name is an honour to that order—I mean Ebenezer Elliott. In an address sent by Trades Unionists of Sheffield in 1834, Elliott says—'You came among us as a rich man among the poor, and did not call us a rabble. This is a phenomenon new to us. There was no sneer on your lips, no covert scorn in your tone.'

These words show us how working men were treated some thirty years ago. It was in reply to this address that Mr. Owen made a remark which is an axiom in the best political liberalism of these days; he said '*Injustice is a great mistake.*'[1] It is not merely wrong, wicked, malevolent, hateful; it won't answer, it won't pay. It is a blunder, it is a disgrace as well as a crime.

Mr. Owen was an apostle, not a rhetorician. He never looked all round his statements (as Mr. Bright now does) to see where the enemy could come up and pervert them. He said 'man was the creature of circumstances' for thirty years, before he added the important words '*acting previous to and after his birth.*' He had the fatal ideas of the New Testament, that equality was to be attained by granting to a community 'all things in common'—at the commencement. Whereas this is the result, not the beginning. You must begin with inequality and authority, steering steadily towards self-government and the accumulation of the common gains, until independence is secured to all. Mr. Owen looked upon men through the spectacles of his own good nature. He never took Lord Brougham's advice 'to pick his men.' He never acted on the maxim that the working class are as jealous of each other as the upper classes are of them. All that he did as a manufacturer he omitted to do as a Founder of Communities. As a manufacturer, even Allen, his eminent Quaker partner, wrote to him, 'Robert Owen, thou makest a bargain in a masterly manner!' Dr. Bowring allowed that the only time Jeremy Bentham ever made money, was when he was a partner of Mr. Owen. In after life Mr. Owen was really reckless of his own fame. No leader ever took so little care in guarding his own reputation. He lent his name to schemes which were not his. The failure of Queenwood was not ascribable to him. When his advice was not followed, he would say 'Well, gentlemen, I tell you what you ought to do. You differ from me. We will not quarrel. Carry out your own plans. Experience will show you who is right?' Then failure came, for which he was not responsible, but it was ascribed to him. The public knew nothing of Executives which he withdrew from. They only knew Robert Owen, and whatever failed under his name, they inferred failed *through him*. Mr. Owen was a general who never provided himself with a rear guard. While he was fighting in the front ranks, priests might come up and cut off his commissariat. His own troops fell into pits against which he had warned them. Yet he would write his next dispatch without it occurring to him to mention his own defeat, and he would return to his camp without missing his army.

Mr. Owen's fault was that he was always playing at world making—no, I retract that word. I will not say 'playing'—he was too earnest a man for that—but he was always dreaming of world making. Now, to sweep the world clean and begin again is a rather extensive undertaking. It would be a great interruption to business. And it is difficult to pack up the human race and put them out of the way, while the world is being cleared. So the world objected to the operation, and Mr. Owen never had his way. But let us not be too hasty to condemn Mr. Owen for this idea. He was a young man and had commenced as a theorist when the first French Revolution broke out. He saw France and America both make the attempt of reconstituting society. Things were so bad, politically and religiously, that nobody had any hope and little chance of amending them. Many men besides Mr. Owen thought it better to begin again. When Pope, the poet, who suffered from great constitutional debility, stumbled, and nearly fell as he was getting into a boat, he exclaimed, by way of apology to the waterman—'God mend me!' 'I think, sir,' answered the waterman, 'God had better make a new one!' This was the opinion of most political Reformers when Mr. Owen was young. Their only hope was in a new state of society. Even the present Queen's father said, when introducing Mr. Owen to a public meeting in the Freemason's Hall, London, so late as 1819—'It may be doubted whether the permanent safety of the British Empire does not depend upon the measures which may be speedily adopted to ameliorate the condition of the working classes,' and these measures he called upon Mr. Owen to explain.

It is difficult to judge yet the great act of Mr. Owen in 'denouncing all the religions of the world,' as he did in the City of London Tavern in 1817. It was part of his plan. It was a deliberate act. He told his religious partner, Mr. Allen, the Quaker, that he would do so two years before. This act arrested the acceptance of his social system. From being a Social Reformer, Mr. Owen commenced to be a Religious Reformer, and, being a thorough man, he did by the Church as he did by the State—he proposed to reform it altogether. For this work, Mr. Owen appears to me to have made no adequate preparation. He followed the instinct of his conscience without calculation. The ominous meeting in the Rotunda of Dublin in 1823, sealed the fate of his Social Reform, and condemned his schemes ever after to the hands of the minority. The great powers of society set their faces against him, and the people were too poor to carry his ideas out. The greatest person of distinction who best understood Mr. Owen, and who did not desert him on account of his irreligious views, was the Queen's father, to whom we have before referred. He said at one of Mr. Owen's meetings, two years after he had denounced all religions, 'If I understand Mr. Owen's principles, they lead him not to interfere to the injury of any sect; but he claims for himself that which he is so desirous to obtain for his fellow creatures—"religious liberty and freedom of conscience"—and this he contends for, because his experience compels him to conclude that these principles are now necessary to secure the well-being and good order of society.' This is excellently put, and is really all Mr. Owen meant. Being always a Theist, he was logically in error in denouncing 'all religions.' His province, as it appears to me, was to defend humanity against the abuses of religion, and maintain, as the Duke of Kent puts it, 'religious liberty and freedom of conscience.' However, Mr. Owen thought differently, and nobly he acted up to his convictions. Like Paine, he threw away worldly honour and renown for the sake of conscience. His courage was of the highest order. He quailed before no tumult—no disappointment made him despair. He was ready to lead an army, and he was equally ready to lead a forlorn hope. And when he had retired from the world, and was stretched upon his solitary bed in Newtown, and all his toils and visions were over, and the sands of life were ebbing fast, and a few short hours would close his long account with the unheeding world, the clergyman who called upon him asked him 'whether he did not regret the waste of his life upon fruitless efforts and unaccepted schemes?' The old philosopher's eye brightened, and he answered:—'No, sir; my life has not been spent uselessly. I have proclaimed important truths to the world, and if they were not regarded by the world, it was because the world did not understand them. Why should I blame the world? I am in advance of my time.' The clergyman admitted that he never saw more consistent philosophy than was manifested by the brave old man.

It was Mr. Owen's idea that the existing system would fall to pieces of its own weight, and he astonished people by naming the time when this would happen. He was wrong about the time, but right about the fact. Is not the system always falling to pieces? What is the meaning of our panics, pauperism, and 'great social evil'? Did not Ireland fall to pieces when three millions of people perished of famine? Has not our Indian Empire fallen to pieces in a very tragic manner within these twelve months? The system in some part or other is daily tottering and falling, and has to be repaired and renewed. Mr. Owen did not believe in the renewal of society. In this he was wrong. His own views enabled this repair to be made. They were more practical views than even Mr. Owen thought. His own dream of a science of society which he entertained in 1817 is adopted in 1858 at Liverpool. The nobility who deserted him in 1823 now take up his ideas—they deny his name and work by methods of their own—but they work with his materials and in his field.

There are three principal misapprehensions current upon Mr. Owen's views—by the political economists who regarded him as interrupting the course of society—by the clergy who held that he taught false views of the formation of character—by newspaper writers who considered that he sought to bring about an impractical state of Communism. The best correction of these errors is to state what his views were on these points.

1. The old terror of political economists was that Mr. Owen wished to interfere with the means by which twenty millions of mouths were fed. He did not propose to interfere with the means, but to improve the means. At present the twenty millions are not engaged, and never were engaged, in any concerted action to fill their mouths, but are scrambling for each other's loaves, lying in wait to intercept each other's fortune, and not unfrequently cutting each other's throats by the way. Mr. Owen thought this system might be improved—the world has now come round to the same opinion.

2. What Mr. Owen maintained as to the formation of character was that the circumstances in which men were placed exercised an influence upon the mind for good or for evil. Nobody doubts this now. Mr. Buckle, in his brilliant book on the 'History of Civilisation,' has established this truth beyond dispute. Mr. Owen said, if you want better men, place them in better circumstances, raise the wages of the poor—diminish their labour—better their food—improve their dwellings—increase their knowledge—let science serve them—let art refine them—give them wholesome recreation, and secure them moderate competence. This was not orthodox gospel, but it is a gospel very much wanted in the world.

3. When a great painter once executed a picture of the deluge, all the world went to see it: and they found on the canvass nothing delineated but a boundless waste of water, and one solitary spar projecting above it, upon which a single snake had crawled. What could tell the tale of desolation so well? All the agony and hopelessness of a doomed and drowned world were pictured there. So now, if any man would picture the hollowness of our present civilisation, he has only to pourtray a vast crowd of men with a solitary gallows standing above them, on which some poor wretch—perhaps a woman—is hanging. There you behold at once the falsehood of our civilisation—the poverty of social science—the incompetence of government—the feebleness of education—the weakness of the Church. We first rear the criminal and then strangle him. We ought to speak with moderation of the triumphs of Christianity so long as the Gallows is the conspicuous companion of the Cross. Mr. Owen never ceased to say we ought to manage these things better, and the world called him 'a man of one idea.' He was thought to be a man of one idea because he had but one way of stating it. You might as well call Newton a man of one idea because he merely discovered the law of gravitation—that was one idea, but it was capable of boundless and sublime applications. In the same manner Mr. Owen's idea of the influence of physical circumstances is applicable to every detail of human condition. Mr. Owen's great Communistic idea was, that the ordinary conditions of subsistence, and dwelling, and clothing, ought to be guaranteed in common to all: that moderate labour, on the part of the many, and moderate attainments in the science of society on the part of the few, would enable this to be done. He saw that there would always be a savage element in society so long as the lower classes were left to scramble like barbarians for the supply of their physical wants. So long as labour is presided over by want and death, civilisation will alternate between splendour and tragedy. And history shows this to be true. It was urged that to have food, shelter, garments, and knowledge in

common, would ruin everything, enervate everybody. This is said still, although we have old things and are having new things in common, without these results. Communism simply means that state of society in which the common fruits of intellect, art, and industry shall be so diffused, that poverty shall be impossible and crime unnecessary. And we are every day attaining to this. The laws of the universe are common. Light, and sky, and air are common. Life and death are common. In the hour of his birth the young prince screams for air like any pauper; and unceremonious Death who has the *entrée* of the poor-house, walks into the parlour of the gentleman without sending in his card. The noble building is now open to the gaze of the shoe black as well as to the connoisseur. Works of highest art and books of rarest value are now being made accessible to all. Fire offices insure the cottage or the mansion. The careless are as secure as the careful. Life insurance is another form of equality. The strong and temperate are made to use their prolonged lives to pay up premiums which go to the progeny of the weak and the reckless. The virtuous and the vicious, the base and the noble, are all declared equal in the sight of the law. The same police watch over the life of the scoundrel and the patriot. Before civilisation began, the weak had to take care of themselves, and had to get strength or discipline. Now the feeble and the stout, the coward and the brave, are equally protected. In savage times a man had to take care how he got into a quarrel. In all danger, whether he sought it, or whether it was thrust upon him, he had to defend himself. It was the reign of animal competition. The law has done away with this competition. The apparent effect of this is to encourage the coward and the sneak. That personal daring which made the inspiration of Homeric song, which made Sparta a name of energy through all time—which still makes the blood tingle in the pages of Sir Walter Scott, is no longer a daily requisite or means of renown. A man need not either carry arms or use them. He neither requires personal bravery nor discipline. A set of men are paid to defend him. He has only to call the police. An old warrior of the romantic days would rather die than utter the craven cry. If a man gets into a disputation he is not allowed to settle it in honest hot blood, but must refer his quarrel to the decision of a cold-blooded magistrate, who will probably give the decision against him, and compliment his enemy. How the hot blood boiled—how courage blushed with shame—how the pride of manliness was stung, when craven, cringing Peace, in the name of law, first put valour down! But we all know now that the peace-maker was right. There is plenty of exercise for courage without our expending it in broils and bloodshed. The equality of the law has produced justice—and the equality of competence will lead to happiness, security, and morality. Society will not be disorganised, though Co-operators and Communists should succeed in finding that condition of human society, in which it shall be impossible for a man to be depraved or poor.

Note

1 January 15, 1834.

4

"INDUSTRIAL CO-OPERATION", *FORTNIGHTLY REVIEW*, JANUARY 1866, 479–488, 491–493, 497–499.

Frederic Harrison

[Frederic Harrison (1831–1923), was born into a wealthy family in London. He attended Wadham College, Oxford, where he first encountered the work of Auguste Comte, whose "positivist", pseudo-scientific "Religion of Humanity" shaped profoundly his subsequent thinking on social reform. [Christopher Kent, *Brains and numbers: elitism, Comtism, and democracy in mid-Victorian England* (Toronto: University of Toronto Press, 1978); Martha S. Vogeler, *Frederic Harrison: the vocations of a positivist* (Oxford: Clarendon, 1984)] For a while, he was employed by the London Working Men's College founded by the Christian Socialists in Bloomsbury and was friendly with G.J. Holyoake who introduced him to northern co-operators. [Royden Harrison, *Before the socialists: studies in labour and politics, 1861–1881* (London: Routledge & Kegan Paul, 1965)] In this extract, Harrison presents a critique of the "Rochdale model", arguing for clearer definition of the relationship between co-operation and socialism. He recognises that affinities persist between them, as co-operation is not merely about material gain but like socialism provides a culture for many supporters akin to a religion. This helps explain its success and resilience, clearly demonstrated during the recent Cotton Famine. But unlike socialism, Harrison argues, co-operation is necessarily involved in market relations and this generates contradictions. Subordination of the producer and prioritisation of the store leads to a reliance on slave grown cotton, for instance. Most damagingly, Harrison suggests that there is nothing intrinsically different about this form of joint-stock enterprise and capitalist forms; pecuniary gain is frequently the most important motivation for co-operators. The conflict between idealism and commercialism has yet to be resolved and remains a question "on which its supporters are wholly divided", as co-operative manufactories treat workers as "hands". Harrison doubts the ability of workers to run large-scale industry unaided, believing in the necessity of the principle of authority, as did John Ruskin. In the end, Harrison was thoroughly pessimistic about the movement's wider ambitions and drew a clear distinction between co-operation or "bastard Communism" and authentic forms of socialism or communism.]

Now, in dealing with co-operation, it is happily possible to speak in a much more judicial and critical spirit than it is in speaking of unionism. Trades' unions are still the object of so much ignorant hatred and of such cowardly calumny, that a friendly writer is forced into an attitude of controversy and almost of advocacy. With co-operation, it is very desirable that its weak side should be insisted on at least as fully as its strongest. Its partisans and even the public are rather inclined to exaggerate its importance. During the recent elections one must have been struck to see how many candidates on both sides, who guarded themselves from betraying a single definite opinion, loudly proclaimed themselves in favour of "co-operation." Doubtless it would have been as much to the purpose to have proclaimed themselves staunch adherents of the penny post, or ardent friends of the half-holiday movement. Of course, as the Legislature has, and can have, nothing to do with co-operation, it was totally out of place in candidates' addresses. And perhaps every one of them would have shrunk with horror from the great revolution which "co-operation" really is in the minds of its most active apostles. This, however, proved that it is considered a safe thing to profess; and serves to indicate interest in social questions. But as it is beset by no prejudices whatever, it is only right that its value and its defects be impartially brought out; and that its adherents may not mislead themselves as to its promises . . .

The case of Rochdale is naturally the most striking that can be taken. There the Pioneers Society alone now numbers 5,200 members, with a capital of £71,000, and an annual business of £200,000. Associated with it is the Corn-mill Society and the Cotton Manufacturing Company, both owned and worked principally by the same class. The effect of this movement on the town is most obvious. During the worst times of the cotton distress the Pioneers was unshaken. The material prosperity and well-being of the whole town has received an impetus from it. The "store" has affected for good the moral, intellectual, and industrial tone of a large city. Its mere existence is sufficient to make it almost safe both against either great demoralisation or great destitution. The importance of this work is recognised by all classes of the inhabitants. There have been no more zealous friends of the movement than the clergy, many of the municipal officers, and both the late and the present representative in Parliament. The Rochdale movement, which dates from 1844, owes its origin and its success to a knot of men of very remarkable character and ability. There were amongst the founders some men of real mercantile genius—men who might have made their own fortunes ten times over—which they united with the power of inspiring and directing their fellows. Some of them are still at their post at Rochdale, rich in nothing but the gratitude and esteem of their fellow-citizens, for whilst they might easily have raised themselves amongst the great millionaires of Lancashire they were contented with giving prosperity to a city and new energy to the working classes of England . . .

No reasonable observer, however, can imagine that accumulating savings, avoiding debt, obtaining good and cheap food, or the "making a pound go a long way," is the sole feature, though it is the main feature, of the co-operative system. Co-operation now numbers a large and highly-organised band of propagandists. It forms a new "persuasion" in itself, with all the machinery and enthusiasm of a religious sect. There are men who devote themselves to preach and extend co-operation, just as there are men who devote themselves to awakening souls or advocating temperance. In every society there are men who give their time, labour, and often the savings of their lives, to found and establish a new "store," or to bring their neighbours to look on the system as a vital truth. The "pledge," the abolition of slavery, free trade, and "Bible religion," have never been preached with more systematic activity than this has. It has its organ, its lecturers, its "conferences," its dogmas, its celebrations, and it would not be an English institution if it had not its testimonials and its subscription funds. It has developed a style of thought and speech which is strangely akin to that of a religious movement, and in co-operation tracts the system is expounded in phrases which are in familiar use with reference to sacred subjects. The nucleus of many a flourishing society consists of men who have a strong impulse for social improvement, and whose motives are at least as strongly the benefit of their fellows as that of themselves. No one can read the *Co-operator* regularly without seeing that it records a movement in which some of the finest characters and spirits amongst the working classes, from one end of England to the other, are absorbed; without admiring the energy, perseverance, sagacity, and conscientiousness which these efforts display; without learning to respect the spirit of union, faith, and self-sacrifice which they frequently exert. The constant acts of benevolence, of unflinching patience, and of well-deserved confidence, with which co-operative records are full, are truly touching. Co-operative poetry alone forms a literature in itself; and in the *Co-operator's* pages one may often read a piece full of terse, vigorous lines, which, if not exactly a poem, is eloquent versification. Nor can any man of feeling or discernment witness a really worthy co-operative celebration—see those Lancashire or Yorkshire workmen, with their wives and children, meet in their own hall, surrounded by their own property, to consider their own affairs—hear them join in singing, sometimes a psalm, sometimes a chorus—listen to the homely wit, the prudent advice, the stirring appeal, and feel the spirit of goodwill, conviction, and resolution in which they are met to celebrate, as it were, their escape from Egyptian bondage,—no one, if present at such a meeting, can fail to recognise that co-operation, if not a moral or social movement in itself, has had the benefit of many high, moral, and social tendencies to stimulate and foster it.

In short, the best testimony for co-operation, in its form of the "store" system, is this—that in every leading town, men recognised as the most able, conscientious, and energetic of their order amongst the working classes, will generally be found active supporters of the "store;" and those amongst the independent and educated classes who sympathise most earnestly and wisely with the welfare of the working classes, will be found to acknowledge its claims and services. No man of generous feeling can help being moved to admiration when he recalls the homes which have been saved and brightened; the weight of debt, friendlessness, destitution, and bad habits which have been relieved; the hope and spirit which have been infused into the working classes by this single agency—the co-operative system. It has come successfully through the trial of the cotton distress; it is spreading into every corner, even every rural village in England, and is firmly established in Germany and France.

It is precisely the great influence which co-operation now exercises, and the very high qualities which are devoted to its extension, that render it the more essential to examine it closely—to know exactly what it can and what it cannot do—what are its defects and its dangers. The men who have founded and support these institutions are far too straightforward and resolute to fear any honest judgment upon their efforts. The last thing that they would choose would be any attempt to shut out the truth from themselves, or any one else, respecting the system; and once convinced of the fairness and goodwill of the counsellor or critic, they will attend to genuine counsel or criticism with patience and impartiality. In this spirit the following remarks are offered by one who has more than a mere goodwill for the movement in its legitimate sphere, and as a material expedient; who has a strong esteem and sympathy for it, its objects and its adherents; who recognises in it and them some of the very best grounds of hope now extant; and who desires only to define somewhat more closely the true scope and limits of co-operation. The time seems now to have come when this must be more accurately realised in the minds of the founders of the movement. It will not live unless it rests on a basis of consistent and acknowledged principle. Above everything, all are interested in avoiding any sort of misconception about it. Co-operation must have a reason for the faith that is in it. To assist in this end, the following pages are written; not as being, in any sense, the individual opinion of the writer, but as developing the system of industrial life planned by the author of the motto which stands at the head of this article, and as part of the system which bears his name.

Let us come at once to the key of the whole position. Co-operation, it is usually said, is designed to elevate the condition of labour by associating capital with labour, and by giving to labour an equal interest with capital in the results of production. It is also said (and with truth) to be in a flourishing condition, and to have firm ground to rest on. Now what is the case actually? Flourishing as co-operation clearly is in a pecuniary sense (with the exception of a very small number of manufacturing societies to be noticed presently), the whole of the co-operative societies throughout the kingdom are simply "stores," *i.e.* shops for the sale of food, and sometimes clothing. These, of course, cannot affect the condition of industry materially. Labour here does not in any sense share in the produce with capital. The relation of employer and employed remains just the same, and not a single workman would change the conditions of his employment if the store were to extinguish all the shops of a town. In such an extreme case, the workmen would still be hired for wages in the ordinary competition of labour, for the shops do not employ any of them. The cloth, flour, tea, and meat which the store now supplies, have all been made under the same conditions as before, and are simply purchased in open market in the ordinary way. The cotton goods sold at the store have probably been grown by the labour of negroes, and manufactured under the merest rule of competition. If co-operation (so far as the stores are concerned) were developed to a point beyond the wildest dreams of its friends; if it absorbed the entire retail trade of the country, and there were no such thing as a shop left for rich or poor, it would still, for any direct effect it has, leave the "labour market" just where it found it, for not a single article would be *produced* (though all would be distributed) in a different way from heretofore. Hence a "store," as such, does not affect the true labour question directly. So that what we mean when we say that "co-operation" is a great movement, is that working men have devised a highly convenient and economic plan of buying their food.

No doubt there is the whole *indirect* effect of this system, the freedom from debt, the accumulation of saving, the business experience, and all the countless other advantages which we have set forth and urged in preceding pages. No one can overlook them, and scarcely can exaggerate them. But these are in themselves purely economic arrangements of practical convenience, and cannot affect the social conditions of labour otherwise than as economic arrangements can. The practice of savings-banks is a highly useful economic arrangement, which has done a vast amount of good. So is the penny post. The ready-money principle is a valuable rule. The practice of accumulating savings, of not living up to one's income, the habit of regular economy, of giving a fair price for a sound article, as also the habit of early rising, are excellent bits of worldly wisdom to which the successful man often attributes his wealth. But these things, useful as they are, especially as contributing to a rise in life, are not vital movements of society or new revelations. In fact, they form merely the mode in which the capitalist classes have amassed their wealth, and they are often most conspicuously practised by men who have won and who use their wealth in the worst way. The very men with whom labour has had the hardest struggle, are just those who exemplify the value of these rules. And it is significant that the men who are the most earnest advocates of this species of economic prudence, are just the men who are known as the most hardened followers of the barrenest schools of political economy, to whom competition is a sort of social panacea and beneficent dispensation. It can hardly be that industry is to be regenerated simply by the working classes coming to practise the penny-wise economics of the getters of capital. It is much to be desired that this useful kind of prudence was more common. But if co-operation is to end in simply putting £5 or £10 into safe investments for working men, it is scarcely worthy of the fervent language which addresses it as a new gospel of the future, or of poems to celebrate its noble mission upon earth. We might as well expect them to be produced about a goose club.

There is no mystery about co-operation, nor, indeed, anything very original. Railways and joint-stock companies in general are simply co-operative societies; so is a goose club, so are all the clubs in Pall Mall. The new working men's clubs are so still more, and this admirable movement possesses also a great many of the advantages of the co-operative system, and is free from some of its defects.

In fact, wherever a number of persons join their small capitals into one capital, of which they manage to share the profit or the benefit (a system as old at least as the Romans), a true co-operative society exists. No doubt there are no companies (or very few) in which the subdivisions of shares are so small and the facilities so great as to enable working-men to invest out of their savings. But that is only an accident. It is quite easy to conceive a joint-stock company with very small shares, for some petty local object, very much connected with the working class—and many land and building societies are thus connected—which would be (many of them now are) classed strictly as co-operative societies. There are plenty of such little speculations, got up by pushing men of the people, owned and managed by them and their friends, which figure in the long list of the co-operative roll. They are very useful institutions, which bring a good dividend to the prudent investor—and so are gas companies. Now the "stores" offer a number of useful and incidental advantages which very few companies do. But in principle "stores" are joint-stock companies for the sale of food and clothing. As such they are doing a vast amount of good; but the industrial question is not solved, or even materially affected, because working men have devised and developed a very useful form of the joint-stock company system.

But as we have shown above, a man must be very short-sighted to see nothing more than this in the system as it now exists. There is a great deal more, only it is entirely subordinate and very indefinite. There is a wide-spread wish for social improvement, a spirit of self-sacrifice, and an unselfish enthusiasm which is very general in the movement. Gas companies do not subscribe to help each other in difficulties. Railway companies are not given to educational funds. Directors do not usually give their services gratuitously. Joint-stock companies' meetings, when they declare a dividend or dead loss, do not straightway sing a hymn, and appeal to each other, with tears in their eyes, to stand like men to the Limited Liability Act. There is something in this movement not explicable by love of cash. But all this amounts to saying that some very noble, earnest, and powerful spirits have thrown themselves into the movement. It is part of the social feeling and the strong sympathy which marks every effort of the genuine sons of labour in England, and, indeed, in Europe. But if it is a true part of co-operation at all, it is a part so indefinite, so ill-understood, and so very much disputed, that it cannot be said to be more than an adjunct. In itself, simply, co-operation is a joint-stock system for the association of small capitals. This has been practised by the rich for centuries, without any particular moral or social result. The prospectuses of new companies contain everything except homilies on the beauty of association. But the moral and social spirit which undoubtedly often accompanies co-operation is so very little defined, and is so devoid of any principle, system, or recognised rule whatever, that it cannot keep its ground beside the practical clear end of a good dividend. Co-operation may mean either the making and saving of money, or the joint labour of all for all. It may also mean partly one, partly the other. But if so, the relative proportions and limits of these two must be determined. Until this is done, co-operation is a mere form of pecuniary investment.

Now this question is all the more essential because no candid friend of the movement can deny that it is one on which its supporters are wholly divided. Most societies have within them more or less distinctly two parties, the one the men who look on the system as an economic, the other as a social, instrument. The one are sincerely desirous to become and to see their fellows become small capitalists; and then, in the words of one of the addresses, "the great problem of social economy is for the working classes to keep themselves with their own money." These men look on anything else as communism, and they are strict political economists. The other party fervently desire to see a system in which the share of capital in profit is reduced, and in which capital freely devotes part of its profit to labour; and these men are disciples of some kind of socialist scheme, and very often previously Owenites or actual communists. The latter are the more enthusiastic, the former are the better men of business. Both are useful, but they differ, as the discussions and divisions in the societies show. At present the economic school always carries the greatest weight and a majority of votes. The result is generally a friendly compromise; and an address which opens with a fervent call to the members to "elevate themselves by making money," closes with a motto in verse.

> "Each for all, and all for each,
> Helping, loving one another."

There is, however, a certain poetic vagueness often about the social element. Facts and acts are distinct; and, I believe, there is now no co-operative society existing which gives any substantial part of its income to *others than the members who share the capital*. There are, however, unmistakably two real sections in the co-operative world, and also in its friends: those who desire to see the privileges and power of capital extended to working men by their becoming capitalists; and those who desire to see working men relieved, by capital being deprived of much of its privileges and its power. These two parties, though quite friendly, are widely different, and at present, in the division list, the former have their way.

In the face of this great fact, which contains the key of co-operation as a social system, it is needless to consider the value of the general principles which are vaguely supposed to be connected with it. They can have no stability, for they do not rest on any accepted set of truths, or any recognised principle of action. One man writes to ask the *Co-operator* if Sunday trading is not contrary to the "true principle of co-operation." The editor of that useful and instructive periodical plainly considers that alcohol is; and he vigorously calls to order a "store" which ventured to sell beer. Of course, co-operation has no more to do with teetotalism than it has with Methodism. Now, if "co-operation" means a general term for all the moral and prudential virtues, or rather for what each man takes these to be, it means nothing. Nothing so vague can make any great effect. The thoughtful men amongst the working classes know well that for the permanent improvement of their order much more remains than that some should save a little money, and all buy cheaper and better food. Social wants require social remedies, and such things are mere delusions unless they are based on sound social philosophy. Modern life is not so simple a thing that it can be reformed by prudent maxims, with or without fine sentiments. Nor is our industrial system so feeble a matter that it can be moved by vague professions of good-fellowship. Stripped of this, co-operation is one of the best, perhaps far the best of economic expedients for increasing the comfort, health, and happiness of the poor man's home; but as such it cannot claim to have solved or even dealt with the industrial problems of society. As a system under which labour is to gain a new position, and stand on fairer terms with capital, it has yet everything to do; for it has neither done nor even suggested anything tangible.

We have hitherto purposely kept out of view the real manufacturing societies. These *are* co-operative societies which are employers of labour. Here, then, the system does grapple with the position of labour and capital. But what is the result? As a test, the experiment is scarcely favourable. The manufacturing societies are extremely few, they are not yet exactly successful as speculations, and they do nothing but *pay the labourer his ordinary market wages*. They are chiefly flour-mills and cotton-mills. Now the flour-mills have paid large and regular dividends, have done a considerable business, and have been admirably managed, and of course have had their hard times. But these are not strictly manufacturing societies; they supply chiefly their own members and other co-operative societies, and may be more properly classed with the "stores." The amount expended in labour is extremely small compared with that for raw material and plant. They naturally employ at times workmen unconnected with the society; but I have never understood that mere workmen employed by them ever receive anything but the market rate of wages, or any particular advantage, privilege, or perquisite. Nor do I think any societies in the kingdom remunerate their ordinary workpeople in any other way than the usual mode. Frequently these people are shareholders, but very often are not; and in any case the society, or rather company, wanting labour, goes into the market, and gives the price of labour as fixed by competition; just as a railway company does. The fact that the holders of the shares in the "store" or "mill" are for the most part (they are not always) real working men, is a very important and interesting fact; but it does not affect the conditions of labour, or add appreciably to the wages of their "hands."

The flour-mills apart—which are very successful and useful modes of making money—the other manufacturing societies are insignificant, until we come to the cotton-mills. Here and there an association of bootmakers, hatters, painters, or gilders, is carried on, upon a small scale, with varying success. The plate-lockmakers of Wolverhampton (who have been recently carrying on a struggle with the competing capitalists so gallantly) are another instance. But small bodies of handicraftsmen (or rather artists) working in common, with moderate capital, plant, and premises, obviously establish nothing. The only true instances of manufacturing co-operative societies of any importance are the cotton-mills. During the great cotton fever which preceded the distress, several mills were started or projected. Some of them for a time seemed promising. The great Lancashire famine, however, came on them almost before they had got to work; and it would be impossible to draw any inference whatever from them. Some of the mills, however, never got to work at all. Some took the simple form of ordinary joint-stock companies, in few hands. Others passed into the hands of small capitalists, or the shares were concentrated amongst the promoters. In fact, there is now, I believe, no co-operative cotton-mill owned by working men in actual operation on any scale, with the notable exception of Rochdale. The Rochdale mill deserves consideration by itself. Rochdale, it is well known, is in a special sense the cradle of co-operation. As Mr. Holyoake tells us in his admirable account of its rise there in 1844, "Human nature must be different at Rochdale from what it is anywhere else." Its rise may be distinctly traced to the influence of Owenism, and some of its leading promoters there, besides being men of real industrial genius, are deeply imbued with many valuable principles which Robert Owen upheld. The Rochdale cotton-mill once bid fair to be an extraordinary success in a commercial view. Their buildings are not surpassed by any, and equalled by few, in the county; their management has been cautious and able; their credit stands in the money-market even higher than that of neighbouring capitalists; they weathered the storm of the cotton distress perhaps better than any, being almost the last to close and the first to open; and they are now running full time. They have, in fact, proved that it is quite possible for a cotton-mill (at any rate) to be worked on the largest scale, with a successful result, on the co-operative principle.

What, however, they have not proved is the possibility of a mill being wholly owned by those who work it, and of labour receiving more than the ordinary market share of the profits. The mill was founded on the principle of dividing all profits (after satisfying all expenses and the interest on fixed capital) equally between the shareholders and the workmen, every £100 received in wages counting in the distribution of the dividend the same as every £100 invested in shares. This principle was a real experiment to institute a new condition of labour. The mill had not worked long, however, before (in 1861) this principle, after a severe struggle, was abandoned, and no efforts of the minority, backed by many influential friends of the movement, have succeeded in restoring it. This, therefore, in the great home of co-operation, has for the present decided the issue. The question how to give the labourer a larger share of the profits has failed of solution. A body of co-operative capitalists, it is there seen, hire and pay their own workmen on the ordinary terms of the market, and under the rule of simple competition. This is the greatest blow, in fact, which the system has ever yet sustained, and is one which, if it cannot be reversed, stamps it as incompetent to affect permanently the conditions of industry. In spite of all efforts which faith, hope, and charity make to conceal it, this decision has planted a deep root of division amongst the co-operative body, and has broken the confidence of their most zealous friends. Some of the most active friends of the movement as loudly justify it as others loudly condemn it. And a long controversy has been carried on with great energy and no result. But a vote of the whole body of co-operators would undoubtedly show for the economic party an overwhelming majority . . .

If there is one thing which the progress of civilisation more continually develops, it is that the direction of capital requires entire freedom, undivided devotion, a life of training, and innate business instincts. All our complex forms of industry involve sometimes, in the directors, engineering or practical genius, a sort of instinct of the market, and a life-long familiarity with an involved mass of considerations, partly mechanical, partly monetary, partly administrative. The head of a great production is like the captain of a ship or the general of an army. He must have scientific knowledge, technical knowledge, practical knowledge, presence of mind, dash, courage, zeal, and the habit of command. It is all very well for working men to buy butter and tea prudently, and even to superintend the agents who buy it for them. But it is ridiculous to tell the hammermen at a forge that they can successfully carry on Whitworth's engineering business, or build the *Great Eastern*. Conceive the London and North-Western Railway managed by its stokers, porters, and ticket-clerks, or the Peninsular and Oriental Steamboat Company carried on by a committee of seamen, or the Bank of England managed by its ordinary cashiers! These are extreme cases, but they strikingly explain the real defect of the position. What is the limit? Where does the business become so simple that it can be managed by the mere workmen whom it employs? Arguments on this subject are almost ridiculous, were it not that the extravagant pretensions of some co-operators seem to call for notice. In a word, no sensible man will deny that the great industrial occupations would come to disastrous ruin were it not for entire secrecy, rapidity, and concentration of action, and that practical instinct of trade which nothing but a whole life and a very difficult education can give—and even that can give only to a few.

It profits little to argue that the bulk of the workmen, though unfit to manage, are very fit to superintend the management. He who is unfit to manage is not fit to direct the manager. The only course open to inexperienced men undertaking a complex manufacture would be to trust themselves blindly to a skilful director. But if they do, they are simply in his hands, and the independence and value of their owning the capital is at an end. It cannot be turned both ways. Either the manager is controlled by the shareholder, in which case success is endangered, or he is free, and then they lose responsibility and practical power to affect the management. You cannot *buy* the inspiring authority any more than the electric will of a great military or political chief. It is impossible to *hire* commercial genius and the instincts of a skilful trader. Nor must it be forgotten that the success of great trading companies proves nothing. They are companies of capitalists, the large majority of whom are by the habits of their lives trained to the skilful employment of capital, and versed from childhood in the ways of trade. And even these men practically entrust the whole management blindly to a few great capitalists among them, any one of whom might very well own and direct the whole concern. The fact that an association of *capitalists* can manage a gigantic interest does nothing to prove that an association of *workmen* can. A company of merchants, naval men, and financiers, whose whole lives have trained them to it, can manage the

Peninsular and Oriental undertaking. Does that prove that a company of able seamen could?

But this is to repeat for the hundredth time the objections against Socialism and Communism. There is no need now, or in this country, to expose the unsoundness of these. But co-operation, whilst sharing in many of their defects, wholly forgets the high aims which make these systems noble in their errors. The great-hearted and misjudged enthusiasts who taught them, really grasped the industrial evils in their fulness, and resolutely met them with a cure. They saw that the root of the evil was the extreme power and selfishness of capital. They met it by destroying the institution of individual property, or by subjecting it to new conditions and imposing on it new duties. In Communism, where labour and capital were alike devoted to the common benefit; in Socialism, where labour and capital are radically reorganised, whatever else of evil they might contain, the relative condition of the labourer must certainly have improved. But co-operation is a compromise which reduces none of the rights of property and imposes on it no new obligation. Starting from the same point as Socialism—the anti-social use of capital, and the prostration of the labourer before it—it seeks to remedy all its consequences by making more capitalists. It faces all the risks which beset the subdivision of capital amongst a mass of inexperienced holders, and then does nothing to guarantee more justice in the employment of that capital in the aggregate.

The subdivision of the capital, after all, is a mere mechanical expedient. It must be temporary. The aggregation of capital, the accumulation of wealth in the hands of the more skilful, is one of the most elemental tendencies of society. The prudent *will* grow rich, the rich *will* grow more rich. It is, in truth, one of the primary truths about human labour. Communism boldly says—Let none grow rich. Co-operation simply says—Let more grow rich . . .

Co-operation concerns itself solely with the re-distribution of capital and its produce. For the employment and the duties of capital it has not a word.

Capital has its beneficent as well as its sinister side. It is a power for good far more than for evil; and if co-operation too often forgets the formidable power of aggregate capital, whether owned by many or by one, by rich or poor, it too often puts out of sight the noble functions which capital in a single hand can exert. As the possession of vast and free capital in a single skilful hand enables it to be used with a concentration, rapidity, and elasticity which no corporate capital can enjoy; so in a conscientious hand it is capable of yet more splendid acts of protection, providence, and beneficence. There is nothing chimerical in such a supposition, and nothing degrading to those who benefit by it. It does not consist in the giving of money or the distribution of patronage. A great, free, and wise capitalist—and England happily can show some of the noblest examples—whose mind is devoted to the worthy employment of his power, can in countless ways, by advice, help, example, and experience, promote the welfare of those about him, raise their material comfort, their domestic happiness, their education, their health, their whole physical and moral condition; can act almost as a providence on earth, and that by means as honourable for them to receive as for him to use. Every one knows that some of the largest estates, and some very large manufactories in this country, are now successfully carried on in a spirit which provides in a very high degree for the welfare of all concerned. The feeling of honest pride, confidence, and goodwill with which these efforts are met on the part of tenants and workmen, is as elevating to them as it is to their employers. It would be a perversion of mind which could see anything mean in so noble a relation as this. It would be preposterous to suppose that the sense of duty could be as lively and personal on one side or the other, where the capital is owned by a company. No responsible manager of a society could feel or venture to show the same munificent care for his people that many landlords and many manufacturers now do. No association could or would be ever voting sums for those benevolent purposes which the conscientious capitalist carries out day by day. As little could it do so as the Board of Admiralty could inspire the sense of sympathy and devotion which binds a captain like Nelson to his men. This is a conviction almost as old as society itself, which it needs more now than some phrases about "Self Help" and "Mutual Co-operation" to eradicate. Socialism, it is true, and still more Communism, did claim to substitute for this spirit another as strong, or even stronger. But that was by boldly reconstructing the social system, by instilling new habits, and instituting a moral education. But the bastard Communism—of breaking capital into bits—which some advocate as true co-operation, leaves the whole force of these sentiments out of sight. It weakens the power of capital for good far more than it weakens its power for evil. The morality and education of capital it passes by. It subdivides it, but does nothing to elevate it. Right, useful, necessary often, as the principle of association and co-operation is, indispensable as it may be as an adjunct and resting point, it will still remain as true as ever, that on any large scale, and for the highest uses, concentrated and not associated capital will command the greatest practical success, and develop the most noble moral features both in employer and employed.[1]

It may be asked, is there any need so closely to criticise a spontaneous economic movement which has an obvious practical value? Is it necessary again to repeat objections against Socialism as a system? The answer is that there is real need for it. The co-operative system is so great a success that any illusions about it would be very dangerous. It is now absorbing men of such high qualities and influence, that if not well directed it will prove positively pernicious; and especially so, since it is being advocated with such exclusive claims and such extravagant language as befits only a new social system. The present writer yields to none in his warm sympathy and respect for the movement as regards the "stores" and associated artificers. He knows and has seen how very much good it is doing. But that good is wholly dependent on its true limit and use being understood, and he has long seen with regret that some of the very best leaders and friends of the working classes are throwing themselves exclusively into it, as if it were a new gospel, destined to revolutionise the conditions of industry. As applying on any large scale to manufactures, it seems to the writer a feeble echo of Socialism, with many of its defects and few of its ennobling aims. On this side it is a crude compromise between the claims of labour and of capital—the hybrid child of Plutonomy and Communism.

Note

1 It will be seen that no notice is here taken of the system originating in Paris, advocated by Mr. Mill, and adopted by Messrs. Briggs and Messrs. Crossley, in which a portion of the profits is freely given by the capitalist to the labourer, or a share in the capital is made over to him. This, the most hopeful fact in our industrial system, the best of all schemes of industrial improvement, is not co-operation at all. It wants every feature of co-operation. It is not self-help by the people, for it is a wise and spontaneous act of munificence from the capitalist. No efforts of the labourers can advance its introduction. The capital is not sub-divided, but remains practically in one hand. The management is not democratic, but remains also in one hand. The labourers are not partners, and have no control for good or evil over the concern. It is the free gift of a bonus to the labourer—a wise, a just, and a promising system—but not co-operation.

5

"THE LAND! THE LAND!", *CO-OPERATIVE NEWS*, 5 OCTOBER 1872, 505–506.

William Pare

[William Pare (1805–1873), the son of a cabinet maker, was born in Birmingham. He helped found the local Mechanics' Institute and played an active role in the Birmingham Political Union during the agitation that preceded the Great Reform Act. Pare was elected to the first Birmingham Town Council in 1836 and was appointed the city's first registrar of births, marriages and deaths in 1837. He was converted to Owenism after reading William Thompson's, *An Inquiry into the Principles of the Distribution of Wealth most conducive to Human Happiness* (1824), and he remained a keen Owenite for the rest of his life, helping to found the first Birmingham Co-operative Society in 1828, briefly visiting the Ralahine community in County Clare, Ireland, in 1832 and acting as governor of the Owenite community at Queenwood in Hampshire between 1842 and 1844. He acted as trustee of Thompson's estate, left for the purposes of founding communities (Thompson's remaining family fought for the estate and eventually won) and was Owen's joint literary executor (along with Dr Henry Travis) when Owen died in 1858. In the years that followed, Pare did all he could to keep the Owenite faith alive. He wrote regularly for the developing co-operative press, reacting positively to the popularity and success of Rochdale co-operation but reminding readers of the wider goal. "We must not be content to remain a nation of mere shopkeepers . . . co-operation must result in an entire reorganisation of society", he wrote in the *Co-operator* in 1868. [J.F.C. Harrison, *Quest for the New Moral World. Robert Owen and the Owenites in Britain and America* (New York: Charles Scribner's Sons, 1969), 239] Pare organised the first modern Co-operative Congress in 1869 and published many articles in the *Co-operative News* after the establishment of the newspaper in 1871. The article reproduced below is an excellent example of Pare's passionate belief in the continuing relevance of the Owenite vision.]

TRUMPET-CALL TO THE CO-OPERATORS OF GREAT BRITAIN AND IRELAND.

IV.

THE LAND! THE LAND!

Comrades,—Some one there must be in our ranks constantly to bear the "Excelsior" flag; and for the nonce I shoulder it.

Whilst you are busying yourselves in discovering and practising the most economical mode of laying out for your sustenance the wages you have earned in competitive mills and workshops, where your labour is hired at the lowest possible price by the capitalist, in order that he may make the largest possible profit (*i.e.,* something above and beyond interest for his capital, and remuneration for his services in direction and superintendence), it is desirable that you should be constantly reminded by your leaders that these economics of distribution are but the A, B, C of co-operation—the mere leading-strings or go-cart, so to speak, by which infant co-operators learn to walk. Just as you have saved or are saving the profits of a whole army of needless middle-men heretofore employed in exchanging, transporting, and distributing that portion of the wealth you have created, which under the "everyone-for-himself-and-devil-take-the-hindmost" system you are permitted to retain, so must you save that other share which now falls to the lot of the capitalist in the shape of profit (as above defined) for setting and keeping your labour in motion when it suits him so to do.

How this may be best accomplished I have in part indicated in former "calls." It should not—*must not*—be attempted by following the haphazard course of the competitive system—making articles on the speculation of their being in demand in the general market when made—but by producing for the supply of known wants in the co-operative market—that is, to meet the steady demand of the members of your own body in those necessary articles which enter into their daily consumption. By steadily and persistently following this course, you will gradually free yourselves from that chaotic confusion into which ever and anon the productive resources of our populations are thrown, for want of something like systematic arrangement and co-operative effort.

But this action which I recommend pre-supposes a federated union of societies. It is idle to dream that it can be otherwise effected; and it is most gratifying to find that this fact is being more and more realised. I gather this from the reported proceedings of the various district conferences, and from the correspondence in the *News*. I hope to see the day when it will be esteemed a privilege for a society to be permitted to join the Wholesale federation, and to be represented at the Annual Congress, and continuously by its Central Board. The benefits conferred by each may well make the union with them felt to be a privilege.

I believe it will be found that larger benefits will attend the carrying on of production in its various branches by, or under the surveillance of, the Wholesale Society, than by separate organisations. But if separate organisations be resolved on, then undoubtedly they should be brought about by the subscription of the necessary funds by the societies, and not by individuals, for unless this be the case, a low, grovelling selfishness, instead of a high and ennobling socialism, will be fostered.

As, however, some difference of opinion exists as to the part, if any, which the Wholesale should take in production, it may well form one of the subjects for discussion at the Congress next year.

But whatever may be resolved in this respect, if the order of production be maintained upon which I insist, there can be no doubt that the several commodities produced will be most easily and economically distributed through the medium of the Wholesale.

Can anything be more barbarous and wasteful than for each manufacturing society to be sending a traveller round to the stores throughout the kingdom to sell its goods? It is pitiable to read the story of the Hebden Bridge Fustian Cutters as to this waste of their resources in search of markets in their early days, and painful to find that the managers of very many of the stores received them so coldly. May we hope that these ignorant and evil days have passed, and that the true fraternal spirit of co-operation will reign from henceforth.

All this, however, is but exordium. My chief object in now writing is to press upon you the necessity of at once attempting something higher and nobler than anything you have yet achieved. Let those who are yet ignorant learn; and those who have learned ever bear in mind that co-operation is destined to effect an entire revolution in the objects and aims, and consequently in the whole life and character of man. Assuredly co-operation will introduce and perpetuate that blessed time which prophets have predicted and poets have sung, when "the lion shall lie down with the lamb," and when "there shall be none to hurt or destroy, in all God's holy mountain."

What a solemn mockery it is whilst dwelling in this turmoil of competitive strife to pray daily, "Thy kingdom come, Thy will be done on earth as it is in heaven," if, wrapping ourselves up in individual selfishness, we care only to better our condition, and some of us hardly that!

No, my friends, if God's kingdom is to come and His will be done, of a verity, so far as we are concerned, we must separate ourselves entirely from the present cold, heartless, devilish system of society, and leaving its hideous body and soul destroying towns, associate ourselves in convenient numbers on new and healthy sites, surrounded as far as possible by everything which is good and beautiful, and under arrangements for conducting all the business of life which shall necessarily lead to the greatest happiness, not only of the greatest number, but of all.

This will be accomplished by the acquisition—at first by a few, your leaders, but ultimately by all—of the knowledge of the causes which lead to evil and of those which lead to good; and the constant and consistent application of that knowledge to practice, by eliminating, and in the future preventing, in as far as in us lies, all and every the causes of evil, and instituting and preserving the causes of good only.

In the "good time coming," human labour, instead of being a curse to be shunned, will be a blessing to be sought. Why? Because instead of long, monotonous, health and life destroying toil, allied with ignorant and vicious associates, often under repulsive conditions and sometimes smarting under a sense of injustice, it will—by being shared by all, by being alternated in kind, aided by all possible mechanical and scientific appliances, undertaken in company with intelligent and agreeable comrades, and surrounded by all that is attractive—become simply an agreeable exercise. Or, where from the very nature of things this cannot be, and there is need for any disagreeable, difficult, or dangerous occupation to be undertaken, the enlightened public opinion of a well trained and grateful community will set its especial mark of approbation on those who chivalrously undertake it as the benefactors of their species.

In those days, instead of the low sordid greed, cunning, lying, and cheating attendant on our present trade and commerce, a spirit of frankness, truth, and justice shall pervade all our dealings. A time, indeed,—

> When every transfer of earth's natural gifts
> Shall be a commerce of good words and works.

Well, then, what steps are to be taken to gradually bring about this happy state of existence which I am glad to believe some of you are panting for?

It is time, I say, that we laid the foundations of a co-operative village, and that we may among other matters, give to co-operators and the world at large a living example of the vast benefits which may be derived from associated homes; conspicuous among which will be the relief of women from the drudgery of present domestic life, with an increase of comfort and a saving of expenditure which few who have not studied the subject would credit.

Advantages of other kinds there will be, far too numerous to be dwelt on in this address. One, however, which I have endeavoured to force upon your attention several times during the last few years is to my mind so important that I cannot refrain from again pressing it upon you. Such a well ordered village community, with all its accessories, when in full action will become a normal school, wherein the children, not only of the resident members, but of outsiders, will be rationally trained, physically, mentally, morally, and practically, to become real men and women, instead of the miserable fragments of humanity we find at present. Mental and muscular labour will be alternated, so as to render both agreeable, instead of the *ennui* and fatigue produced by the prevailing system. The school, the workshop, and the farm, will form the curriculum of study, and will be made to illustrate each other. And by the time the children have attained their majority it will be found that their light, but well-directed and mechanically-aided, labour will have paid the whole cost of their maintenance and education from birth.

Comrades, I ask are not these advantages worth striving for—worth a sacrifice, if need be, to attain? Let those who think so do their utmost to realise them, and to bring about a conviction in others. Explain it to your wives, daughters, and sisters; talk it over with your fellow-members; make it a question to be discussed at your conferences; so that some speedy action may be taken, and we may not be maundering over it for years, as we have other questions which, when heartily taken up, have been made a success.

Let a portion of the surplus capital of the societies be devoted to the purchase of an estate, say in Lancashire or Yorkshire, or other suitable locality, of some two or three thousand acres, in the centre of which should be placed the dwellings for about five hundred families, artificially arranged, together with the public buildings. In close proximity should be the gardens, orchards, and ornamental grounds, and at convenient distances the farm buildings and ordinary workshops. In addition may be a mill for the production of cotton, woollen, silk, or other fabrics; or manufactories for other articles consumed by yourselves, and distributed through your wholesale societies.

The surplus produce of the farm in like manner may be sold to the stores, and the cultivation of the land on improved principles will attract some of the more advanced labourers from the agricultural districts, who are preparing themselves for co-operative effort, and who will gladly unite with you in such a really effective work. I purposed, when commencing this address, to have pointed out some, at least, of the many advantages to be derived from an improved system of farming, with a larger command of capital and other facilities which can rarely be compassed under the present isolated system, but which will be most facile under co-operative arrangements. This, however, must be reserved for another occasion. Meantime, I beseech you ponder well the rude outlines I have now given you.

I conclude by offering you my heartfelt congratulations at the progress which our principles are making. By the latest news which has reached me from home, I find that the first commoner in England, the Speaker of the House of Commons, has pronounced for co-operation. Alluding to the relations of employers and employed, in an address to his labourers at the recent "harvest home" on his estate at Glynde, in Sussex, he is reported to have said: "My opinion is that we shall never have a settlement of that question until the labourer receives, in some shape or other, a share, though it may be a small one, of the profits of the business in which he is engaged. I refer not only to those employed upon farms, but to those engaged in mining, in manufactories, and in trades of all kinds." Bravo, Mr. Speaker! Hear, hear! As the *Examiner* says, "Progress so rapid is enough to make Owen's ghost rub its eyes."

WILLIAM PARE,
Hon. Sec. to the Central Board.

6

"CO-OPERATIVE VILLAGES – CO-OPERATION AND COMMUNISM", *CO-OPERATIVE NEWS*, 12 FEBRUARY 1876; 19 FEBRUARY 1876, 81, 93.

George Dawson

[Little is known about George Dawson of Sheffield, who contributed the following letter to an on-going debate in the pages of the *Co-operative News*. In it, Dawson acknowledged the continuing influence of the ideas of old Owenites such as Dr Henry Travis and his faith in "co-operation in the highest sense, or communism" in creating a just economy and society. However, according to Dawson workers in Sheffield had sketched out their own plans independently, before Travis had published his work. Travis' text is not identified in the letter but was most likely *Effectual Reform in Man and Society* that had been published the year before and which had attempted to substitute the awkward sounding word "Effectualism" for socialism, communism and co-operation. [J.F.C. Harrison, *Quest for the New Moral World. Robert Owen and the Owenites in Britain and America* (New York: Charles Scribner's Sons, 1969), 238] In his letter, Dawson asserts that many men and women were ready to come together to effect such a change, which should not be dismissed as a "purely ideal or Utopian" aspiration but one made eminently practical by the joint-stock form of organisation. Like Travis, Dawson looks to the co-operative movement to provide the necessary capital to develop such initiatives, sadly lacking at present, however, despite the ambitions of individuals such as J.T.W. Mitchell, who along with other co-operative leaders had recently addressed a meeting in the city.]

CO-OPERATIVE VILLAGES.—CO-OPERATION AND COMMUNISM.

Sir,—I feel inclined, if you will allow me, to say a few words upon the above subjects; only, from the brief time at my disposal, I am afraid they will be very hurriedly and imperfectly put before you.

    The question of co-operative villages—or communities, as I prefer to call them—is one which I take the deepest interest in, and would like to follow up its discussion in your pages, only that other matters have a prior claim upon my time and energies. I rejoice that the subject has been brought forward; and, strange to say, has begun to occupy the attention of many persons, in widely different places, at the same time. Yet I regret that so few of those who are known to take a deep interest in the subject do not see it to be their duty to join in the discussion, give us their views, and practically aid in converting their ideas into a consolidated and realised fact.

Whatever we may think of, or how we may agree as to, the theoretical or practical value of Dr. Travis's plans, the appearance of his book just at this time, when so many are becoming impressed with the need for some change, is quite remarkable, and would lead one to suppose that things were working together "for good" finally, and shortly to result in the realisation of some such scheme as we have in view. Previous to the appearance of Travis's book, a small circle of friends in Sheffield had met, and conceived a plan similar in all its leading principles to that of the doctor; and, after discussing several schemes for raising capital, finally adopted that of "shares." And, on the first night of the adoption of this plan, 380 shares were promised to be taken up by six persons present at the time; and many persons outside offer to take shares, should our idea ever be realised.

Then, the horrid condition of society is such as to lead all thinking men to the conclusion that things are so very bad that something must be done, either to end or mend our present barbarous and unchristianised state.

As Mr. Holmes stated in his able address here last Monday, and again says on page 55 of last week's *News,* that the wealth of this country is increasing at a tremendous rate; whilst the number of the population, or producers, amongst whom that wealth is divided, is not increasing in a proportionate degree.

If this increasing wealth is not being divided so equally amongst those who earn it as it should be, it must be monopolised by the few capitalists, who do not earn it; and who, therefore, have no moral claim to possess it. As Mr. Holmes says, in 1868 the producers were 13,321,000, and they produced £825,000,000. Of this £825,000,000, 10,962,000 producers receive £324,000,000—£29 a year, or 11s. 2d. weekly; and the 2,359,000 receive £501,000,000, or £216. 12s. each yearly, or £4. 3s. per week, in sums varying from £60 to £8,500 a year. Is not this an awful fact to think of—this unequal and unrighteous division of wealth?—which means an unequal division of God-given comfort, health, knowledge, morality, and length of life.

When will men see and work out the mottoes of communism (and especially co-operators) "that in all labour there is profit," "that the labourer is worthy of his hire," "that he who will not work neither shall he eat." Think what all this wealth would enable these 13 million workers to do, if it was only divided "fairly" amongst them. The so-called "benefactor" of mankind—the rich employer—made rich out of the wear and waste of the lives of his employés, is really no benefactor, but a monopoliser of the wealth and comforts which belong by right to others. In a properly organised state of society there could be no millionaires, no paupers, no persons dying of want, or short of all the necessaries and comforts of life. It is a disgrace to a nation calling itself "Christian" and "Bible loving," that a man or child may die from sheer want. And it is equally a disgrace that one man should be the possessor of one or four millions, for the possession of this by the latter is the cause of the death from want of the former. No man can become rich—as society is—without someone becoming poorer; and he who owns thousands he cannot use, is only the complement to the one who is dying for want of food and fire.

And co-operation in its highest sense, or communism, is the cure for all this; but not that kind of co-operation which gives the capitalist 10 per cent, and then another share after that, whilst to labour it gives only the usual wages of the trade and 1 per cent of what is left after the do-nothing capitalist has satisfied his rapacious appetite. But a system of co-operation, where labour and capital may have each their fair share and no more, where all labourers may be upon a common level as far as human nature will permit, where all may be surrounded by the conditions which tend most to morality, intelligence, and health, where it will be easy to do right and difficult to do wrong, where all the blessings of the present state may be kept, and the curses and vices left behind. This is no purely ideal or Utopian state. There are numbers of men and women who are so organised as to be "a law unto themselves," and whose lives are exemplary, and who find it easy to live as they should do, who long for a happier, healthier, and more perfect society, and who, if left to themselves, could form without difficulty such a nearly perfect society. There are numbers of such—to say that there are not is to paint human nature as blacker than it is—and why should not these people betake themselves to more pleasant scenes and conditions, and by means of intelligent and advanced co-operation or communism create for themselves that form of existence which would be free from the ills which are eating the very life blood out of present society?

There is no reason why they should not do it, and nothing that I can see which forms any insuperable obstacle. Co-operators admit that they have wealth, some of them almost a surfeit of it, which wealth is doing but little, as they admit, to improve or remodel society; yet with that same wealth turned into another channel they could start a movement which would bring about a complete revolution in society, and would prove the greatest moral and reformatory movement the world has yet seen.

I was surprised and glad to hear Mr. Holmes take such an advanced view of co-operation; and draw a picture—if not in such bold lines as I could wish—of what might be done by co-operators if they would only think of some higher work than that of selling bacon and sugar, and higher results than that of a 2s. divided. Certainly, that is something; it is a good deal; but, at that rate, co-operation may go on for generations and accomplish but little.

A co-operator getting 2s. "divi." from his store, and yet living amid and surrounded by all the present unnatural conditions of society, cannot do much for himself or his fellows.

The movement had to begin, of course; some of the wisest and boldest have shown the rest what can be done; and it is now time for these wisest, who have achieved so much, to take another and a greater stride forward, and beckon the rest to follow.

These wisest and most far-seeing men should put their heads together, and, with the help of their great wealth, found "a new beginning of society"—a form of society more honest, equable, healthy, and moral than any we have yet seen. If they will not, they should be ready to assist with their surplus wealth those who are ready to sacrifice time, money, and life in making the experiment. It has often been said *àpropos* of past movements—and I now repeat it as applicable to ours— "Now is the time."

Everything appears favourable, and pointing to certain success. It only requires some one to resolve to start.

Some one has said, "It took co-operators twenty years to save their first million; five more to save the second; while they saved the third million in a year and a half."

Now, at the same rate, what will they save in the next year, and the next? And what is all this wealth doing? Is it possible to put it to any higher use than the one it is now serving? I think it is.

Messrs. Holmes, Mitchell, and Butcher, when here the other night, each showed their hearers how they might better their condition, and that of society in general, by taking a more advanced view of co-operation and its powers. One of them showed that in 15 years—I think—the whole railway system of England might be purchased by co-operative means; and Mr. Butcher pointedly and humorously showed them that the workers, and not the idle employers, were morally entitled to the best food, the best homes, the highest comforts of life, and I agree with him entirely. This is communism, as I call it—call it what he will. As one of the speakers said, society might be turned upside down by means of co-operation. I agree with him, only, that as co-operation is, it would take a long time—ages almost. And the result would come much sooner if these same men would, in some corner of the land, give outsiders a practical example of what could be done in that way.

I am sorry I haven't time and space to give a lengthy review of the remarks of these three gentlemen, to show that their ideas contain the germs—more than the germs—of principles which, if carried, would completely reform society. It appears to me, that after all, after 1,800 years' preaching, the practical worker— not the parson and preacher—is to be the means used in bringing about the millenium. In a town like this, of milk-and-water co-operation, where co-operators can't, by force or by surgical operation, get advanced ideas into the brains of their committees, it was refreshing to hear such wise, broad, and advanced views—and took one's mind pleasantly away from candles and soap to far higher subjects. I hope the Sheffield co-operators may benefit by their visit. They certainly needed all the advice they got.

I beg to thank you, Mr. Editor, for myself, and friends here, for your very suggestive and advanced article in the *News* for the 5th inst. Co-operators should be proud of an editor of their journal who is willing to point them to the great prospects of the future, rather than hold them back and preach contentment. Every idea in that article, and more might be realised in a year, if co-operators would only resolve to make a start. This question has been discussed at the debating class of the Reform Club here on four Saturday nights, and very animated have been the discussions.

We "communists" laid our principles before the class, much as you and Dr. Travis lay them down; and, though every opponent "ardently desired to see our scheme realised," they all voted it "impracticable." The objections were generally very amusing, as objections to all new reformatory movements are. One chief objection was, that in such a state of society, where no single employer could pocket all the profits, men need not work so many hours, and leisure time was a curse to a man, leading him to sin and crime. That, I believe, was the chief objection urged. But the objector's reasoning faculties were too weak to show him that there were other antecedents and concurrent causes besides leisure time to make a man vicious and to make bad use of that time.

The soldier employs his leisure time badly, because he can hardly do otherwise. The soldier's position and surroundings would not be those of the man in a model village where all must work, and where the public-house and other temptations would not exist. In speaking of the economics of a co-operative village, I spoke of the common cooking kitchen, the common washhouse; and in pointing out our present wasteful use of fuel, I said why should we not, in such a village, be able to warm our rooms by simply turning a tap, as we turn on and off our gas light? This was laughed at by these members of a "Reform Club," whose eyes see no reform save that to be obtained by the circuitous route of voting for A in preference to B. Yet, Mr. Editor, you use the same illustration in your article. These same persons will read your article, and may not laugh at that.

They said—would it not be better for us to remain and assist in removing all the evils of society we spoke of, to remove intemperance, remove poverty, reform parliament, reform church, reform this and that?

I asked if it would not be better to reform all these, so far as we were concerned, at one blow, by removing ourselves away from them, and creating society anew for ourselves, with the vicious elements left out; and then, if we succeeded, others would be induced to follow our example. Most of the evils of society are inflicted by society upon itself, and they could be removed, but not in the way we are at present working for that end. Society is ever at war with itself. We call ourselves great, glorious, intelligent, moral, free, and we are great in sin and crime, and selfishness and shams. We are glorious, as getters of wealth and despoilers of one another. We are intelligent, in having amongst us some of the most ignorant and benighted beings upon the earth. We are moral, with a morality that festers and stinks—a morality so rank and shallow, that no man hardly dare trust his brother. And we are free, with a freedom that grinds and goads the worker for the enrichment of the rich, and treats the resulting poverty as a crime. We call ourselves civilised, christianised, and all that is good, and send out men to point the heathen to heaven, and we are as bad as bad can be, and don't know the way to deserve heaven ourselves. We send money bags, not brains to represent us and make laws for us in Councils and Parliament. We let the first-born (as savages often do) and not the morally fittest, wear the crown and inherit the wealth. We put the rich and not the poor into the best seats at church; and we pay bishops to tell us to wait till we get to heaven for our share of the pleasures, whilst they make sure of theirs here, lest they should miss that in the future.

We allow men to get fat upon our sweat and toil, and live in grand houses, and wear fine clothes, and we are content with a cottage and fustian. They tell us we may walk in their grounds, and view their houses, and pictures, and plate (which we worked for), if we will only "not touch," and "keep off the grass." And we bow our heads in gratitude, and we keep our fingers off *our* pictures, and our feet off *our* grass, thinking they are another's.

We allow men to rob us of that which is the birthright of everyone—the soil; whilst we, in consequence, have to turn to the poorhouse, and die in disgrace. We allow the rich—that is, those who have got our share as well as their own of wealth—to live in the West-end and the country, who die at the rate of 11 or 12 per 1,000; whilst we live in the East-end, in the slums, and die at the rate of from 24 to 36 per 1,000; and all this is necessary to keep them rich and us poor.

We shudder when we read of a battle with 10,000 slain; yet in London 20,000 a year are wilfully killed, and 200,000 wounded. And in Liverpool the number is greater in proportion. Our drink traffic alone slays tens upon tens of thousands a year, and yet we will not stop this preventible slaughter. It costs us £150,000,000 a year—sufficient to place every pauper in the country in co-operative villages in an independent position.

Our non-producers and idlers, who cost the nation most, live an average of 55 years at least: we, the producers, live from 17 to 30 at most.

We allow children to be born and die before five years of age at the rate of two out of four. In 1859, 184,264 children under five died, as did 105,629 under one year. In ten years, 1851–60, two million children under five years of age died. And yet we have a state-supported church, and a state-supported system of medicine. Doctors—and our present uncivilised state of society—are responsible for these deaths. And things are getting worse instead of better. Ignorance of parents is one cause of these deaths. In one town alone thirty gallons of laudanum are sold each year, to be given to infants; enough to kill 6,000 men. If society was true to itself such ignorance would not exist. If doctors did their duty, they would instruct the people better; if they know better, which I doubt. 300 children are found dead in the streets of London each year. What is the cause? Poverty and crime. Poverty the cause of all; a wicked and unequal distribution of wealth.

In the reign of Henry VIII. 72,000 persons were hanged for petty thefts, most of them committed through poverty. Have we mended matters since then? We don't hang them certainly; but what about the actual poverty?

How many hundreds of thousands of agricultural labourers and their families have been for years living in the lowest condition of want; and yet each labourer is of more worth to the nation than ten dukes.

7,000 people a year die in the London workhouses, and 82,000 in its public institutions. How many die in the whole country? And yet we bow our heads in reverence to those curses of society—rich men—who have locked in their coffers that which would save nearly every one of these miserable beings.

Every town possesses lairs and dens called houses, where every physiological and sanitary law is outraged, and where the poor try to live, and die in the struggle. If cows and horses died at the same rate that human beings do, the nation would go into hysterics, and no rest would be obtained until the rate was reduced; but the death of a horse touches somebody's pocket—the death of a poor man, woman, or child touches no such pocket. Would to God it would touch some hearts! In 1854 Lord Russell said 35 per 100 of the people could neither read nor write. Whose fault was that, Lord Russell?

Our criminal class costs us two millions and a-half a year. Suppose they were all producing something; what a difference! Yet it is society's own fault that they are not. Crime is everywhere; we are taught it in school, in church, in chapel, and in the shop. Our food is adulterated, our water is poisoned, our air is unfit to breathe.

The richer we get the bigger we build our cities, and the more unhealthy they become; the more keen and deadly the competition, the faster we die. Civilisation (so called) and demoralisation and death go, at present, hand in hand.

43,000 women work at field labour and similar revolting trades. In a co-operative village they need not do that. 50,000 females are constantly walking the streets of our towns, driven mostly by poverty to lead lives of shame. If they had their share of wealth few would do that. In a communistic village all necessaries as well as comforts would be found them, and a congenial kind of employment.

And so we might go on and fill a book, to show that England is not so bright or so happy as she lyingly pictures herself to be. It is only the few who are happy and prosperous, and only the few who can be, in the midst of such temptation and vice, good and virtuous.

Re-model society, remove its shams, its vices and sins, or rather the causes of these, and you will have a happy England.

And to do this you must begin in a small way; and a community commenced to-morrow, with the help of all this surplus wealth of which co-operators boast, would and must be a success, and be a start towards the redemption of society.

Milton-street, Sheffield.   GEO. DAWSON.

7

"MODERN ENGLISH COMMUNISM", *CO-OPERATIVE NEWS*, 25 AUGUST 1877, 448.

W.H.C.

[The unknown author of this contribution to a debate in the *Co-operative News* also attempted to elide co-operation with socialism and communism. The letter details "the trial of Communism about to take place" in Sheffield, which supporters hoped would prove its validity to the doubters. The social critic John Ruskin had purchased thirteen acres of land four miles out of Sheffield at Totley in Derbyshire, which he rented to a group of local communists for an experiment in co-operative life. Co-operators were fond of citing Ruskin's famous dictum in *Unto This Last* (1860): "Government and Co-operation are, in all things and eternally, the Laws of Life. Anarchy and competition, eternally, and in all things, the Laws of Death". However, although Ruskin proved a trenchant critic of capitalist consumerism, he had no faith in working-class control, believing instead in the inviolability of the principle of authority or "mastership". [David M. Craig, *John Ruskin and the Ethics of Consumption* (Charlottesville: University of Virginia Press, 2006)] The anonymous writer of the letter reprinted here had visited the community at Totley with a party of secularists, criticised the farmhouse and hoped that E.T. Craig – manager of the Owenite community established at Ralahine in Ireland in the early 1830s – would be approached for advice on its redesign. Although the affair ended badly, with friction between the autocratic Ruskin and the working-class communists (the former eventually withdrawing his support), this letter underlines the sustained interest among co-operators in attempts to supersede the capitalist system that were more far-reaching than shopkeeping, however fragile and partial. [The story of the Totley communists can be found in W.H.G. Armytage, *Heavens Below. Utopian Experiments in England, 1560–1960* (London: Routledge & Kegan Paul, 1961), 293–299; Mark Frost, *The Lost Companions and John Ruskin's Guild of St George: A Revisionary History* (London: Anthem Press, 2014), 133–143.]]

MODERN ENGLISH COMMUNISM.

What's in a name? has been asked over and over again a hundred times. It has also been said by someone that "words are vehicles to convey thought"; but then words are so pliable, and can be made to mean just what the writer or reader wishes them to mean. Take infidel or heretic, and what an awful signification attaches to those words in the minds of many, more especially of the superficial sort—people who allow others to think for them. And this word communism conjures up in the minds of some all sorts of terrible ideas, when, if people would only take the smallest trouble to inquire, before hastily coming to a conclusion on this or any other subject that comes under their notice, they would save not only themselves, but a host of others, an amount of senseless anxiety—aye, and senseless talk, too, that renders them simply ridiculous in the eyes of those of riper judgment.

But when we speak of communism to many who do know its meaning, we find even such persons treating it as Utopian and impracticable, telling us that people will have to be made over again, just as though human beings were like a piece of granite rock, and as incapable of change; whereas we are continually meeting with persons advanced in life whose ideas now are as opposite as the poles to what they were only a few years since. Others will direct our attention to Lanark, Harmony Hall, and Ralahine, as specimens of failure. As well might they call to mind the numerous shipwrecks that occur as failures in navigation; or the bankruptcies that appear in our newspapers day by day as the failure of commerce.

Such incidents are but the weak links that exist more or less in every chain of human construction, and as such they are regarded by the thoughtful and intelligent; because principles do not depend upon accidents for success, and the miscarriage of any scheme—having truth for its foundation—is only affected by hindrance for the time being, the ultimate issue is certain; and the shrewd man of business ever avails himself of the failings of his fellows—they are as beacons to him, warning him of the rocks upon which others have split—and by so doing he pursues a path of safety till success rewards him for his toil.

Communism no doubt has hitherto failed to create a general interest in its principles, but many things have to be considered that account for this lack of interest, and also for the failure attending the numerous trials that may have been made at different periods of the world's history.

Taking our own country into consideration, and what are the difficulties that have stood in the way, one of the hindrances to its success in the past arose from this fact, that the pioneers were men who dared to differ from the popular religious teachings of the day, hence they were termed infidels; that of course was reason enough for the masses to reject it, and when it is also considered that the law and the press were against communism (because it sounded the knell of the privileged classes), together with the difficulty of communication either by post or road, it is not to be wondered that so little progress was made; and when the general ignorance of the masses at those times is also taken into consideration, it is easy for us to conceive how difficult it must have been to disseminate a thorough knowledge of the principles of communism.

Let us hope that with the increased advantages possessed by the present generation, these principles (which I hold to be essential to the true progress of the race) may become more widely known and understood; for knowledge is power, and power rightly wielded must ultimately raise the people to the normal condition in which every human being should live.

I have often heard it stated—and I have believed it—that men were to be found who would carry out the principles of Communism, if only the means were at hand to give them a fair start. Well, the opportunity now presents itself; and in such a manner as few were prepared to expect, not even the most sanguine; so that the old cuckoo cry of "Ah! it won't come in our day" ought to be banished from the vocabulary of all who profess and call themselves Socialists or Communists. And as this will be read mainly by those who for the last forty years have been endeavouring to establish a system whereby the masses can be raised to a much higher level than they could have attained by the old methods, I trust that an amount of earnest interest will be manifested in the trial of Communism about to take place—and of which I have to speak at some length—that those who are now engaging in it may be encouraged by co-operators and socialists in a most unmistakable and brotherly manner; inasmuch as the outside world are only too ready to throw every obstacle in the way of social progress.

Prophets are never wanting to prophecy evil, whenever real earnest workers set about work of reform, and especially so of that kind of reform which happens to be much in advance of the prevailing opinions of the day.

Co-operation in trade is a great success, and a blessing to thousands; yet it has been predicted to fail a thousand times. Co-operation in manufacture, to a limited extent, has been a success, and who but the superficial will dare to predict its failure in the future?

Now communism, pure and simple—as I understand it—is but the logical ultimate of all preceding forms of co-operation; because it is the only normal condition of existence in which man can love his neighbour as himself. This may appear startling to many, but will be endorsed by those who have made it a subject for study.

But as my purpose in this article is to bring before the readers of the *Co-operative News* the latest phase of communism, and not to discuss the question, I will call their attention to what has already appeared in this and other newspapers relative to what Mr. Ruskin has done for the people of Sheffield.

It will be remembered that an extract was copied from Mr. Ruskin's *Fors Clavigera* a short time since, showing what Mr. Ruskin had been doing with the property he came into possession of at the death of his father, and one of the items mentioned in the statement given in *Fors* was somewhat as follows:—"That Mr. Ruskin had purchased thirteen acres of land for the sum of £2,200, to be let to a body of communists in Sheffield at a rental of about £70 per annum, in order that the principles of communism might have a fair chance of being tried."

In order to ascertain to what extent the affair was progressing, I paid a visit to Sheffield a short time since, and found the party numbering between twenty and thirty persons of all ages—of varying professions and different creeds—orthodoxy, heterodoxy, and no doxy—but all were imbued with the spirit of earnestness and determination to put their faith into practice; and as in all associations we find radical and conservative parties, so in this instance I soon discovered the two sections, combined with a strongly-marked individuality of character peculiar to most large manufacturing towns.

Happily the conservative element (I use the word in the sense of being cautious) predominated to a considerable degree, which, under their present circumstances, is rather to be commended than otherwise; as it only too often happens when a number of persons acquire property on very easy terms they are apt to be reckless in the use of the same; this cannot be said of our friends in Sheffield.

However, there is no doubt they mean work as soon as they have passed through what may not inaptly be called a state of gestation. Their ideal, no doubt, is lofty—as most ideals are—but the realisation of it will probably have to be postponed for a long time to come; for who ever heard of an ideal being reached—even the most moderate in their expectations? I remember once hearing a minister of a Presbyterian church remark that "there was even more pleasure in the attempt to obtain an object than in the actual obtaining of the same." Because, in our eager striving after any one thing we have set our minds upon, the expectation increases in intensity as the object is approached; so that, when it is reached, a reaction sets in—a kind of unstringing of the bow; in fact we find that our ideal falls somewhat short of our anticipations. Nevertheless, we must have ideals, and the loftier they are the more pure our lives become, as they stimulate us to exertion, enabling us to overthrow all obstacles that attempt to bar our way.

I found, upon inquiry, that the future home of our friends had been obtained under much more favourable circumstances than as stated in the public newspapers; that the rent had been rescinded—that Mr. Ruskin had generously offered to erect all suitable buildings for dwellings and workshops, and also to lend them £500 free of interest, for seven years, the said £500 to be returned at that period, or they are to show cause why. Now could any terms be more favourable? Are they generous beyond all praise?

The day following my arrival was Sunday, and I found a large party of Secularists and others were to pay a visit to the estate. It was a glorious day—it was as though the gods had been propitiated, or rather St. Swithin, for he evidently intends giving us the full benefit of his forty days' control of the elements. Our train left the Midland station about 9 a.m. for Totley and Dore—a station situated four miles from Sheffield, and one-and-a-half from the new settlement. On a reference to any ordinary map it will be seen that the property is situated in the beautiful county of Derbyshire.

On alighting from the train I was informed that the greater number of visitors were expected in the afternoon, so that I found myself in company with the elect. I mentioned, incidentally, my intentions to those present that I purposed publishing a few observations concerning them, which met with disapproval from the more modest of the party, while others thought it might benefit them. The objections arose from a diffidence of being paraded before the public at such an early period of their existence.

The road from Totley station to "Parker House Estate"—better known as "Badger's Farm" (the latter name being derived from the late owner, the former being its real name)—lay pleasantly situated along the base of a range of hills upon our left, while to our right and stretching far away the land was beautifully undulating, and covered with crops of waving corn interspersed with meadows, woods, &c., and beyond this could be seen other ranges of hills extending to the horizon.

Suddenly we turned to the left to take a short cut across the fields, which brought us to a lane leading up to the promised land. Here we found our progress considerably impeded by a very steep incline; and if our friends find the rise in Communism as steep, they will necessarily progress but slowly, but perhaps all the more sure, for we invariably take a good foothold of *terra firma* when ascending its rugged sides.

Having traversed a short distance upward and onward we entered upon the Parker House Estate, which consisted of 13 acres of grass land, small garden, a farmhouse, and out-buildings; the latter constructed of stone, and rather old-fashioned, both as regards their exterior and interior appearance. If Mr. Craig had been with us he would have found fault at once with the low ceiling and ventilation; although a good ventilation can be had by opening a door on one side and window on the other; but here, again, comes the other difficulty, viz., the draught, which remedy is as bad as the disease. Well, let us hope Mr. Craig may have a voice in the new buildings that are anticipated.

The ground, occupying as it does an elevated position, commands an extensive view of the surrounding hills and valleys; the scenery is at once picturesque and beautiful, the only element wanting to complete the picture being water, small coppices and woods abounding on every hand. The land is admirably adapted for a variety of occupations to be carried on simultaneously—such as farming fowls, sheep, pigs, and cows, according to the tastes and requirements of the community. A portion would grow sufficient vegetables and fruit for them. These things, combined with the manufacture of such articles as can find a ready sale, cannot, under wise management, fail to secure success to the undertaking.

The subsoil is chiefly clay, beneath which I should imagine stone can be found, as all the neighbourhood abounds with a kind of hard, blue stone, of which most of the houses and other structures are built. Thus it will be seen our Communistic friends are indeed exceptionally circumstanced. They have one of the best of landlords, for where can the man be found that will let land free of rent, erect suitable buildings, and lend cash into the bargain, free of all interest? Then, again, the selection of the site, elevated so as to obtain pure air, a delightful scenery, sheltered on the north and east by yet higher ground, the south and west sloping downwards towards the sun when in his prime; also a good running ironstone stream at the lower part of the ground that can be utilised for driving machinery—all these to be had for the using of them. Failure under such conditions will argue only one of two things—either total depravity or total incapacity; but failure must be an "unknown quantity" to our friends. Obstacles must act as spurs to stimualte them to greater exertion; difficulties must create in them a stronger determination to succeed, inasmuch as the eyes of the world will be upon them; they will be like a city set upon a hill, unto which people will turn their attention, some to criticise and laugh at, others to praise or blame.

The only occupants of St. George's Land (the property belongs, strictly speaking, to the St. George's Company, the master of St. George being the trustee) were two married couples and a single man, the latter a very intelligent Scotchman—but who ever knew a Scotchman this side of the Tweed otherwise? Their occupation has hitherto consisted of preparing some of the ground for gardening purposes, and getting in a crop of hay, which appeared in good condition. Of necessity there will not be employment for all the members until the necessary buildings are erected, which can scarcely be accomplished under twelve months at least.

In acquainting myself with the various members, I met with one, a venerable-looking old gentleman, whose peculiar vernacular indicated his acquaintance with that very worthy sect called the "Society of Friends." I found in him a man of superior intelligence, and one likely to be of great use to the Communists, even if he remains as an outside member, which, judging from his age and other circumstances, I think will be the likely course for him to pursue. At present he acts as their adviser, for which he appeared well adapted. I was rather surprised to find they had not completed the rules of the society, and other matters also presented themselves to me that appeared open to criticism; but that is not to be wondered at, when a fair view is taken of all the circumstances by which they are surrounded. Still the bare mention of these matters so far may be of service to them, even if I am mistaken in my opinions, because we are as a rule benefited by public opinion—that is, if we are willing—in fact, I know of nothing so wholesome to any community as friendly criticisms of what appear to the critic the weak points of those whom he attempts to criticise.

My earnest hope and best wish is that success may attend them in the undertaking; and, at some future period, I trust other visitors may be able to give our readers an account of Communism at Parker House Estate, such as shall convince the most obdurate sceptic that its principles are superior to any that have ever yet been tried.

Of one thing, most thinking minds are all agreed upon; that the present condition of society cannot last much longer. That excessive riches should exist side by side with abject poverty is as intolerable as it is true; and that enlightened reason on the part of the masses will cease to tolerate such hideous evil is also true.

In taking leave of our Sheffield friends, I would entreat them to regard themselves as the modern pioneers of a new era of freedom from the powerful grasp of the privileged classes. Thus viewing themselves, they will be the more likely to exercise a wise watchfulness over their words and actions, lest there should be any room for the enemy to assail them, seeing they will of necessity be beset by hostile critics on all sides.

Let "Excelsior!" be their motto and "Fidelity!" their watchword, and, with the material advantages which they command, they will become the saviour of their fellows.

W. H. C.

8

"ADVANCED CO-OPERATION, THE SOCIALISM OF ENGLAND", *ENGLISH SOCIALISM* (MANCHESTER: ABEL HEYWOOD, 1879), 1–7.

Henry Travis

[Dr Henry Travis (1807–1884) was born in Scarborough and trained as a physician. A prominent Owenite, he spent time at the Queenwood community in Hampshire and later acted along with William Pare as Robert Owen's joint literary executor. Like Pare, he continued to argue for the relevance of Owen's ideas throughout the 1860s and 1870s, contributing regularly to the co-operative press, including Henry Pitman's *Co-operator*, the first co-operative periodical with a national circulation. In the main, Travis was content to rehearse uncritically Owen's views, though believed that more emphasis was needed on the role of free will and human responsibility. [J.F.C. Harrison, *Quest for the New Moral World. Robert Owen and the Owenites in Britain and America* (New York: Charles Scribner's Sons, 1969), 236–239] The pamphlet reproduced below – which was afterwards bound in with Travis's last published work, *English Socialism* (1880) – illustrates his reconfiguration of the Owenite idea of "Community". In it, he outlines his belief in the usefulness of joint-stock companies with limited liability to enable workers to move beyond shopkeeping towards "advanced co-operation". [A useful discussion of the opportunities opened up here is Donna Loftus, "Capital and community: limited liability and attempts to democratize the market in mid-Nineteenth Century England", *Victorian Studies*, 45/1 (2002), 93–120] Although Travis emphasises how all classes are likely to benefit from this "new order of things", he is in no doubt that its success will depend on the backing of "the most intelligent of the working classes". Interestingly, Travis refers to these new social forms as "little co-operative commonwealths", an early usage of a term which in the singular was to become a decade or so later the frequently stated ambition of both the socialist and co-operative movements.]

ADVANCED CO-OPERATION, THE SOCIALISM OF ENGLAND.

THE ADVANCED form of co-operation to which many who take part in the present great co-operative movement look forward, and which many of those who feel interested in other social reforms will learn, it may be hoped, to anticipate as the chief end of their united proceedings, and the greatest good by far which can be realised for humanity, themselves included, will be an improved state of society, a system of social co-operation, by which all who enter into it will be introduced to a life in accordance with the dictates of the highest goodness, and, therefore, in the highest degree conducive to the happiness of every individual.

It will be realised by means of new self-supporting social arrangements, in which permanent, useful, and well-remunerated employment will be provided for the working classes first, under influences most favourable to their improvement and happiness, and which, economical but beautiful in their early construction, for those who are now in poverty and in want of employment, will be gradually developed and made still more attractive for those who are now in more favoured positions, and to suit the improved character which all will acquire under the new influences in ideas and surroundings to which they will be subjected in these new arrangements.

It will be based upon a new and very superior intellectual and moral education for old and young, under the guidance of the knowledge of the effects of influences in the formation of character, and of enlightened and unexclusive benevolence consequent upon this knowledge, or the intelligent desire that the rational happiness of every individual should be promoted to the utmost possible extent—knowledge and good feelings which of course the old must acquire before they can be efficient educators of young or old, or can assist efficiently to improve the character and condition of the population.

The new arrangements may at first be constructed by joint-stock companies, with limited liability, to whom they will be a most desirable form of investment. And various other means will be adopted to provide the funds required for the extension of the system, as the benefits to be derived from it by all classes of existing society become known. The interest for the capital employed in the construction of the new arrangements will be provided for by the surplus productions of the associations placed within them. And in due time the capital may be repaid, and the arrangements may become the joint property of the societies by whom they are occupied.

A commencement of this new form of co-operation should now be made as soon as possible by forming an example of the new arrangements. For the new system and its advantages must be seen in practice before it can be generally understood and believed to be possible and desirable. When one example can be seen in operation, the immense advantages—economically, educationally, and socially—which will be obtained by the new mode of living will be so obvious that the rapid extension of the system will certainly follow, and the chief thing to be considered will be that its development shall be regulated beneficially for all existing interests, in accordance with the enlightened and, therefore, unexclusive benevolence which will be the guiding influence of all its proceedings. The example of the successful communities in America has only shown that wealth may be produced in great superabundance, and the moral and physical evils of the competitive state of society may be to a great extent prevented, by co-operative communities under the influence of peculiar sectarian creeds, sufficiently binding to induce the societies who adopt them to live harmoniously together, but which can never be generally accepted. A system of social co-operation worthy and likely to be imitated by the world at large can only be realised under the influence of the new and very superior intellectual and moral education referred to above—an education by which men of all creeds—Christian, Jew, Mahomedan, &c., &c.—will be enabled to acquire the spirit of enlightened benevolence, the true religious spirit, which will bind them together in mutual good-will, whatever may be their differences of theological belief. While men are so unintelligent and so defective morally as to feel mutual animosity on account of their differences of opinion upon theological subjects, they can never realise a well-ordered and happy state of society. The knowledge of the effects of influences in the formation of character will enable those who can apply it in the regulation of their social feelings and conduct to raise themselves out of the intellectual and moral deterioration of sectarian ideas and feelings.

The construction of the new arrangements should be undertaken by the possessors of capital, and by those who are accustomed to direct extensive business operations, and will be so in the advanced stages of the change; and the new education, within the new arrangements, should be directed by men and women the most competent—intellectually, and morally, and practically—who can prepare themselves for the task by acquiring the knowledge and the good feelings of the co-operative character. But it seems likely that these persons will not be induced to take the lead in the new proceedings, and that the most intelligent of the working classes, who are better able to appreciate the gross injustice and the direful evil consequences of the present system, and the strong need which exists for effectual remedial measures, will be left to provide the capital and the business acquirements necessary for the initiation of the new order of things. And their co-operative stores, and trades unions, and benefit societies, and clubs, and other associations of various kinds, have enabled many of their leaders to acquire the business ability, and may soon be made the means to provide the capital required for the formation of an example, when the leaders who are competent in other respects can be induced and enabled to acquire and apply the knowledge which will be the peculiar humanising and harmonising influence, the means of intellectual and moral elevation, upon which the system of social co-operation will be based.

But so long as men imagine that any plans of social co-operation can be satisfactory in their results which are not based upon the education of old and young under the influence of this knowledge, they cannot possess the intellectual and moral qualifications necessary for the realisation of enlightened social co-operation. This is the great point upon which the schemes of FOURIER and of other foreign social theorists are fatally defective. They do not include the knowledge by which alone men can be enabled to acquire the enlightened good-will towards all of the true co-operative character.

The formation of an example and the progressive development of the new system by the multiplication of these co-operative communities, will be greatly facilitated by the fact that these new associations must be limited in numbers, and may be formed without interfering with existing institutions, as joint-stock companies of any other kind are established. For each society must be neither too large nor too small for the advantageous combined performance of the different departments of the general business of life—productive, distributive, educational, and general—to provide food, clothing, dwellings, instruction and improvement, amusements, &c., in the most advantageous manner for a socially organised community. And this most advantageous number will probably be from 300 or 500, as a minimum, to 3,000, as a maximum. The smaller number of persons, therefore, within the new arrangements, of suitable extent, will suffice to exhibit to the world the advantages of social co-operation. And when one of these communities, or little co-operative commonwealths, can be seen in operation, with the harmony, and good order, and abundance of the most useful wealth, and happiness, consequent upon the improved character of the people and the new social arrangements and general proceedings, it will naturally be imitated. For the public will then be enabled to see how easily and how beneficially for themselves and society generally, the poor and the working classes will be enabled to provide abundantly for all their reasonable wants, and how easily they will be educated to be intelligently kind and just and truthful in all their social proceedings, when they are placed within suitable surroundings, under the guidance of competent persons by whom their proceedings will be superintended in the spirit of enlightened brotherly and sisterly kindness and justice, until they can be educated intellectually and morally to be competent to adopt the system of self-government, in the same spirit, which will be the most conducive to the happiness of all.

And when it shall be seen how easily and beneficially this can be done for and by the poor and the working classes it will soon be seen how advantageous it will be for all classes to be enabled to become intelligently kind and just and truthful in all their social proceedings, and to "learn and labour truly to get their own living" by well regulated, useful employments in co-operative social arrangements. It will be seen how much better this will be for every member of the human family, even for those who are now the richest and in the highest positions, than the degrading life of selfishness and disunion, and mutual opposition and injustice, and mutual deception, in which all, from the highest to the lowest, are now involved, and the frivolous and useless pursuits and display and rivalries with which the time and thoughts of the higher classes are so much occupied. And no limits can be assigned to the improvements which may be made upon the economically constructed arrangements of the first communities for the working classes.

The co-operative trading societies and other associations of the working classes may provide abundant capital for the formation of an example when their members in sufficient numbers are disposed to apply their savings to this best of purposes, and to place them in this most safe and permanent of investments under good management. The land may be purchased, or may be obtained upon long leases; and the surplus of useful objects required for the payment of interest, and rent, and taxes, and all other external expenses will easily be produced by these communities, and will readily be disposed of in the markets of the outer world, of which, except for the sale of this limited portion of their productions, these new societies will be independent. And as the change becomes more developed the means for the multiplication of the new communities will easily be found by the then more enlightened influential classes of society and by an enlightened and elevated public opinion. And the transition from the present to the new state of society will easily be regulated to be highly beneficial for all classes and individuals, in all its stages, by the new public opinion which will thus be formed, and will be guided in all its proceedings by the spirit of benevolence, enlightened and expanded by the knowledge of the effects of influences in the formation of character. Many questions arise for consideration in the preceding statements, which must be correctly answered, and which the reader must enable himself to answer correctly and clearly before he can understand the subject. The replies to these questions will be given in other tracts which will shortly be published.

HENRY TRAVIS.

Part 2

POLITICAL ECONOMY

9

THE ECONOMIC ADVANTAGES OF CO-OPERATION SUBSTANTIATED. A LETTER ADDRESSED TO THE REV. NORMAN MACLEOD, D.D., PROVING THE TRUTH OF THE LARGE PROFITS FROM CO-OPERATIVE ECONOMY, AS STATED AT THE GLASGOW MEETING OF THE ASSOCIATION FOR THE PROMOTION OF SOCIAL SCIENCE (LEEDS: DAVID GREEN, 1860), 12–18, 21–23, 25–26, 29–30.

John Holmes

[John Holmes was a trustee of a successful co-operative flour mill in Leeds – the People's Mill – and a frequent speaker and writer on co-operative issues. In the introduction to this pamphlet, Holmes explained that it had emerged from discussions that had taken place at the inaugural meeting of the National Association for the Promotion of Social Science held in Birmingham in 1857, a Liberal middle-class think tank that provided an important forum for the propagation of co-operation and opened up an important space for dialogue across classes in Victorian Britain. [For this body see Lawrence Goldman, *Science, reform and politics in Victorian Britain: the Social Science Association, 1857–1886* (Cambridge: Cambridge University Press, 2002)] During the debate at Birmingham, which had concluded that co-operation represented the best solution to the problems of credit and debt that bedevilled working-class lives, Rev. Macleod had stated that, "It mattered not what name it was called, whether Co-operation, or Socialism, the results given were the results needed; and the way was the Socialism of the Scriptures". Unsurprisingly, most of Holmes' pamphlet consists of an argument about the greater efficiency of co-operation compared to competition, enabling improvement of both the material and the moral status of working-class consumers. Interestingly, however, Holmes ends with a long quotation from the influential chapter from J.S. Mill's *Principles of Political Economy* (1848) entitled "On the Probable Futurity of the Labouring Classes" (Book IV, chapter 7), which looked forward to nothing less than generalised co-operation, a form of socialism from below. [For Mill's engagement with socialist ideas see William Stafford, *John Stuart Mill* (Basingstoke, Macmillan, 1998).]]

In October, 1857, the Association for the promotion of Social Science held its first meeting at Birmingham. I submitted a paper on the "Economic and Moral Advantages of Co-operation in the provision of food, instanced in the People's Flour Mill Society at Leeds, and in the Rochdale Co-operative Pioneers' Store." The paper was got up and read on the 15th October, entirely upon my own responsibility. The Directors had not only nothing to do with it, but few of them knew of such a paper being prepared, until announced as having been read, in the public journals. To tell the truth, not a few of the Directors were then, as now, at difference with me upon various methods of procedure. As a Trustee, I had access to the books, and from thence obtained the figures: of the other facts and conclusions I had ample experience. Knowing, therefore, anything stated would be submitted to a severe criticism, both by the public, and also our own officials, I was the more careful to be accurate, apart from a wish, as a friend to Co-operation, not to damage it by erroneous statements. The same views actuated me in extracting from the Rochdale reports, books, and friends, the facts and figures given concerning them at Birmingham. An Abstract only is published in the Social Science Transactions, vol. 1, p. 567. Returning to Leeds, some of the Directors requested me to read to them the statements made at Birmingham; and as it was only reasonable to allay jealousy, as well as to give any information upon matters which concerned them especially, I did so to a very full meeting of the Directors, called for the purpose. Knowing how general differences of views prevailed among us, you may judge my surprise, when instead of a very possible vote of censure, a vote of thanks was tendered; and because they approved of the *truth* of the facts and figures, it was unanimously requested I would permit them to print the whole, with notes and explanations, for the purpose of being circulated among our own members, (free), and to the public at a low price, in order to publish to the world what Co-operation had done so far as it had been tried. This was done accordingly, and first beginning with our own members, the paper was pretty extensively circulated. Leeds, Yorkshire, and many other districts had the statistics at the end of this letter, then first published. They have been frequently reprinted, and are now continued; and if not true would be contradicted at once by our members, and by scores who owe Co-operation no thanks for what it has done. On no occasion, however, and by no competent authority have the facts ever been challenged. No miller has ever publicly disputed them here, or at Rochdale, although published in papers, and lectured upon in meetings. Had there been a fallacy, hundreds would most gladly have denied and disproved; and that this has not been done, may be fairly accepted in Scotland, as proof that the statements are borne out by facts.

Referring to the paper, page 6, you will find it stated as a summary, that "during the last five years, the average capital has been £7,689, and the returns, £56,930, with profits per annum of £1,788. Capital has been turned over seven and a half times yearly, at a profit of three and a half per cent. upon returns, or *twenty-five per cent.* upon capital." This proves the statement of the profits up to that time; and it must be understood, that not only had we the difficulties of Cooperation within itself, and members to deal with, but we had at the time to compete in the markets with the use of a very low Egyptian corn, which we did not use on principle; although we could have gained 2d. to 3d. per stone, amounting to thousands of pounds thereby. Again, under the head of pecuniary results, you will find stated at page 7,—"During the nine years of the operations of the society, the business has risen from £22,000 to £70,000 per annum, at the rate of 350 per cent. over nine years; and capital has accumulated 100 per cent. over subscriptions, while members have withdrawn in the shape of bonuses, 175 per cent. more than all the capital subscribed. The rule of profit, however, can scarcely be calculated, because for the first five years we sold "at as near prime cost as possible. Yet, if we take the former state of the markets into account, it cannot be less than 50 per cent. per annum upon capital; and if we add the real increase of value to the consumer, in consequence of an acquired and guaranteed purity, the gain to members and the public must be more than that enormous interest!"

Under the head, "Costs and Economy of Working," the preceding reduction and economy of forty per cent. are fully borne out; so that we need not to go over the details again for the first nine years of working. At present, i.e. 1860, I am bound to state we are not working so economically as we have done. Costs will vary with expenses, and these have always a tendency to increase. Among the extras adding to our costs just now, is the interest of £800,—a sum laid out by unanimous vote of the members, to purchase a plot of land, in order to extend. We expect shortly to have the said land, now laying idle, covered over with productive buildings and offices, enabling us to increase our operations, and so economise expenditure. Other causes not necessary to mention, have lately turned unfavourably upon us; but these, similarly situated, private enterprize would have had equally to contend with. Co-operation has its seasons of success and failure, and the latter must be borne if we would reap the fruits of the former. Thus much for an experience at Leeds; where in the economic result we are not singular...

It is not necessary, to bear out your estimate, that I should do more than prove the facts stated, about the advantages of Co-operation. It may be left to the advocate of private enterprise to explain how it is that they cannot at Leeds grind flour for less than 2s. 6d., and they say they cannot. In Co-operation, as we have no secrets, I will in a few words explain how it is that we can thus economise. First, we have a large and well ascertained market of demand at once. Instead of seeking customers, they seek us. Second: we deal only for ready-money, buying and selling. Third: capital is furnished by the members. Fourth: by agreement members conform to time and mode of purchase. Fifth: no advertisements, puffs, or expensive shops or show are required; and sixth: integrity in all transactions is our interest. We thus avoid costs of trade, in seeking orders, losing by debts, of collecting, or by lawsuit. Half the number of salesmen, carts, and horses, will do the work usually required. Adaptation of supply and demand, and capital, enables us to economise in the best possible way. Arrangement, and surveillance, called out by the interest of each, is perpetual; talent, and skill, and knowledge, are developed, and freely tendered, which would be very costly to pay for; and in many ways that can only be realized by observation, advantages are common by Co-operation which *cannot* be acquired by competitive enterprise. Of course, to all this there are drawbacks, and not a few. I know them well, and have no wish to underrate our difficulties and disadvantages. I know the envy, hatred, and uncharitableness of numbers; the discontent of others—the ignorance of many, &c., &c. I know the ingratitude of the mob, and the fickleness of the people; but still, with all these costs to contend with, here we have the fact of our economic success. And though these societies were to be torn in pieces to-morrow by internal dissension, still, what they have achieved is to-day a fact; and a fact that will as seed planted upon the receding waters of prejudice and error, be found after many days, in superior fruits...

The benefits of Co-operation are not limited to the provision of flour only;—but as people require meat as well as bread; groceries, coal, hats, coats, shoes, and clothing of all kinds; at Rochdale they have set the world an example of how well Co-operation can supply these necessaries, and economise in the supply. In the provision of these goods, from 1844, the dealings have risen from £710; at a profit of £32 17s. 6d. to £104,012 in 1859, with a profit of £10,739. The last balance of the Rochdale Store for the quarter ending 18th September, 1860, shows returns of business amounting to £37,885 6s. 6d., with a nett profit of £4,341 14s. 4d. (capital £30,000), which shows nearly 15 per cent. profit upon returns, or better than 55 per cent. upon capital, per annum, in the store department. Now, we think this not bad, and at least a full justification to all or any of the estimates held out by what we stated, of the economic benefits of Co-operation. I have again to point out, that this does not arise from either low articles being sold, or unduly high profits being made. As in the case of flour, superiority in our trading consists in the superior economy attained by Co-operation...

And yet, as before said, these superior achievements of Co-operation are now actual, even though they disappeared to-morrow. We who know what Co-operation can do, know it can do very much more than anything it has yet done. We know there is a power in arrangement, and an economy of power, yet never called out. The great mass of the people are totally ignorant of even the name of Co-operation. Hitherto the cultured among political economists, have opposed and doubted its effects. Even the most active and enlightened among the officials and directors themselves, admit they are but children at school, learning what is practical; and feel like untrained workmen, awkward in the use of good tools. At a glance—what a change, an economic change, would follow the prudent development of Co-operative enterprize, demand and supply...

To use the very accurate words of Mr. S., "to elevate from a lower to a higher—or rather, from a loose to stricter habits"? Is it an illusion that thousands who once feared to face the creditor, and dreaded the sight of a dun, and a bailiff, have now no such fear or dread?—but instead of being deeply in debt, can at call fall back upon from twenty to a hundred pounds in their Co-operative savings bank? Are better houses, furniture, and the *best* of clothing and food, illusions? or the 5000 volumes in the library, the 200 daily, weekly, or monthly publications; the microscopes, telescopes, and even opera glasses, free to the use and enjoyment of the Rochdale members, illusions? O for such *illusion* all over England and Scotland. Nay, let me hope the Social Science meetings at Glasgow may reverse the evil, and make it *real* SCOTLAND first, and England second; for Co-operation has no jealousy. O for the honest feeling of pride, and perfect independence and freedom, in the use of the wealth and luxury that these men have now acquired by Co-operation, and which in that acquisition, they have learnt to *use,* and not to abuse...

Satisfied of the principle, and of the facts also, I yet with great deference, and with reservation in relation to circumstances, submit this view of Economic Co-operation against the opinions to the contrary. But not sanguine of these results being obtained without time and patience, and strict conformance to the necessary conditions of business, I do not think success will be so certain in this department of action, as in those instanced; indeed, I fear already some are going on too fast, and that people are joining Co-operative societies in anything but a Co-operative spirit. Undue selfishness, in many cases, is rife among those who are members of Co-operative societies. Already a movement is going on to alter the constitution of them, so that the capitalist may get richer, and the poor be kept poor. This movement may possibly succeed for a time, but it will certainly destroy itself. When the mass have no interest in the results, it will be vain to expect their united action and economic support; and such is the danger its friends see. Co-operation will do more than it has done, if people will but let it: but it will be wrong to blame Co-operation for failure, wrought by its bitterest opponents, under the guise of being its friends. I hold, however, that the circumstances and requirements of the age are tending to draw out and to require an extension of the principles of Co-operation: it is but a matter of education and time, for its application into all forms and conditions of modern requirement. Progression works tide-like—one forward wave and then perhaps several backwards, in reaching up to the mark; but the master wave rolls at last. And although we see many failures in action, the grand principle of "each for all," must in the ultimate prevail. This is the very fulcrum of civilization; and Co-operation is the present advanced instrument of this progressive *Christian* principle...

Against the results above described, "the immorality, anti-social feelings, and painful sense of individual insecurity prevailing, and corrupting all society, and even extending to the Commons' House itself," (the highest court which should correct abuses), we have no other, at least no better remedy, than the moral and economic principles of Co-operation. These have proved themselves efficient to produce a correction of many of these evils, and would, we believe, prove still more so, by extension and development. Under the pressure of these evils, that the people should be dissatisfied, is not to be wondered at. The opinion that Co-operation in application would be an *efficient* remedy, is commended by the highest authorities in political economy. The following opinion of John Stuart Mill, is to the point:—

> "Though the existing associations may be dissolved, or driven to expatriate, their experience will not be lost. They have existed long enough to furnish the type of future improvement: they have exemplified the process for bringing about a change in society, which would combine the freedom and independence of the individual, with the moral, intellectual, and *economical* advantages of aggregate production; and which without violence or spoliation, or even any disturbance of existing habits and expectations, would realize, at least in the industrial department, the best aspirations of the democratic spirit, by putting an end to the division of society into the industrious and the idle, and effacing all social distinctions but those fairly earned by personal services and exertions. Associations like those which we have described, by the very process of their success, are a course of education in those moral and active qualities by which alone success can be either deserved or attained. As associations multiplied, they would tend more and more to absorb all workpeople, except those who have too little understanding, or too little virtue, to be capable of learning to act on any other system than that of narrow selfishness. As this change proceeded, owners of capital would gradually find it to their advantage, instead of maintaining the struggle of the old system with workpeople of only the worst description, to lend their capital to the associations; to do this at a diminishing rate of interest, and at last, perhaps, to exchange their capital for terminable annuities. In this or some such mode, the existing accumulation of capital might honestly, and by a kind of spontaneous process, become in the end the joint property of all who participate in their productive employment: a transformation which, thus effected (and assuming of course that both sexes participate equally in the rights and in the government of the association) would be the nearest approach to social justice, and the most beneficial ordering of industrial affairs for the universal good, which it is possible at present to foresee."
>
> —*Mill's Political Economy,* vol. ii, 4th edition, pp. 353–4.

10

"LAND, FREE TRADE, AND RECIPROCITY", *CO-OPERATOR*, 4 DECEMBER 1869, 836–837.

John Parker

[This article by John Parker, about whom little is known but who wrote regularly for the *Co-operator*, also demonstrates the influence of J.S. Mill on co-operative thinking. Acceptance of free trade ideology has often been regarded as evidence for co-operators' incorporation into a liberal worldview, yet this extract indicates that some of them had a far more subtle view of the issues involved. Just a few years after the establishment of the Cobden Club seemed to symbolise the hegemony of free trade finance, its benefits were being publically challenged on many fronts. [Peter Gurney, *Wanting and Having: Popular Politics and Liberal Consumerism in England, 1830–70* (Manchester: Manchester University Press, 2015), 315] Parker's intervention emphasises just how partial free trade is in its operation, but also rejects doctrinarism: "Neither absolute protection nor absolute free trade can prove at all times and in all circumstances a benefit to nations and industries", he argues. Further than this, Parker questions the way in which landownership, the money supply and taxation are all subject in effect to forms of protection, to the detriment of the majority. Private ownership of land is singled out as especially harmful, and here Parker's criticisms are entirely in line with longstanding radical discussion of the problem of the land. [Jamie Bronstein, *Land reform and working-class experience in Britain and the United States, 1800–1862* (Stanford, Calif.: Stanford University Press, 1999)] The real difficulty with the policy of free trade for Parker, then, is that it does not go nearly far enough: "Our legislative Solons commenced their free trade policy at the wrong end of the series of national interests. They freed the produce of the foreigner, whilst they enslaved the labour of the citizen at home".]

Land, Free Trade, and Reciprocity.

As free trade principles are now being questioned as to their beneficial influence on the industry of the nation, and on the social condition of the people, it may not be out of place to inquire how far the *pros* and *cons* keep pace with all the bearings of the subject in question. Free trade—according to the strict meaning of the term—is something very different from that adopted by English statesmen. If the principles of free trade be not judiciously applied to certain—or even to existing—interests, it is quite possible that though they will in some instances prove beneficial, yet they may in others prove disadvantageous. No writer in modern times has made such a careful analysis of the effects of free trade policy on the prosperity and wealth of nations, as John Stuart Mill: yet this profound and able writer is compelled to confess that a free trade policy has its limits, and is not applicable under all circumstances. "The only case," says he, "in which, on mere principles of political economy, protecting duties can be defensible, is, when they are imposed temporarily—especially in a young and rising nation—in hopes of naturalising an industry in itself perfectly suitable to the circumstances of the country."—(Principles of Political Economy, p. 556.) Even Sir Robert Peel himself, after he had become a strenuous advocate of a free trade policy, had to set it aside when he deemed it necessary to put an export duty on our coal, in order to economise its consumption. Dr. Buckland and Mr. Warburton had concurred in their opinion as to the exhaustibility of coal in England; and as their opinion weighed much in the estimation of free traders, Peel discovered that protection—if judiciously used—might, in this instance, be a benefit to the nation. Such was the policy of Sir Robt. Peel in 1842 with respect to our coal; and why he should swerve from that policy in 1860, and give France the benefit of English coal without imposing a duty upon it, is one of the mysteries which frequently associate themselves with the policy of all great minds. This gracious act of the Government of 1860 cheapened coal to Rouen and Havre, but made it dearer to British consumers. The free exportation of coal to France has been a benefit to the coal owners of England, but no permanent benefit has been bestowed on any other portion of the community. Indeed, so far as a partially free exchange of commodities between England and France has been achieved by the treaty of 1860, it may reasonably be disputed whether the productive classes of England have received any appreciable benefit therefrom.

What did France give us in return for our generous conduct? Well, England allowed her wines, silks, and kid gloves, to be freely sent to her markets; but France refused to admit the silk manufactures of England on equal terms. The silk manufactures of England, when exported to France, had for a certain period of time to be loaded with a 30 per cent. duty; and what was still more galling to English manufacturers, France continued her export duties on the raw material. But what has it availed English workmen that the wines and silks of France have been freely admitted into English ports? The wardrobe of workmen's wives in England is seldom graced by the presence of silks, nor is her husband's larder often replenished with wine. Wines and silks are unseemly things in the dingy domicile of an English labourer, where rags, hard crusts, and water make up the complement of his humble fare.

Free trade is ruled by principles that have yet to be properly applied to British industry and commerce. Neither absolute protection nor absolute free trade can prove at all times and under all circumstances a benefit to nations and industries, either in their infantile condition, or even in their matured forms of existence. Every nation and every branch of industry is governed by surroundings that require the delicate touch of philosophic minds when a free trade or protective policy is contemplated.

It is urged by some that although many of our exchanges with France are not confined to articles really useful to the operative classes, yet there are exchanges truly beneficial to Englishmen. True, we have taken from France since the treaty an almost annually increasing quantity of agricultural produce. According to returns, we received from France during the three years preceding the treaty, cattle to the number of 11,900; sheep and lambs, 2,094; butter, 91,172 cwts.; wheat, 8,459,164 cwts.; wheat flour and wheat meal, 4,653,549 cwts.; potatoes, 1,673,172 cwts. During the last three years of the treaty, we have received from France, cattle 68,904; sheep and lambs, 53,581; wheat, 4,126,949 cwts.; wheat flour and wheat meal, 5,507,427 cwts.; potatoes, 2,970,581 cwts.

In the export of all these necessaries, there has been a steady increase, wheat excepted. But what does this avail the English labourer? Is it a real benefit to the labouring population of England that one-fourth of its food should be produced by the foreigner? This is a grave and important question, and ought not to be hastily answered, either by protectionists or free traders. John Stuart Mill affirms that "that country is the most steadily as well as most abundantly supplied with food, which draws its supplies from the largest surface." Granted; but why should the policy of England prefer the land and labour of foreign nations to her own? Why not employ our surplus labour and barren acres at home? Can our agriculturists not compete with the foreigner? And can the soil of Great Britain and Ireland not produce food for thirty millions of people? Such are the questions that grow out of the present policy of our legislators, the condition of our land laws, and the social condition of the people.

I am willing to admit that a great boon was conferred on English operatives when our importations of food were freed from the duties imposed on them. This wise and liberal policy extended the area from which the industrious classes of England could draw their food, stimulated our agriculturists to greater activity, and cheapened the poor man's loaf. But why is it that, notwithstanding all the advantages our free trade policy has bestowed on certain interests, we do not further extend a similar policy? Why do we free the produce of foreign nations from duties in English ports, allow capital to compete with capital, labour with labour, and strenuously adhere to a protective policy for the land of the nation? But protection does not stop here. Our banking system is as truly protective as the corn laws were previous to their repeal. The Act of 1844 cripples our commercial transactions by making banking capital, banking issues, and banking facilities a fixed quantity. The provisions of that Act do not allow trade to measure the issues of the bank;—the limited issues of the bank measure the trade.

When the capital of the nation is increasing at the rate of one hundred millions annually—and this accomplished by increasing trade and commerce—it is evident that during periods when gold and silver are scarce, an extension of banking issues must be requisite for the nation. Our banking monopoly forbids this; and, what is equally as glaring and impolitic, it claims for itself alone the right of issuing convertible notes. Here, then, is protection in one of its most odious forms. Then, again, we have protection thrown around the fixed and floating property of the nation.

The taxation of the nation is not equitably levied on capital and labour. Is it not monstrous that labour should pay upwards of 40 per cent. of its annual income in the shape of indirect taxation? Every family of four persons pays not less than £13 a-year as duty on the necessaries of life. How are families with an annual income of £40 or £50 a-year to procure the necessaries of life, when nearly one-third of that income is filched from them by the protective laws of the monied and ruling classes? Let the annual incomes of our landed proprietors and manufacturers be taxed to a similar tune; and England will soon wipe out her national debt, and would soon be required to re-model her system of taxation. The labour of Englishmen will never be free, so long as the present laws of taxation are allowed to prey on their industry. With a monopoly of banking, with a monopoly of land, with high prices of food, and with an unjust mode of taxation, we need not marvel at the pauperised condition of English operatives, and the flagging prosperity of some of our branches of industry. It is not free trade principles that are at fault for such a state of things in England. It is the protective policy still cherished and maintained by monopolists and legislative enactments. Our legislative Solons commenced their free trade policy at the wrong end of the series of national interests. They freed the produce of the foreigner, whilst they enslaved the labour of the citizen at home. In what consists the freedom of English operatives? Labour is employed or kept idle at the caprice of capitalists. The land of the United Kingdom is securely locked up against the free operations of labour and capital; and every addition to the power of machinery keeps intensifying the competition of labour. What labour most requires, is reciprocity of trade at home. The interests of our landed proprietors are too much protected; that of labour too little. On this account free trade with the foreigner, in many instances, is a positive disadvantage to English workmen. Access to cheaper markets abroad does not compensate the industrious classes at home for the loss of labour they sustain. Englishmen want reciprocity of interests at home. Let the land and other natural sources of labour and wealth be laid open to our starving and half-employed operatives; then will free trade principles be able to prove their utility in equalising the rights and privileges of the great industrial powers of the nation.

No better definition of Free Trade was ever given to the world, than that by Sir Fitzroy Kelly. "Real freedom of trade (said he) consists not merely in the repeal of protective duties, but in the right to buy, to grow, to manufacture, to import, to use, to exchange, to sell—unrestricted by any fiscal or arbitrary law." In my estimation, the great error of those now denouncing free trade, is to be found in the fact of their ignorance of the real causes of the inactivity of our manufacturers, and of the distress of the working population. With a wider knowledge of facts, and a better acquaintance with the principles of political economy, they will find that it is not free trade, but protection, that lies at the root of many of our social evils.

11

THE LOGIC OF CO-OPERATION (MANCHESTER: CO-OP PRINTING SOCIETY, 1873), 6–11.

G.J. Holyoake

[Holyoake's pamphlet illustrates how co-operative ideologues played an important role in bringing the consumer into the discourse of political economy. Despite Adam Smith's famous dictum in *The Wealth of Nations* that "consumption is the sole end and purpose of all production", the role of the consumer was largely ignored within classical political economy, with William Stanley Jevons' attempt to change things in the 1870s generally regarded as cranky by his peers. [Sandra Peart, *The Economics of W. S. Jevons* (1996)] Despite this marginalisation within professional discourse, co-operators like Holyoake brought the consumer to the fore in the last third of the nineteenth century. In this work, Holyoake stakes out his position in an internal debate on producer co-operatives that was intensifying within the movement, navigating between "individualists" who stressed the autonomy of productive enterprises and "federalists" who wanted all production to be controlled by the CWS. Supporters of the former believed that labour should receive a percentage of any profits as bonus, while those who championed the wholesale maintained instead that everything should go to the mass of consumers. Here Holyoake argues the case for giving consumers a dividend on purchases from co-operative productive societies. Although he eventually declared wholeheartedly for profit-sharing, a cause that attracted a good deal of support from middle-class intellectuals and businessmen who hoped it would ease capital-labour antagonisms and provide an antidote for state socialism, Holyoake's pamphlet illustrates how co-operators sought to speak for working-class consumers and mobilise them for social and political change. [Peter Gurney, "The Middle Class Embrace: language, representation and the contest over co-operative forms in Britain, 1860–1914", *Victorian Studies*, 37/2 (1994), 253–286] This challenged the hegemony of the producer that marked both political economy and the ideology of the new socialism that emerged in the following decade.]

Co-operation is an industrial scheme for delivering the public from the conspiracy of capitalists, traders, and manufacturers, to make the labourer work for the least and the consumer pay the utmost for whatever he needs of money, machines, or merchandise. Co-operation effects this deliverance by taking the workman and the public into partnership in every form of business it devises.

Of course I do not want anybody to repeat this definition, because it is a savage, uncomfortable definition. I shall make it milder in a minute. I make it savage now, because I want it to be sharp and clear. Sharp, so that it may cut its way into minds where no co-operative ideas have yet found admission. And clear, because clearness is everything. The only thing Napoleon I. ever said that I admired was his perpetual injunction to his secretaries, "Be clear." With that, anybody is something. Without that, nobody is anything. The mild—no, I hate the word "mild"—the pacific way of defining the thing in question is to say that co-operation is a scheme of industry in which the results are obtained by concert, the profits divided by consent, and the public made a partner with capital and labour, instead of the victim of the needs of both, as occurs under competition.

In each definition, observe, the service of the public is the aim of co-operation. When I said capitalists and traders were engaged in a conspiracy against the public, I wanted to mark that, under a system of competition, every man regards his neighbour as a sheep to be fleeced, and commonly fleeces him. We live in a society of thieves, whom competition licenses to plunder; and he who does it most adroitly is said to have "great business capacity." I always looked on co-operation as the great device of industry which was to save us from ourselves. I always look on co-operation from the side of poverty. Co-operation was not invented to make the rich richer, nor to put a new power into the hands of insatiate individualism, but to save the poor wife in the mechanic's cottage, the poor gentlewoman in her stinted household. I regarded it as the "Good Goddess of Poverty" of whom George Sand sang, who was to save the people evermore from need and greed and despair.

Let us look at the march of co-operation from the poor household point of view.

The poor mechanic in 1821 said: "The shopkeeper conspires against me, and makes me pay a good price for articles which are not always good, but are always dear."

Co-operation—which, like the steam engine, was not brought to perfection at once, and was then rather feeble—said: "Don't trouble, my poor friend; we will create shops in which shareholders shall displace shopkeepers."

After many years' experience, the Poor Householder rubbed his eyes, and said: "I don't see that I am much better off. A co-operative company of conspirators has displaced my old enemy, the shopkeeper, and charge me as much as he did, and I get no richer. I am sorry now that I quarrelled with my old neighbour, the shopkeeper, who did no worse than others, and would have done better had he known how. But these confederated co-operators said they did know how, and don't do it." And the Poor Householder went back to the shopkeeper, and stores went down.

Then a sagacious weaver in Rochdale, twenty years later, turned the thing over in his practical head, and said: "Let us take the Poor Householder into partnership.

Let us share profits with the purchaser. It is he from whom we get all on profits, and by giving him one share we shall secure a good thing for ourselves."

As soon as this was done, the Poor Householder had reason to bless the name of co-operation, and he came back to its stores; and he has enabled it to build halls which no shopkeeper can rival, win a great name, and take a mighty stand in the land.

In course of time, co-operation, which then discovered that the secret of its policy and power was the service of the public, took it into its fertile and good-natured head to try co-operative manufactures. Then it found the Poor Consumer, who stood staring at it as the Poor Purchaser once stared at the stores.

Yet it did not occur to co-operative production to invite the honest fellow into partnership.

At last he took courage, and said, "What are you going to do for me?"

Then Productive Co-operation, having some respect for the unregarded fellow, answered: "We will form a joint-stock company. Then you will see what you will see. We will stop the individual capitalist from taking everything. We shareholders shall all co-operate, and share the profits. Co-operation for ever, we say!"

Well, they did that for many a year; but our old friend the Consumer found himself getting no fatter, and he said one day to his joint-stock patrons, "Do you know, I don't feel much better."

"Don't you see," they replied, "that we have extended co-operation? It is a great thing to extend the principle!"

"Yes, I see that," said the Poor Consumer, "but I don't exactly see what I get by it. I only see a set of joint-stock conspirators who make me pay as much as before. Can't you put co-operative production on the same footing as co-operative distribution, and give the Poor Consumer a turn the same as you did the Poor Purchaser?"

"You are a very stupid person—not to say troublesome," said the Joint-stock Co-operators; "but as we want your custom we will make a great co-operative concession to you. We shall give all workmen a share of the profits. Now, sir, we guess you are well satisfied at last. If labour is taken into partnership with capital, is not that co-operation? If not, we should like to know what is."

Well, this was done, and deservedly great was the rejoicing thereat. In some cases workmen were permitted to take shares, as at Halifax. In better cases, as at Whitwood—workmen who did not take shares received a mitigated recognition that labour had rights as well as capital.

While Co-operation was blessing the inventor of industrial partnerships, and whilst its ears were filled with delicious applause, echoing from every camp of labour, it descried its old acquaintance, the Poor Consumer, coming up again still sharp in nose and pinched in the cheek—looking a little less disconsolate than of old, but still far from satisfied in his mind.

Co-operation had for once a kindly word, as it always had a latent respect, for him whose forefathers, during a thousand generations, never had before known a disinterested friend; for no persons cared for the Consumer unless they wanted him to buy something.

"What, come again?" said Co-operation. "What's the matter now?"

"Well," said the imperturbable applicant, "I am come to ask when you are going to do something for me?"

"Why," cried astonished Co-operation, "what more can we do? Don't you see that capital and labour now co-operate together with co-equal advantages? Do we not unite the energy of individualism with the concert of co-operation?"

"As to individualism," answered Consumer, "I don't know what to say to that. It never did anything for me. I thought co-operation was designed to get rid of individualism, and substitute for it the concert of all for the advantage of all. Individualism is 'for itself and the devil take the hindmost,' and as the 'hindmost' is always the public, the devil gets more than his share."

"Ah," says Co-operation—who has some common sense, but has not got it always ready—"there is something in that. But you are not the public." "Then who am I?" said the Poor Consumer. "Where will your manufactories be if I don't turn up to buy their produce? Just where your stores where when I stayed away from them. To whom do you go for orders? Who pays your prices? Who keeps your mills and mines going? Who makes you rich but the Consumer? And the Poor Consumer is the public, who in the end pays all because he is the many. Oh, narrow-head Co-operation! You have still got individualism on the brain. You still secretly regard me as a person to be kept at a distance—as the outside party, who is to pay the prices out of which the dividends are to come; you still think that all you share with me you lose. So thought the old store-making co-operators. So they kept me out until at last the stores went out themselves." Co-operation, who was a good deal amazed at these retorts, said to the speaker, "You have a fluent tongue, and not a bad memory; but I am not so sure that you are so good a prophet. You ought to remember that co-operative production is a much more difficult thing than co-operative distribution—requiring more capital, higher skill, and involving greater risks than shopkeeping. The shopkeeper only requires to know a good thing when he sees it; the manufacturer requires to know how to make it."

"Admitting all that," answers the Consumer, "is co-operation intended to benefit me or not? That is what I want to know. I see a manufactory conducted by a single master. He goes on the individual system. I know what his object is. He is a conspirator against my pocket. He means to get out of me the highest price he can for whatever article he sells me. Then the co-operator comes forward and professes to be my friend, and tells me he will deliver me from that conspirator. I am much obliged to him. But what does he do? He forms a joint-stock company, who indeed co-operate among themselves to share the profits of my original adversary, and charge me the same prices as he did. The one-master system they replace by a hundred-master system; and in lieu of one conspirator, I am assailed by a joint-stock company of them. To make matters better, these confederated individualists take into partnership the workman, and share profits with him; and now I am assailed by a more formidable company of conspirators; for the workman, my neighbour and my friend, he has joined the compact against me. He co-operates, indeed, with the loanholder and the shareholder for his own advantage; but they all co-operate against the consumer. They all look to the public to pay. True co-operation commences with proposing a partnership with the public. Individualists conspire against the public. True co-operation serves the public, and delivers the consumer from the conspirators of competition."

"Ah!" in an awakened tone, exclaims Co-operation, who can see the right thing when lucid intervals occur, "I suppose you mean the scheme which the co-operative printers of Manchester have lately adopted—that of giving 5 per cent to loan capital, because it is withdrawable, and 7½ per cent to share capital, because it is not withdrawable, and dividing the remainder of profits in three equal portions, one to shareholders, one to workpeople, and one to customer—is something like what you have in your mind."

"Yes," exclaims the pertinacious Consumer, "that looks a little nearer the right thing. That scheme does recognise the consumer, and co-operation will find that it will pay to recognise that querulous creature. But printers always were in advance of mankind. All the cleverness of the world passes through their hands into type; and if wisdom is not born with them, they catch it from their copy."

12

"SUGGESTIONS FOR CARRYING OUT THE PROPOSALS FOR THE EDUCATION OF CO-OPERATORS", *CO-OPERATIVE NEWS*, 4 NOVEMBER 1882, 743–744.

Ben Jones

[Benjamin Jones (1847–1942), was the son of a dyer's labourer and a power loom weaver from Salford. He started work aged nine, was appointed salesman and assistant buyer for the Co-operative Wholesale Society in 1871 and worked his way up. From early on he was a keen educationalist, as this paper read at a southern section conference demonstrates. Jones and others were trying, with the aid of academics active in the University Extension movement such as the historian Arnold Toynbee, to get retail societies to make educational provision more systematic. [Brian Simon, *Education and the Labour Movement, 1870–1920* (London: Lawrence and Wishart, 1965)] He notes in his address a recent meeting at Newcastle where the idea of an education in "culture" was promoted by university men. While Jones broadly supports this development, he underlines the importance of an education in "the principles and practice of co-operation, for without these, it is possible they may not always have the necessary leisure to enjoy the culture which is to be given them". His ire was directed particularly at Dr R.D. Roberts, secretary for the Cambridge system of local lectures, and the class aspect of his rejection of "culture" in the narrow sense was made more explicit in the discussion which followed, William Nuttall of the CWS, for instance, ridiculing university professors and stressing the importance of co-operators remaining independent in education as in everything else. Above all, Nuttall argued, co-operators needed an education in political economy to enable them to understand why such a yawning gulf existed between rich and poor and how this could be changed. In his summary, Jones agreed in the necessity of an education in political economy as a critique of the status quo.]

SUGGESTIONS FOR CARRYING OUT THE PROPOSALS FOR THE EDUCATION OF CO-OPERATORS.

It is gratifying to see the comparative rapidity with which co-operative public opinion has declared itself on this subject. It was only in June last year, that the Southern Section resolved to call the attention of the other sections to the necessity of some action being taken. In December, statistics were placed before the United Board, showing the surprisingly small amount of educational work done, compared with what was generally understood. At the March meeting, the Board unanimously approved of systematic action being taken to extend and develop educational work, and agreed that the subject should be discussed at the Oxford Congress.

At the Congress, papers were read by Mr. Toynbee and myself, and the delegates were unanimously in favour of educational extension. Since Congress, these papers have been discussed at numerous conferences, with almost unanimous expressions of assent from the delegates; and at the last United Board meeting, a series of proposals were approved, copies of which have been placed in your hands.[1]

These proposals have been referred to the sections, who will no doubt carry them out as far as they can see their way to doing so. Of course each section will carry them out in the way it deems best, and in a large body like ours, there is certain to be considerable differences of opinion, both as to what it is advisable to do, and as to what it is possible to do. Already these differences have manifested themselves. The Scottish Section consider the proposals too elaborate and complicated; but it is to be hoped it will not, and I am sure it need not, hinder them from carrying out many of the proposals, if they cannot see their way to carrying out all. On the other hand, their near neighbour has pleased the advanced division by a sudden and agreeable change; from being the most apathetic section in educational matters, they have swung round to the other extreme, and appear determined to make amends by being the most energetic in the future. They have lately held a meeting of co-operators at their headquarters in Newcastle, which was addressed by Professor Stuart, and Messrs. Roberts and Morton, of Cambridge. At this meeting, a course of education was advocated, which should embrace what was called culture. The *Co-operative News* reports Mr. Roberts as saying: "Education might be considered under two heads. There was in the first place, the education which was with a view to the daily work, which they might call 'technical education;' on the other hand, there was the education which was with a view to the leisure time, which they might call 'culture,' " He then went on to say: "The subjects with which the university dealt, however, were more with a view to culture—with a view to giving wider interest, to making it possible to obtain out of leisure time, the highest possible intellectual pleasure." A resolution was passed in favour of the scheme propounded by these gentlemen.

Although it is an ambitious undertaking, I heartily hope they will succeed in carrying out all that is proposed; but I also hope that they will, in addition, teach the principles and practice of co-operation, for without these, it is possible they may not always have the necessary leisure to enjoy the culture which is to be given them.

If the report of Mr. Roberts's speech is accurate, there is one portion not altogether so pleasing, since it contains a mis-statement. He says, "at the meetings of the Co-operative Congress at Oxford, the question of education was dealt with in certain papers, but in reading those papers, he saw that the view of education which was taken by the writers was education in the principles of co-operation. That was a most important and legitimate thing, but it seemed to him far too narrow an idea of education." (Cheers.) Mr. Roberts is certainly under a misapprehension. I cannot understand how he has got the impression. Mr. Toynbee distinctly advocates an education which will fit co-operators for the citizenship of a great country like England; and I, while urging that education in co-operation shall be the first charge on the funds of co-operators, fully agree with anything being done afterwards, if the funds will only admit of it. There is all the difference between insisting on a certain subject having our first attention, and having our exclusive attention. The difference is so palpable, that if I did not believe it to be impossible for a university man to do such a thing, I should have considered the statement at Newcastle as only a cheap expedient to elicit a cheer...

Mr. R. NEWTON...

The paper was excellent in a double sense. It not only showed the necessity of providing themselves with more education, but at the same time showed them the means by which they might acquire it...

There was no difficulty in young co-operators now-a-days getting information. The older ones had had to struggle like sparrows in winter, after crumbs of bread, the result being there had been a great waste of time in reading, because they didn't know what to read, or how to get what it was desirable they should read. They wanted men to take up this subject of co-operation and work it out. Working men ought to study how they can beat work out the conditions of their being, so as to get these conditions into their own hands. (Hear.) Some professors of political economy looked upon working men simply as so many bars of iron, not as common and equal factors...

Mr. NUTTALL wished to say to Mr. Acland that be never read a list of the universities and the names of their professors, without feeling that there was an immense amount of time and money spent upon men to very little practical purpose. (Laughter.) He wished to be clearly understood. He agreed to some extent with the people at Newcastle, that the education of these gentlemen was an education of culture, and not of utility. It was not an education that would assist working men in their efforts to improve themselves, and that was what they were looking forward to. He knew Mr. Acland would be pleased to see what was needed. They could not serve themselves and the nation better than in trying to master the subjects they wanted in their daily work in the world. Working men had to earn their bread. When they had done that, then there would be time for culture, perhaps. The first step was to teach them how best to earn their bread. (Hear.) Unless they did this they would be called simply theorists...

For himself, the more he read about these questions, the less he felt he knew. He never in his life felt more ignorant than he felt that day, and his difficulties increased every day. And the further they advanced, the more they would find themselves beset with difficulties. It was when they left the distributive and came to the productive, to national and international questions as affecting working men, that the difficulties were perceived in their true magnitude. He never felt pleasure in seeing working men leave the means of getting a living for themselves to mere capitalists. It seemed very strange they should do this. They should never let capitalists get into the position of being able to dominate labour. They should themselves arrange how labour should be employed and paid. They should themselves decide whether they should find occupation at home, or should seek it abroad. These were questions which would necessarily spring up when working men began to study matters affecting their own interests for themselves. He didn't agree with running down dividends. He admired the man who admired dividend, but he admired him most who considered the means of getting it...

They could not do better than by establishing classes and teaching them themselves. If there was one thing more than another they should interest the scholars in, it was political economy. They knew that it dealt with them, and they should deal with it. He never ran down dividend. It meant accumulation of capital. But when they stopped there, he condemned the stopping business. (Hear.) They had two classes of men in the society. One owned and lived without much work; the other worked very hard and lived very little. If he had his way he would order it so that everyone that eat should earn what he eat. How this could be done would be shown by a careful study of the subjects suggested in the paper before them, and this was the question above all others, which working men are interested in solving. (Cheers.)...

Mr. B. JONES then rose to wind up the discussion, and was received with cheers. It was a very pleasing and satisfactory thing, he said, to see a question one had taken an active part in promoting, progressing so well as this question of education, which, in its present aspect, he had been connected with from the first. From being a United Board matter, the subject had now become of general interest, and was being warmly discussed all over the country. This was one of the most hopeful features of the movement at the present time. (Hear, hear.) On looking over his notes on the discussion, he found the task they had cut out for him an exceedingly simple one. They seemed pretty nearly all of a mind on the subject, and left him very little to answer. Mr. Newton had referred to political economy. That was the secret of the whole thing. His paper really dealt with political economy, but he had put it in simple and homely language that could be easily understood. It would have been an easy matter to have used a mass of unintelligible jargon that would have had no meaning whatever to many, and would have conveyed no more to those versed in the science than the simple remarks in his paper conveyed to all. He had abstained from doing this, believing that the simpler the language, the more forcible and substantial would be the lesson conveyed. (Hear, hear.)...

The essence of the whole problem was this, that the great bulk of the wealth of this country belongs to the few, and the work has to be done by the many. They didn't want to take their wealth from the few, but let them have only a proper rate of interest for what they had at stake in the world. At the present time, through the ignorance of the working classes, capital received more than double what it was entitled to receive, according to the doctrines of political economy. If working men would but get the necessary knowledge, they might very soon put this right, and very materially improve their position by the very process of applying the principle of political economy to the reduction of the wages of capital. This showed the necessity for the education of co-operators.

Note

1 These proposals were given with the report of United Board meeting in the *News* for September 16.

13

INAUGURAL ADDRESS DELIVERED AT THE TWENTY-FIRST ANNUAL CO-OPERATIVE CONGRESS . . . 1889 (MANCHESTER: CENTRAL CO-OPERATIVE BOARD, 1889), 3–5, 7–13, 28–30.

Alfred Marshall

[Alfred Marshall (1842–1924), Professor of Political Economy at Cambridge University, was one of the most influential economists of his age. From the first Congress in 1869, co-operators invited middle-class intellectuals to preside over these annual meetings, and Marshall spelt out the reasons why he supported the movement at Ipswich in 1889. He regarded co-operation as a perfect compromise between socialism and collectivism on the one side – which was making rapid progress in the 1880s – and capitalism and individualism on the other, educating workers about business and imbuing them with useful moral qualities like thrift. Marshall accepted that the worst aspects of unregulated competition needed to be curbed and was no advocate of hedonistic consumption, approving of the movement's hostility towards credit and advertising. [David Reisman, *The Economics of Alfred Marshall* (London: Macmillan, 1986); *Alfred Marshall's Mission* (Basingstoke: Macmillan, 1990)] Interestingly, he also regarded co-operation as a protection against capitalist trusts whose main purpose he argued was "to increase the fortunes of the rich", an idea that struck a chord among co-operators as the final extract in Part 2 demonstrates. In fine, Marshall considered co-operation as representative of what he called "economic chivalry", a line he developed in a later address that argued "economic chivalry" could bring about "true Socialism", thereby making Marx's bureaucratic socialism more unlikely. ["Social Possibilities of Economic Chivalry" (1907), in A.C. Pigou (ed.), *Memorials of Alfred Marshall* (London: Macmillan, 1925), 346] Marshall's presidential address certainly indicates the pull of liberal political economy for co-operators but also its limitations; it was no accident surely that individuals from within the movement were honoured as congress presidents from 1892, the first being J.T.W. Mitchell who, as the extract in Part 4 shows, had rather different ambitions for co-operation.]

Co-operation is many sided, and can be looked at from many points of view. There are, in consequence, many definitions of it, all having much in common, but each bringing into special prominence some aspect of it which appeals with special strength to some one or other of the many different classes of minds who are attracted by it. It is of course necessary to agree provisionally on some formal definition of a co-operative society for administrative purposes. But a movement which, though so great, is yet so young, is in danger of being cramped by the too rigid insistence on any hard and fast formula; and I would wish, instead of defining it, to describe the general notion which I have formed of it. I regard it as the typical and most representative product of the age; because it combines high aspirations with calm and strenuous action, and because it sets itself to develop the spontaneous energies of the individual while training him to collective action by the aid of collective resources, and for the attainment of collective ends. It has points of affinity with many other movements; but it is like no other. Other schemes for developing the world's material resources are equally practical and equally business-like, but they have not the same direct aim to improve the quality of man himself. Other schemes for social reform have equally high aspirations, but they have not the same broad basis of patient action and practical wisdom. What distinguishes co-operation from all other movements is that it is at once a strong and calm and wise business, and a strong and fervent and proselytising faith.

The cardinal doctrines of its faith are, as I have said, not peculiar to it: they are shared more or less by other movements. They are, I take it:—Firstly, the production of fine human beings, and not the production of rich goods, is the ultimate aim of all worthy endeavour. Secondly, he who lives and works only for himself, or even only for himself and his family, leads an incomplete life; to complete it he needs to work with others for some broad and high aim. Thirdly, such an aim is to be found in the co-operative endeavour to diminish those evils which result to the mass of the people from the want of capital of their own; evils which take the two-fold form of insufficiency of material income, and want of opportunity for developing many of their best faculties. Lastly, the working classes, though weak in many ways, are strong in their numbers. They have a great power in their knowledge of one another, and their trust in one another; and they can much increase this force, for by joint action they can make their little capital go a long way towards getting a free scope for their activities, and towards emancipating them from a position of helpless dependence on the support, and the guidance, and the governance of the more fortunate classes. And though the beginning of such a movement may be small, it has in it the seeds of growth, because it will educate the working classes in business capacity, and in the moral strength of united and public action for public purposes.

Now this co-operative faith, as I understand it, differs from the faiths of many social reformers in two respects. On the one hand it is more prosaic, and more ready to take facts as they are, it does not substitute for them brilliant products of a poetic imagination. And on the other hand, the virtues to which it appeals are the virtues of those who hold the faith. It is not a claim that the virtues of others should induce them to divide equally all round the advantages which they have already acquired.

I do not mean that the co-operator is very likely to consider the existing arrangements with regard to property as the best possible. He may probably think, as I myself certainly think, that the rich ought to be taxed much more heavily than they are, in order to provide for their poorer brethren the material means for a healthy physical and mental development; and he may think, as I certainly do, that the rich are in private duty bound to contribute freely to public purposes far more than the taxgatherer ought by force to take from them, and to confine within narrow bounds their expenditure on their own personal enjoyment, and that of their families. But the point I want to insist on is that any beliefs which the co-operator may hold on questions of this sort do not enter into the co-operative faith, because that relates to the duties of co-operators themselves, and not to the duties of others towards co-operators. The co-operative faith is a belief in the beauty and the nobility, the strength and the efficiency, of collective action by the working classes, employing their own means, not indeed suddenly to revolutionise, but gradually to raise, their own material and moral condition...

Well, what is the explanation of this huge trade? It lies chiefly in the fact that more effort was wasted in doing things that it was not worth while to have done at all, in the old-fashioned retail trade, than in any other business to which working men had access. It is possible that if a co-operative society of working men had been able to penetrate the mysteries of the trade of law in its application to real property, and had been able to cut away all those complications that are more trouble to everyone, and more cost to everyone but the lawyers, than they are worth, there might have been an even more striking curtailment of wasted effort. But however that may be, retail trade was the one accessible business in which there were great economies to be effected. Retailers, as a body, kept far more shops than was necessary, spent far too much trouble and money on attracting a few customers, and then in taking care that those few customers paid them in the long run—the very long run—for those goods which they had bought on credit, or in other words, had borrowed; and for all this they had to charge. The smallest shopkeepers were those that spent most of their time in looking after their customers, and least in handing goods over the counter. It was those who were nearest the condition of the working men who performed the most unnecessary services for them, and charged them the most for so doing. In some cases a retailer would sell at long credit what he himself bought at long credit from a wholesale dealer, who himself perhaps bought at credit from the ultimate producer. The manufacturer had to charge high for the risks and trouble, as well as the locking-up of the capital; the wholesale dealer, starting from this raised platform of high prices, piled up a good percentage more for a similar cause; the intermediate dealer did the same, and perhaps, finding the retailer in his power, added a little adulteration extra; the retailer, having the workman in his power, added on, perhaps, a little more adulteration, and, anyhow, a great increase of price.

Now the co-operative store bought for cash, and as nearly as possible at the fountain head; it required no advertisements; in its earlier stages it paid next to nothing for shop front; and in its later stages when it had a somewhat expensive shop front, it put a great many businesses behind it, or in successive stories over it. Its customers, regarding it as their own, would not mind mounting many steps, or waiting a little for the assistants on a Saturday night, or at any other time, when there happened to be too few to get through the business quickly. The customers were the proprietors, and had no inducement to adulterate their own goods; and the time which they spent on attending meetings of the society and managing their own business was in a great measure saved from the time that used to be spent in considering whether it would not be better to change their shopkeeper, or perhaps in lamenting that they were in his power and could not do so.

Now, my object in dwelling on this oft-told tale is to show that the success of distributive stores does not prove that there is any magic in co-operation which will enable the working classes to undertake difficult businesses without the aid of picked men of a high order of business ability. Those whom the stores have thrust to the wall are chiefly men who did not get very high earnings, although they charged high prices. The system of co-operative retailing has such great inherent economies that it is likely to succeed if carried out with good faith and honesty and average good sense: the more business genius it has the better it will succeed, but it can flourish fairly well without business genius...

But the advantages of the Wholesale are still further increased, when it produces in one of its own departments the goods which it sells itself to the distributive stores. Such a department as the boot works at Leicester, or the biscuit works at Crumpsall, can avail themselves of the splendid resources of the Wholesale for buying much of their material. The department has a supply of capital which is at once unlimited and never too large; for the great bank in which the Wholesale keeps its own reserves, and those of many distributive societies, will always allow to it as much capital as it wants, and never force it to pay for more. It can offer practical constancy of employment to its workers, for when trade is slack the Wholesale will, of course, give the preference to the goods of its own department, and leave the other producing firms with which it deals to bear their fretting under the ragged edge of inconstant work as best they may. Again, the department need have no very great anxiety about those fluctuations of prices which make the career of most of its rivals so full of strain and stress. If one year it makes a fortunate purchase of raw material, and the Wholesale can credit it with a sale price for its finished commodities, pitched on a much higher basis, the gains all go into the common purse of the Wholesale; and if, at another time, the markets go against its buyers, so that when wages and all other expenses have been paid, and a fixed 5 per cent. allowed for capital, the balance sheet shows a loss, there is no disturbance of the ordinary routine. Departments which, if they had been independent businesses, would have been sunk by accumulated losses in their early years, have been carried through the waters by the strong hand of the Wholesale; and, having emerged safely, with their lessons of failure behind them, are in fair years making high net profits: these profits go to strengthen still more the already strong hand, and enable it to undertake new tasks, and to help other struggling departments through their temporary troubles.

With these advantages the Wholesale has risen to a position unique amongst all the achievements that have been wrought by the working classes in the history of the world. The mere size of the business which they have to control gives a largeness to their ideas. It compels them to extend the range of their thought over the whole country, almost over the whole world. It is an education in itself to any member of a local society to have to consider whether his representative on the Wholesale is to advocate a forward policy—whether, for instance, he is to support a proposal for starting one more new line of ships of their own, or for opening a new foreign depot in addition to those at Calais and at Rouen, at Copenhagen, and Hamburg, and New York. He feels a healthy pride as he turns over the pages of his "Annual," and sees prints of one splendid building after another of which he is part owner; as he reckons up the acres of flooring in his warehouses at Manchester, or asks whether there are many buildings in the city that are finer than his London branch, with its high clock tower.

And when he looks forward, his ambition may reach out a long way unchecked. He may reason that if the belief should extend that all goods sold in the stores, whether high class or low class, are honestly what they pretend to be; that they are sold at least as cheaply as the tradesman can sell them; and that there is a dividend of, say, 2s. in the pound thrown in at the end of the quarter, the sales of the retail stores may perhaps grow to three or four hundred millions a year. Every increase in their sales would increase their power of consulting the tastes of a great variety of customers, and so retaining those who are now drawn off to shops that follow special lines of their own; and it would increase the variety of the orders which they could give to the Wholesale. And if the growing loyalty to co-operative principles, which induced individuals to buy more largely of the stores, induced the retail stores to buy more largely of the Wholesale, they would by their very increased custom enable the Wholesale to extend its operations, to sell to them more cheaply, to provide them with a larger choice of goods, and thus to increase their inducements to buy almost everything from it.

The powers of the Wholesale as a dealer would therefore be increased much; but its powers as a producer would be increased out of all proportion. For now, though it can vie with any in buying direct from the packing houses of Chicago and the flour mills of Minneapolis, it cannot enter upon any manufacture for which there is not a very large working class demand; since many purchasers when buying manufactured goods prefer the variety offered by a long street of shops to the charms of the dividend at the stores. Not being able to sell largely, the retail stores do not buy largely; and being themselves compelled to seek for variety, they will, as a rule, buy only very small quantities of any one particular pattern, whether it is a co-operative product or not. Co-operative manufacture on a large and varied scale is thus like a cocoanut: it has a very hard shell; but when the shell is broken, there is plenty of good food to be got within. There is a charmed circle to be entered if individual co-operators would buy manufactures so largely from their stores, and their stores would buy so largely of co-operative manufactures, that co-operative manufactures became so various, and the stocks of them held by the distributive stores became so large, that there would be scarce any temptation to seek variety in the outside shops.

It is a most fascinating picture. The retail societies, if properly supported by the private individual, and the Wholesale, if properly supported by them, have within them greater economies than have ever been claimed by the plausible promoters of those Trusts of which we have heard so much lately. But while the purpose of those Trusts was to increase the fortunes of the rich, by means which perhaps might be fair, and perhaps might incidentally benefit the consumers, this further development of the great co-operative federation would be a means by which the working classes would help themselves. Its strength would be a moral strength; would rest on a broad basis of democracy and of equity; its gains would be divided out among all consumers, those consumers being in great part the producers themselves, consuming in proportion to their earnings, and earning in proportion to their efficiency. Raising its high head far beyond all other business undertakings, it would stand forth to challenge the admiration of all ages, the glorious product of working men's hands and working men's heads, of working men's providence and working men's enthusiasm for a great and good cause. It would, in a greater or less degree, act up to all the cardinal principles of the co-operative faith, as I understand it...

I have come to the end of my time, and yet have touched the fringe of only a small part of the great problems which you have set yourselves to solve. The days of romantic chivalry are past. Knights-errant no longer rescue imperilled maidens from the castles of terrible giants, or slaughter dragons that vomit volcanoes of flames; but there is as loud a call as ever for courage and a chivalric self-sacrifice for great and worthy ends. Those who are full of the co-operative faith have to endure the disappointment of seeing themselves out-voted by numbers who care for little that is co-operative except the dividend; and still they have to keep their courage, and to keep their temper, and to fight the good fight time after time till they win. I am told by those who know, what I should have otherwise expected, that there will be in this hall to-day many of the truest and bravest knights of that great order of modern chivalry—co-operation; and they must sometimes wish that the doors had not been held so widely open for those worshippers in their great temple whose devotions are exclusively paid at the shrine of dividend, who stay eagerly watching to see whether the golden image that dwells there will hold up its fingers at the end of the quarter to signify 2s. 3d. or 2s. 4d.; and care for very little else. But to them I would repeat the noble motto of the English Wholesale: "Labour and Wait."

They and others who are not here to-day may wonder that I have not put more into the foreground the great issue as to whether the employés of a co-operative society should share in its profits. I have not done so, partly because my time was short, partly because there seems some danger of its overshadowing what I regard as a still more fundamental question. Profit-sharing is a great end, but it is also a means to an even greater end. It certainly tends to award to the worker a better and juster share of his work than he would otherwise get; but, taken by itself, it does not go very far towards that end. Unless it is used also as a means towards a better organisation of industry it is apt to become little more than a change of form, nearly as much being taken off wages at one end as is added on at the other under the name of profit-sharing. But even so it compares not unfavourably with the best result that can be reached without it, even if the spirit of the employers is liberal, and they try to pay not as low wages as they can, but as much as the business will bear; and if as their business extends they promote their old employés as rapidly as possible to higher posts at higher salaries. It is true that those employés who have been more than five years with one firm are, taking all England together, much better off than they would have been if the firms for which they had worked had barely kept their heads above water; and there is much more indirect profit-sharing, and solidarity of interest between employer and employed in the non-co-operative world than at first sight appears. And I must further confess that when any abstract or "metaphysical" principle—the term is not mine—is applied to settle rigidly what share of the profits should go to labour and what to capital, and what to the consumer, I find myself unable to follow it; whether it is put forward in the interests of labour or of the consumer. Nevertheless, I regard the movement towards the direct participation by the employé in the profits of the business as one of the most important and hopeful events of modern times, and as one of the best and most valuable fruits of the co-operative spirit.

It is the most convincing outward sign and symbol, and the most efficient means, of a true desire to associate the worker in the business, to keep warm his interest in it; to induce him to take a pleasure in advancing its prosperity by all means, whether they fall within the technical limits of his ordinary work or not; to offer him, as far as may be, education, and opportunity and scope for a worthy ambition to act not merely as a hand, but as a thinking and thoughtful human being. Profit-sharing is a good means towards this great end; and he has not lived in vain who has helped to overcome the obstacles which impede its general adoption.

14

THE MARRIAGE OF LABOUR AND CAPITAL (LONDON: THE LABOUR ASSOCIATION, 1896), 1–3, 6–8.

Hodgson Pratt

[Hodgson Pratt (1824–1907) was a civil servant in the government of India before becoming an advocate for international peace and co-operation. Pratt was a vice-president of the Labour Association, an organisation formed in 1884 by G.J. Holyoake and middle-class devotees of profit-sharing such as Edward Owen Greening, Aneurin Williams and Henry Vivian, to contest the CWS model of consumer power and promote productive enterprises based on worker co-partnership. What this term meant was left conveniently vague and many profit-sharing ventures received backing from the Labour Association, many sponsored by employers as docile alternatives to trade unions. This pamphlet was originally delivered as the opening address at the annual exhibition of co-operative productions organised by the Association and held as part of the National Co-operative Festival at the Crystal Palace, Sydenham. [Peter Gurney, *Co-operative Culture and the Politics of Consumption in England, 1870–1930* (Manchester: Manchester University Press, 1996), 67–69] Pratt's address is a clear expression of the belief that profit-sharing ventures would render state socialism avoidable, healing the harmful breach between capital and labour whilst avoiding the violence of revolutionary change. Although it is the case that the Owenite socialist William Thompson had argued for the creation of "capitalist-labourers" in the 1820s, co-partnership bore little resemblance to this ambition and was understood at the time by the majority of trade unionists (though not all – see the extract below by Tom Mann) as merely a cynical employer strategy.]

FRIENDS,

We are met here to-day to inaugurate the Annual Exhibition of goods produced by industrial societies in which the workers are partners. This Exhibition is organised by an Association whose special object is to awaken public interest in a comparatively new system of industry, which it believes will work a mighty but peaceful revolution in society, and render a lasting benefit to all. This Association addresses itself to workmen, to employers of labour, and to the public at large.

When it is remembered that three-fourths of the whole population of our country are wage-receivers, it will be clearly seen how all-important it is that the position of those wage-receivers should be placed on a satisfactory footing. In the light of the fact mentioned by Mr. F. A. Channing, M.P., at the opening of a similar exhibition last year, that position cannot be considered as satisfactory. He stated that, in the two previous years, strikes and lock-outs had involved a loss of wages to the extent of eight millions sterling! There are very many other facts, well known to us all, which show that a complete change is needed in the relations between capital and labour. Of those three-fourths of the population who are wage-receivers, how many are living under healthful and proper conditions of existence; how many are able to enjoy a decent competence in old age; how many can look forward with certainty to having say a pound a week from the age of sixty? How many of those three-fourths have the certainty that, at any time of their life, they may not be turned adrift from their employers' workshop, and so deprived of the means of livelihood, without any fault of their own?

These are questions which it is impossible to answer satisfactorily, and which have therefore occupied the attention of social and political reformers, of philanthropists and statesmen for many years past. It is because there has been no adequate answer to these questions that the doctrine of State Socialism, especially in Germany, has so widely spread; regarded as it is in some countries as a danger to the whole fabric of society and as involving a fatal war of classes.

Amidst the numerous theories and experiments which have been made during this century in order to bring about a more equitable and human, and therefore a more stable, condition of society, we have had those of Robert Owen, and Charles Fourier, and these have been followed by what is called the Co-operative Movement of Great Britain. In accordance with the traditional prudence and the practical character of our countrymen, they have tried a bit-by-bit reform, and they have resorted to independent associations for mutual help, instead of asking for State help or having recourse to a social revolution carried out perhaps by force.

The working classes of Great Britain inaugurated their own redemption by organising their own consumption; and by keeping the profits of the trade in the primary necessaries of life in their own pockets. Their success in Distributive co-operation, *i.e.,* in Consumers' Stores has been marvellous. It is an unparalleled instance of the power of wise organisation carried on by working men. The 1,700 societies have a million and a quarter of members; an annual trade of forty millions sterling; and a profit for themselves of five millions. This form of association has enabled thousands of men to save, who were never before able to accumulate anything for old age; and they have done it without the least difficulty, many of them being enabled thereby to purchase their own dwellings from the profits.

Nevertheless, from the very nature of the case, Distributive co-operation could not do more than this. It could not change the deplorable relations of capital and labour, the two great factors of industrial production. Those relations may be described, like the condition of Europe, as consisting of an armed truce or open war. The capitalist always tries to get as much work out of the workers for as small a wage as the latter can be induced to take; and the worker is always trying to get as much wage as he can induce, through his Trades Union, the capitalist to give. The former wants as long hours of labour as he can get, and the latter wants as few hours as possible.

Could any state of things in human society be more absurd and unnatural than this? Well: it is the object of the Labour Association to convince the British community that the whole of its members suffer from the alienation and contentions of the two partners to all production—the capitalist and the worker. This Association next proceeds to show that the remedy for this disastrous position is to be found in a true union and wise co-operation between the owners of capital and the providers of labour. There are two forms under which this happy marriage may be effected, which they call "The Co-partnership of Industry." In one form great Captains of Industry, as Carlyle called them, are recommended to share profits with their employees and to pay those profits in the shape of share capital—the holders of it having, of course, with the responsibility of capitalists, a voice in the control and management. This arrangement is specially known under the title of Industrial Partnership.

The other form of productive co-operation is that in which all the capital has been found by workmen, either employed in the society or by their brethren in other societies, or by members of Trade Unions, and by Co-operative Distributive Societies.

The next thing that the Labour Association does is to make it plain to the world that this great reform is not a visionary dream, but that it has been actually carried out with increasing success in a great variety of industries. Many of these, I am happy to say, are well represented in the fine Exhibition which we open to-day, and which is a great object lesson of the future of industry...

I have perhaps been invited here to-day because I have during the last seventeen years worked my eight hours a day on behalf of international unity and concord. National unity and concord are surely no less essential to prosperity and progress. Peace is the very condition of true life, as necessary as the atmosphere to all living things; but there is no peace without justice. The relations of the producers of wealth—the capitalists and the workmen, must be established on that basis. The present conditions of industry involve injustice in many forms: there is an unfair share of the profits of labour; there are the great evils of "sweating;" of exhausting conditions of work; very little hope for the toiler in his old age, and a natural discontent with his lot. The whole community is responsible for this state of things, and suffers from it. The remedy rests partly with the workers, partly with the great employers, and partly with the millions of consumers. Will the latter continue to be indifferent as to the conditions under which the cloth they wear, the furniture they use, the coal which they burn at the fireside, have been provided? We are all members one of another; and we must recognise that fact in our daily practice, as a great moral and religious truth which lies at the basis of human society. Practical brotherhood must be realised, for the sense of that brotherhood actuating us incessantly is necessary to a conviction of the fatherhood of God...

In concluding, I wish to refer to the men who have built up co-operation in our country. It is a true and noteworthy fact that you may know something of the inherent goodness of a social, political, or religious reform from the character of the men who promote it. A great cause attracts great men, and makes them nobler by its influence. Well, in no movement for "bettering the world" (as the Rochdale pioneers said) have I met men who have so much impressed me as being inspired by a great ideal, and by being ennobled through it as in the co-operative revolution. It owes its success in the past, and it owes its growth in the present, to such men. It has attracted workers of very different training and spiritual temperament. Let me speak of some few of those who have departed, such as Owen, Kingsley, Maurice, Hughes, Craig, Lloyd-Jones, James Hole, and William Pare. Many of these I have known, and I attended the meeting held in 1869 for the foundation of the Co-operative Union. It is impossible to speak of Edward Vansittart Neale without an emotion which almost incapacitates one from doing justice to him. He was one whose character was of the finest type in its unselfish devotion to the welfare of the working-men of England. He was a man of high culture, and of abilities which would have enabled him to earn distinction in his profession of the law: he sacrificed his entire fortune, sought neither fame nor emolument throughout his life, and attached himself to an obscure cause. In my many interviews with him I never once heard him refer to himself, or anything he had done. I must hurry on. In his friend, Tom Hughes, we find a chivalrous, clear-sighted man, who was one of the few to speak on behalf of the North at the time of the American Civil War. In his friend and comrade, John Malcolm Ludlow, we have another man of the same high type, whose touching words at the Co-operative Alliance Conference last year must remain in the memory of us all. Who that ever heard the splendid oratory of that self-taught leader, Lloyd-Jones, can ever forget the enthusiasm with which he inspired us? Have we not still with us Edward Owen Greening, whose clear demonstration of economic facts, whose strong organising faculty and sincere faith in co-operation are known to us all? These men are well represented in the younger brothers who are daily doing more and more excellent work. Let me mention my friends and former colleagues, J. J. Dent and B. Jones, as examples of the power which belongs to men inspired by great truths, and having striking ability to apply them in action. Have we not at our side in this meeting such men as Vivian, Blandford, Aneurin Williams, and A. K. Connell, who, from the vantage ground of past labours, are carrying on the splendid work of the Labour Association? But I must go back for a moment. Have we not among us one of the fathers of co-operation, as energetic and vigorous as the youngest among us, George Jacob Holyoake, whom we all regard with admiration and affection? His genius gives to the stalest argument new force and brilliancy. May we not say that the "new moral world" is in sight? How soon it shall be realised depends upon the encouragement given to the workers by their countrymen. We look to the latter to give that sympathy in a practical form, in the shape of capital and custom. With all reverence, I say that I believe this to be Divine work, for God desires that truth, justice and mercy shall reign on this earth. I think I cannot more fitly conclude than by quoting the following words from that great and noble teacher, Mazzini:

> "Working men, we live in an epoch similiar to that of Christ. We feel in our inmost souls the need of re-animating and of transforming modern society. We seek the kingdom of God on earth, as it is in heaven—or rather that earth may become a preparation for heaven, and society an endeavour after the progressive realisation of the Divine idea."

HODGSON PRATT.

15

RESOLUTION AND DISCUSSION ON TRUSTS, *THE 35TH ANNUAL CO-OPERATIVE CONGRESS, 1903* (MANCHESTER: CO-OP UNION, 1903), 345–347.

[By the time this resolution was passed at the 1903 Annual Congress, co-operators had been anxious about the rise of capitalist monopoly for almost two decades. They were fearful of the effects on trade and condemned the covert operations of trusts, syndicates and combines (the terms were often used interchangeably and without much precision) as particularly harmful for working-class consumers, fears that were strengthened by J.A. Hobson's important work, *The Evolution of Modern Capitalism* (1894). Such forms, co-operators maintained, were in effect reinventing the old immoral trade practices of regrating, engrossing and forestalling, and ought to be curbed by law. Indeed, it was the rise of monopoly capitalism, as well as the effects of total war, which eventually drove co-operators to break with liberalism decisively, enter the political arena and establish the Co-operative Party in 1917. [Sidney Pollard, "The Foundation of the Co-operative Party", in Asa Briggs and John Saville (eds), *Essays in Labour History, 1886–1923* (London: Macmillan, 1971)] The 1903 resolution, which was passed unanimously, urged the movement to educate consumers about the dangers posed by private monopolies. W.H. Berry who moved the resolution pointed to their deleterious effects on consumers but also stressed how monopolies or trusts were opposed to the co-operative movement in principle and would try therefore to snuff it out. Co-operation or "the people's trust" was the only real defence against this threat he argued, an idea that was taken up and amplified within the movement over subsequent decades. Ongoing and accelerating changes in the economic structure of society proved the optimism of the sometime Liberal-Labour MP Fred Maddison who contributed to the discussion was somewhat misplaced.]

Mr. W. H. BERRY (Southern Section) proposed the following resolution:—

That, in view of the rapid growth of trusts and other combinations of capital controlled by, and in the interests of comparatively few persons, this Congress believes that such attempts at monopoly are a menace to the well-being of the community; and urges all co-operative organisations, when arranging propaganda work, to endeavour to counteract the influence of such combinations, and to strengthen our movement to resist any attempts which may be made to retard its free growth and development. Further, we believe that the influence which in many places has been exerted to prevent individuals from joining co-operative societies is an interference with personal liberty which ought to be resisted by every means in our power.

Mr. Berry asked for the indulgence of the delegates, because time would not allow him to deal with all the points of the resolution. The history of the trust movement began a hundred years ago when small shopkeepers were gradually merged into great companies; there was then a long period of ruthless competition with these huge trusts and combines. The magnitude of the trust movement was so great and its effects so far-reaching, that it had become a prominent feature of the world's industry, and some of its characteristics were not creditable. One of the first effects of the trust movement upon many industries was to artificially force up prices, although the cost of some raw material had declined. Wages had not varied materially, but there was a tendency in the combines to give a higher remuneration for exceptional ability. Socially and commercially, the trust movement was opposed to the co-operative movement. Trusts were organised in the interest of the few, whilst the co-operative movement was organised in the interests of the many. He thought that in the future we should see a large extension of this trust movement, and it seemed to him that, as co-operators, we must see to it that we maintain and extend the people's trust—organised by the people, for the people, and under the control of the people. Co-operators had to consider how best they could strengthen their own movement; and he suggested to them that the dangers to their movement were greater within than from without. The danger to our movement was the want of knowledge amongst our members. One thing they should keep in view was the importance of getting members to understand what the co-operative movement was, and what these trusts also were. Supposing, for instance, when the huge tobacco combine was contemplated it had been successful and the trust had brought its prices down to a penny per ounce, what would co-operators have done? Would they have been content to pay their 4d. per ounce, or would they have paid a penny per ounce for a time and paid more than 4d. per ounce when the combination had captured the trade. Co-operators must stick to their principles, and the question of capital should not be considered until they produced everything for themselves and paid for the highest ability which could be obtained.

Mr. J. T. BROWNLIE (Woolwich) seconded the resolution. He said that this was a question of so much importance, it well became the United Board to call the attention of Congress to it, and urge committees of societies to take it up. Some said co-operators had nothing to fear, that the co-operative movement could fight and beat the trusts. He ventured to say they knew nothing of the trusts, or they would not say any such thing. The trusts had come to stay, unless co-operators could take the means to control them. Co-operators would have to take up their rightful position, not only in municipal affairs, but in political affairs as well. The trusts were looking at the co-operative movement and its large turnover, and were saying, here is another thing we shall have to tackle. Co-operators would have to exercise their rights by using their votes to capture the administrative and legislative machine. He appealed to them to take every opportunity of exercising their rights as citizens, and understanding what these trusts really meant.

Mr. J. T. HARRIS (Brotherhood Trust) believed these trusts were the greatest enemy of the co-operative movement. The boycott had fizzled out too soon; but these great combines were really menacing to the movement, and co-operators were not sufficiently alive to their danger. One great danger was the amount of capital they employed. Another danger, and a vulnerable point, was the small numbers employed in the co-operative movement. How very few co-operative members were employed in the movement. If the trusts wished, they could organise a very efficient boycott, by refusing to give co-operative members employment. Co-operators must employ more and more of their own members, and then they would be independent of the trusts. Many of our members were ignorant of the tendency of modern times, and the dangers which threatened the movement. In our propagandist work we must call attention to this point. If co-operators were loyal they could build up a true people's trust which would be impregnable to all attacks from outside. He hoped co-operators would discuss this question at conferences so as to understand it, and hasten the time when we should produce not merely one quarter, but the whole of our consumption.

Mr. G. I. WALKER (Sunderland) asked why co-operators were continually prating about fighting trusts, whilst nearly every society was shutting out its members' capital, which was going into the hands of the private traders. Co-operators should create capital, so that they might fight the trusts. If they were to capture British trade and do something worthy of the name of co-operation, they must enter the arena of competition, go in for the manufacture of engines and ships, and enter into mining operations. There were brains and money enough in the co-operative movement to create a people's trust. We must employ all our own capital to break down the barriers against its profitable employment. Why were we making dividends? Was it to send men to Congress, or on a holiday tour, or to build convalescent homes and orphanages. We must by means of education qualify ourselves to meet competition in the open market...

Mr. F. MADDISON (Blackpool Printers) said this was a most important question, and he was glad that it had been placed on the agenda. He hated all trusts and monopolies, because he believed in freedom. He asked them, however, not to exaggerate the situation, not to become alarmists, for, in his opinion, there was nothing in the industrial situation in England to justify anything approaching a panic. So long as they could draw upon the markets of the world for their supplies, the whip hand of the trusts would always remain in their hands. The trusts grew in America because before a trust was formed the people who promoted it put up a tariff wall. They first got the tariff right, and then they went ahead in trust. If they only retained the same inlet that they had for these shores for their supplies, though they might have to fight the trust, and probably would, their success was practically assured. There was only one antidote for all trusts, and that was competition. The trust was no danger so long as they opposed it with another trust more efficient. The co-operative movement had got to oppose all trusts by greater efficiency, and if they could not provide greater efficiency they were beaten, and so they should be. The great law of progress involved that. There was no reason why they should be beaten, but don't let them advocate the idea of monopoly in the movement. Let them allow for variety. Don't let them think that one mould must necessarily do for them all. They were proud of their Wholesale Societies, but they were also proud of other attempts—co-partnership attempts, and let them be sufficiently broad-minded to show that in the co-operative movement which was resisting monopoly they could have variety of co-operation. One word about industry. Let them go into the outside world of industry, and take their co-operative principles with them, and assert before trusts or any one else that labour would never be satisfied as a mere wage-earning—it must also have interested work, and interest in its work.

Part 3

CLASS, DEMOCRACY AND THE STATE

16

"DISCUSSION AT HALIFAX", *NOTES TO THE PEOPLE*, VOL. 2, 1852, 793–806, 823–829.

Ernest Jones and Lloyd Jones

[This debate that took place over two nights in late January 1852 clearly exposed the growing tensions at this time between varieties of co-operation and socialism. Ernest Jones (1819–1869) was an early disciple of Karl Marx who came from a landed gentry background, trained as a barrister and played a leading role in late Chartism. [Miles Taylor, *Ernest Jones, Chartism, and the romance of politics, 1819–1869* (Oxford: Oxford University Press, 2003)] Patrick Lloyd Jones (1811–1886) started his working life as a fustian cutter, and then served as an Owenite missionary and lecturer before converting to Christian Socialism in 1850. For Lloyd Jones, co-operative success proved the power of working-class association and their ability to check market abuses, such as adulteration, through their own efforts. Anticipating Ernest Jones' chief line of attack, he denied that he rejected political solutions to the problems faced by the poor, but argued instead for a plurality of approaches. For his part, the Chartist leader denied that co-operation as presently practiced offered any way out, insisting instead that it would "lead them back into a greater gulph of misery than that from which they were trying to emancipate themselves". Co-operation was merely a mirror image of competition for him and thus destined to prove disastrous. The prioritisation of politics did indeed prove to be Ernest Jones' main card, one that he played repeatedly, and he read his opponent a long lesson in radical political economy to support his negative assessment of co-operation. Following Marx and Engels' excoriating critique in the *Communist Manifesto* (1848), Jones ridiculed the efforts of the Christian Socialists, accusing them of having "emancipated one or two wage slaves, and turned them into monopolists and capitalists", and taunting, "What carried the Reform Bill? Was it a pat of butter? No! it was political power". Whether Jones' characterisation was entirely accurate, the separation of the political domain from the social and economic continued to be a marked feature of the labour movement post-mid-century.]

A full report of a discussion which took place in the Odd Fellow's Hall, St. James's Road, Halifax, on Monday and Wednesday evenings, the 26th and 28th of January, 1852, between Mr. Ernest Jones and Mr. Lloyd Jones; when Mr. Ernest Jones undertook to vindicate the following propositions:—

1st.—"That Co-operation cannot be successfully carried out without first obtaining the Political Rights of the People."

2.—"The errors of the present Movement. Showing that it carries within it the germs of dissolution; would inflict a renewed evil on the masses of the people, and is essentially destructive of the real principles of Co-operation: instead of abrogating profit-mongering, it recreates it; instead of counteracting competition, it re-establishes it; instead of preventing centralization, it renews it, merely transferring the *role* from one set of actors to another."

FIRST NIGHT'S DISCUSSION.

MR. LLOYD JONES, who rose and said, It would perhaps be as well if at the commencement of the discussion he explained to them the reason why he was there. They were aware that the Co-operative Movement had been opposed by his opponent (Mr. Ernest Jones), and that he (Mr. Lloyd Jones) had been a party engaged in that movement, and approved not only of the principles, but of the practices of that movement; and also that that movement had not been forced into a premature existence by the agitation of any orator, or by any parties seeking to promote a selfish purpose, but had grown up amongst the people themselves, and partook of whatever of justice, fairness, and honesty there was amongst the people everywhere. Therefore any justice, fairness, or honesty that was in it had been put there by the people themselves, and not by anybody outside of them. He not only came there on as a matter in which he himself was interested, but he came to vindicate what he believed to be honorable and honest proceedings upon the part of those who called themselves co-operators. Previous to doing so, he would endeavour to make himself clearly and distinctly understood. Standing before them to justify that movement was not to him personally a matter of pleasure, not personally a matter of profit. It was because he wished to see that movement successful for their sakes—because he wished to see no misunderstanding going abroad in relation to that movement—because he wished to see them by their own efforts helping each other, and bestowing upon each other, by the influence which they could give each other, when associated together for business purposes. It was only because he wished to see that self-development, that moral and intellectual development, and that increased comfort which he believed that movement would bring to them—it was only for that reason that he was there before them that night to vindicate it. Now, what was that movement? Let any man for a moment imagine that a number of the inhabitants of Halifax, Bradford, Rochdale, or any other town; that scores and hundreds of the working-people of Lancashire and Yorkshire, associate together, as is the case in almost every town in Scotland, and many of the towns in the Midland, Western, and Southern counties of England. He would say that any man who put to them the possibility of these people spontaneously putting into existence a movement, a business, a principle that had dishonesty for its foundation, was doing a great wrong to the intentions and the honorable character which he (Mr. L. Jones) believed to belong to the working people of this country. Now co-operation meant, that a number of people, not strong enough to do business isolatorily, should unite to do business collectively. As a matter of principle they saw so much of scrambling, of personal injury and individual suffering in the competitive system as at present carried on—that those people believing themselves to be too weak to grapple with those things individually, had united their means for the purpose of meeting and overcoming them. This co-operative movement then was based upon that principle, that individually you are not strong enough to grapple with the evils of the position that you occupy, and that you have united your means—you have clubbed your intellects to meet that which singly you could not meet. It is co-operation in men's minds—people, not kings and governments—the people have united for the purpose of self-employment, and then there is co-operation for the purpose of distributing amongst the people those articles which they require for their daily and weekly consumption, seeing that amongst the manufacturers great wealth is acquired by trading with and upon the people, by using the people for individual purposes. Thus uniting capital they give to labor its due participation in the advantages of its use. They believed that large fortunes had grown up in the hands of a few people, and that those fortunes were not used—never had been used for the purpose of giving to the people their fair share of that comfort and happiness which, through large means, could and ought to be enjoyed by the people. They had in their town, and every town, a large number of manufacturers who had very small beginnings a few years back. Those who have these establishments use their money in connection with the labor of the people, dispose of the article that is produced, and take to themselves the profits of the transaction, giving to the honest-working people just as much wages as they can command when idle fellow-laborers are competing for the job. This is an evil. This state of things is not founded upon justice. There ought to be no desire in the breast of any man to injure or rob his fellow-man. No man having faculties and moral powers should be so used, because he is accidentally rich. When a man sees his family destitute of the comforts of life—his children growing up in ignorance,—when he knows this, and has a desire to educate them, through a pure love to his own family—through a pure desire to elevate those who depend upon him, he has a right to use all the power he possesses for the purpose of doing that good to his family which they demand. He cannot meet those evils singly,—he cannot meet the manufacturer singly,—he is completely powerless by himself,—he has only to discover some new method of producing the article, as well as to improve those methods, to hit upon any plan of putting labor into the streets—of cheapening production, and his end is answered. He cannot compete with the rich manufacturer singly. They therefore said to the people, seeing that you cannot compete successfully singly, that it is naturally the tendency of capital to press more and more upon labor, and deprive it more and more of its fair share of that which it produces, it is the duty of the laborer to look to his right, and to say that he is assisting his brother to do that which he could not do in his weakness,—he asks them to unite and render that strong aid, in order that they may do that upon principles which has never been done for them before. He believed that every working-man that united with them with that intention, did that which could not be in any sense considered criminal. For if a man could, by association with his fellow-men, be induced to give up spending his money at the public-house, and unite with his honest, sober neighbour, he had at least done something that was not blame-worthy, and ought not to be condemned by his fellow working-man. Now, the first effort of the co-operator was to unite himself with his fellow laboring-man to get the machinery by what capital they possessed between them into their own power. Small parts at first—very small indeed; but still let them get as much as they can into their power, using it for their own purposes, instead of allowing it to remain in the power of others, to be used against them, and to their injury. Now this was co-operation for protection, as far as they could carry it; and he was not ashamed to tell them that he was engaged in this work—that it was his business entirely to see what could be done for the purpose of putting working-men in that position. In London they had several associations of working-men who were carrying out their views by capital advanced to them, in some instances, by subscribed capital in others; they were using their own portion for their own undertakings, disposing of that which they produced, instead of promoting capital by taking the whole of the profits they were giving only to capital that which was deemed its fair share of the profits. Well, now, that was the first form of association—for producing the things that are needed. That was the kind of association by which the working-man is necessitated to be made the master of his own position, where the machine shall not displace him, but shall be made to work for his good, and for the comfort of his family—where he should not be stunned in his position, but by taking hold of that instrument the people stand upon this earth and say, we are men and not dogs, and we will not be content with the lives that dogs lead. Under the present state of things, this distributive principle is entirely in favor of the interest of the seller and against the buyer; it is the interest of the seller to get all the profit from the man who buys and to impose upon the ignorance of the men as much as he can. It is his interest to adulterate every article that will admit of the process of adulteration.

He was not now speaking of a man's duty, which was to live an honest life in this world, if he could do it—but in the businesses of society, the leading of an honest life was a complete impracticability. He could read them extracts from the "Lancet" to show that everything they used was adulterated not only by the small shop-keepers, but by the large and most respectable. In some things the adulteration was as large as ten per cent. and even fifteen per cent. of matter, scarcely worth anything of itself, that was introduced into the articles they used every day. Not only does the man who does it commit a moral wrong, but he injures the man, financially, upon whom it is practised. If they earned a pound a week, the shopkeeper stole five shillings out of it. They paid, say, one shilling for a pound of coffee, and half of that was chicory, which was not worth three pence per pound—therefore they were cheated, because, if the articles were fit to use, they might as well have them separate and at their own prices.

It was doing them a wrong, morally, and also as regarded their health, that they should have put upon them, adulterated articles mixed up with wholesome food, which they ought to get for their money. The co-operators say "we cannot all become shop-keepers;" the individuals are merely retail purchasers, and say, 50, or 100, or 700 in one town join together and send the whole of their capital into the market to make the wholesale purchase—they take themselves above the adulterations of the retail traders, they go and buy at the wholesale price everything which they need for the consumption of their families—to do that equitably, each man must bear his share. It is not right for one man to say, I will give five pounds, and another, I will give five shillings. Every man must be on a fair footing—there must be no shrinking of duty. They must agree among themselves to put down five shillings, or five pounds, or whatever they might consider necessary to do their business. They then went to the market, and the goods were brought into the shop wholesale. First of all they were secured from adulteration, because they had a right to a share of any profits; and having given the consumption, and having taken into the shop the custom of their family, they had found the two things that made a profit—capital and consumption. If they had all the wealth in the world and bought things they could not sell, there would be no profit, inasmuch as they had not taken the first necessary step to secure it. Well, then, having found the capital and the consumption, the principle of the co-operative stores was, that at the end of a quarter, having sold their goods in the meantime, free from adulteration, at a fair market price—they then counted up and saw what profit they had made—that is, how much, under the ordinary circumstances, would go into the till of the retail dealer—perhaps it is £100. They might then agree to divide it amongst them; perhaps it is ten per cent. upon the whole, and every man receives that according to his fair proportion of expenditure, and fair claim upon it. It might be urged that this secured them from adulteration; for if they adulterated, they would be cheating themselves by putting low priced things into better articles. But then every man has a right to examine the accounts from the fact of his being a sharer in the profits, and that right of investigation precluded the possibility of any man behind the counter doing false things, because of this continual supervision, of the accounts. In some stores they deal with the public who have given them no capital. Suppose now in Halifax there are a hundred people who have clubbed their money and opened their shop, and they have fifty customers that do not belong to them—perhaps they cannot trust them—but go into the shop with the miserable vice of suspicion in their minds—they would rather die than be one amongst the co-operators. He knew that Mr. Ernest Jones thought it was unfair that their profits should be taken from them. You throw the gate open and invite all to come and deal with you. You invite them to come and do as you have done; you tell them to bring their custom and to bring their capital, unite with you as brothers, and, at the end of the quarter, to take with you the fair share of the profits of your dealings. It has been urged against you, as an instance, that at Padiham in building a mill for their looms—they prescribed the number that should join in that. He wished to explain this to them. Any man would know that at the commencement of a shop the arrangements were always made on a larger scale than necessary for their first requirements because they would expect the business to increase. Now, a man going to invest capital for manufacturing purposes, says, "I have so much capital, I shall want so many looms." They must close their arrangements, and, if any other party wants to do as they are doing, they must commence another mill in the neighbourhood. There is no absolute exclusion in this—it was necessary that their limits should be circumscribed. He thought he had now given them the definition of the co-operative movement as far as it had gone, and he would now tell them his connection with it. They saw that the retail shops could not get into the wholesale markets with that knowledge of business which was necessary—and in the best possible manner: and they saw that another step was actually necessary, that was a centre where the best goods might be bought by a man of good judgment so as to remove all the people from the chance of being defrauded in the wholesale markets. Another reason in favour of this was, that the central depôts supplying themselves with articles which they needed for their own consumption, could take from them such articles as they manufactured in their localities, and at their centre in London or Liverpool, they could work all those goods in the ordinary methods of exchange. There were two reasons for establishing a central depôt, and that is in London, for the purpose of supplying all those businesses all over the country at a central connection, and furnishing them with such goods as they might rely upon as to quality and price. He was as much in favour of political power as Mr. Ernest Jones, and wished to see them in possession of all the political power that by their united efforts, or otherwise, they might be able to get. Suppose he was to say to parties engaged in the tee-total or any other great movement, "Gentlemen, you cannot get that until you have got political power," did they think he should be a wise man in saying so? He knew that some fine speeches might be made about great grievances and other things; but they had looked so much at political grievances, so much at the short-comings of the government—that they had not looked at their own. When he heard them talk about political power he could go the whole length with them, although he never made a speech on it. He signed their petitions and his heart and soul was in the movement, but he would say to the Chartists make the Charter your first aim. They did not ask them to put co-operation before their political movement, but let them not imagine, whilst they were struggling politically for their enfranchisement that they might not do something locally for their social emancipation. Every man to the work in which he has most faith, and the realization of their expectations would come in due course. The time being up Mr. Lloyd Jones resumed his seat, and

Mr. ERNEST JONES then rose and addressed the meeting. He said he wished expressly to explain to the audience that in rising to take part in the present discussion he was not one of those who thought co-operation a wrong thing. He was one of those, on the contrary, who believed that their social regeneration could not be established unless it was established upon a system of co-operation; but he was one, at the same time, who believed that that system of co-operation could not be carried out, unless they first did away with the obstacles that lay in its way. He was one of those, moveover, who thought that the present system of co-operation was one that even if those obstacles were removed would lead them back into a greater gulph of misery than that from which they were trying to emancipate themselves. In the first place he believed that co-operation even on a good basis, could not be carried into effect as a national remedy without political power to precede it. In the second place he was one of those who believed that the present system of co-operation was merely a recreation of the present system of profit-mongering, competition and monopoly. At the same time he hoped there would be no misapprehension entertained as to the estimation in which he held the present members of the co-operative movement. He believed that they were an honest well-meaning, reflecting and good body of men; but he believed that they were being misled; as the well-meaning, aye, the intelligent, the intellectual and the honest of all ages had so often been, by leaders who did not understand the evils and vices inherent in the system which they no doubt honestly recommended; and by not being able to perceive the downward slope of misery that they were tending towards while fancying they were ascending the heights of social happiness. Now he did anticipate that since the first part of this discussion appeared to have been allotted to this point "That Co-operation cannot be carried out successfully, without first obtaining the Political Rights of the People; he did anticipate that his honourable opponent would have shown that it could. Therefore he (Mr. Ernest Jones) humbly conceived that he had failed to assail that part of his position—that he had scarcely touched upon it. On the contrary he had endeavoured to show them what the present system was, and he had most erroneously described that system. He, (Mr. Ernest Jones) would draw their attention to the first part of the subject and touch upon a few points that had been brought forward by his worthy opponent; who had told them that the fundamental part of the co-operative principle was its productive element—to produce, to manufacture, to grow corn, to manufacture cotton clothes, and to make machinery. The next point he described was the distributive principle, the shop-keeping portion of the business. Now, let them see how far they could carry their productive system out, (and this was the most important branch of the co-operative principle,) without having political power. They combine—they associate—for the purpose of production; they must have money so to do. In a co-operative store a few of them might club their pence together and might buy the articles they required, and sell them to themselves, and to the public also, making profits, with a comparatively small amount of capital to begin with, length. But the capital they required for the productive portion, was infinitely greater than that required for the distributive branch—they had to buy land, to build, or to buy a factory and purchase machinery and the raw materials required for their manufactures, and they would need a large amount of capital. They clubbed their pence for this purpose, but how was it to be carried on, on a large scale? They required the co-operation of many for the starting in business of a few. They might co-operate to buy land, but the land bought by the many would locate only a few. So in the other branches of production. Now they next looked for the reproductive principle: where was it? Let them take the case of the Amalgamated Iron Trades. The co-operative money of the many, goes to buy a business for the few. All those who subscribe will not be those who are set up in business, but, for the £10,000 subscribed by 12,000 people only 200 or 300 will be set at work.

The reproduction of the capital again would be stopped by the competition of the capitalists, to meet which would require all the resources of the co-operative concern. Thus the reproduction of the capital of these few was prevented from this circumstance: they have got to compete with the capitalist who lowers his prices in competing with the co-operative manufacturer. The capitalist compels all his wages slaves to work for less and the co-operative manufacturer is obliged to lower his profits in order to compete with the monopolist, who lowers his wages. Thus there are two insuperable difficulties for the present co-operator: it requires the capital of the many to set up the few—their few cannot reproduce that capital, owing to the resources being crippled by the competition of the rich; and that very competition, by lowering wages win the labor-market, prevents the remainder from repeating the experiment.

If they turned to the laws of political economy they would find they never could propound a national remedy, unless they increased the real riches of a country; its food—not its cotton clothes, and machinery. Secondly, if they increased the manufactures without extending the market for them! the demand, in the same degree in which they were extending the supply—they must inflict an injury. Now it rested for his opponent to show that he *did* extend the demand. But while foreign markets were beginning to be closed against us by foreign competition, and while we were thus increasing the supply without increasing the demand, what would be the result? The coming down of prices and wages, and the spread of misery and destitution. Let them suppose that their co-operation was to succeed to some extent—and suppose that it was based on right principles, could they do good more rapidly than their enemies did evil? What brought wages down? The surplus labour of the market. As long as the capitalist could throw surplus labor into the market, so long would he have the working classes at his feet. As long as there were men starving and men wanting work—the capitalist would have wages-slaves. As long as he had wages-slaves, he could undersell the co-operator, and thus prevent him from reproducing his capital; and prevent the low-paid multitude to spare from their daily bread enough to compete with him by co-operation. Now if their co-operation could stop surplus-labour from flowing into the market they had solved the question. Unless they could bucket the surplus labor out of the sinking vessel of society more rapidly on the one side than it was flowing in upon the other, they must endure miserable failure. He therefore asked his opponent to tell him whether they could do that by their co-operation. If not, to confess its inadequacy to the end proposed. They could not. Every year the small farms were being consolidated into large, and the surplus was marched into the labor market. Every year increased machinery displaced human labor and the surplus was thrown into competition. Every year the labor of the woman more and more superseded the labour of the man and an added surplus was cast into the streets.—Every year the labour of the child succeeds the labor of the adult and an additional surplus is turned into the market.—Every year the population greatens, and another surplus is thrown into the world by the hand of God and nature.—The labor surplus, lowered labor's-wages, and the people's means of emancipating themselves grew smaller. As their wages fell, they subscribed less, and at the time they required most, they got the least. He called upon his opponent to show—that co-operation would take that surplus-labor out of the market, and that co-operative capital would increase and accumulate instead of decrease with the decease wages, and the competition of the rich. Again: if they increased the manufactures without increasing the demand they glutted the market, brought prices down, and with them, wages, thus diminishing their own powers of production, and the purchasing powers of the public. Let these points be settled, and the question would be arguable—at the present time it was scarcely arguable. But suppose they had Political Power:—by trying co-operation before they got political power they were putting the cart before the horse. The co-operative cart was very good when laden not with profit-mongering, but with christian co-operation. It was very good for piling their sugar, tea, and coffee in. But they would stick in the mud of competition and misrule—theirs was the cart—but political power was the horse that must pull them out of the mire.

With political power, they could secure the poor-lands, which had so long been in the possession of the porpoise bishops and pastors. They might club their pence together until eternity before they would be able to get one capitulary estate from one fat bishop; but by a people's parliament they could do it in a single hour.

What could they do without capital? They were obliged to borrow from the rich—and mix wages-slavery with debt-slavery. Political power would give them capital, without debt. The rates, tithes and taxes of this country amount to one hundred and one millions of pounds sterling; and suppose they were to confiscate the tithes of the church—and turned their attention to the armaments of the country—to the seventeen millions for army, navy, and ordnance, if we are to have a standing army let us have an army of seventeen millions, let every man be a soldier to garrison his own cottage. A People's Parliament would say, let those who contracted the National Debt pay for it. Thence would come the capital for co-operation—from priests, usurers and slayers, without infringing the rightful property of any solitary man. He asked them if they, the Chartists, were not the best co-operators, after all? Then co-operation would be safe—for the laws would be made to protect it, instead being made to destroy. They might then do that in one session for which they might struggle for a thousand years under the present state of things, and the millenium would find them no nearer to their object. He put it to his opponent to tell them whether this was not the easiest and quickest way of gaining their end? whether political power was not the best way to gain co-operation? He (Mr. Ernest Jones) was not an enemy to the truth of co-operation—but to its errors: He only propounded a different co-operation. His opponent said they should co-operate together and put the profits into their own pockets and that they should also take the profits of the public, and put them into the pockets of the members of the store. He (Mr. Ernest Jones) did not want them to stop co-operating until they got political power—he only wished them to co-operate upon a true social system and not upon an anti social one, as at present, which ought to be scouted by every socialist in the country. His opponent had thrown out a very bold word in reference to the present system, he had stood forward as the champion of their "practices," He (Mr. Ernest Jones), would now analyse the system. His opponent told them that their co-operative stores were established for the purpose of buying in the wholesale market and returning to them at the end of the quarter their fair share of the profits. He said you have no interest in adulterating your food, for if you did, you would be cheating yourselves." Now these stores sometimes, sold to the members generally to the public also. Take the first case:—where they went into the market, bought at the wholesale prices, and sold to themselves. Would you not suppose that they would sell at the wholesale price? But they sold at the retail price and at the end of the quarter they found that they had "cheated themselves" out of the difference between the wholesale and retail prices. They actually with their eyes open charged themselves too much and paid themselves back at the end of the year. He had heard of people cheating others, but it certainly was a funny thing for a man to cheat himself.

They are interest-mongers, and yet they lose the use and interest of their money for a whole year or a quarter. But they not only cheat themselves, they cheat others also. He contended that the present system of co-operation was a system of profit-mongering as great, and greater in one sense than that of the shopocracy of this country. He was not in love with the latter, but he would say if he was to be cheated at all, he liked a man to tell him of it plainly and then there was an end of it, but he did not like a man to tell him he was doing him a great favor and then to be cheating him all the time. Mr. E. Jones being told the time had expired,

Mr. Lloyd Jones commenced by saying, as his opponent had concluded with a statement of what he conceived to be an exceedingly funny thing done by the co-operators, he would at once explain the fun of that mode of doing business, and state to them the much funnier thing which his opponent preferred. The people in the co-operative stores agree to buy their goods at the wholesale price, and then sell to themselves at the ordinary market price. They cheat themselves for the sport of the thing, and then they give back to themselves, as a good joke, the amount out of which they have cheated themselves. Now did any of them ever put a shilling into the Savings' Bank?—did they ever cheat themselves in any investment whatever? If so, they committed the same sort of joke—a capital thing to be laughed at, but a very good thing to do. The other joke was this: Mr. Ernest Jones likes a bold piece of roguery—he was sorry to hear him say so. Although the co-operator might be considered a very foolish man, he made restitution at the end of the quarter; and that was a good old custom. His opponent liked the man who adulterates, and then did the funnier thing of allowing him to give you nothing back. That might be a good joke for Mr. E. Jones, but it was no joke at all for them. Depend upon it they preferred their own joke,—for they lost nothing by it, but won a little. He would now explain to them what Mr. Jones, with a loud voice, set before them, and seemed to think a wonderful thing, namely, that co-operation intensified competition by bringing new competitors into the market. He asked his opponent if he meant to tell them that the co-operator never worked before—that he was just now made for the purpose—that his labor was brought into the market for the first time? He would tell them that the co-operator was a man who was seeking to regulate his own labor, and not to increase the products of the country, nor intensify competition. That he was made first as a competitive tool, but was now an instrument used by himself. He would tell them now, in a co-operative movement they could not create competition, and how it was impossible to do so in a co-operative store. The thing is very easy of explanation, and very plain and practicable. Suppose a hundred people begun as distributors, he would show them, how out of that competition could not by any possibility arise. What do they speculate upon? Upon their own business. If the public came they served them; but it was the continued effort of every one connected with those stores to indoctrinate the public into their principles, and turn them into ordinary members. In Rochdale they began with 30, now they were 700; in Padiham they began as 12 now they were 200; in Halifax they began as 25, and now they were much increased. Your object is not to make a profit of your neighbour, but of your own transactions; and if your neighbour comes to you as an ordinary dealer, you treat him as such and your doors are open to him. And if you could take a whole town into co-operation you then limit the extent of your co-operation. What is a shop or store? A place where you bring together such articles as men need for their consumption. In one place it is a clothing concern, in another a shoemaker's, and in another a hatter's, and you dispose of your machinery to those who use it for productive purposes. Suppose it finds you with everything you want. The consumption of a country is what keeps the poor at work. If you give over consumption you may as well give over producing, and so long as you possess consumers, you see the grand object of having a centre organization, so that the consumers shall have the election—the protection of those goods which they require. You start with 700 members; they want a certain number of pairs of shoes, besides the productions of the tailor's shop, and the factory—they will want machinery. There are 3000 factors in Rochdale; they require a supply of two pairs of shoes in the year. Do you say to the shoemaker, when he has organized that consumption, "You can go where you like to be consumed,"—you can say to them, "There is a market for your shoes." The co-operators bring them into connection with all the feet of the establishment, and say to them, "Produce the shoes that the feet wear out." So that they now saw that the store was not in its imperfect state, a place for selling with a view to profit, but for organizing the consumption of the people. And in the same way they may command the production of those things necessary to supply that consumption. Now he would tell them there was political economy there. They need not go to Moses and Son for their shoes, when they could command the consumption of any number. Seeing that every one of your stores accumulating capital as a reserve fund for purposes beyond the shop to put into operation the labor that may be thrown out of work; and there is a consumer ready at hand to take the article that is produced. Let them reflect upon the matter. Here are tailors in their town, who have no means of coming into contact with each other that they may exchange their labor; but are in the hands of the ordinary manufacturers. If you have these stores there is a capital accumulating, as nothing is more easy than for those who manage these stores, knowing what they are about,—to organize the labor of those hatters, shoemakers, and tailors, and put them into communication with each other through the medium of the store, and enable them to exchange when, under ordinary circumstances they would have been idle. He wished to show Mr. Jones that this was not so frightful a thing as he imagined. He knew it was difficult, but then there never had been a great thing done in the world without difficulty. Large manufacturers that had begun with small means had grown strong by the labors of their workmen. Fourteen years ago, 17 men in Leeds clubbed all they could together, and it made £1100; and they have gone on, each man doing his own particular work—the smith doing his work—the pattern-maker doing his, &c., and these 17, except two, remain, and are stated to be worth £30,000, accumulated by their own labor. Mr. E. Jones preferred the bold-faced robber who took all the profit. He said: No—let the people take it themselves. Their's was the first step; and let the man who had a yard before him unoccupied clear it before he stepped up and asked for another. Let him not act the part of a coward, and say, "I won't take that unless you will let me have another. Let every man conquer every difficulty, political and social, as soon as he can, and not stand back and do nothing because he cannot do everything. His opponent said, they would get them out of the mud, and it would give him great pleasure to see Mr. Jones coming with his immense power to pull them out. Talk of the power of the parsons—there has been a power of talking—a power of bombast that has led away the hearts and understandings of the people most shamefully to the wasting of their time. They were the best co-operators said Mr. Jones, and would help them—he would say, help yourselves gentlemen. You boasted four years ago of a petition signed by 7,000,000, and you are now voting for your executive and muster in all England and Scotland, 1600 votes. Help yourselves. He grieved that this should be so. The men who boasted of being liberal did he see them on all occasions doing the most liberal things—did they support the liberal press as they ought? Ye who say you do all good things, where is your own newspaper which Mr. Ernest Jones is trying to call into existence? If you were prepared to do what you could, you would have ten newspapers instead of one. If you knew your own interests and how to settle them, you would not have other men writing your newspapers at high rates. It was a source of grief to him to see the working-classes lying at the feet of the people.

The *Chairman* here interrupted Mr. Jones and said he felt it to be his duty to call him to the question, as he was now dwelling upon matters that had no connection with it.

Mr. Jones then resumed, and said, The Chairman of the discussion must leave the discussion of the question to the disputants. It was the office of the Chairman to keep time, and Mr. Jones and himself were to be supposed to understand the question and settle that between them. Now, he did not put these things in anger to them, but in sorrow—he put it as an argument to them with a feeling of shame, for he would gladly to-morrow see them doing their work well, and as honest men. When they told him that if they had political power they would do a great many things; but would do nothing until then for their own improvement—then he told them they were hypocrites, and not true men. The true man did the good to the extent of his power at the moment of its existence, and at the first opportunity for its accomplishment. He had tried to explain what co-operation was, and he had one request to make of Mr. Jones that was according to the rule of debate that he would introduce no new facts into the discussion which could not be answered for the night; but let such be brought in during his next speech, so that he (Mr. Lloyd Jones) might have an opportunity of answering them in his last speech.

Mr. Ernest Jones rose and said, He expected that his worthy opponent instead of dwelling on generalities and descending to personalities would have attempted to answer those questions which he put to him, namely, Whether they could take the surplus labour out of the market as fast as it came in? Whether they could unlock the monopolies of land and machinery and money, currency, credit and exchange, which kept that surplus in existence? Whether it did not take the co-operation of the many to locate or set up the few? Whether the competition of the capitalist did not prevent the reproduction of the co-operators' capital? Not one of these questions had his opponent answered. Instead of that he had given them generalities and dwelt on personalities connected with a public question. He should at once proceed with his argument. He had said that it was a remarkably funny thing that men should charge themselves too much and pay themselves back at the end of a quarter, and his opponent had asked them if they ever put money into the Saving's Bank, and told them it was exactly the same thing as putting it into a co-operative store. Now it would be much better to put their money into the Savings' Bank at the commencement, and not cheat themselves for a year out of its use and interest, and then pay themselves back the capitalist alone. He had alluded to the stores that merely sold to themselves, and he was told that he liked the people to deal with a rogue who did not give them anything back at the end of the quarter. He did not state that he liked a rogue; but that if he was to be cheated at all he preferred, so to speak, the honest rogue who told him his intentions, to the man who said he was doing him a favour and was doubly cheating him all the time. He (Mr. E. Jones) would direct their attention, to what he was proceeding to advert on at the close of his previous remarks. The stores that sold also to the general public at the retail price. The members pocket the difference between that and the wholesale price at which they bought. It might be right for the parties to overcharge themselves and put the profits back into their pockets; but was it right to overcharge the public. If they returned the difference to each member at the end of the quarter, why not do the same with the general public?

His opponent might say,—those who started the concern gave the public unadulterated food—they found the capital, and were therefore entitled to any advantages which might accrue therefrom,—and that this was based upon the rights of capital. He (Mr. E. Jones) denied that capital had any rights! man had *all* the rights—capital had none. But the members had no claim, even on this ground: Suppose they paid 5s. or £1 each, towards supplying themselves with unadulterated goods at the wholesale price; by selling to the public at the retail price their capital was soon doubled—if they succeeded. What increased it?—the public—out of 50s. the member found but 5s. Why, after all, it was the public that found the capital—but the member who grasped at all the gain. Where do their reserved funds come from? From the public. If £30,000 profit have been realised in so many years by seventeen men in Leeds (as Mr. Lloyd Jones had sttaed) the general public had been cheated to fill the pockets of those men, who, calling themselves co-operators, had become profit-mongers and capitalists. Thus, what did their co-operation effect in its present plan? It enabled a few men to rise from the ranks of labor, and to live in idleness out of the earnings of those who lived by work; and how? Thus: they buy at the wholesale price, and sell to the public at the retail price, and they pocket the difference, and at the end of a year they gain so many pounds (if successful.) Another year they pocket an additional sum; they extend their transactions until at last they become small capitalists, like those £30,000 gentlemen, to whom his opponent had alluded, they are enabled to give up work and live upon their large dividends—upon the interest upon the money that has passed over their counters from the men who lived by toil; so that their plan of co-operation enabled a few to rise above the mass, and live in idleness out of the earnings arising from those who lived by work. He (Mr. E. Jones) maintained that a man had no right to take that from society for which he did not give back the full value: that no man ought to receive a reward beyond the fair remuneration for his labor and his time. By his opponent's plan, if a few men have got a little capital to trade with, they appointed one man at 6s. per week and his keep, to do the work, while the members do no work whatever, as far as the store is concerned, but still divide profits, dividends, and bonuses among themselves. Now, they came to another point: his opponent said that it is impossible that they could monopolise or compete, and that they were always extending their concern. At the Padiham Mill there were seventy-seven men subscribed twenty-five pounds each to commence work, and then passed a law to exclude any more members. And why? because we are told that when you start a new trade you are obliged to set limits to your transactions. But then you do not refuse to set limits to the subscription of capital. Instead of only the number of looms required for seventy-seven members—they had eighty additional looms beyond what they needed for themselves—they had extended their concern and yet they adhered to their rule of not admitting any more members. They would allow a man to go and work as a wages-slave at ordinary market-wages, but not unless he paid a premium of £8 for the benefit of the rich capitalists. His worthy opponent had altogether neglected this point of the question—that these concerns must compete with each other:—first they have to compete with the capitalists, and then to compete with each other afterwards. It was impossible for them to compete successfully with the monopolist who had the power of driving wages down to starvation pittance, owing to the labour surplus in the market. The capitalist could undersell the co-operators, so that the latter must lower their profits to starvation point—or give up their business. Again: the present system of co-operation made it the interest of the co-operator to prevent the spread of the principles. Take the Padiham factory: do its members wish another factory to start up on the opposite side of the street? No, that would not be convenient for them. Already there are too many mills—there is too much supply for the demand, and if they keep increasing the supply without increasing the demand, they must begin to compete. They must have customers, and if there are not enough to divide equally, then he who can must get the larger share, and the rest must perish. This must be the work of the present plan of co-operation, which must result in competition and eventually in monopoly. He asked his opponent to show how it could be otherwise unless he increased the demand for the article at the same time he increased the supply—and he further asked him to show how he would increase the demand. There was, however, another point of which it was most essential to take cognizance, that is, what would be the sound basis of co-operation? If instead of a mill being started upon the isolated principle, a grand national co-operative movement was set on foot, where interest could not clash with interest, if the co-operative mill here had an identity of interest with all other co-operative mills elsewhere. How was that to be brought about? By this means. Instead of the co-operators pocketing all the profits accumulated, and becoming new capitalists, let all that is realised beyond the working charges including the just remuneration for time and labor, be appropriated as a fund for the establishment of additional co-operative stores, mills, farms, and workshops. Let those 17 gentlemen engineers who have pocketed £30,000 say we will merely take as much of the profits as we require to carry on our business and remunerate our labour, and give the rest for the purpose of raising our poor weak brethren from the wretchedness in which they are sunk,—for all that we get beyond what justly remunerates us belongs to the public, and they alone have a right to it, since from them it comes. Accordingly, the £30,000 we have beyond what is necessary for our own wants shall be devoted to commence another co-operative store to emancipate another lot of our fellow working-men. We will build another mill, or buy another farm, and take within its precincts those wages-slaves who are too poor and too weak to emancipate themselves. We have been fortunate enough to extricate ourselves, and like good Samaritans we will now help others to do the same. The new mill or farm out of its returns should give a fair support in return for fair work, and the accumulating surplus should again go to start a third mill or a third farm. That was co-operation. His opponent's plan was isolation. That was brotherhood—his opponent's plan was competition and hostility.

Mr. Lloyd Jones then rose and said;—A great part of his opponent's speech had given him great pleasure, inasmuch as it was the outpouring of an exceedingly benevolent spirit. It was calling upon all men who, by the proper use of their means, accumulated any description of wealth to use that for those who stood in need of it. He acknowledged that that was an exceedingly benevolent speech, and if men would do it, the world would be a great deal better than it was; but really if the socialist co-operator—a man who is trying to do all the good he can—has not turned good Samaritan, have you who profess so much benevolence? Pray why are you not turning good Samaritans for somebody else's sake as well as your own? He did not believe they were Samaritans—he believed that nine-tenths of them would rather take from the man wounded than give to him. He did not believe in good Samaritanism, he did not see it in society, no political party carried it out, and until he saw the work instead of hearing the talk of the Samaritans he would not believe in it. He would explain to them how that large profit on the Rochdale store could result from five shillings. You put your five shillings into a Savings' Bank, and at the end of the year you get two and a half per cent. upon it; but you put it into the co-operative store and let it be used to supply you with the things you need, and you make a profit upon all the money you laid out previously to joining the store. You may turn that over twenty or thirty times a-year, and you are making a continued profit—not upon your five shillings alone; but by taking all the money required for your current expenditure to the store and making it operate as manure to give vitality to it for you at the end of the quarter or year. His opponent had said they were growing into great capitalists; and yet in a previous speech he said they never could grow into great capitalists, because those who were already great capitalists would never give them the opportunity. Now he should like to know how these two statements could be reconciled. If they were not capable of growing rich by a proper management of their own resources, and putting themselves into the position of those who are now great capitalists, then they never could accomplish the frightful things to which his worthy friend had alluded. If a man spends fifty pounds a-year upon a large family and puts five shillings into the co-operative store as a member, he gots the benefit of the interest on the fifty pounds which he lays out in goods which might be a profit of £7 10s. upon his expenditure; which formerly went into the pocket of the shopkeeper with whom he dealt. Suppose poor men did make it—they sell unadulterated articles at market price, and their profits are less than at other establishments that adulterate. The average profits of the stores is one shilling, sometimes one shilling and sixpence, and it has reached two shillings in the pound, never above, and in many cases it has been nothing at all. After all there is some sense in the joke; if you spend fifty pounds at the store you get two shillings on each pound, and that is five pounds at the end of the year, a handsome thing; but you get nothing from the overgrown capitalists with whom you deal—he gets all the profit upon the expenditure of your family. He meant to say that these profits put together in a common fund might now be used to good purpose for the benefit of the people, when they have wisdom enough to do it. If the members take the profits at the end of the quarter, his opponent said they ought to do the same by the public as themselves. He (Mr. L. Jones) said no—because the public did not supply the first condition to make that money; they invested no capital in the concern, therefore the public have no right to it. Would any man tell him if he put by his spare money for the purpose of entering into a business to make a profit, that because his neighbour chose to come and take advantage of his money, that he had a right to say he had as much interest in the concern as himself? His neighbour came to his shop because his tea or coffee, &c., were much better than he could get anywhere else, and was he then to give him part of the profits upon his goods. No as fond as they were of jokes they never submitted to jokes of that description. Mr. Ernest Jones' plan is first-rate if he will put it into practice. He (Mr. L. Jones) complained of him as an imaginary co-operator. As a Samaritan he wished to see him practice instead of preach. He would show then how the difficulties to which his opponent referred might be removed. Suppose they co-operated for the whole consumption of Halifax, Huddersfield, or Leeds, they had all the great capitalists fighting against their co-operative mills and stores. Could not those who had an interest in the business say to the large capitalists you shall not beat our small ones, because we, the consumers, have united, and we will not have your stuff, but their's. Could not the people say, "We will have that which is produced by the work of our brothers, who are reduced to starvation." Thus the organization of the consumption of the people is taken into their own hands; and they say "We will have those things which we need from our co-operative mills, because they are produced by our own brothers who are worthy to emancipate themselves from social serfdom; and we will therefore give the preference to our fellow workmen." Why is the consumption of the people in the hands of the capitalist? Because the people are not organized. He put this to his opponent as a practical solution which is now being worked out by co-operative stores. And those who encourage all co-operative efforts are doing this upon a business basis settled between themselves. And they deal with each other, and are doing so more and more every day. His opponent asked what men were getting with co-operation; and told them that those 77 men in Padiham shut out all the rest of the town. But he would tell them they sought to make them themselves 80 men, and the whole town could not furnish the additional three; and they shut up because they could get no more members. They said, "We have done this work: if those other men who would not help us want to enjoy what we enjoy, let them subscribe their money, and build another weaving shop. We want to do our work in a practical manner, and to put our business upon a business foundation; because success in business must have the conditions of success, and all the fine talk in the world will never get it unless you do that which is necessary for the transaction. But they charge £8 for letting a poor man work. Don't you think that when a poor man can get into another mill for nothing he would be a great fool to go and give them £8. Why do they do this? Because every man is admitted into a share of the profits of the establishment, and therefore a compensation was required by the man who invested his capital, but did not work. You go in on these conditions, because co-operation puts out the idea of using a man as a mere producing tool; they want to give every man an interest in the productiveness, prosperity, and success of the establishment; and he thought if those men contributed, as Mr. E. Jones, had stated, £25 to start the concern, and if they admit others at £8, they are putting them to an advantage above themselves, and there is no injustice in it. Would it not be miserable to ask a man to work for you, and give you £8 for the use of your loom, unless there was some advantage on the other side to make up this. But it is said the large capitalists will and must beat us down, and they were asked if they could take the surplus labor out of the market? Now there were a great many things that they could not do. He would give them the moon every night if he could, but he could not, as it changes, and is sometimes small and sometimes large, which they could not help. They would take all the surplus labor out of the market to-morrow if they could; but they could not do that. So then because they could not take all out they were not to take part. Because a house is on fire, and you cannot jump out of every window are you not to jump out of one? If you give a man £5 profit at the end of the year upon his consumption, which he never had before you give him the means of increasing his productions, and by distributing that money you give them the means of consuming many things they could not before, and also a means of increasing the productiveness of the country. He was there to tell them what co-operative men were doing, and to tell them not to neglect the opportunities at their disposal, for they were doing an injury to themselves; and whilst they were crying out against those who were taking advantage of the opportunities which they were neglecting; they were doing a sin against those men. His opponent said it was their interest to keep the people out; but where was the interest? In Rochdale they began with 30, and went on to 700. It was in the aggregate the strength that he received, by giving the same strength to another man which that man gave to him, it was by the aggregate of that strength, used in unity, that they would be enabled to lift themselves above the difficulties of this life, and occupy that position on the earth which they ought. This is the work of co-operators. Co-operation does not stand in the way of the political enfranchisement of the people. They believed that co-operation was the thing needed; others believed that political enfranchisement was the best thing for elevating the people. Let both labor unceasingly to gain that which they believed to be best. But he would say they benefited the people when they took from the class that oppressed them the £5 which was returned to the working man who was a member of a co-operative store; so that he might have more means at command for the education of his children, and for promoting the comfort of his family.

Mr. Ernest Jones said he had asked his opponent whether they could take the surplus labor out of the market?—whether they could unlock that monopoly which drove that surplus into the market?—whether they could undersell the capitalists? or if not, whether they could compete with them?—whether it did not take the co-operation of many to emancipate the few?—and whether the competition of the rich would not prevent the re-production of co-operative capital?—whether, if the concern were successful, the system did not lead to capitalism and monopoly?—whether the isolated system did not lead to competition among co-operators? He would leave the audience to judge whether these questions had been answered. He stated that they would increase the production if they increased the number of productive agencies by factories, without increasing, in the same proportion, the consumption, or demand for the article. He admitted they might increase the demand to a slight amount; but the increase of production would be greater than the increase of consumption, and consequently they inflicted as great an evil as that which they were trying to abolish. His opponent charged him with saying, at one time, they would become great capitalists,—at another that they would fail. What he (Mr. E. Jones) said, was this: that they could not succeed; but that their very success would be an evil. If they succeeded they became capitalists by accumulating profits; and the way to redeem the people was to distribute not to centralize wealth. Thus, in case of success, they inflicted an evil on society; but that they must fail and be ruined in competing against the rich, he thought he had shown; and thus they inflicted an evil on themselves. They could raise a few men here and there into capitalists without the emancipation of the great masses; but they could not do—they never had done more; and by so doing he contended they did their best to create a fresh system of capitalism and monopoly. His opponent had taken the argument which he applied to the isolated store, and wanted them to believe that he had applied it to the whole. His opponent had admitted that they could not take the labor surplus out of the marke. In that admission Mr. Lloyd Jones had given up the whole case. There was the point—that was what put them down, and enabled the monopolist to undersell them; because he took the advantage of the impoverished population of wages-slaves, in a two-fold manner:—by driving wages down he stopped their sources for raising new capital; and by underselling thro' the means of cheap labor he forced them to waste the capital already subscribed. Therefore co-operation must fail. Mr. Lloyd Jones promised to give them the the moon every night, if he had it in his power; he (Mr. E. Jones) prayed that he would not give them moonshine (laughter.) For was it not moonshine to pretend to put a stop to wages-slavery, and at the same tell us he could not put a stop to that by which wages-slavery was created, namely—labor-surplus? If you cannot remove the cause, you cannot remove the effect. Indeed, Mr. Lloyd Jones's moon was laboring under an eclipse.

He (Mr. E. Jones) must now digress to answer some statements of his opponent. Mr. Lloyd Jones admitted they had passed a rule at Padiham to exclude more members—but said it was done because the public would not come. Then, if they would not come, whence was the necessity to pass a rule for keeping them away? No! the fact was, as soon as they found they had money enough to start their mill, they shut out the public that they might have all the profits to themselves. His opponent had wanted to make them believe that the poor men at the additional looms shared in the profits: they did not—they got four per cent. for their money, and common wages—so that they had to pay eight pounds for permission to work at market wages in the Christian co-operators' mill: whereas at the capitalists they could get work and the same wages for nothing. So much for his opponent's attempt to mislead the audience. His opponent had told them the co-operators never made more than two shillings in the pound—that they could not clear more than about £5 in the year, on their own purchases—and, therefore, that they could not grow capitalists, and that they were not profitmongers. Then he (Mr. E. Jones) asked where came the £2000 here and the £1000 there from? Why! from the public. It could not be from their own purchases—it must be from the purchases of others. From the amount surcharged on the general customer, and from their brother workingmen. "Oh, but," said Mr. Lloyd Jones, "the public don't supply the first condition. They don't find the capital." Did they not? What did the members find? Five shillings a-piece. What did the public find for the members in one year? £2000. Who found the capital now? Was this fair dealing. The member makes a payment of five shillings once, and receives eternally—the public pay eternally and never receive at all. His opponent alluded to a mutual exchange between neighbouring towns as an antidote to competition. He would touch on that before the discussion concluded. Unable to shake these arguments, or alter these facts, my opponent swerves from the question and addresses remarks which are of a personal character to the cause of which I am one of the humble advocates. He asks us what we have done? Did we support our press, and ought we not to have ten papers instead of one paper? We have papers—we have had papers, and we will have more—but where are your papers; and what has become of them? Do you support them? No, not even the "Penny Christian Socialist," could you keep alive! (Cheering, which was suppressed by the Chairman.) What have you done in the cause of human progress or redemption? You may point to your isolated localities where you have emancipated one or two wages slaves, and turned them into monopolists and capitalists. But what general good have you conferred upon society? What was it that carried the repeal of the Corporation Act? Was it meal-tubs? No, it was political power. What carried the repeal of the Slave-trade? Was it a candle-box? No! it was political power. What carried Catholic Emancipation? Was it a cake of soap? No! it was political power. What carried the Reform Bill? Was it a pat of butter? No! it was political power. What is it that is driving on the middle class tyrants and the aristocracy to a semblance of reform, and leading them to confess that man is man, and that they must concede something of their rights to the people? Is it your co-operation that they fear—no, it is ours; for you co-operate with pence and we with men. We the political organizers, who don't talk, talk—talk Christian Socialism, and under the cover of talking, slip the sovereigns into our anti-christian pockets all the while, we promise you fair labor—without an £8 premium. We say with political power we will give you the chance—the means of co-operation. What use are all your theories of, without the means to carry them out! You are mere theorisers—we are men of business and facts. You want land and money capital. Political power will give you the land without infringing upon the rights of any private individual. Political power will give you the capital. But you taunt us with our weakness. You say, we are only 1,600, strong. But who has made us so. You! by drawing off after your desert-mirage, portion upon portion of the working-classes. With your Trades-Unions, and Co-operations, and Financial Reforms, you have taken the brave crew out of our ship in little boatfuls, and launched them on the troubled sea of capital—though we still have some to keep our flag up at the mast-head—but where will you be when the storm of panic comes, and the proud vessel of monopoly bears down upon your shallops? How will you weather dull trade, short time, panic and commercial crisis? Nay? that, which is your weakness, is our strength. It is the heart and brain, and not the purse that gives the strength. It is thought and intelligence, not money-bags, that make nations free. No commercial crisis can drag intelligence from the mind, no panic can tear truth from out the heart! With dull trade your sovereigns diminish—with dull trade our recruits increase.

In a political struggle, the chances are in our favour. In a money struggle they are in the favor of our enemy. In the latter he has £1000 to every one of ours; in the former, we have 1000 men to every one of his.

END OF THE FIRST NIGHTS DISCUSSION.

THE discussion was resumed on Wednesday night, the 28th of January, the attendance being even larger than on the previous night.

Mr. LLOYD JONES then rose and proceeded with his address, and went on in a somewhat similar course of remarks to those which he made at the commencement of his opening speech on the Monday night. He called upon his opponent to prove that the co-operative societies were doing anything that was either false in principle or fraudulent in practice. His opponent, he contended, was frequently wrong in his facts, and false in his logic. He now came to a fact or two that had been put forward on the last night. They had been charged by political reformers with being the cause of their weakness—with having taken the best part of their people from them. Now let them understand him, they had never sought to take a single man from any public cause in the country—either out of the Temperance Society, or any other society; all the members they had had came to them without being sought, and they came because they found the co-operative movement was a better cause than the one in which they had been engaged before. He did not believe he had ever given more than half-a-dozen lectures on the subject. He was anxious to succeed as a business man; and he did not neglect his own business; for he considered he would be a fool if he did. His opponent had said that the co-operators would become weak when a panic came, and they would become strong. Now there was a profound meaning in that statement. As business men they must suffer when a panic came, for they knew of no charm by which they could free themselves from liabilities. His opponent said, in a panic they became strong by political organisation, now, if he had insulted them by telling them that their cry for the charter depended upon the condition of their stomachs, and that it was not a set of principles to be advocated by thinking men; but by men who came out in the face of day, when out of employment and hungry, who came out to utter a mere cry like groaning beasts of burden who were not fed and shouted before the public—if he had told them that they grew weak by abundance; they would have charged him with insulting them. But he believed there was much truth in it; and that many of their noisy meetings had been accurately described by Mr. E. Jones. It had been said that the political nostrums of their opponents was to go before their social one: and that it would pull them out of the mud. (Hisses, and cries of question.) They were told to stand on one side when they proved that their opponents were going backwards and not forward, then he would say "God help them." He was sorry that any agitation should have to depend upon the hunger of the people. He did not want the hungry multitude, but the men who thought, and who would do the right thing necessary. When a panic came the working-classes were ready to turn out in millions. Suppose they had the suffrage—suppose they got all they wanted with regard to political power, could reliance be placed upon their decision that they would do all that was right to all parties in the state? His opponent told them to look at the associations in Paris, put down at the point of the bayonet. This was not the fact. Similar associations were put down at Lyons, but in Paris they were all open and going on. But if this was not so, what did it prove? Why, that universal suffrage had allowed the government of France to perpetrate so gross an injustice. Yes, the French people had got universal suffrage, but did they know how to use it? And were the English people wiser than the French? He would say to the honor of the people of France, that bad as they had been, the injustice alluded to by his opponent, was not committed by them. Immense injustice had, undoubtedly, been done in that country—murder, perjury, confiscation of property had taken place, liberty had been destroyed, and at the foot of all was universal suffrage? Why was this? Because the people had got more than they know how to use, because they were the dupes of those who did not tell the truth, because they did not reason for themselves or rely upon the unchanging principles of justice in their dealings with each other. His opponent ridicules them because they had no newspapers, he (Mr L. Jones) would tell them they did not rely on newspapers. He held in his hand a printed statement of the Halifax co-operative flour mill, the profits amounting to £836 14s. 7½d. He did not say it was wise for them to divide the profits. But how many men were worse Chartists, or teetotallers, or worse husbands and fathers because they belonged to the flour-mill? Supposing there had been only one miller in Halifax, would the people have been any better off for that individual putting the money in his own pocket? Suppose they took a number of men and put them in those stores—some behind the counter, and others managing the concern in different ways; they made those men stronger men than they were before. They were then able to meet the shopkeeper on his own ground. The working-men who joined these stores could each say, I am a shoemaker or a worker in iron, but I am also a shopkeeper, I am as good as he and know where his goods are brought from, and can go the same markets. There was another thing. Under the present system half the working-classes were slaves to their shopkeepers, who supplied them with what they liked, because of their dependent position. He had no hesitation in saying that the working classes, taking them head by head throughout the country, were mortgaged for a fortnight by this degrading and ruinous system. But this was not the case at the co-operative stores. They gave no credit, the people were required to be prudent and careful, and if the establishment of such places was only to teach them the simple virtue of prudence, they were very much calculated to elevate their characters and social position. He brought these things forward to show that this thing was not false in itself, but that it would bring them into the enjoyment of many blessings and comforts. He concluded his speech by saying they did not want to bring the people out at a time of famine, but under the influence of their own feelings as reasonable men to do a reasonable work.

Mr. ERNEST JONES then expressed his surprise that his honorable opponent should have been talking about newspapers, and France, and the numbers of the Chartists, and not on the propositions in dispute. He would remind him of them. They were, that the present system of co-operation was vicious in principle, and pernicious in its results. It was vicious in principle, because leading to competition and monopoly. Secondly, he (Mr. E. Jones) maintained that it must fail, even were it placed on a just basis, to emancipate the people, but would perish before the hostility of the rich, and leave the working-classes worse off than it found them—unless it were preceded and accompanied by political power. Thirdly, he had maintained that political power was the only adequate means for social regeneration; and, fourthly, he had propounded a system of co-operation in consonance with the principles of truth and justice. He wished the audience to remember that this was the question, even if Mr. Lloyd Jones forgot it. He had said that the present movement was based on a system of profitmongering; would his opponent be kind enough to give them a definition of what profit-mongering was! If not, he would. Profit-mongering was to take more for a thing than its value, and put the difference in your own pocket. You had a right to charge for the cost of the material, for the time devoted to it, and for the labor bestowed on it. By that time and labor you had a right to live. And the fair price for that time and labor, was a fair maintenance for him who bestowed it. Everything charged beyond that was profitmongering. Could his opponent deny that? Well, then, since he could not, he would show him that the present co-operative plan did profitmonger, and pretty handsomely too. He held in his hand the rules and regulations of the Bradford Co-operative Stores. One of its first rules (said he) is to furnish the members with provisions and clothing at prime cost. This was fair enough. You club together your 5s. and you get your articles at prime cost. Then you add the expenses of management, you are justified in that; but don't take any merit to yourselves because you pay yourselves the expenses connected with selling to yourselves. Next, you pay yourselves five per cent. interest on the money you lay out in the stores; well, nobody could grumble at that, but when you have done that you have done all that you ought to do, you are not profit-mongers if you go no further than that. But what do you do next? The next thing you do is to sell to the general public all goods at the ordinary market price, and then take the whole of the profits from them, without even being so merciful as to give them a little per centage in return. What is the result? In the course of time, if you are successful, your profits accumulate, you begin to be aristocrats of labour—you still work in the market for your bread—but presently you make profits enough to live without work—you take profits from the stores, but do no labor in the store—one or two shopmen do the work—you pay them 6s. per week, and their keep, as you know—and merely perform the labor of walking to your shop to take your dividends, such dividends consisting of your surcharge beyond the value of the article. Now, then, what have you to say, to show you are not profit-mongers as arrant as the shopkeeper you decry.

He next went on to show that the system was ruinous in its tendency if directed to manufactures—powerless if directed to land. If, said Mr. E. Jones, you start a factory, you do not shut up the factory of the rich man at the same time you open one for yourselves! you are not strong enough to do that. If you do not, you increase manufacture, and do harm. Mr. L. Jones had asked how they could increase production, because new men were not created for the purpose. I will tell you:—consumption under the present system depends on the means of buying. The rich make the people poorer more rapidly than you can make the poor rich—with increased poverty the purchasing power diminishes—you keep increasing the supply of goods, while the market for those goods is thus becoming smaller—now tell me, how will you find your way out of the dilemma? That's what beats you! But you yourselves increase this very evil by your fallacious remedy. I will admit you may create a benefit for the moment; by employing temporarily a few more men than were employed, but the benefit is purchased at the price of a permanent and increased evil. Here lies the political economy of the case: you increase the amount of production without increasing the market for the produce at the same time. Thus you glut the market—you bring the prices down, and, by bringing the prices down, you must bring your profits down in competition on the one hand, and the wages of the wages-slave on the other. So much for co-operation in manufacture. Now for co-operation in land. Can you unlock the monopoly of land? You want to buy the land—it is not to be bought. A political law of primogeniture, settlement and entail locks up the greater part. Club your pence to eternity, and see if that will cut off an entail. Political power alone can do it. But some land does come into the market. How do you stand with that? the difficulties increase the further you go. You want to buy land, and club your pence together. You are earning six, eight or twelve shillings a week; are you out of that able to spare enough to locate yourselves on a farm and emancipate yourselves from wages'-thraldom? You see that the co-operation of the many is required to locate the few. Suppose you have all clubbed together with the hope of each getting a farm: it will buy land enough to locate only a few. After your first effort how are you to go on? The more you want to purchase land the less your means of doing so become. The more you want to purchase it, the dearer it becomes, for the greater the demand for land the more it rises in price, and you cannot increase the supply—land is not india-rubber. Meanwhile, you cannot deny that wages must keep falling, under the present system and that you cannot prevent the surplus from flowing into the market; you have admitted it; then you cannot prevent the downward tendency of wages. You are getting poorer and poorer. Your means of buying grow smaller and the land grows dearer at the same time. Thus the distance keeps increasing between the acres and the man. The speaker concluded by calling on his opponent to answer these points, to refute these arguments, instead of talking about newspapers, or leading them to France.

Mr. Lloyd Jones said, they were told they would glut the market, had there not been gluts in the market without any co-operative mills or workshops? It had been said, a fool might in one minute ask a wise man questions that would take him hours to answer. Machinery in its complicated nature for the production of textile fabrics, 100 years ago, was equal to twelve millions of men; but during the last hundred years, mechanical appliances had increased to as much as seven hundred millions of men. Suppose that machinery, instead of being in the hands of the competitors, was in the hands of the people themselves; instead of these great mills being in the hands of a Mr. Smith or a Mr. Jones, they were, as they proposed to make them in the course of time, the property of the people, who instead of being the laborers, should become the extenders and the owners of machinery, by the capital put together on the co-operative principles. The £2000 that has been made by the co-operative stores in Rochdale, was made as a profit upon the business. Suppose that Mr. Jones or Mr. Brown belonged to it, and after paying expenses, took all the surplus to the bank and placed it there to Jones' credit—he would have given no amends to the people for making these profits; but that £2000 was given back to the Messrs. Jones, Smith, Robinson, &c. who stand connected with the stores as members; and those who divided the money amongst the members, said "take it home and it will enable you to increase the the consumption of your family." (Cheers.) But was that profit-mongering. You join a co-operative store, and lay out a pound, and five shillings is made upon it, and it costs a shilling for management and they give you four shillings as your fair share of the profits. To call that profit-mongering was cant and humbug. He would be plain with Mr. E. Jones, and tell him that, although he has brought forward the rules of the Bradford stores, in his conscience he must have known that the rules bore quite a different construction to what he tried to put upon them. It was for the people to find out if this swindling was going on.—First of all, it was said, they got their goods at prime cost; obtained five per cent. upon their subscriptions, and then divided the profits; and these they got by plundering the public, and putting all into their own pockets. Now, he should show them they did not do so. Mr. L. Jones here read the rule, showing that their object was to get their goods at prime cost, adding only the expenses of management, and such management as the society shall deem fit to benefit their moral and social condition. The shop-keepers never talked of that! Then again all goods must be sold at reasonable market prices, and the surplus profits, deducting working-expenses and 5 per cent. interest on the shares, shall be divided half-yearly amongst the members, according to the amount of purchases by each; but the rule did not say according to the amount of purchases of the public. The thing was quite plain, and how his opponent could misunderstand it, he was quite at a loss to know. Now he would show them what was done with the, so-called, plunder from the public; there was a law in reference to that. All fines and forfeits, and profits on all goods sold to the public, after expenses are paid, shall go to form a reserve fund of the association; and that was what Mr. E. Jones called dividing the profits, and putting them into their own pockets. They divided and put into their pockets the profits of their own purchases, and that of the public into a reserve fund: but, said his opponent, "give that to the public." He said, no! these men found the capital, and were doing what the public would not not do for itself. Suppose they open a store, somebody must distribute, and could those individuals be paid without profits. They had all the risk, and care, and management, therefore, it was most absurd to expect that they should return the profits received from the public. They might be good-natured in doing so: but they would be very foolish. He asked his opponent to give an instance where the public had been shut out from becoming members? Had they been shut out of Halifax, let any one try and see whether or not.

MR. ERNEST JONES said his opponent had endeavoured to vindicate profit-mongering, by showing that the profits went into one man's pocket instead of that of another. A nice distinction—while they still came, as before, out of the pockets of the people. So much for his opponent's moral logic. As to the Bradford Store, his opponent had said the members did not put the profits in their pockets, because they went to the Reserve Fund. What was the Reserve Fund? a fund to extend business. It was pocketing profits in another way. Not one word had his opponent said in refutation of the insuperable difficulties that beset co-operation, under our present system. But he (Mr. Lloyd Jones) had told them to "suppose" they had become possessed of machinery? What a fine thing, that would do for them. So it would—But he, (Mr. Lloyd Jones) would like to do something more than "suppose" it. He would like to see it, and to hear how it was to be done. Ah! that was always the case with those superficial rhetoricians, who surfeited the people with fine theories, and shadowy imaginations. Suppose it, indeed! That was no answer. Show how it is to be done—despite the obstacles he (Mr. E. Jones) had pointed out. These shadowy schemes, these miserable failures had been the case from Harmony downwards (hear, hear), Harmony an eternal disgrace to any country, and in which Mr. Lloyd Jones took so conspicuous a part. (Loud cheers). His opponent had asked him to bring cases where the public had been shut out of co-operative undertakings. He had brought forward the case of Padiham—but not only did they prevent the public from being admitted, they expelled the very members themselves. In Castle Street, London, nine men expelled eleven by a mere juggle. He would now explain his plan to them.

Suppose a number of you men in Halifax commence a co-operative store. Having clubbed your subscriptions together—you buy in the wholesale market and sell to yourselves and the general public (for he could not see why they should exclude the general public, from any benefits they might offer). You have one of two courses open to you, either to sell to the general public at the wholesale price, the same as to yourselves, merely adding thereto the cost of management and distribution, to cover your working charges; or you charge the market price to them and keep the surplus which you devote to a fund, until it is accumulated sufficiently large, to enable you to commence another store, or a co-operative farm or factory; and in that factory, or farm, or store, you set other wages-slaves at free remunerative work. These labor on the same conditions after receiving the fair day's earnings, for the work, the surplus goes to repeat the experiment, and so they might go on adding fresh stores, and mills, and farms, proceeding in geometrical progression, till they gradually spread the means of happiness to the great bulk of the people instead of isolating the profits, until they made an aristocracy of labor and of gold (loud applause). The co-operators of the present movement, pretended to be Christian Socialists. (cries of no, no), Well, but he contended that this was the noblest plan of Christian Socialism. Could any body say there was anything wrong in this plan? which he proposed? (shouts of no, no.) Is there anything you can object to in this plan. (No! from Mr. Lloyd Jones.) His opponent admitted there was nothing wrong in this plan—he had said on Monday, that it was "first rate." On this plan of co-operation (said Mr. E. Jones) you would be able to do something for your three hundred poor brothers' that are to be turned out of their work in Halifax. (cheers). Then why don't you try it? If you confess it is better than yours, what is the reason, you don't try it? (hear, hear). Because there is profitmongering in the one, and no profit-mongering in the other. The public do not support you, because they have no confidence in you, and they see that the professions of the parties who are at the head of the stores are not to be believed. Why do you in Halifax employ master shoe-makers; when you have got two shoe-makers in your own store, and don't employ them? (cheers). But you think you are making head-way because here and there a store is flourishing upon illgotten gains. Don't deceive yourselves. You have not begun the fight yet. You are competing only with the small retail shop-keeper at present. And even with him, you cannot compete. I hold in my hand a paper signed by David Willman, and two other persons in Halifax, stating that they can buy their goods cheaper and better from small shop-keepers in their neighbourhood, than from the Co-operative Store in Cow Green. (Shouts of "we can," and applause). What will it be when the retail shop-keeper, ground down between you on the one side, and the capitalist on the other—leaves you naked to the arrows of your mighty foe? They are still the interposing guard—when it is gone, how will you stand? You say you are undermining the capitalist. Castle Street undermining Moses? Not you? While labor saved forty millions, capital has made two thousand four hundred millions. That looks like undermining. Why, before the fight begins, you are growing proportionally weaker every day! It is a gross and melancholy delusion, to mislead the people by sophisms, such as the leaders of the present Co-operative Movement are now doing.

Mr. LLOYD JONES on rising to deliver his concluding speech said he would take first of all the reference which had been made to the co-operative business, in which he was for some time the acting agent, and which had been pronounced a dead failure. Presuming it was all true what his opponent had said about him, they ought not to fall out about it, they ought to shake hands and cry "quits." He would not bandy the charges which had been brought against him. How were the Castle Street Tailors to compete with Moses & Son? Now does Mr. E. Jones mean to say that you people will do nothing for principle—but that you will do everything for personal profit—then he would say the chances are that Moses and Son will always beat the Castle Street Tailors. If you will give up all principle and not deal with your fellow-working men, but prefer Moses & Son, then the game is up and they have it all their own way (hear, hear, from Mr. Ernest Jones). We (said Mr. L. Jones) will tell you what you ought to do, and if you do it not the sin is upon your own heads. If you give those men the preference because they are working out the flesh and bones of your wretched fellow-creatures; if you do this along with society at large, then he would say, "Society, you are a great scoundrel!" you are mean slaves because you can make a profit by it. Now, he confessed the Castle Street Tailors did sell dearer than Moses & Son and such like establishments, and why? There is a firm in London which pays 1s. 3d. for making a coat, and the Castle Street Tailors pay 14s. If you say you cannot drag your brethren from slavery unless the co-operators could compete with such establishments, then he said they could not do it and the sin rests on your own heads. He would tell them what they did in the co-operative stores—they go into the market with cash, and never buy with credit; they do not adulterate the articles they purchase, they do not offer mocha coffee, as one great shop had done, and then you find but two ozs. of coffee, and all the rest is chicory. Do you want to submit to a juggle of that kind—you may get cheapness by it; but it is that system which has been your ruin and ground you down to the earth; but the co-operators will not join in a juggle of that kind; they would sooner shut up their stores tomorrow, for they can work as well as you can. Why don't they give the reserve funds, accumulated from the profits derived from the public and commence other stores for the benefit of the public? because you are a mean lot of fellows and won't allow them to do it; you want back your profits for your own benefit. You do wrong in doing so—you do wrong to capitalise every penny but never divide them. If the co-operators won't do that which Mr. E. Jones recommends, do it for yourselves, and don't talk of what is best and most Christian-like; but so long as the co-operators are doing better than you—hold your tongues—for shame you ought to do so. You want political power. Act like reasonable men and do what you can for yourselves until you get it. There is not a man that joins the stores, that does less to obtain political power, than he did before, but they are not the men to be dragged into a political agitation that is not creditable. If the co-operators do not deal fairly with their stores, towards all who deal with them, then open you, another store in the same street, and capitalise your profits for the sake of setting up other stores for the benefit of the working classes. (hear, hear). Mr. E. Jones in his plan said, buy land, and get machinery, and organize for political power. But you will not catch us political birds, by putting such political chaff on our tails, (laughter). When will you get your political power? Do you know you have to ask the capitalists and the monopolists for political power? Why; you are going to smother the bishops (laughter). The bishops get a great deal more, and you get a great deal less than you ought to have. But do you know what the great manufacturers of your towns have got out of the labour of the people? Oh! you never inquire into these things. You count up what the bishops get, but do you know what the rich capitalists get?

Your eyes are open to the abuses of government; but to the evils that exist around you, your eyes are shut down. It is every man's duty to elevate himself without injuring his fellow man. If you will prove that you can practice a better thing than the co-operators they will bless you and pray for your success, But (said he) you are hypocrites and will not do the best you can for yourselves and your families. Suppose you get political power there are still doubts as to whether you will use it with discretion; you are not angels. Then allow co-operators to work in the way they think best. They will fight in the co-operative movement, and allow you to fight for political power. It is said that the co-operators are substituting one set of profit-mongers for another. But that cannot be profit-mongering, when they give to each member, a fair share of the profits on the goods they purchase. It is not profit-mongering to make the profits received from the purchases of the public &c., into a reserve fund, for the purpose of opening a central store. No man can class the two things together as one and the same. The increasing capital of the stores, will be the means of putting you at work. It is not Moses & Sons, and the slop shops that the co-operators compete with, but with other concerns, as, Nugee & Stultz &c., and the great masters.

If you will give the preference to your brothers, instead of the slop shops, which work out the blood of your fellow creatures, then the game is on a fair footing. Set your face in the right direction; put your heads to the work, do the little that is before you; and when you have gained strength, go and do other things, that require doing. Do justice to all; emancipate yourselves; your destiny, is in your own hands, and if you see the way, and will not walk in it, the blame is upon your own heads. (loud applause).

Mr. ERNEST JONES said it was truly amusing to hear the answers which had been given to the questions he had propounded. He had told Mr. Jones that profitmongery was to charge more for a thing than it cost you, labor and time included, and to put it into your own pocket. He had told his opponent that they could not save society by co-operation, because the evil increased more rapidly than they could effect good. Surplus labor and machinery spread misery more rapidly than co-operation created independence,—therefore co-operation must sink in the long run. He told them that co-operation could not prevent surplus-labor, because the co-operation of many was required to save the few, and then the means of the remainder were exhausted by low wages. That the very increase of manufacturers, caused by co-operation, would undermine the co-operation that increased it, by glutting the market, and reducing wages. That they could not increase the market, because the market meant not men but money, under the existing system. That they could not obtain land, because political power locked it up on the one hand, and poverty kept off the people on the other. That while increasing poverty prevented the subscription of new capital, the reproduction of that which was already subscribed would be prevented by the profits being swallowed up in competition with the rich. They had heard his opponent. The ablest debater of the present co-operation plan had been before them, arguing its defence. All that could be said for it had been said; and he submitted that his (Mr. E. Jones's) arguments had been unanswered. His opponent had admitted they could not take the surplus out of the market; he had admitted they could not umdersell the wholesale dealers like Moses, &c.: he had confessed that if the public preferred paying less to paying more, co-operation must fail. In these admissions his opponent had given up the case. The whole hinged on them—there was nothing more to argue. But, said his opponent, the public have philantrophy and generosity enough for the sake of Samaritanism to pay dear to the co-operators, instead of cheap to Moses. Have they (said Mr. E. Jones)? A little time ago you told us we were "a mean lot," and that we would not support you unless we got large profits. Now you tell us we're such angels we'll pay dear instead of cheap, from pure virtue! Now, the fact is, it don't depend on your will at all. (Hear, hear). You are too poor. You *can't* go to Castle-street—you *must* go to Moses. You can't go naked—you have just money enough to afford a coat from Moses, not money enough to afford a coat from Castle-street, and therefore to Moses you must go against your will, and cut the throat of your fine theory of co-operation. You say you will compete with Nugee and Stultz. Not you! It is the slop-dealers you will have to compete with, for they are making a slop-shop of the world; and the wholesale dealer is devouring the retail tradesman. (Loud applause.) But they were asked how they would get political power? They were getting nearer and nearer to it every day; they were going forward, and not backward, as his opponent would have them to believe. They were going on strongly and hopefully, step by step, and they had faith in principles which told them before long the political rights of the people would be extorted from the inflictors of their political wrongs. What (he asked) brought Cobden and Bright into the field—love of liberty? No! fear of truth. (Cheers). What brought Sir Joshua Walmsley into the field—to do something for the people? Dread, lest the people should do something for themselves! (Loud applause.) What brought Russell into the field? The hopes of keeping others out of it. And at this moment they were asked to follow social delusions, when realities were bowing ready to their grasp. They were taunted with their apathy and weakness. Yes! that old giant, the Charter, was on a sick bed. But why was he there? Because he had been attended by a lot of quack doctors and old women, who drugged him with their nostrums, and soporifics, and narcotics—threw him into a lethargy, and then chuckled "he is dead." But he is waking up again! He is walking over the hills of Yorkshire, and looking down into your co-operative profit-nests, and turning them inside out to the broad light of day and common-sense. He tells you—"There is great commotion on the Continent! England itself is imperilled! (though I am not one of those believing in invasion;) but, in such times—what is Government obliged to do? It must throw itself upon the people, and to make the reliance worth anything the people's rights must be conceded. If the people instead of now availing themselves of the opportunity presented, go on grubbing in meal-tubs and candle-boxes," the Government will set them at defiance, and the game be lost. (Loud cheering). What has the co-operative system done? They have been for the last thirty-six years getting money, as they say. Why have they not grown rich? So far from having acquired a competency they are no nearer the end than when they began. They are nothing but a signpost, which, instead of directing the people aright, is turned the wrong way, and leading them backward to the guilds of the dark ages. (Loud applause.) But what will political power not achieve? While you are mending the breeches of a bishop's footman we shall be dividing the poor-lands of the bishop himself among the poor. (Immense applause.) I am not hostile to co-operation, but I do affirm this—that if a man has a given amount of capital, enough to compass one enterprize, and divides it among two, he will fail in both. So with you. You have a certain amount of strength, power, and resources—you require it all to get political power. If you fritter two-thirds of it away in trade's-unions and co-operations, you will achieve nothing. Now, then, you have got to choose which you will play—the certain game, or the fallacious one. But we, too, are co-operators. We, too, invite you to our co-operative factory. But there we deal not in cotton, devil's-dust, or shoddy. There we weave political enfranchisement, decked with the rich embroidery of social right. (Loud cheers.)

The discussion having closed,

Mr. L. JONES rose to move a vote of thanks to the Chairman, when he was met by shouts of "Vote! vote!"

THE CHAIRMAN said he had been informed that there was a minute on the books of the Committee that no vote should be taken.

Several persons here intimated to the Chairman that that was incorrect, and a general demand for a vote followed.

Mr. URIAH HINCHCLIFFE then moved, and Mr. JOSEPH FELL seconded, that a vote should be taken.

THE CHAIRMAN then called upon those who were of opinion that Mr. ERNEST JONES had proved his propositions to hold up both hands, when a perfect forest of hands was held up.

The contrary was put, and the Chairman then declared that an immense majority of the meeting were of an opinion that Mr. Ernest Jones had proved his propositions.

A vote of thanks was then moved to the Chairman by Mr. Lloyd Jones, seconded by Mr. E. Jones, and carried amidst loud cheers; after which the meeting separated.

17

CO-OPERATION V. SOCIALISM: BEING A REPORT OF A DEBATE BETWEEN MR H.H. CHAMPION AND MR BEN JONES (MANCHESTER: CENTRAL CO-OP BOARD, 1887), 6–23.

[This debate illustrates how the contest between socialism and co-operation became more heated after the founding of the Social Democratic Federation along with other socialist organisations in the 1880s. The son of a British army officer, Henry Champion (1859–1928) attended Marlborough College and served as a lieutenant in the Second Anglo-Afghan War. He converted to socialism and joined the SDF in 1883, becoming the party's first secretary, though he fell out with Henry Hyndman, the founder of the SDF, eventually being expelled a year or so after he debated with Ben Jones at Toynbee Hall in London. [Martin Crick, *The History of the Social Democratic Federation* (1994)] Champion freely admitted the movement's successes in the debate but maintained that "mere Co-operation" only benefited "the highest class of workmen". According to him, generalised co-operation could only be achieved by state socialism. Meaningful change he asserted would depend on "a certain amount of paternal legislation" as a great many workers were not only too poor to associate but were also too "degraded" and "brutalised" to act for themselves. Jones in turn questioned Champion's claim to be a democrat, as he desired nothing less than a benevolent autocracy. Jones strongly contested the idea that "State action (was) the highest form of co-operative action", insisting instead that "State control was like a rod of iron; voluntary co-operation was like a fluid". The question of the role of the state in effecting social and economic change was one that continued to divide socialists from co-operators over subsequent decades.]

Mr. CHAMPION, who on rising was received with cheering, said that he had that evening to advocate the merits of Socialism as against those of Co-operation; to try and show them that the merits of Socialism were superior to those of Co-operation as a remedy for the evils of society which probably everyone in that room deplored. He would commence by saying that it was hardly fair to entitle the discussion "Socialism *versus* Co-operation," because the principles of the two things were in some degree similar. Mr. Jones was an advocate, and a well-known one, of a system of Co-operation by individuals for the purpose of carrying on retail trade and manufacturing industry. He would be able to show them that that had been done, with a good deal of success, by many thousands of people prior to the last two generations, in this country, and there he was entirely with him. He could say that individuals who had co-operated had benefited their own condition a good deal, but when Mr. Jones went on to say that an indefinite extension of that scheme would put an end to the social evils which now afflicted society he could not agree with him, feeling, as he did, that he (Mr. Jones) was wrong. He did not object to the Co-operation of individuals, but he did not think it sufficient, and he would try and show why. Mr. Jones, and the Co-operative Societies with which he was connected, were performing one piece of social reorganisation very effectively—eliminating middlemen and other unproductive classes of society—but they were also at the same time taking away the property and business of a large and respectable class of the community, the shopkeepers and retail dealers, and would do so more and more every year. Supposing the process were carried on indefinitely, and all retail trade and all industry carried on by representatives of Co-operative Societies of that kind, it would be for Mr. Jones to show why the effects of competition between these Co-operative Societies should not be quite as bad as the effects of competition between individuals. He thought it would. Mr. Jones's reply probably would be that there was no reason why you should not have a Federation of Co-operative Societies. His (Mr. Champion's) reply would be that that was exactly what he was striving to bring about. They would then have society organised as Socialists wished to see it organised, but for the fact that they would be paying part of the proceeds of labour to two entirely unnecessary classes of society; that was to say, those to whom the rent of the ground on which the shops stood was paid, and those who drew their interest. His object was to get rid of all the idle and useless classes in society. He contended it was not an efficient remedy, because it would still leave a large number of persons who would be mere parasites of the community, as he believed they were now. They would be doing nothing, and would be appropriating the profits of other people's labour. Mr. Jones objected to the taking away of other people's property, to the nationalisation of the land or nationalisation of property, and to the taking of the land by the State. He (Mr. Champion) would say unless they did so they might reorganise society to some extent, but the worker would not get the full benefit of his work. That was his first objection to mere Co-operation. It was not a complete answer to the Social Question. He would further say that the scheme of Co-operation only benefited the higher class of workmen, and, as a matter of fact, it hardly touched those for whom he had the most sympathy—those who were the most helpless. It would be very possible for the population of a mining village, or for factory hands, to combine in that way and carry on the business. It would be very easy for them; and as to the lessons of combination and co-operation, they were very good indeed, but the evils affecting the poorest and most ignorant classes Co-operation could not touch, until, at any rate, they were raised to a higher level than they were at present. He contended that it would be useless for Mr. Jones to go out into the streets and preach the gospel of Co-operation until Socialism had procured shorter hours, better food, better houses, and a clearer understanding of this question. He did not think Mr. Jones and the Co-operators appealed to a very high sentiment in their Co-operative work. Anyone who had read the last few lines of Mr. Jones's pamphlet would see that the purposes for which Co-operators combined was not to raise their fellow-creatures who were below them in the social scale, while the foremost point in the mind of the Socialist was the raising of those who were lowest in the social scale. That was practically all the objections he had to urge. He would endeavour to show them, in a very few minutes, how the Socialists on the contrary proposed to benefit, by another form of Co-operation, just those very classes which somehow would have to be raised before they would be able to govern themselves, or to secure for themselves the profits which were now being taken out of their labour by other people. Many of them knew what was the general idea of Socialism. They knew that society was divided into two classes—those who lived on property, and those who lived by labour. Seeing that the class which lived on property had the control of the whole political and industrial machine, seeing that they worked that machine in their own interests, and seeing that those interests were directly opposed to those of the class which lived by labour, he would say they could not have a really satisfactory state of society until the distinctions between these two classes were abolished. Fuse them into one, one working-class bulk together. These individuals, these classes who lived without doing useful work, took away from society without putting into it, and consumed without producing. Socialists wanted to get rid of that distinction of class, and they said that could only be done by putting the whole of the control of the legislative machinery into the hands of a purely Democratic State, and by that Democratic State using its power for expropriating the middlemen, landlords, and capitalists. Then industry should be as quickly as possible reorganised on a collective basis under the control of that Democratic State. He did not think it could be done very rapidly. He wanted Mr. Jones to show how his plan of co-operation could affect the political application of social theories to immediate legislation. In the *Globe* newspaper of the previous Saturday was to be found a list of the Board Schools, and the number of children who came to them insufficiently shod, clothed, and fed. He took the trouble of calculating the proportions, and found that the proportion of children who came without sufficient boots was 33 per cent, with insufficient clothing 30 per cent, insufficiently fed 34 per cent. He wanted to know how Co-operation was going to give those children all they needed before they grew up to be citizens capable of providing for themselves. He came to the question of houses. It was admitted by every one that private enterprise in that department had absolutely broken down; that the State or the municipality must interfere, must undertake the erection of houses because private enterprise would not provide adequate or wholesome house-room for the masses of workers in great centres of industry. Co-operation would not touch that even if carried out to its ultimate result immediately. He would say that it laid with Mr. Jones to try and show them if his plan of Co-operation was an efficient remedy for these things, how, where, and when it could be applied at once, for he was an impatient man; he was not content to go on waiting in the hope that in three or four generations time these evils would be put a stop to. He did not say that they could be put a stop to at once, but he did say they might begin at once, and he wanted to see a beginning. If Mr. Jones differed from him in principle he must also object to those departments in which the State had already interfered. If he objected to the theory of Socialism and its application to the practical politics of to-morrow, he must object to the practical politics of yesterday, such as the intervention of the State for limiting the hours of labour in factories, and in the matter of elementary education, in regard to the employment of women and children in mines. Would he or would he not be prepared to defend the State compulsory shortening of hours of the tram-men in the Metropolis? They could not co-operate to free themselves. They could not combine in trade unions. If they were to strike, their posts would be soon filled by the unemployed. He wished Mr. Jones to understand that he considered the co-operators were doing good work, but when they said that their scheme was an efficient remedy for all the evils from which society was at present suffering, then it was that he disagreed with them. Mr. Jones would say, probably, the points to which he most objected were those of expropriating the persons who now hold property. His (Mr. Champion's) answer was that though he might advocate expropriation, did not Mr. Jones confiscate property by taking away the trade and the living of shopkeepers, as was being done by the Co-operative Societies? If they did not believe him they had only to ask any shopkeeper who had been competed against by Co-operative Stores. (Laughter.) Mr. Jones would probably object to compulsion. He (Mr. Champion) would say that the power of persuasion was perfectly useless—it was inadequate to teach persons who were so degraded and so much brutalised, as many of our people unfortunately were, and therefore they had to be subjected to a certain amount of paternal legislation. The poorest even knew what they wanted. They wanted more of the physical enjoyments of life, more material comforts, more ease, more rest, but owing to their surroundings and their circumstances they were quite unable to get them for themselves. It was rather by beginning at the other end that all those men who sympathised with the claims of labour should combine for the purpose of using political power to wrest industry from the people who now hold it. They (the Socialists) would begin at one end, Co-operators would begin at the other.

Mr. JONES, in his reply, commenced by stating that he and Mr. Champion had each agreed to distribute to the meeting pamphlets representing their respective views. These pamphlets formed the basis of the discussion that night, not, as the chairman had stated, to try and solve all the difficulties and defects in the constitution of society, but simply to try and ascertain clearly and definitely what the difference was between Co-operation and Socialism, and whether Socialism would do more than what Co-operation professed and tried to do. He and Mr. Champion had had two hours' conversation the previous Wednesday night, for the express purpose of trying to arrive at the points of difference between Socialists and Co-operators. He wished those present to bear that in mind, and, the first thing they had now to do was to settle where they were. In this preliminary conversation, Mr. Champion said he represented his own views, which might or might not be the views of other Socialists—he represented himself alone. When Mr. Champion had expressed a doubt as to whether the pamphlet, "What is Meant by Co-operation,"[1] really represented the views of co-operators generally, he (Mr. Jones) told him that his attendance there on this occasion had been officially approved by the Central Co-operative Board—the representative organisation of the co-operators; and that if Mr. Champion were to send that tract into any city, town, or village, and have it read to an assembly of co-operators, he would not find five per cent out of their nine hundred thousand members who would disagree with it. They then settled the points of difference between Co-operation and Socialism.

As Mr. Champion had told them, he did not object to co-operation, and he disagreed with and strongly disapproved of those Socialists who went about London and the country trying to persuade people not to become co-operators. Further, Mr. Champion only objected to co-operation on the distinct grounds (as he believed Mr. Champion told him) that it was not sufficiently effective, that it would not do its work fast enough, and that Socialism would do it much faster. Now, Mr. Champion had not proved that that night. (Applause.) Further, Mr. Champion had said that by Socialism he meant not only co-operation as they understood it, but two things which he mentioned that evening; first, expropriation, or confiscation of all property, except what could be devoted to personal use, or personal enjoyment; secondly, the organisation of all production and commerce; from the building of ships to the slaughtering of horses and the boiling of cat's meat; and from the control of vast commercial operations, to the selling of penny novelties in their streets; all these operations should be under the control of Central Boards, elected by the people. Thirdly, Mr. Champion believed in physical force to hasten the day when those Socialistic plans could be put into operation. That last was a point Mr. Champion had left out of sight that evening, but he (Mr. JONES) was not going to leave it out. Only in that day's *Times* they had one Socialist saying—"For five years we have been looking for bread, and given stones; might they not get brickbats in return?" They had another Socialistic saying—"We will oppose the truncheons of the police with revolvers and chemical preparations." Well, they knew that Socialists had tried force against force. Socialists had been in prison, and he believed some were in prison at the present time. That was one of the ways in which Mr. Champion hoped to hasten the day. Mr. Champion was of opinion that physical force must be met by physical force; and he went to the extent of saying—"I reserve the right to hang my opponents, if I get the opportunity, and I fully admit their right to hang me." There was a full and definite statement. (Laughter.)

Now, they should look at the question in this light—They had had their unscrupulous "bloated aristocracy," as Socialists would say, retarding step by step the progress of people to something like a state of equity. At length opponents of progress had come to the conclusion that it was no use offering direct resistance any longer. But, although they had got apparently something like a democracy, the democracy was not yet in the saddle. Although they had nominally the power as a democracy, the aristocracy still retained the power. He would therefore put it—Supposing any one of them were a member of that "bloated aristocracy," and he saw his privileges disappearing one by one, while something like equity was being restored to the nation, would he not set his wits to work to see how he could prevent it? If he saw direct resistance was no longer available, would he not try indirect resistance? It had been done times out of number in history. These opponents would try to increase the velocity of democratic progress, in the hope that the people might be carried past the path of equity, and be pushed over a precipice to as low a point as they had started from; or, as a friend of his had said, "from the heaven of anticipation to the hell of realisation." Now physical force was a two-edged sword, and if those who wanted to get what was right advocated the use of physical force, and admitted, as Mr. Champion did, that it might be used against them, how could they, a minority, a disorganised and unarmed minority compete successfully against a majority, well organised, well armed, and with all the sinews of war with which to resist that unarmed minority? Therefore, if the well armed majority could have only a plausible excuse for saying that force should be employed, had not they then the right to say "They shall take who have the power, and they shall keep who can." "We will put you into chains of servitude again, and we will take care that you, the democracy, shall no longer have any power?" He would put it to them whether that was not a possible state of things which might come out of this Socialistic agitation for physical force?

The Social Democratic Federation said that all these Socialistic states of things should be managed by means of elected bodies. Of course, Democracy meant the government of the people by the people. Now, if they had elected bodies, the majority must rule; so that supposing the Socialists were by some stratagem able to get supreme power to-day, then, by their Democratic principles, they must, to-morrow, resign that power into the hands of the people. How, then, could they make the majority act in the way the minority wished? (Cheers.) Did they not see that Mr. Champion was on the horns of a dilemma? (Cries of "No, no.") He (Mr. Jones) would then repeat it. The minority could only get over the majority, and make it conform to its views against its will by force. Now, anybody would admit that. Then, the majority must be kept down by the minority. But in a Democratic state of society the majority exercises its power according to its own inclination, and the minority has to give way. Did they admit that? Therefore, either the Social Democratic Federation must strike out the word "Democratic" from its title, and substitute "Despotic;" either Socialists must do away with the freedom of election, and substitute a benevolent autocracy, "paternal government," as Mr. Champion injudiciously termed it, or they must make up their minds that they could not consistently or effectually use physical force. If Mr. Champion was deprived of his weapon of physical force, which they would see was altogether inconsistent with another article of the Socialist's Democratic Creed, how was he going to hasten on that state of things which Co-operators said could only be brought about by raising the standard of equity, and under it carrying on the work of voluntary association. He and Mr. Champion agreed upon one thing—the value of education; and if Mr. Champion admitted that they must take the people step by step of their own free will, he (Mr. Champion) admitted everything that co-operators claimed, and which they were trying to carry out.

He would now take State expropriation of property. Mr. Champion did not advocate that state of Socialism which Mr. John Burns advocated. Mr. Champion was not going in for that state in which a man could not have a guinea orchid in his buttonhole. Mr. John Burns objected to these things, but Mr. Champion did not. Mr. Champion would expropriate all interest and profits, and admit the State as the sole receiver. Mr. Champion would not prevent the action of supply and demand on the rates of wages, only with the slight exception of what trade-unionists did already. He would have a minimum of wages, and a maximum of hours. No man should work for more than a certain number of hours. Mr. Champion would not interfere one iota with the high salaries which were being paid, for instance, to the officials on their railways. If he understood Mr. Champion aright, Sir Edward Watkin could continue to be chairman of his three or four railway companies. He could have his houses, his pleasure grounds, his park, his horses, his groom, his butler, and his domestic servants. No hindrance would be placed on these by Mr. Champion, so they could see what a mild Socialist he was. A man with a family of two, and another with a family of ten, would each receive the same wages according to Mr. Champion's proposals. If that were Socialism, co-operators were far ahead. They began at the beginning. They believed that the standard of equity must be raised, that they must teach prudence and forethought; and teach people to consider what would be the results of their actions.

The CHAIRMAN here announced that each speaker would now be allowed three quarters of an hour in which to question his opponent. He called upon Mr. Champion to put the first question to Mr. Jones.

Mr. CHAMPION said he would like Mr. Jones to reply to his statement that even if Co-operation were carried out universally, those who did the work would have to keep those who did no work—living on the rent of land or interest on shares—and provide them with the means of living.

Mr. JONES, in reply, said Co-operators stated distinctly that capital had a right to remuneration, for capital was stored-up labour; but when Mr. Champion and his friends went to the unemployed and said, "all the stored-up capital of this country has been produced by their labour," then they were wrong. A large proportion of the stored-up labour of the country had been produced by invention. He agreed with the Socialists that it had got to a large extent into wrong hands; but two blacks did not make a white. Co-operators said that every Co-operator ought to be possessed of a certain amount of capital, and they showed how he could get it. They also showed how it could be made fruitful. They could lend it on such terms as to be remunerative to those who borrowed it. They clearly foresaw a state of things which would make even Mr. Champion quite satisfied. People would some day be glad to lend their capital for nothing, on condition that those who borrowed it took care of it and returned it when wanted. (Laughter.) In

1862 their Co-operative members numbered 90,000; in 1887 they had 900,000. In the twenty-five years their numbers had been increased tenfold, and this, he thought, was good work. In the same period they had multiplied their trade fifteen times, their capital seventeen times, and their profits twenty-two times. And yet Mr. Burns said that Socialists for five years had been asking for bread and got only a stone. He (Mr. Jones) would reply that Co-operators had worked for twenty-five years, they were drawing £3,000,000 per annum of profits and interest, and were likely to get more. They did not believe in separating themselves from the people. They believed in the principle of "a little leaven leavening the whole lump." If only the wealthy classes would stretch out a helping hand, and be content with an interest of 4 per cent for their money, they could build houses for the working classes in London, and, at the existing rentals, present them with the freehold in less than twenty-five years from the present time.

Mr. JONES then asked Mr. Champion the following question:—"If, as I believe, I have shown that he cannot hasten the Socialistic work by physical force, and cannot hasten it by compulsion, but must depend upon voluntary effort like Co-operators, does not he then thoroughly approve of the Co-operative programme?"

Mr. CHAMPION said the matter of physical force seemed to excite Mr. Jones's ire a good deal. Mr. Jones seemed to think that he (Mr. Champion) was concealing it from those present. He believed that its discussion would have a salutary effect upon those who were too easy in circumstances to believe that there was a spirit of revolt in those who were suffering. There was a better social feeling springing up between the upper and lower classes, but there were a great many people who were very selfish whom it did good to know that there was a spirit of revolt among the people who were oppressed by them. He would say any cause which was worth arguing for was worth fighting for in the last resort. If Mr. Jones had 900,000 Co-operators, why did they not come forward and say something for the men who were out of work? They surely ought to have a natural sympathy for those people. Mr. Jones and his friends were not appealing to as high an emotion as the Socialists were. What Socialists wanted was State compulsion—backed up by batons and bayonets for the matter of that. It had become absolutely necessary in other departments, and should be put in force. Mr. Jones believed in force being used to put down one dishonest action, and why not the other. Equity compelled them to imprison the thief and the pickpocket, equity also should compel them to punish the man who took away their labour and did not give them a fair reward for their work. Mr. Jones had said he believed the time would come when people would lend the Co-operative Societies money for nothing; "the bloated aristocracy" who held the land of this country he did not think would lend money without interest. Mr. Champion then asked Mr. Jones whether Co-operators approved of State interference on Socialistic lines?

Mr. JONES replied that Mr. Champion had not defined what he meant by Socialistic lines. There was no doubt whatever that all laws were Socialistic in a certain sense. If Mr. Champion meant did he approve of compulsory expropriation of land, of buildings and money, &c., he answered No.

The CHAIRMAN said he thought what Mr. Champion meant was, did Mr. Jones approve of what had been done by the State in limiting the hours of labour of women and children and in other directions, and, if he did, did he approve of a further limitation?

Mr. JONES said he approved of the Ten Hours Factory Act, he approved of the Shop Hours Bill, and he approved of similar measures. He would use compulsory means to enforce equity, unless he clearly saw that compulsion would produce greater evils than the evils which the compulsion was meant to remedy. He would say the Socialistic methods would produce greater evils than it proposed to remedy. Mr. Jones went on to say that when a co-operator was asked how he would apply his principles in a certain case he could always do it. Assuming that Socialists would try to do the same, he would ask Mr. Champion how he would allow a man who had worked compulsorily eight hours per day to use his leisure time? Might he make anything for sale or exchange, or anything at all?

Mr. CHAMPION said, in answer, that he should have no objection to his making anything so long as he did not put it on the market and compete with the factories. He should object to his doing anything which would tend to lower the working man's standard of living.

Mr. CHAMPION asked Mr. Jones, in view of the awful suffering that existed, how much suffering he wished to see before admitting that it was justifiable to resort to physical force?

Mr. JONES replied, "I wish to see none."

Mr. JONES asked Mr. Champion whether a man who had made anything for his own household use should be at liberty to dispose of it at any time to anyone else?

Mr. CHAMPION made reply that anyone present would see that one individual might make a sofa for himself, and his selling it would not have much effect upon the market or disorganise industry. ("Oh!") He would ask Mr. Jones what was his opinion of State organisation for unemployed labour?

Mr. JONES replied that he would prefer voluntary Co-operative organisation of unemployed labour. He thought it was quite possible to organise them on co-operative lines and to devote them to useful work. If he had more leisure at his command he could devise schemes for giving employment to the unemployed of this city, and carry them out successfully. Mr. Champion would allow a man to make a sofa or a chair, or as many as he liked, and exchange them, so long as they were for his own use in the first instance. Millions, of course, might do the same. Where would Mr. Champion draw the line?

Mr. CHAMPION replied that he would use compulsion to prevent the exchange where it was found not to be beneficial. He thought it might be left to the common-sense of the people. He was in favour of industry being put under collective control, and he would increase that control as far as possible. Mr. Jones had said he was in favour of co-operative organisation of the unemployed. Was not State action the highest form of co-operative action?

Mr. JONES said he did not deny that the State was a form of Co-operation, but it was too rigid, and not sufficiently flexible to adapt itself to all the purposes of society. State control was like a rod of iron; voluntary co-operation was like a fluid (water). A rod of iron placed along an uneven piece of ground left cavities, but water filled every cavity and nook; and the advantage of voluntary co-operation was that it would adapt itself to every exigency of life; while State Co-operation would do nothing of the kind.

Mr. JONES said he would like to ask Mr. Champion whether he considered it justice to allow the present owners of 5,000 acres of land, and of a half-dozen mansions in different parts of the country, to retain that property for their own personal use and enjoyment, while any poor, miserable wretch who only rented two rooms would have to pay a rent to the State for the use of them?

Mr. CHAMPION replied that what they, as Socialists, objected to was not so much the possession of the land by the individual, but the use of it for the purpose of squeezing labour out of the working man. They would not interfere with those who held land or houses for their own use. The Duke of Buccleuch would be allowed to remain in possession of his 2,000,000 acres of land, if he could show that he wanted them for his own use, and not for making profit from others. Property used for the purpose of making a profit would be the first to be taken away. Mr. Jones had stated that State Co-operation was like a rod of iron, whilst voluntary Co-operation was like water. He quite agreed that State control was very inflexible; the only difference was that he was able to show from what the State had done in the housing of the poor, giving work to the unemployed, &c., that let its action be as inflexible as it may, it would do away with their evils for a time. He wanted Mr. Jones to show how his flexible Co-operation would deal with these very practical questions. Though they might not press upon these 900,000 persons who voted for the Liberals and Radicals, they did press very hardly upon the persons with whom he sympathised.

Mr. JONES said Mr. Champion could not get his State Socialism at once if these lives were endangered; but these lives were not in danger. Poor-law relief and private charity prevented their lives being in danger, except in very rare cases. Its effect upon society could not be disputed. They might hiss at the words "poor-law relief" and "private charity," but poor-law relief, if they cared to do so, could be increased without State Socialism in the sense in which Mr. Champion advocated it. If Mr. Champion could do anything to stir up private charity so as to lessen the amount of human misery, he would be doing good work. If Mr. Champion could increase poor-law relief, without doing a great deal more harm, he would be doing good work. State Socialism did not save lives; but Co-operation found employment for and raised men up, and was doing its share to promote general prosperity.

Note

1 "What is Meant by Co-operation." To be had gratuitously, from the Central Co-operative Board, City Buildings, Corporation Street, Manchester.

18

TRADE UNIONISM, CO-OPERATION, AND SOCIAL DEMOCRACY (LONDON: TWENTIETH CENTURY PRESS, 1892), 10–16.

Harry Quelch

[Son of a blacksmith's labourer and a seamstress, Harry Quelch (1858–1913) grew up in poverty and began his working life at the age of ten. He joined the Social Democratic Federation when it was founded and replaced Hyndman as editor of the party's newspaper, *Justice*, in 1886. [Chūshichi Tsuzuki, *H. M. Hyndman and British socialism* (Oxford: Clarendon, 1961)] Quelch was skeptical about trade unionism, and as this pamphlet shows, he believed that co-operation was equally problematic for labour. Typically, he accused co-operation of only reaching better off workers. Quelch's indictment of the movement for its "absolute failure to materially change the economic conditions of working-class life" was based on his experience of London, where co-operation made poor headway owing to the structure of a labour market characterised by seasonality and irregularity of earnings, but exactly the same could not have been said about northern industrial towns, where the "divi" helped great numbers of working-class families make ends meet. Despite making serious criticisms, there is also a genuine attempt at understanding, however. "In its inception co-operation was socialistic, and its originators were Socialists", acknowledges Quelch, and he admits that contemporary enthusiasts can still be found who believe in "universal co-operation", but they are inevitably overwhelmed by mere dividend hunters and consumers who have to buy cheap goods. Indeed, if co-operation did become universal in scope then it would be nothing less than Social Democracy, so it would be better if both co-operators as well as trade unionists accepted this now and become Social Democrats, Quelch argues. Pervading the essay is the sense that the impoverishment of the working-class consumer is inescapable within capitalism, a natural corollary of the iron law of wages.]

It is much to be feared that to a large extent the "new" unionism is only the "old" unionism applied to unskilled labour; that the ideals are no higher, and the means no better adapted to the end. That is to say, the new unionism is only trade unionism, not Social Democracy. While trade unionism recognises the present system of society, justifies capitalism, and defends wage-slavery, and only seeks to soften the tyranny of the one and assuage the evils of the other, Social Democracy aims at destroying the whole system. It is chiefly as a possible means to this end, as an educational influence, as a means for sufficiently improving his position as to make the workman discontented with that position, that trade unionism is useful from a Social-Democratic point of view.

What is true of trade unionism is equally true of co-operation. It is most valuable to those among the workers who are best off. The artisan, earning a regular weekly wage, has not only a better opportunity of becoming a member of a co-operative society than the more precariously-employed and more poorly-paid labourer, but the advantage to him is greater by reason of his having more money to spend at the store. Even where the poorer individual is able to continue his membership, the relative position of the two remains unchanged, but in many cases the poorer members have to sell out, and then the affair becomes simply a joint stock company of the more fortunate, the race being once more to the swift, the battle to the strong. This is the case where co-operation has been commercially successful, and where it has been thus successful it has done more than any abstract argument could do to demonstrate its absolute failure to materially change the economic conditions of working-class life. But in London distributive co-operation has not been phenomenally successful.

For this there are several reasons. Most Londoners of the poorer class purchase their commodities in small quantities, the number of small shops near their dwellings rendering simple and easy a practice which is engendered in most cases by casual and precarious wages. Then again the co-operative stores have to compete with large private stores, where the margin of profit is small, and the proprietors of which have all the advantage on their side. A co-operative store starts with the object of saving for the consumer the profits of the middleman, and supplying, as far as possible, pure, unadulterated goods; but the profits of the middleman are made by advantage in the market, by adulteration, and by sweating. Consequently the co-operative store is unfairly handicapped—as the private store keeper, with a small margin, it may be, but with a large aggregate, of profit, is able to sell cheaper—and cheapness is everything. Of course people should buy good goods, even if they are dear, and not cheap and nasty, but they do not. Low wages compel the poor to buy the cheap, shoddy commodities, the production of which keeps wages down and intensifies poverty. This is the accursed round of commercialism. Low wages create a demand for the worst kind of articles of consumption, and this demand is supplied by overwork, by sweating, and the worst paid labour and most inferior workmanship.

It is just as useless to preach to the poor the advantage of buying unadulterated goods at co-operative stores—when you can get them even there—as it is to pass resolutions at Trade Union Congresses against sweating. Who is the chief patron of the sweater but the workman? Fancy a docker buying a suit of clothes that has been made by fairly-paid labour! It is not because they like shoddy clothing, bosh butter, sanded sugar, and birched tea, that the workers buy these things; it is because they can afford no better. And it is because they can afford no better, because there is a market for them, that these things are produced. In nine cases out of ten a workman would never buy a suit of clothes at all if he waited till he could pay such a price for it as would allow even a reasonable amount to be paid for the labour expended in making.

Under these circumstances it is not possible for a co-operative association to successfully compete with the private trader and at the same time supply superior and purer commodities to its customers, and act fairly towards its employés. It has for some time been a standing complaint at Trades Union Congresses that certain co-operative societies are unfair employers. They employ non-union labour and pay less than trade union wages. In its inception co-operation was socialistic, and its originators were Socialists. Likewise, very often, those who start a co-operative society are enthusiasts, who are prepared to make sacrifices, to resist the pressure which impels the poor to buy cheap goods and nasty, but after a while others come in who are mere dividend hunters, who, while willing to draw dividends and profits, will not even patronize their own store, unless they can purchase there as cheaply as of the individual trader who cuts down prices by adulterating his goods or sweating his hands.

But while co-operation has not been particularly successful in London, it has met with very considerable success in other places. A commercial concern which started some fifty years ago with a few pounds scraped together by a few poor men, and which now comprises a million members and realises annual profits to the tune of three millions cannot be described as anything but a success. And yet it is this very success as a commercial concern which demonstrates the failure of co-operation, as a means of emancipating the workers. Nevertheless, this was the hope of many of the original advocates of co-operation. They imagined that, starting as a small store, or a small workshop or factory, this co-operative society would grow and grow until it absorbed the whole industry of the world—until we had universal co-operation. If it had not been tried, people might still believe in the possibility of arriving at such a consummation, but it has been tried—and has been successful as a commercial undertaking—but it has absolutely failed to produce any appreciable improvement in the condition of the working classes. To many co-operators, doubtless, this is a matter of no concern. So long as the store affords them a safe investment for their little savings, pays them five per cent on their investments, and a dividend on their purchases, as well as offering these on terms as reasonable as can be obtained elsewhere, it serves all the ends which, to their narrow minds, are desirable. To these there is nothing to be said. They are really not co-operators but capitalists. And yet there is no doubt that they form the overwhelming majority of the so-called co-operators of to-day. To them the commercial success of co-operation must be a source of intense gratification unalloyed by the knowledge that it has lamentably failed to approximate to its high ideal.

But it is only in connection with that ideal that we are concerned with co-operation here. It does not interest us that co-operative stores enable the lower middle class and the aristocracy of labour to purchase more economically, if not more cheaply than they otherwise could do; that co-operation affords another opportunity for thrift on the part of those who have something to save. The important thing for us is the consideration as to whether co-operation has done anything for those who, because of their poverty, have always had to buy "cheap and nasty" when they were able to buy at all, or whether it has given the opportunity of thrift to those who have hitherto had nothing to save. We must here regard co-operation, not as a commercial enterprise, but as a factor in social progress, and in this connection we are bound to arrive at the conclusion that it has effected nothing and is absolutely valueless, except to a certain extent as an educational influence. As an educational agency it has, like other gigantic joint stock undertakings, demonstrated the uselessness of the individual capitalist and given workmen an object lesson on the facility and economy with which they themselves, when organised, can manage the most important industrial enterprises, without a master. Doubtless also from the moral point of view, co-operation has had some educational effect. But that is all.

It is urged, of course, that co-operation has done good in eliminating the middleman. It has become fashionable of late years to denounce the middleman. But his elimination does not always benefit those on whose behalf the outcry against him is generally raised. So long as the workman is robbed of all but a subsistence it is of little importance whether the chief robber shares part of the spoil with an underling for relieving him of some of his dirty work, or whether he sticks to the whole "swag" himself. This has generally been the effect of the abolition of the middleman. In the work of production, the amount saved by his elimination has not been added to the workers' wages, but to the employers' profits; and in the distribution of commodities it has not meant reduced prices for the consumer, but enhanced profits for the merchant or manufacturer.

But, it may again be urged, the ordinary workman can, if he likes, become a shareholder in the "co-op." So he may become a shareholder in a railway—if he likes; but this does not make the capitalist domination of our railways less a fact. Even were all the workmen in a district shareholders in the co-operative society, the better paid among them would still "have the bulge on the others," as Uncle Sam would say. In a co-operative store, as elsewhere, the man with two pounds a week is worth just twice as much as the man with one pound. The two-pound man can spend twice as much and save twice as much as the one-pound man. And, generally speaking, instead of levelling up, all that co-operation does is to increase and intensify this difference, with the result that in very many cases the co-operative societies are composed almost exclusively of the artisan class, who look down with contempt on the poor labourer who cannot even afford to be a co-operator.

In some provincial districts practically the whole of the work of distribution is carried on by co-operative stores, and the small shopkeeper is comparatively unknown. This has not, however, made any material difference to the great mass of the workers in those districts. They work as hard and live as hard as the workers in centres less favoured by co-operation. They appear to experience the same difficulty in making both ends meet, and look forward with eagerness for their "divi" in order to pay rent or buy clothes, or to supplement their wages in some other way. In very many cases, too, mill-owners and other large capitalists are also shareholders in the co-operative society.

It comes to this, then, that neither Trade Unionism nor co-operation, on present lines, can solve the great social problem, why the most industrious are the poorest—nor can they emancipate the workers. Of course if Trade Unionism developed into a universal federation of labour and seized the political machinery in order to organise industry and control production and distribution, it would be within measurable distance of that emancipation. But that would be Social Democracy; and useful as Trade Unions may have been and are, they are not socialist organisations nor are their members Social Democrats. In like manner, if Co-operation were to become universal, to include all workers in its ranks, to regulate the amount of work according to the needs of the community, and devote its efforts to supplying these needs instead of to creating profit, it would be near securing the same end. But this also is Social Democracy, and co-operators to-day are not Social Democrats. Logically both trade unionists and co-operators should be Social Democrats. A trade unionist, who believes in trade unionism, would surely like to see it spread and spread until the whole community was one vast trade union, with elected delegate committees, carrying out rules made with the consent of the whole of the members and controlling the whole of the political and economic forces in the interest of the members, until there was not a blackleg or knobstick on the face of the earth. Surely too, the co-operator who has any faith in the principles of co-operation, would like to see them universally adopted, not alone by individuals but by nations, until we had a real national and international co-operative commonwealth. In either case the result would be Social Democracy—a democratically organised community having control of its own economic and social forces and using these for the common good.

As a matter of fact, however, neither trade unionists or co-operators generally speaking, believe in or even understand abstract principles. The trade unionist regards the capitalist employer as a necessary factor in the social economy of the world, and as a really beneficent being, so long as he pays trade union rates of wages and respects trade union rules—quite oblivious of the fact that the very position of the capitalist makes his interests, beyond a certain point, diametrically opposed to those of the workman.

It is to the workman's interest that the whole of his fellow workers should be employed. It is to the capitalist's interest to employ as few men as possible, not merely with a view to economy but because the competition of a large number of unemployed has a salutary effect in keeping down the wages of those in employment. It is to the interest of the workman to get as much wages as possible. It is to the employer's interest to pay as little as possible for his labour.

With all this, however, the average trade unionist will have nothing to do with the wild revolutionary Social Democrat who would abolish the capitalist altogether, but rather regards the latter as being on the whole a decent sort of fellow, who only needs a little pressure to be put on him to induce him to concede all that is necessary.

But while the ideal of the average trade unionist is to make terms with the capitalist so as to make wage-slavery tolerable, the ideal of the average co-operator is somewhat lower, his desire apparently being to transform a number of workmen into petty shareholding capitalists. That is why I, who am a trade unionist and a co-operator as well as a Social Democrat, am more ardent for trade unionism than for co-operation, because trade unionism does, at any rate, mean even now, the organisation of workmen as workmen, and not as capitalists or on the side of capitalists. Trades unions, aiming at improving the position of workmen as such, constantly find that they have in spite of themselves to enter into conflict with the employing class, as witness the late strike of the Durham miners and of the Engineers. Here the unions in both cases were most conciliatory towards the employers. This conflict will go on and deepen. Unconsciously men will find themselves forced into the class war in which the the workers with their organisations will be on one side, and the capitalists on the other; and from which conflict only can Social Democracy be evolved.

Co-operation, on the contrary, though regarded by the individual trader as an enemy, does not necessarily enter into conflict with the capitalist at all. Indeed, so far as it transforms workmen into shareholders it forms a bulwark for capitalism, the same as the creation of small landholders or any other class of small proprietors would do. As educational agencies both trade unionism and co-operation have done an immense work. In addition to this, through trade unionism workmen have had many thousands of pounds additional wages, which but for their unions they would never have had. The pity is that so many held aloof, and have been content to participate in the gain, without assisting in the work, and that those who have done the work and secured the gain have not turned their gains to greater advantage. As I said over and over again to the men when they were out in the strike of 1889, the lesson of the need and power of organisation which they appeared to have learned by that strike was far more valuable to them than the mere material advantage of a rise in wages, which after all was individually inconsiderable, and which will disappear on the first decline in trade. Even now as a matter of fact, the employers are trying to filch it from them. Unfortunately this lesson appears to be almost forgotten already, and we seem to be again approaching a period of apathy, to be again succeeded by another conflict in order to oppose or to recover a reduction in wages.

Is it not time that we combined and strove for something higher, wider, and more far-reaching than this? Let the trade unionists unite, combine, federate; not for constantly squabbling with the capitalist over the spoil which the workers alone create, but to secure for the latter, organised, the control of their own tools and raw materials—of the mines, the railways, the factories, the shipping, the land—of all those things which only have value through their labour. Let the Co-operators co-operate with each other, with Trade Unionists and Social-Democrats for the same object. Let us all agitate, educate and organise to form the workers of the world into a gigantic trade union, an International Co-operation, a Social-Democratic Commonwealth.

19

CO-OPERATION IS REASONABLE SOCIALISM (MANCHESTER: CO-OP UNION, 1894), 1–8.

W. T. Carter

[Little is known about Walter T. Carter, apart from the fact that he was an active member of the Reading Co-operative Society and spoke regularly at co-operative meetings. This pamphlet is the text of an address he gave at a district conference held in the city, in which he makes a strong case for eliding socialism and co-operation, though not without a swipe at those groups that were claiming the socialist ground. Carter's analysis and rhetoric recalls the Owenite critique, though he does not refer to this directly. For him, the system of competition demoralises all classes, creating enervating luxury at the top of the social scale and brutalising poverty at the bottom. [See Noel Thompson, *Social opulence and private restraint: the consumer in British Socialist thought since 1800* (Oxford: Oxford University Press, 2015)] The answer to this state of affairs is education and co-operative practice. Education he argues should instil "the ideal of citizenship"; enabling workers to better understand the duties of the community to ensure their well-being in the home, the neighbourhood and the workplace. Change of this kind is "what I understand to be the true aim of real Socialism", he observes. Co-operation is the most promising means of overcoming "Individualism" and the resulting inequalities that generate conflict because it resolves successfully the tension between self-interest and community well-being. Defined in this way, co-operation is nothing less than "reasonable Socialism", inclusive, peaceful, and gradual, certainly, but no less committed to a radical reconstruction of the social, economic and moral order than more recent "unreasonable" varieties, such as that represented by the Social Democratic Federation, which engages in "wild and incoherent declamation". Despite what its modern socialist detractors say therefore, co-operation is, Carter emphatically maintains, "Socialistic in origin; Socialistic in character, Socialistic in government, and Socialistic in purpose".]

To those who earnestly interest themselves in the happiness and contentment of *all* classes of the community, the present condition of society would appear to be very far from being satisfactory. Whether one peers down to its lowest strata, or examines with clear, honest eyes its upper crust, he will find—in this very much to deplore and to make him ashamed—in that, much to excite his feelings of compassion, remorse, and indignation. In the latter, he will witness all the shameless evils that result from luxury and unlimited means of self-indulgence; in the former, he will discover that there exist all the evils that follow hopeless and unchanging poverty—squalor, wretchedness, apathy, and even indifference to life. As he reflects on this two-fold picture, he recognises that this condition of society seems to have attended every age of civilisation, and yet he cannot in his heart believe that it is a necessary resultant. On the contrary, he feels, and must feel convinced, that the tendency of civilisation if left to its own natural course is to secure to every individual the fullest development of his faculties and capacities, to encourage him to devote their exercise for the common good, by enabling him to fully enjoy the fruition of his skill and industry. In every age great thinkers have protested against the evil policy of hindering that development, and depriving the toiler the just reward of his labour; for this, in the main is the great barrier to *his* progress and the well-being of the State. In the present time, all good and right thinking men have come to the conclusion that this barrier must be removed, and removed with as much certainty, quietness, speed, and equity as the habits, customs, and predilections of the people will permit. If these stand in the way—and stand in the way they do and will—they must be overborne in the people's best interests. It appears to me that the only sure way of removing these obstacles is by education. By education I mean the training of every man to the ideal of true citizenship. If he grasp this ideal he will at once realise to himself his own importance and value to the community in which he lives; the opportunities and the means that are his to bless it by diligence, honest work, and the culture of whatever talents he may possess to their highest capacity. He will become proudly conscious that he is not a mere thing that the community may, with reckless disregard to its own welfare, treat with contemptuous indifference and neglect, but that the community has also high and imperative duties towards him, the persistent neglect or failure honourably to discharge becomes ultimately a disgrace or a peril to it. The community must also see that to him shall be given all adequate means and every facility for developing, from his childhood, his faculties and capabilities for the common good, that every opportunity shall be opened to him for applying his best faculties and capabilities in the promotion, not of his individual advantage only, but of the general good, and, above all, that the fullest rewards, which are his due, shall be secured to him in just proportion to his contribution to the common welfare, and also that his general surroundings shall be such as shall promote and maintain his general health, his comfort, and his pleasure. Thus education will enable him to clearly understand that his own best interests are the best interests of the community it is his privilege and highest duty to serve, and that the best interests of the community are the conservation of his interests, by whom it is faithfully and honourably served.

By such a training it may reasonably be expected that it would naturally result in a complete alteration of our present ideas affecting the duties and rights of employers and employed—of our present methods of the production and distribution of wealth—and, of the best means of securing to all the freest and fullest enjoyment of the beauties of Art and Nature. The hard-working toiler, now struggling hopelessly to obtain even the barest means of existence, would then be immensely relieved of his sordid anxieties, and be rendered free to take his rightful place in the social world, and give due attention to the duties that fall to him as a true citizen of a free and happy community.

To bring about such an alteration is what I understand to be the real aim of true Socialism.

The principle of the past has been free and unfettered Individualism. Each was to do his best for himself. Every child was trained up in the spirit of self-interest as his motive-power. It was supposed that if this principle were acted upon the greatest advantage would accrue to the State. But, in practice, this principle of self-interest led to unrestricted competition, which is only another name for incessant war between every single individual, and to the adaptation of every artifice that a state of war only is held to justify, for the purpose of over-reaching and ruining his opponent. The successful ones in this internecine strife made themselves stronger by taking from the defeated the very means by which they could provide themselves with the necessaries and comforts of life. They were thus compelled, from sheer necessity, to labour for the profit and advantage of those by whom they were beaten, and to accept such remuneration as they were pleased to grant. And, even amongst the fallen ones, there arose between each a more bitter rivalry to secure for himself permission to labour by under-selling each other in the labour market. The stronger ones had to continue the fight among themselves, until they found the struggle too fierce even for them singly to maintain their position. It became necessary, therefore, for each to combine with others. So groups were formed, called companies. This change wrought greater ills for the weaker ones, until they learned how to form combinations too. The strong ones knew they could beat the weaker, while they could deal with them singly, and foresaw the difficulties that would come if the units were permitted to unite. So they strenuously endeavoured to prevent that union being allowed. But without permission they did unite—till in course of time the permission came. Then a more devastating struggle ensued, because of the larger areas of the battlefields and the greater numbers and strength of the combatants. These struggles became so frequent and prolonged—the results always so doubtful, the sufferings endured so intense, the disturbance and loss to the community so tremendous—that it began to dawn upon many minds that the principle of Individualism was not only a wrong principle but a very evil one. It disintegrated society, made each man the other's enemy, and, whilst it brought increased wealth and power to the few, reduced the masses to poverty and impotence. It had lasted so long with an ever-continuing and increasing strife and disaster that the public mind and conscience began to be awakened. It began to see that a new principle must be adopted, and that, owing to the very complexed state of modern society, it would be most prudent, most wise, and least dangerous, that the methods of carrying out the new principle should be evolved from the old.

The end to be attained must be the common good, without sacrificing the interests of the individual.

Now this change might easily be effected if all men were perfect, without different passions, different desires, different powers of thought and action. But every individual does differ in these; and it is good that these differences do exist. Wise men will recognise it when they attempt to formulate a scheme for adaptation by human beings. Fools and madmen only attempt to ignore it. Do what man may, each will endeavour to do what he believes will best promote his own interests. Now, if a method could be devised by which, while he is left free to do so, and yet be constrained to place the results of his efforts into one common fund, so to speak, out of which his reward proportionate to his contribution to that fund could with certainty be secured to him, the object of the new principle, Socialism, would be attained. The great lesson that each then would have to learn would be that he must not act as he pleases, but as he ought, as an important unit of a great whole—the community. He must learn to act in the spirit of the sublime motto, "Each for all," and the community, in that of "All for each."

Many methods have already been devised, each having its own field to work in; but, though good, and probably sufficient for the end it proposes to attain, is too much limited and restricted to produce the general result desired to be achieved. Thus there are Trades Unions, Friendly Societies, Building Societies, and many others; but of all the schemes that have been submitted to humankind for adoption, none seem to me so well adapted for every phase of society—none to meet the exigencies of society I have alluded to with least friction—none so far reaching, so *little disturbing,* and so effective—as Co-operation. It is Socialistic in origin, Socialistic in character, Socialistic in government, and Socialistic in purpose. It is equitable—satisfying every sentiment of honesty, justice, and morality—simple in practice, practicable and thoroughly effective for the purpose it has in view, which is to enable every worker to provide as much for others as for himself all the materials necessary to satisfy fully their bodily requirements, and to secure for others, as well as for himself, every opportunity for the highest culture of their minds—to ensure that all workers, as well as himself, shall receive the just and full reward for their efforts to promote the common good.

Under Co-operation no act can an individual perform as a member of it, without the others associated with him participating in such benefit as may accrue therefrom, and no advantage that the whole corporation has gained from the collected actions of its members, but each will have secured to him his just share, which is equitably measured by his contribution to the general result. It takes men as they are, and by force of precept, constant exercise, and moral obligation it makes their selfish propensities (for it is natural to every man to possess selfish instincts) naturally work out the good of the whole. It takes from no one what he by past legal sanction possesses. It does not suddenly overthrow any existing institution. It, by a slow but sure process, dries up the channels, through which the streams of the results of past and present labour flow, to the enrichment of the few, but diffuses them among all who had a share in producing them. It is training, and thus qualifying, men to play their proper part as good citizens, to take an active interest and share in the management of the affairs of their locality—be it large or small—and from the experience they might thus gain to be able to wisely and prudently control the destinies of their nation, and impress their will on the world at large. Such are the possibilities that may reasonably be expected to naturally issue from the Co-operative method of working out the principle of Socialism.

When we consider the smallness numerically, and the status commercially of its originators, and compare its present position, its wondrous growth in fifty years in spite of its detractors and of its own shortcomings in management, we are filled with justifiable pride and gratitude. This growth is no imaginary thing, as you may be convinced by a careful scrutiny of the official returns by the Government. It has not grown without having to encounter much fierce and strenuous opposition. It has not grown without having to surmount great disasters. It may still have many imperfections, arising mostly from inexperience, which time will remove. But the fact remains, and can be denied by no one, that it has triumphantly succeeded in face of many other rival organisations professing to have the same object in view. So, I think, we may feel assured that the method of Co-operation is the best in the field, and that what it has achieved for the toiling masses goes to show that the principle of Socialism is a right, just, and beneficent principle, and that the Co-operative method is the right one to pursue to secure its general adoption. But the opposition to its further progress is not yet over, nor is it less strenuous. Traders do not like it because Co-operation has taken the commercial field upon which to work out its object. Yet Co-operation did not enter into direct competition with them, since it refused, and still refuses, to undersell them. Traders have more reason to complain of each other on that score, rather than of us. It may be that they are the more angry with us because they have seen we can do without them—by doing for ourselves what they were accustomed to do for us. They find they are no longer a necessity.

But the most strange obstacle to the further progress of Co-operation arises from the apathy and indifference to it displayed by working men themselves, and from various rival organisations by which they have formed. These organisations, such as the Social Democratic League, Social Democratic Federation, and others, profess loudly—no doubt sincerely—that their object is to bring about Socialism; but their impatience of evolution and their wild and incoherent declamation have done much to bring wide-spread contempt, ridicule, and discredit on the very principle of Socialism itself. From what I have heard their advocates say in our public streets, and from what I have read in the various pamphlets issued by them, I am not surprised that society is uneasy in regard to them. Their ideas seem to me subversive and destructive without any compensating advantage to be gained in the end. To me they are like Samson of old, who, in his blindness and strong rage, pulled down the pillars of the temple in which the moneyed enemies of his time and people were assembled, and thus destroyed the temple which rested upon them with all the lords in it and *himself*. So they would, in their blind mistaken way and in their rage of impatience, by unreasonable methods destroy the foundations upon which the great temple of society rests, and with one fell swoop scatter all the accumulations of the past, to which they, with all other members of society, are justly heirs, and which it is their common duty to increase and pass to their children, and appropriate to themselves whatever in the scramble that would follow might come to their hands.

It has been said by some of them that no man ought to receive higher wages than another—that all men should be paid alike the same wage, no matter what their capabilities. Would this be equitable? Would it be just to pay to the experienced, the skilful, the industrious workman no more than to the inexperienced, unskilful, and idle? Would this be reasonable Socialism? Who would be satisfied with such an arrangement? Would it be probable that the community would obtain the best service that each individual could offer? Co-operation declares "That every worker is justly entitled to receive that full amount of wages that would be a fair equivalent to the value of his work, AND his equitable share of the profits that accrued from his skill and industry. It may be that there are some co-operators who have not yet reached this ideal, but education and experience will enable them to see its righteousness. Acrimonious speeches on their failure to see as others see it—aimed more or less at particular individuals—will not hasten, but will delay the time when even this difference of vision will pass away.

Some say there should be no interest. Well, if money be lent for the purposes of trade or manufacture, by which the borrower may make a profit, has not the lender a right—a just claim to a share of that profit?

It has been said by some there should be no rent. Well, Co-operation makes it possible that no rent should be paid. It enables a man to buy his own house, and become his own landlord, and if he likes to conform to the old custom of receiving rent, he can do so easily. If he has two pockets, he has only to take his rent out of his own (tenant's) pocket, and transfer it to his own other (landlord's) pocket. So the difficulty about paying rent is easily disposed of. He need pay rent to no one but himself.

Others say it is wrong to make profit? As men are constituted there must be some inducement to enterprise. Will any one enter on any undertaking, be it large or small, without some prospect of advantage to be gained? What a stagnant world it would become if there were no stimulant for exertion other than an abstract sense of moral obligation, and yet Co-operation overcomes even this objection. For practically co-operative bodies do without profit, since they distribute all the net profits they make on an equitable basis among those who make it.

Now, I would ask these opponents of ours engaged in the same field of work, to consider this: Co-operation was devised by working men, is sustained by working men, exists only to promote the best interests of working men, and is governed solely and entirely by working men, chosen by working men themselves, and in the interests only and purely of working men. It proceeds on the line of least resistance, while they proceed on lines that provoke the most violent and stubborn resistance.

Thus thinking, I believe Co-operators have a fair and just claim to the active and earnest support of every worker, be he what he may. At the least, Co-operators have a right to expect that he who calls himself specifically a "Socialist" will avoid in his public utterances speaking against a method which has undeniably wrought so much good to the toiling masses; which has brought (and continues to bring) to their homes so many comforts they would never otherwise have had the opportunity to enjoy; which has done so much (and continues to do) to raise the social status, the moral, and even the political, influence of every worker; which is capable of making men good and useful members of the body politic; but the aim, scope, and possibilities of which they do not yet seem to understand, realise, or to appreciate.

May I, in conclusion, express your hope that they and all workers may soon see their way to come within the pale of Co-operation, and share in the glorious record of successful work that Co-operation has made, and give their powerful aid to its further progression and expansion. Then they will be able to proclaim with us, with all their fiery zeal and enthusiasm, to an unbelieving world of Individualists that Co-operation is reasonable Socialism.

WALTER T. CARTER.

20

THE CO-OPERATIVE MOVEMENT IN GREAT BRITAIN (LONDON: SWAN SONNENSCHEIN, 3RD EDN, 1895), 224–241.

Beatrice Webb

[Beatrice Webb (1858–1943) initially published her important study in 1891 under the maiden name of Potter. Having worked on Charles Booth's investigation of poverty in London, she was guided through late nineteenth century co-operative culture by leaders of the Co-operative Wholesale Society such as Ben Jones and J.T. W. Mitchell, whom she greatly admired for their business acumen even if she was sometimes disgusted by their eating habits. [See Beatrice Webb, *My Apprenticeship* (London: Longmans & Co., 1926)] Webb's reading of co-operation helped shape the influential Fabian socialist interpretation of co-operation developed in partnership with her husband Sidney over subsequent decades. [Royden Harrison, *The life and times of Sidney and Beatrice Webb: 1858–1905, the formative years* (Basingstoke: Macmillan, 2000)] She took the "federalist" side in the debate on producer co-operation within the movement, arguing that independent co-operative workshops would necessarily degenerate into small capitalist concerns and backing the CWS's version of consumer hegemony. However, unlike Jones and Mitchell, Webb believed that voluntary co-operation, even when driven forward by the CWS, would always remain severely limited and could not therefore bring about socialism more generally. For this to happen, the state had to play a leading role, run of course by bureaucratic experts' who would usher in an economy and society based on "collectivism". A number of co-operators (see the extract by Percy Redfern, Chapter 23 below) were prepared to go some way along this track, but most recoiled, committed as they were to maintaining the movement's independence and fearful of the dangers of state control.]

CONCLUSION.

I WILL assume, in the remarks with which I propose to end this slight sketch of the British Co-operative Movement, that we, like the early Co-operators, are socialists; that we accept, as the Ideal towards which we are tending, a state of society in which all citizens will serve the community with wholeheartedness, the community remunerating them, in return, according to the personal expenditure needful to the full and free use of their mental and physical faculties. Without this desire for, and faith in, a possible socialist state, these observations will appear uncalled for. I should therefore advise the student who desires only a matter-of-fact statement of past or present events, or the philosopher who is satisfied with society as it at present exists, to close the book, as the few remaining paragraphs will afford him no nutriment, and may even supply an irritant which will effectually prevent the comfortable digestion of the preceding narrative, and of the statistics contained in the Appendix.

Have we citizens of Great Britain then any certain ground for faith or even for hope that through the concurrent action of the Co-operative and trade union organization we shall attain Robert Owen's New System of Society; a state in which the earnings of all workers will represent efficient citizenship, while all citizens will render willing service according to their highest ability? The answer, I fear, is no longer doubtful. Even if Trade Unionists and Co-operators worked in unison, voluntary association, though an admirable training and convincing example, would be found wanting as a sole and all-sufficient method of social reform.

For the Co-operative movement, though a striking and imposing example of a complete solution of the administrative difficulties of an industrial democracy, forms at the present time an altogether insignificant part of the national industry. The total capital of the country is estimated at ten thousand millions. Only twelve millions of this is administered by voluntary associations of consumers. But the enthusiastic Co-operator will ask: why not develop the voluntary system of democratic Co-operation until it embraces the whole field of industry? It may be well, therefore, to inquire briefly into the probable social and economic limits to the further extension of this form of democratic self-government.

The first barrier to an indefinite extension of the Co-operative movement under the present social system are the conditions of life of certain classes. Men living below a certain standard of life, or in isolation, populations continually shifting their abode and changing their occupation, are incapable of voluntary association, whether as consumers or producers. The hand-to-mouth existence of the casual labourer, the physical inertia of the sweater's victim, the vagrant habits and irregular desires of the street hawker, and of the mongrel inhabitants of the common lodging-house—in short, the restlessness or mortal weariness arising from lack of nourishment, tempered by idleness, or intensified by physical exhaustion, do not permit the development, in the individual or the class, of the qualities of democratic association and democratic self-government. We need no demonstration of the truth of this fact; it is the burden of complaint at Trade Union and Co-operative Congresses. Thus, I imagine, it is no mere coincidence that Co-operative and trade union organizations flourish best in state-regulated trades, such as textile and mining industries; while the wage-earners of Birmingham and London, at work in their homes, or in workshops that escape regulation, are apparently incapable of association as consumers or producers. The labour history of the last fifty years tells us plainly that legislative regulation—the outcome of *compulsory association*—is the only effectual instrument for raising the condition of certain classes to the social plane upon which voluntary association becomes possible. But whether or not we admit that the absence of legislative restriction is the principle cause of this incompetency, it is indisputable that about four-fifths of the wage-earning class are outside the Co-operative and trade union movements.

Poverty and irregular habits form a lower limit to the growth of Co-operation. Fastidiousness and the indifference bred of luxury constitute a higher limit to the desire or capacity for democratic self-government. The upper and middle class, with incomes altogether out of proportion to their actual needs, demand the servility of the profit-making traders and the irregular and diversified production of profit-making manufacturers. The business-like despatch and quick answers of the Store official jar on the sensitive feelings of the great lady, accustomed to the silent subservience and immediate acquiescence of well-bred servants, paid to wait on her pleasure and convenience. The caprices of fashion, the vagaries of personal vanity and over-indulged appetites can find no satisfaction in an organization of industry based on the supply of rational and persistent wants. Moreover, the severe mental strain consequent on the conscientious expenditure of a large income, or the apathy of a mechanical satisfaction of every want disinclines the wealthy customer for the responsibilities of association. Physical nausea and mental exhaustion are the common ailments of the rich, as well as the complaints of the very poor: while the love of personal possessions, and the spirit of rivalry engendered by social ambition, effectually withdraw the surplus energies of the well-to-do classes from any form of democratic association. To bring, therefore, the great bulk of the middle and upper class expenditure within the jurisdiction of the Co-operative movement we should be forced to impose a graduated income-tax amounting to something like twenty shillings in the pound, on all incomes over £400 a year. Propaganda among the rich is as futile as propaganda among the very poor; if the Co-operators "mean business" with those classes of society, they must add certain items to their political programme the character of which there is no need to specify.

The social limits are not the only boundaries of the Co-operative State. The administrative limits are, if anything, more important. For the group of citizens who administer a Store or the Wholesale Society are necessarily the actual consumers of commodities or services supplied through those organizations. Now this special form of democracy does not always form a possible or desirable and administrative group. We cannot imagine the Calais and Dover Line of steamers being owned and managed by the actual passengers. If it were deemed desirable that the community should undertake this service, we should, follow the example of the Belgian Government in the service of the Ostend and Dover route, and the central government would provide a national line of steamers. Again, the most ardent Co-operator who aimed at the communal administration of railways, would hardly contend that the proper administrative group for the London and North Western was the passengers and traders who used it. All persons, whether or no they travel by rail, are indirectly interested in the means of transit as consumers or producers of articles upon which carriage is paid. Hence an important body of consumers would be disfranchised; while the difficulty of gathering together a genuinely and permanently representative body of the different classes of passengers and traders would render a steady and uniform administrative policy impossible. In the single instance of a consumer's organization undertaking the means or transit—the Liverpool Docks—the franchise has been limited to traders paying at least £10 annual dues, so as to form, from out of the casual and scattered constituency of customers, a responsible body of proprietors permanently interested in the good management of the docks. And even on the Mersey Docks Harbour Board the community at large is directly represented by four nominees of the government.

Hence in some of the largest and most important industries an open democracy of consumers forms an undesirable or impossible constituency for representative self-government. But this is by no means the most important administrative limit. In all cases of a national or artificial monopoly the actual consumer is an improper representative of the community. We could not, for instance, endow the farmers and agricultural labourers with the land of the nation; no body of proprietors which excluded any portion of the community would be a satisfactory constituency. If our mineral wealth were to be nationalized, the mines would not be handed over to the colliery proprietors or even to the coal miners. Moreover, when consumption is compulsory, association must also be compulsory. The provision of such articles of universal consumption as water, gas, roads, street-lights, must obviously be undertaken by a compulsory association of consumers, if we desire to maintain an industrial democracy. For instance, if the Sheffield Store had undertaken to raise the two and a half millions recently paid by that municipality for its water-works, it is obvious that the Sheffield Co-operative Society would have become a combination of capitalists making profit or suffering loss by a speculative supply of the wants of those Sheffield citizens who, through ignorance or indifference, remained outside the association. In other words, we should again have returned to the individualist system of industry, with its advantages and disadvantages—a form of society which we are not at present discussing.

And in this example of the Sheffield Store we touch on a financial as well as an administrative limit to the rapid growth of Co-operative compared to other forms of democratic enterprise. While a municipality, through the collective power of compulsory association, can raise millions every year by its assessment on the citizens, the Store accumulates capital at a snail's pace. Compare the 300 millions of property administered, according to Mr. Giffen, by municipalities in 1885 (gas-works alone standing at 21 millions) with the 12 millions of Co-operative capital. To sum up, therefore, these obvious limits to the Co-operative commonwealth, we may state that all the larger forms of national wealth, such as land, means of transit, and all commodities of compulsory consumption—gas, water, sanitary appliances, etc.—are excluded from the possible domain of voluntary associations of consumers.

But the statement of the boundaries of the Co-operative State is not yet complete. The whole national export trade is necessarily excluded. For here it is obvious that administration by an open democracy of actual consumers cannot even exist unless we await the miraculous conversion of the hordes of China and the savages of Africa to the doctrines of Robert Owen. It is, of course, conceivable that the Store system might be developed among other Anglo-Saxon nations with whom we trade, and that a relationship such as exists between the Scotch and English Wholesale Societies might be established in the corresponding central establishments of Australasia, Canada, America, and Great Britain. But other forms of socialism seem likely to obtain in Australasia; and the American people, intent on personal gain, show neither desire nor capacity for any form of government other than a nominal democracy ruled by a corrupt plutocracy. On the other hand, the British Stores and Wholesale Societies might frankly engage in a profitable export trade with the merchants of foreign countries; or they might export surplus manufacture, so as to obtain the increasing return from manufacturing on a large scale in those industries in which they are already engaged. But the danger to the integrity and prosperity of the Co-operative movement of this step is easily demonstrated. All the economic advantages of the control of production by the actual consumers are abandoned. Once again Co-operators taste the forbidden fruit of industry—profit on price. Supposing the profit from the export trade became a considerable portion of their total income, voluntary associations of consumers, able at any moment to limit their numbers, would be sorely tempted to close their doors to new-comers. Thus the Wholesale Societies might be transformed into profit-making machines of capitalist producers, and the habit of trading with non-members abroad might be rapidly extended into the custom of trading with non-members at home. With the quotation of the shares of the Stores and the Wholesale Societies on the Stock Exchange, rising and falling in value with the advent of a new directorate, or the rumour of a foreign war, the whole fabric of the Rochdale system might fall into disrepair, if not into hopeless ruin, by internal competition between societies, or combination among them against the interests of the whole community.

Thus, those of us who believe in the millennium of a fully developed industrial democracy, perceive in the national export trade the last resort of capitalist administration of industry. No mere voluntary association of Co-operators can undertake the export trade. Here again the only possible participation of democratic Co-operation would bring us rapidly back to the individualist system—profit on price for individual gain. Should these industries therefore eventually fall into the hands of the representatives of a democracy, they must obviously be administered by the public organization of the whole people—that is by the State or the municipality. For in this manner only can the profits, which will necessarily accrue from dealings with other States, be accumulated for the benefit, or distributed for the satisfaction of the whole body of citizens.

The limits of the probable domain of the Co-operative State are now all within sight. Voluntary associations of consumers are practically restricted to the provision of certain articles of personal use, the production of which is not necessarily a monopoly, the consumption of which is not absolutely compulsory, and for which the demand is large and constant. Under the present social system a restricted portion only of the nation is within reach of a social democracy—that intermediate class neither too poor nor too wealthy for democratic self-government. Let us attempt to reduce these limits to a statistical form in relation to the total income of the United Kingdom. I must however warn the reader that I offer with all reserve the following estimate, with the hypothetical figures upon which it is based. I use these figures as a convenient form of summing up certain arguments, and not as an accurate calculation of the present or future possibilities of the Co-operative movement.

Let us assume that Co-operators, although unwilling to reduce the incomes of the well-to-do classes by legislative measures, were determined to use their political power to level up the standard of life among the degraded classes to the plane of voluntary association. Assuming, moreover, that in this attempt they were successful, the Stores and dependent federal institutions might then hope to attract the whole expenditure of working-class income within their sphere. Of the 1,300 millions of national income, 500 millions, at most, is attributed by statisticians to the wage-earning class. From this let us deduct 100 millions for rent, gas and water rates, and taxes. The commodities or services which these charges represent, we have already shown to be outside any possible extension of the Co-operative system. Another seventy millions of working-class income is spent in alcohol; no Co-operator proposes to undertake the provision of spirits and beer to the Co-operative world. We have therefore a remainder of 300 to 350 millions. Hence this sum might represent the Co-operative trade. But it is needless to remind the reader that the income of the working class, and more especially that proportion of it which could be spent at the Store, is capable of almost indefinite increase. For instance, the "drink bill" would probably be reduced to a modest pittance if all working men developed the qualities of democratic self-government. And without any recourse to socialistic measures, the gross income of the working class might be considerably enlarged. But there is every reason to suppose that the same conditions of increased intelligence and sobriety among the workers would enable capitalists to obtain larger returns and landlords to exact higher rent. In other words, whatever might be the increase of the total wealth of the nation, the proportionate share of the workers in the national income would, other things being equal, remain the same.

The trade of the working-class Stores therefore might, even under the present social circumstances, increase from the present turnover of 35 millions to the 350 millions of working-class income spent in household provisions. Narrower limits are set to Co-operative manufacturing. A very small proportion of these commodities could be produced under the Co-operative system of industry. Imports of food and tobacco constitute the great bulk of the wage-earner's consumption. Of the remainder, we must subtract what is spent, not on new commodities, but on second-hand articles, which have already passed through the hands of the well-to-do classes, of which there is undoubtedly a large working-class consumption. And lastly we are face to face with the economic limit of the unit of productivity—I mean a sufficiently large demand for any one article to allow of profitable manufacture. For instance, the Wholesale Society has hitherto felt itself unable, in spite of the proximity of its chief centre to the great cotton industry, to undertake the manufacture of cotton cloth. The range of variety in calicoes and prints bought by the working class, render the quantity of any one quality or style demanded by Co-operators too small for profitable manufacture even by their central institution. This unit of productivity is the blank wall which Co-operators have already discerned as the practical barrier to democratic manufacturing. I need not, however, point out that this barrier to Co-operative manufacture would be pushed further and further by the extension of Co-operative trade.

To sum up this rough estimate, therefore, we can hardly conceive that the Co-operative turnover, under the present social conditions, could exceed 300 to 400 millions—a trade which would only admit of 75 millions of capital, should the present ratio between Co-operative capital and trade be maintained. As the working-class capital is estimated at the present time at 169 millions, we shall therefore always be face to face with the present difficulty of using the capital of the working class in the Stores and the Wholesale Societies.

Hence Co-operators are right in asserting that they will always have a superabundance of capital at their command for which the democratic school of Co-operators can find no employment. We may confidently predict therefore, that the individualist school of Co-operators, should I be mistaken in my view of the economic and administrative obstacles to the realization of their ideal of the self-governing workshop, and should they succeed in converting the British working class to their principles, would always have at their disposal a large margin of working-class capital. The custom of the wealthy, anxious to secure quality, and able to pay a good price for a good article, and stimulated to benevolent interest in individualist effort by fear of approaching socialism, might become the happy hunting ground of the self-governing workshop; while the whole export trade might be transferred to industrial partnerships, with their autocratic capitalist administration and profit-sharing wage-system. Thus the various forms of Co-operative enterprise need not compete. The individualist school of Co-operators, in fact, if they surmount purely economic obstacles, will find that their antagonists are the Trade Unions, and not the officials of the Stores or the directors of the Wholesale Societies.

I have refused to consider one limit to the administrative capacity of the Co-operative organization frequently described by the opponents of the democratic form of Co-operation—the centralized government of the Wholesale Societies. First, because I believe that the constitutional structure of these Federations is indefinitely elastic and adaptable. Secondly, because I imagine that the administration of some seventy-five millions of capital, and the organization of a trade of some 350 millions, though an arduous undertaking, is not beyond the capacity of the present Store system, even if the constitutions of their dependent Federations were to remain unchanged.

These then are the external boundaries to the possible domain of the voluntary associations of consumers. But there are also internal obstacles to the realization of the dream of the enthusiastic Co-operator—the absorption by a Co-operative community of the whole of the tribute now levied on the workers by those who "toil not, neither do they spin." A large portion of the income of the community is paid, not for personal services rendered to the nation, but to capitalists and landlords. Co-operators do not escape the payment of this tax. For, like the Owenite communities actually established, the members of the Store and the Wholesale Societies, surrounded by a competitive system of industry, cannot escape the tribute of rent and interest even within their own domain. Doubtless with regard to the interest on the twelve millions of Co-operative capital, it is credited to associates, that is to say, it is charged on the consumption of all members and paid to a minority of capitalist Co-operators. The rent of land, however, is usually, if not always, levied by an outsider, either in the form of technical rent or as interest on the capital expended in the purchase of the freehold. The Bury Store, for instance, cannot escape the tax of Lord Derby's rental; the fact that the Society may have acquired a freehold does not alter the position, since Lord Derby extracts from this community of workers the interest on the capital paid to him as purchase money. Hence the Co-operative system of industry has taken only one step forward in completing the work of the industrial revolution foreshadowed by Robert Owen. Through the open democracy of the Store it has exchanged an individualist for a social administration of industry, and thus secured the profits of enterprise for the community at large. This first step, however, is the most difficult. The democratic administration of industry involves the possession of active intellectual and moral qualities; whereas the inhabitants of hospitals and asylums are equal to the passive receipt of rent and interest. But the British Co-operative movement has left the ownership of land and the means of subsistence in the hands of individuals, whether within or without the Co-operative State. If the English democracy therefore wish to complete the social changes prophetically described in Robert Owen's New System of Society, if they are determined to add to the social production of wealth (brought about by the new industry) to the communal administration and control (introduced by the Co-operative and trade union movements) the communal ownership of land and the means of production, they must use deliberately the instruments forged by political democracy, taxation in all its forms on unearned wealth and surplus incomes, and compulsory acquisition, not necessarily without personal compensation, of those portions of the national wealth ripe for democratic administration. And we have ample precedent for class taxation, and personal compensation, as a method whereby the democracy may acquire or control the instruments of production. A Conservative government recently proposed to use the drink tax to buy out the publicans; a Radical government might suggest a land tax to buy out the landlords, and doubtless Mr. Ritchie, as Chancellor of the Exchequer in a future Conservative government, will impose a graduated Municipal Death Duty on real property, whereby the dwellings as well as the streets might gradually become the property of the corporation. But, like the details of a reformed Poor Law, these measures of relief to a class overburdened with property are without the scope of an essay on that form of democratic industry known as the Co-operative movement.

In conclusion, I would emphatically re-assert that the social, administrative and economic boundaries of the Co-operative State by no means limit the power of Co-operators in our national life. The gathering together of the whole working class in a Co-operative Union on the one hand, and in a Federation of Trade Unions on the other, would make the workers practically paramount in the State. The organization of workers as consumers would effectually prevent any attempt on the part of capitalists and landlords to bribe certain sections of the working class by the promise of high money wages to support a protectionist policy in its legislative form, import duties, or, in its economic form, trusts and capitalist combinations to raise prices. And if the officials of these twin Federations, representing the primeval interests of consumption and production, were to unite in solemn compact, then it would be comparatively easy to weed out of the community those who consume without producing, the parasites of all classes; while those who at present produce without consuming their full portion would be raised to a higher place in the national banquet. That this result cannot be accomplished without resort to legislation, the outcome of compulsory association, has, I think, been clearly demonstrated. But before we can have a fully developed democracy, the nation at large must possess those moral characteristics which have enabled Co-operators to introduce democratic self-government into a certain portion of the industry, commerce and finance of the nation. It is, therefore as moral reformers that Co-operators pre-eminently deserve the place in the vanguard of human progress. While completing and extending their domain to its furthermost limits, Co-operators should deliberately introduce their methods and experience into the administration of the parish, the municipality, the county and the State; thus fulfilling by the sure but slow process of democratic self-government Robert Owen's Co-operative system of industry.

Thus the two distinct bodies of social reformers created by the teaching of Robert Owen—British Co-operators and British Socialists, once again united by a common desire for industrial democracy under the banner of Radical Reform, may accept as a full and complete expression of their aims and methods the noble words of that great democrat John Bright:—"I believe that ignorance and suffering might be lessened to an incalculable extent, and that many an Eden, beauteous in flowers and rich in fruits, might be raised up in the waste wilderness which spreads before us. But no class can do that. The class which has hitherto ruled in this country has failed miserably. It revels in power and wealth, while at its feet, a terrible peril for its future, lies the multitude which it has neglected. If a class has failed, let us try the nation. That is our faith, that is our purpose, that is our cry—let us try the nation. This it is which has called together these countless numbers of the people to demand a change; and, as I think of it, and of these gatherings, sublime in their vastness and in their resolution, I think I see, as it was, above the hilltops of time, the glimmerings of the dawn of a better and nobler day for the country and the people that I love so well."

21

"TRADE UNIONISM AND CO-OPERATION", IN EDWARD CARPENTER (ED), *FORECASTS OF THE COMING CENTURY* (MANCHESTER: LABOUR PRESS, 1897), 31–36, 40.

Tom Mann

[Tom Mann (1856–1941) was born in Coventry, son of a bookkeeper and a domestic servant. He went down the pit aged ten and developed his love of learning through church schools. Joining the Battersea branch of the Social Democratic Federation when it was established in 1895, Mann espoused co-operation as passionately as he did socialism in an effort to bring about a rapprochement between them. He had a truly transnational conception of the struggle for socialism and a deep grasp of the necessity of mobilising workers in their roles as consumers as well as producers. [Neville Kirk, *Transnational Radicalism and the Connected Lives of Tom Mann and Robert Samuel Ross* (Liverpool: Liverpool University Press 2017)] This extract is from an essay he wrote for a collection published by the Labour Press, which also featured essays by figures such as Margaret McMillan and Edward Carpenter. In his contribution, Mann highlights the criticisms of co-operation commonly voiced by socialists, but also points out that "the pioneers of the Movement aimed at superseding the Capitalist system of industry, and replacing it by a scientifically organised system of Co-operation". Although co-operators he admits have had to work within the competitive system and adapt to some of its features, "many hundreds" still believe in "true Co-operation" and the movement is "gradually replacing Capitalist ownership and control by Democratic ownership and control". A particularly hopeful sign according to Mann are the producer co-operatives that demonstrate that workers can manage businesses successfully without the aid of capitalists, thereby undermining the latter's raison d'être. The extract shows that co-partnership could be interpreted as more than merely a capitalist ruse (Mann was a vice-president of the Labour Association), and it also demonstrates Mann's optimism, although his hopes for the emergence of a Socialist Co-operative movement within a year proved misplaced.]

Whilst the work of Trade Unionism proceeds in one direction and Socialist advocacy continues to gather strength, a large field is still left open for those who find satisfaction in voluntary Co-operative effort; and, as we may expect that certain industries although socialised will never be nationalised, but controlled entirely by the Municipalities, so it is quite possible that experience will show the desirability of socialisation in some directions without either nationalising or municipalising. The real essentials of industrial and social well-being are: That no section shall exercise a monopoly power against the rest of the community, and that all shall contribute of their energy to the common well-being in a manner approved of by the community at large.

Now, to take the Co-operative movement as we find it to-day, faults included, what is it? Some Socialists would say it is an institution claiming to be democratic but which is in reality essentially plutocratic, being based upon dividend and interest receiving, and in no material way differing from the ordinary capitalist system. I am not able to speak of it in such terms. I know, of course, that many are connected with the Distributive Store Movement for no higher reason than that of individual gain by the dividend on sales being returned to them, and that others use the movement as a savings bank where they get a higher interest than is possible with equal security elsewhere, and that these have probably never in their lives given one serious thought to the essentials of genuine co-operation. This does not alter the fact that the pioneers of the movement aimed at superceding the Capitalist system of industry, and replacing it by a scientifically organised system of Democratic Co-operation, and although the ideal has been for the most part lost sight of, it is the fact that to-day there are in the Co-operative movement many hundreds of highly intelligent men and women working for the true Co-operation, where shall exist no exploiters by interest, profit, or rent; and if we take the productive side of the movement, although it is still found necessary to recognise the interest-paying system, at least this can honestly be said, that by steady steps they are gradually replacing Capitalist ownership and control by Democratic ownership and control. Instead of relying upon the Capitalist organiser, they as workmen and women have developed the requisite capacity to entirely control the industrial establishments in which they work, and are gradually clearing out the Capitalist financiers. Whatever else may be said, it must be admitted that this is distinctly in the interests of the workers and determinedly opposed to Capitalism. In some 130 different productive establishments in this country, this Co-operative principle is being successfully carried out, and to my mind the time has arrived when the Socialists of this country should forthwith become closely identified with one form or other of Industrial Co-operation.

At present the vast majority of Socialists purchase their personal and household requirements from ordinary plutocratic anti-Socialist establishments. Not less than 3s. in the pound goes to maintain the opponents of Socialism, and if one half of this were diverted into a Socialist channel, to be used as a fund for propaganda or other work as might be agreed upon, we should no longer feel the pinch of poverty in the movement. And see how large a productive trade might be done under such a Socialist co-operative system. It would be a very moderate figure to estimate the Socialist families in this country at 100,000, whose weekly purchasing power might be put down at 25s. each, one half of which would be for commodities manufactured in this country. Certainly, there is nothing to prevent every article of clothing, all bread stuffs and other food, furniture and general utensils, all being produced under genuine co-operative conditions, which would not only finance the movement, but develop a Socialist market of ever-increasing proportions, concurrently displacing the capitalists.

The following extract is from a paper read at this year's Co-operative Congress, at Woolwich, by Mr. A. Williams:—

> Belgium has about 500 co-operative societies in all, of which by far the greater number appear to be consumers' societies. The statistics I have of thirty-two such societies give nearly 19,000 members, and sales of £91,000 a year. The Co-operative Pharmacy of Brussels, included in these, has alone a membership of 12,000, and its sales are nearly £12,000 a year. The most interesting societies are the large socialist bakeries, owned by immense co-operative societies of workers of every calling, which exist in all the principal industrial centres. These are admitted to be well managed, even by those who dislike their politics. Some of them have from 6,000 to 8,000 members: one in Brussels bakes 115,000 loaves a week, and makes a profit of nearly £10,000 a year. It has also a co-operative restaurant, an institution also known in Paris. The Socialist party look upon these societies chiefly as a means of organising and educating the working classes for political and economic emancipation, and of providing funds for their political warfare. They pay no interest on capital: a large part of the profits is devoted to propaganda, but a part is also paid to the consumers in the form of checks exchangeable for loaves. By their means the party has a press, buildings, and the means to fight elections and keep members in Parliament.

Another direction in which the productive co-operative societies have been of great service, in the Midlands especially, is by affording a haven of refuge to men who have been prominent in the labour movement and are boycotted by the capitalists. Over and over again have good men found jobs in one or other of these establishments when, had there been no such refuge, the labour movement in the district must have lost its advocate, and untold suffering would have been the lot of his family. The Trade Union organiser and Socialist agitator is driven oftentimes to starvation for lack of such a means of escape. The very knowledge of the existence of such places in sympathy with the advanced movement and the men identified therewith is in itself a check upon employers.

But, valuable as the movement is in these directions, these are after all only the incidental advantages; the real thing is that the workers themselves become entirely responsible for the control of the Industrial concern, become subjected to disciplinary rules framed by themselves alone, and so are relieved of the incubus of the capitalist exploiter, and give the lie direct to those who have argued that workmen must always rely upon someone outside their ranks to organise trade. Of course they are surrounded by the capitalists' system and conditions, and cannot enjoy the full effects of real co-operation; but every additional factory, workshop, or mill run on Co-operative lines makes it easier for the others to run successfully in the end, at any rate, if not immediately.

As we are agreed that the object aimed at by Socialists and by Co-operators is the Socialisation of Industry, need we be much concerned as to the particular means used to bring this Socialisation about? And whilst we work ardently through Municipal and Parliamentary Agencies, should we not be equally ready to work through Voluntary Agencies also? Already, boots and shoes, clothing of all kinds, furniture, crockery, and hardware, etc., are produced in different districts, and the productive societies are gradually federating themselves together to prevent overlapping, and to render mutual assistance. What is there to prevent the continued and relatively rapid growth of this movement? The chief element of success is a secure market; this can be provided in proportion as Socialists and Labour folk generally are willing to take the trouble to obtain supplies from Co-operative Sources; and as soon as experience shows it to be desirable for any given industry to be municipalised and nationalised, the fact that it is already virtually socialised by voluntary means will render the process a very easy one.

I expect to see Voluntary Co-operation develop on a large scale both distributive and productive, and I hope to see it so develop for the following reasons:—

1. Because it is one of the best means of enabling the workers to obtain the necessary industrial experience to enable them to entirely manage their own affairs.
2. Because in the war between Individualism and Socialism, many of the workers are victimised by the capitalist controllers of the factories, etc., and democratically controlled co-operative establishments affords a ready asylum to such without charity or patronage.
3. Because all work done under co-operative conditions means so much the less under the control of the plutocracy, and is, therefore, a distinct advance towards the complete Socialisation of industry...

The Co-operators, both Distributive and Productive sides, are certain to develop, and a Socialist Co-operative movement will exist in this country inside of twelve months with enormous possibillties. Exactly how the Trade Unionists may be brought into direct contact so as to become part of the Co-operative movement in its various phases is a question I need not attempt to speculate upon; but already in the productive Co-partnership movement the Trade Unionists are exercising a healthy influence. Politically, these same persons are being weaned from mere Liberalism and Toryism, and as they are, and are likely to be, upholders of Parliamentary action, to an ever-increasing extent, they will become supporters of the Socialist Party, which is certain to have a group of members in Parliament after next general election, and will probably gain several seats at bye-elections before the general comes on.

22

CO-OPERATIVE NEWS, 29 APRIL 1905, 493.

Philip Snowden

[Philip Snowden (1864–1937) was born into a family of weavers in the Yorkshire Pennines, working his way out and up by means of teaching and the civil service. He joined the Independent Labour Party soon after it was founded in Bradford in 1893, though his views remained rooted in the causes and culture of liberalism, including nonconformist religious belief, temperance and free trade. [Frank Trentmann, *Free trade nation: commerce, consumption, and civil society in modern Britain* (Oxford: Oxford University Press, 2009)] Snowden was elected Labour MP for Blackburn a year after he made the presidential address to the ILP conference held in Manchester, reproduced below from the co-operative press. In it, he discusses moves to create better understanding between the socialist and co-operative movements. He makes a plea for the continuing unification of "the forces of democracy" that has been successful regarding trade unionism, which has now renounced its earlier non-political stance. However, as yet the two other great working-class associations, namely the co-operative movement and the friendly societies, remain aloof, jealously guarding their independence. Snowden believes that it is vital to get them on side and convince them of the necessity of applying "the principles of co-operation through legislation". State action for Snowden is necessarily superior to voluntary, as it represents a "wider and more useful and more effective sphere". In a wildly optimistic flourish, he prophesises that before the next ILP conference is held in Manchester the co-operative movement and Labour will be allies. It is quite clear from Snowden's address who he thought would be the senior partner in an alliance that failed to materialise before the First World War. Despite his filiations with liberalism, highlighted within the recent historiography, it is important to note Snowden's belief in the superiority of statist methods of reform, a belief that sat uneasily with the majority of co-operators.]

To work in harmony with existing democratic working-class movements—to consolidate them into a powerful working-class political party—has been the object of the Independent Labour Party from its inception, and we can congratulate ourselves upon the fact that that object has been successfully, if not completely, realised. The great trade union movement has now renounced its anti-political attitude, and its members are to-day in alliance with the Independent Labour Party, equally convinced that the great problems of labour can be treated only by a labour party, and equally convinced that the independence of labour is the only way of unifying the forces of democracy, and equally determined that this independence must be zealously and jealously guarded. There still remain two other great working class movements outside the workers' political party, but the continued efforts of the Independent Labour Party and trade unions, aided by the great social and industrial forces and tendencies which are on our side, will, we are confident, soon induce the co-operative movement and the friendly societies movement to recognise their common purpose and common interest with ourselves, and thereby induce them to join with us as citizens in using the power of citizenship to apply the principles of co-operation through legislation to those problems which called the co-operative movement and the friendly societies movement into existence, but problems which are too great to be solved except by the power of an united democracy working through the State. We have never sought to compel the trade unions to accept our ideas. We have tried to convince, not to force. We have tried the logic of common-sense, and trusted to the educating influence of unfortunate experience. This, too, is our attitude towards the co-operators. And it is not too much to say that there are more promising indications within the co-operative movement to-day than were apparent in the trade union movement seven years ago. The membership of the co-operative movement is largely trade unionist. The trade-unionist co-operator cannot be a political trade unionist and anti-political co-operator. His trade unionism and his co-operation are two forms of expressing his belief in the one principle of associated effort, and his labour politics are the carrying of the application of the same principle into the wider and more useful and more effective sphere of State legislation. I read very wrongly the signs of the times if they do not indicate that long before the conference of the Independent Labour Party meets again in this city of Manchester, we shall have the co-operative movement in alliance with the political labour movement.

NO UNWORTHY MOTIVES.

May I, on behalf of the Independent Labour Party, modestly but honestly claim that in our efforts to bring the trade union and co-operative movements into the sphere of political activity, we have been actuated by no unworthy motives, nor by any desire to gain personal or party advantage, but solely by a genuine desire to promote the purposes for which these movements really exist. We have given, and are giving, to these movements more than these movements can give to us. We advocated the principles now accepted by trade unionists when the advocacy earned nothing but hard and unpopular work. We made the public sentiment for labour representation, and we made it easy for men who were then opposed to us, and who have done nothing to make the political labour movement to enjoy the fruits of our agitation. But we willingly forego any personal advantage if the cause gains by our personal sacrifice. There is one thing which the socialist sentiment and enthusiasm inside the trade union and co-operative movements has done which is little appreciated. I am inclined to think that it is the activity, the enthusiasm, the intelligence, the keen perception of tendencies and influences by the socialist trade unionists, as trade unionists, which have successfully kept the trade union movement intact, and effective during the last few years of trial and attack by which trade unionism has been beset. The socialist trade unionists have been the best trade unionists because they have been-socialists. And in the co-operative movement too—and I have seen much of the inside of the co-operative movement during the last few years—I find that the most active, the most useful, the most loyal, and in every sense the best co-operators are those whose adherence to the co-operative movement is based on their faith and knowledge of socialism.

23

"THE CONFLICT OF CAPITALISM AND DEMOCRACY", *CWS ANNUAL* (MANCHESTER: CWS, 1910), 191–192, 196–198, 201–218.

Percy Redfern

[Percy Redfern (1875-1958) was one of the co-operative movement's most important intellectuals in the first half of the twentieth century. Born the illegitimate son of a housekeeper in Leicester, at the age of fourteen Redfern began working as a draper's apprentice, which gave him first-hand knowledge of how consumers were exploited by private retailers. A convert to the "religion of socialism", he read Robert Blatchford's *Clarion* newspaper and joined the Social Democratic Federation in 1895, though switched to the Independent Labour Party the year after. In 1899, he took a clerical post with the CWS in Manchester, soon becoming editor of the CWS's monthly magazine, *Wheatsheaf* and contributing regularly to the co-operative press. In the substantial, perceptive essay from which the extract below is taken, Redfern argues that democracy and capitalism are increasingly becoming incompatible and seeks to correct the common misconception that regards communism as the only alternative, a system considered antithetical to personal liberty. Instead, he argues, society is heading towards "a sane and civilised Collectivism" and he tries to placate anxieties about this prospect. In a sweeping historical and sociological account, Redfern emphasises the anti-democratic ramifications of the growth of capitalist monopoly, finding support in J.A. Hobson's writings. Running through the piece is the urgent need for economic democracy as well as an extension of political and social democracy. For Redfern, the co-operative movement rather than more limited solutions such as profit-sharing or labour co-partnership ("inverted Capitalism"), is the key means by which economic democracy will be brought about. The role of female consumers is central in the transformation of capitalism, which "has unnaturally made production rather than consumption the thing of first importance". Many modern socialists, Redfern argues, have taken a similar line, prioritising the role of class and the interests of organised male labour instead of the interests of society as a whole. Navigating carefully though the overlapping discourses, he defines co-operation as "voluntary" or "pioneer" socialism, a "democratic force in the world of undemocratic Capitalism", and an important strand of a wider "Collectivism" powered by municipal and state intervention.]

THERE are many who will not readily admit any real conflict between Capitalism and Democracy. Capitalism, they would say, is the creator of property, and property is the guarantee of liberty. In America and in the freest countries of Europe the control of industry by the possessors of accumulated wealth exists side by side with modern democracy. In Britain, under the same system of government, private wealth has grown while popular liberties have been extended. According to this view, while social evils undoubtedly exist, they can be met without any interference with the present economic system. Already they are being abolished along the lines of that system. Savings of the people in hundreds of millions lie in the Post Office and other banks. Hundreds of thousands own their own houses; wages are higher; living is cheaper; never were the people better off. And defenders of Capitalism will finally claim that all the working-class movements, with their accumulated wealth, are proof that the present is an order of things equally beneficent to all who will avail themselves of its opportunities.

In the face of this cheerful, and sometimes sincere, optimism the man who persists in questioning the present virtual control of society by the rich and their friends may easily be represented as an envious, indolent, and disagreeable fellow. But the difficulty is, that when he is disposed of so many ugly signs of the times remain. The ever-glaring contrasts of rich and poor remain—to mock at human equality. Rising rents and rising prices press upon the people when they spend their money; unemployment outside the workshop, and the speeding-up of machinery and a severity of discipline within, add fear and anxiety to the original burden of Adam in the earning of a living. Among the smaller business men competition for profits is felt to have reached a demoralising intensity. The swift and ceaseless growth of armaments disquiets all classes. In brief, a hundred social ills, disturbing the consciousness of a people better taught and more closely associated, create a wide, vague sense of wrongs, together with a feeling that a radical change in the present relations of wealth and humanity would go far to alter them.

In the midst of this crude sentiment, definite advances have been made on behalf of the people by certain organised forces of Democracy. The political power which generations of earnest reformers have won for the people has been accepted on their behalf by the big slow-moving Trade Unions, who have realised the advantage of adding it to the power already exercised of industrial combination. Thus, the rule of the rich few not only in home politics but even in foreign affairs (two-thirds of which arise from the propagation of Capitalism in foreign parts), has been attacked in the name of Democracy. Both inside and outside this movement Socialists are active in giving definition and direction to the popular mind, being helped in this by many workers for a larger, fuller, more friendly, and more human world. There are religious people freeing themselves from hypocrisy, artists escaping from patronage, scientific workers demanding a nobler inspiration than the ideals of the battlefield and the market, teachers wanting a less sordid education, and women, especially, with faith in a womanhood free and self-reliant. Co-operators, for the time being, seeking "a policy worthy of our millions," are less definite; yet they, feeling themselves threatened by trusts and boycotts, realise a need of concentration and unity. And since it is so very clear that the vast majority of public-minded English people are of the same stock, and have the same general mind and character, the certainty grows of time bringing a wide democratic union in making the more human ideals at the heart of the people prevail over the tyrannies of wealth and power.

To every manifestation of such a movement Capitalism makes, and is likely to make, a strenuous resistance. Hence arises a conflict with Democracy, in which small issues, that began humbly in the workshop or with the private trader, inevitably widen until they include politics and all social affairs. For, underlying it all is the age-long struggle of class supremacy, with its pride and privileges, against equality, human rights, and the fraternal spirit.

The issue, however, would be simple were it not that the first ideal of the trinity—liberty—is claimed by Capitalism. The old cry was that any alternative to the present system meant Communism. Now, in intelligent circles, that appeal to prejudice is given up. It is too well understood that the actual alternative towards which the times are shaping is a sane and civilised Collectivism. But it is said—and many believe it—that a collective ownership of the sources of wealth would necessarily put an end to liberty and personal efficiency by setting over the individual, in the name of society, a bureaucratic tyranny. It may help to freshen our understanding of a confused situation if we briefly remind ourselves of some main outlines in its historical development...

So the business of making and of buying and selling goods, which once was a Cinderella amongst the activities of men, is now a princess. The last Military Empire passed away with the fall of Granada; Napoleon could not establish another. Tsars, Kings, Presidents, Statesmen, each acknowledge industrial power as the source of dominion. But the descendants of the fellows of her degradation, of the slave-mother, the slave-craftsman, and slave-peasant, the world's huge herded masses of consumers and producers, who give to industry her reason for being and her strength—these have no equal part in her triumph. Instead of the compromise of feudalism developing pacifically into a friendly and a just social order, there was a violent reaction. From a bitter war of old and new came anarchy, and out of that anarchy has come a class despotism, tempered only by a more recent political Democracy.

It is not denied that incalculable advantages have been won. A certain individual freedom has been established; so that no form of social control could now become permanent which did not include personal liberty. Under the mastery of the few, also, the wealth of the world has grown almost beyond measure. In England, even before the industrial revolution, the individualist efforts of landlords, navigators, merchants, and others had led in a long advance from the mediæval poverty of nations. In the early days of mechanical development, too, the rude ability of blunt, direct captains of industry was to be admired. They helped to break down shams, and to force men and States to accept for good some of the realities of nature; and it was they who created the tradition that Capitalism is really friendly to Democracy. And now that all forms of economic control are practically unified in the scientific, world-wide system of Capitalism, its production of wealth, notwithstanding the waste of it, is yet marvellously efficient. But at what cost to the many and to society has come into being this absolute power of the few over the economic forces of the world?

The rulers of capital are now mostly removed from the battlefield of competition. Usually interested in many different companies, a struggle which, for subordinates, is cruelly severe, resolves itself for such magnates into a kind of testing of departments, by which to gauge the comparative use to them of men and things. At the most it occasions a sporting excitement. So far from newcomers imperilling their position, chiefly they render monopoly more secure.

As with land so with capital in its narrower sense: generally speaking, the more that is brought into use the more valuable becomes that already employed. During the Budget discussions of 1909 the contrary has frequently been asserted; but, undeniably, the shortest routes for railways, the richest mines, the best raw materials, the goodwill of the wealthiest markets and buyers, the picked workers—cannot be multiplied indefinitely. Moreover, in modern finance these all reduce to the one thing—capital. As capital, it has one simple end—profit. The ratio of profit to capital has become the sole criterion of stock or share values. Thus from the economic reality of capital as the net human cost of machinery or preliminary labour, as from the moralities of capital, this "capital" of Capitalism is divorced. Reduced to this unnatural simplicity, capital, in the shape of the most profitable investments, is easily monopolised. Thus the day never comes when capital shall be so plentiful that the capitalist will loan it merely for security. On the contrary, the present low values of Consols and other gilt-edged securities chiefly show how much safer have become the more profitable investments elsewhere. So, while capital is concentrating in fewer hands its aggregate profit steadily increases.

The masters of capital are served by trained officers, drawn from the new great middle class of people with incomes from about £200 to £2,000 a year. Beginning with an education superior to that of the masses, and enjoying superior treatment, it is their business to take the capitalists' point of view, to keep up appearances, and to preserve distinctions.

Thus ruled and served, Capitalism scientifically exploits the world. Under their mastery, the peoples of the world are, as workers, continually selling labour in the cheapest market, and, as consumers, buying back in the dearest. Between the capitalists and the people it is always a game of "Heads, I win; tails, you lose." "A good supply of skilled labour," "a big market"—thus Capitalism describes the elements of its gains. But it is the people, organised in civilised society, child-bearing, child-rearing, mutually training themselves in moral habits, working together and spending together—it is they who create by far the greater part of those profits.

In Mr. Chiozza Money's figures, which still hold the field, we see the three classes roughly represented—one and a quarter million of rulers; three and three quarter million of officers and small capitalists, chiefly useful to feed the great; and a thirty-eight million remainder described by him as poor. We see that this majority has never any real surplus of income over necessary life-long expenditure; that the middle class has a moderate surplus; and that the few have always a huge surplus. This is the condition which, by its cumulative effect, has created, and will fortify, a real and (along capitalist lines) an unassailable monopoly of the world. Already, by working out the proportions of Mr. Money's figures, we can see that, while under pure adult suffrage the non-payers of income tax could outvote the million and a quarter rich by 63 to 1, the latter could outbuy the former in a proportion of 543 to 1. But these are for averages; and there are no figures to represent the economic inequality between millionaires and the unemployed. Such odds not only mock at economic and social Democracy, but to political Democracy they are a terrible menace.

Mr. J. A. Hobson, in his "Evolution of Capitalism," has exhibited some of the methods by which monopoly is secured. In America, for example, there has been actually an increase in the number of private businesses. But, on looking closer, the increase is in relatively minor industries, such as boot and shoe making. Behind this outer circle, small groups of millionaires and multimillionaires (chiefly through the industrial trusts, the railways, insurance, banking and finance) control the great essential economic powers—the things upon which all the small men depend. The effect of Capitalism is to create a private monopoly of the main springs that are fed by, and that feed, society, and to leave the possession of the surface wells to be scrambled for...

On the whole we may pronounce it a great gain to Democracy that this country, unlike America, has had a direct inheritance from the Middle Ages. Never here has so entirely prevailed the rule of "Each for himself and God for us all, as the elephant said when he danced among the chickens." Habits and traditions have remained, not necessarily democratic, in the narrower sense, yet acting in restraint of avarice for the common good. Wherever generation after generation has been continuously taught in the name of "the Church," "the State," "the Service," "the Profession," or "the School," to put the honour of a corporate body before individual aggrandisement, the ground has been not only cultivated for its own time, but prepared for future and wider social obligations. To such an inbred sense of honour Carlyle and Ruskin appealed against the Plugsons and the Gradgrinds; and it gave support to Shaftesbury, Oastler, and Sadler in their pure, unselfish work for those little members of society in the factories and mines, upon whom the newer burdens of Capitalism had fallen so crushingly.

But ancient virtue would have been of little avail unquickened by the new spirit of modern political Democracy. While the industrial revolution broke up home industry, it also destroyed for men that isolation of the home worker which still handicaps the political and social advancement of women. A people gathered in the close association of factories and towns who already were being educated for Democracy. The great religious revivals issuing in Sunday and night schools had begun the work; the temperance movement and a militant free press were soon to help; and the Free-thinking party had always a stimulating influence; for the people is a sea that receives many rivers. The Reform Act of 1832 and the Municipal Corporations Act of 1835 limited actual power to the middle class, but could not limit the sense of it; and the franchise was obliged to "broaden down." Democracy speedily proved its human sympathies. To the very followers of liberty Shaftesbury was able successfully to appeal against the official capitalistic leaders of individual freedom. Disraeli's idea of "Tory Democracy" sought to exploit the virtues of such a combination, and Tariff Reformers follow in his footsteps; but what is fine in the anciently descended sense of social solidarity is not to be confined to any party or section. Rather must it be acknowledged as diffused through the nation, influencing totally different persons temporarily to combine with popular forces in furthering, say, social legislation and municipal socialism or in preserving a frank and just public opinion.

But the people have been trained for efforts more direct than those of merely supporting even their best friends. Moreover the industrial revolution forced them to deal with a situation the reverse of that created politically. As citizens they were gaining individual liberty; as workers they were losing it. When one man could at the most employ no more than twenty, no one could become an industrial despot. But the larger and more complex organisation demanded by steam power gave to employers and their agents an arbitrary rule over hundreds. And, while capitalists talked of liberty, gradually there came about the present situation—the tools (machines) divorced from the workers and held by a small rich minority; the many, under a menace of poverty, forced to subject themselves to the owners of tools. This industrial system is, of course, no more democratic than is the political system of Russia; and in its own way it lends itself to precisely similar evils.

From these new circumstances a few of the more clever workers escaped by abandoning their fellows and climbing the ladder of success. They became factory lords, squires, members of the old nobility. At the other extreme men clung to the old system, going so far as to riot against and smash the hated new machinery. The majority, with the usual mutual fidelity and wisdom of natural and permanent majorities, took neither course. They united for mutual defence. Trade unions arose—the first combination of their kind since the suppression of the mediæval guilds and (since they preceded the Factory Acts and the borough incorporations) the first real popular check since the Middle Ages to the triumphant progress of individualism.

Yet for many decades the new force was to remain limited, each union strictly confined to its own trade affairs. Nor was the time ripe for other action. The tyranny of the laws against combination, together with the political indifference resulting from votelessness, made entire freedom from State action the only need; while a generation later the agitation for the repeal of the Corn Laws, overshadowing

Chartism, helped to keep the unionists politically individualists. Only at long last, in our own days, has it been perceived that as the individual is bound up with his class so his class is bound up with the collective actions of the political community. Circumstance rather than logic has taught this, has led the trade unionist to add to industrial combination the power of political union, and thus has brought an independent, and therefore genuine, Labour Party into Parliament.

Under Capitalism the few have gained possession of the means of life of the many, and in trade unions the more advanced of the many have combined to defend their livelihood and their freedom. The Labour Party in Parliament has lifted the issue to a broader level. Where labour opposed the capitalist as an employer only, now he is also faced in his character of social and political magnate; and where an artisan cared only for his own trade, now his organised strength and leadership is appealed to by the poor and oppressed almost the world over. Thus the labour movement is conceived as a whole; and from that point of view some old friends turn out to be new foes, and others, previously under prejudice, are proved to be inspiring friends. It is said that the Socialists have captured the trade unions; but this is a foolish and panic-stricken cry. Neither Socialism, nor the labour movement, nor the Capitalism which both oppose is private property. Each arises from human nature as it is, acting under historical influences, in changing circumstances. The rise of industrial power has given the old oligarchy a new opportunity to assert itself and prevent democracy in industry while circumscribing it in political and social life. The Socialists have urged upon the notice of organised labour a situation which they did not create, and labour has accepted the demands of circumstance. This wing of the democratic host, reviewing its political power, has sought to use that as a lever for raising the working class to industrial liberty. There is no dreaming about Utopia, but rather a slow perception of the actual—a solid concentration upon it.

Hence we have the Labour Party in Parliament setting itself to assert Democracy against Capitalism wherever with its own eyes it unmistakably sees an issue. Thus it has broken new ground with criticism of the old undemocratic secret control of foreign affairs. It has tried to keep politicians firm upon the principle of socialising wealth that society has obviously created. So far from being revolutionary in spirit, it has attended to legislative detail in perhaps too workaday a spirit. Yet where, by instinct and experience, it has felt the need it has proclaimed a revolutionary principle in the "right to work." That right is a human palliative for human misery, and yet is something more. For unemployment, the worst of labour's ills, is also a main prop to Capitalism. It means for the employer an eager supply of labour whenever required, with freedom to select the more efficient, and a power to enforce discipline. But for labour it involves a struggle for place and wages which sets man against man and is therefore demoralising and abhorrent, and at the end of that struggle a compliance degrading, because enforced by fear. So, while the right to work embodies labour's hope of secure livelihood and freedom, to the capitalist it is already Socialism. And the latter does not grossly exaggerate. Go on to socialise all unearned increment, equally from capital as from land, take the worst fear out of the threat of dismissal, continue the developments toward industrial courts, oblige the workshops to be co-ordinated with the nation's schools, secure a minimum wage—and the employer becomes half a State official, while labour, through its voting power, begins to gain that control over its tools which it has lost individually. Bureaucracy might temporarily ensue, but with a people socially enfranchised the human spirit would not long be subdued.

No Socialist Party has captured the trade unions, for the latter have obviously kept to the lines of their natural development. Socialists or no Socialists. What is more to the point is that the labour movement has certainly deflected active Socialism. Great as the labour movement is, it stands mainly for the interests of but a section of society. But that happens to be, amongst the socially unenfranchised, the most advanced section. Consumers suffer also by Capitalism, but whereas the selling of labour is chiefly a man's concern, the buying of goods is mainly a woman's affair. Hence, by an unconscious natural bias the whole weight of the man's superior advancement has gone to increase the importance of the purely labour question. Again, Capitalism, being itself an unnatural system, has unnaturally made production rather than consumption the thing of first importance. And however paradoxical it may seem, Marx and other Socialists (less penetrating than Ruskin), in studying Capitalism, were not Socialist enough to get outside this point of view. They reduced the whole issue to a conflict—a class war—between capital and *labour*, and urged the *workers* to use their political power in transferring capital to a revolutionised society, in order that the conflict might end in all being workers—all collectively owning capital, and all receiving all wealth as the full product of their associated labour. This view is still vigorously propagated as Socialism. But it is so crude a Socialism as to be hardly Socialism at all. It is a mere half-way house between that and the inverted Capitalism of Labour Copartnership.

It is true that the meaning of the word "labour" can be widened to include every kind of human activity. William Morris based all his idealisations on such a view, using the word symbolically—poetically translating it. But in the blunt, busy world this meaning has no currency. "Labour," there, stands definitely for the mass of wage-earners. As the champion of labour, Socialism is, therefore, understood more as a scheme for workers as workers than an ideal for all as human beings. Naturally this intensifies Socialist difficulties with the middle class, whose support is almost solidly given to Capitalism; yet were the latter to become persuaded that "labour" includes organising and directing ability, the objection would still remain. Socialism, narrowly conceived in the interests of producers, practically in the interests of the most highly organised trades, may easily develop undemocratically. Men being what they are—all of us subject to a bias towards our own interests—it is no slight on any body of workers to say that it would mean those trades as a whole—managers and men united—tending (by protective tariffs, statutory wages, fixed prices, and so on) to safeguard their own welfare at the expense of all, and of the community as a whole. If we are to accept

Mr. St. Ledger's recently published study "Australian Socialism," something like it has already occurred on the other side of the globe. Something like it may easily happen here, unless the backward forces of the people exert themselves to secure that the Socialism already shaping itself shall not be a mere truce of capital and organised labour paid for by all, but a true gain to full Democracy.

Perfect Socialism, we have said, is pure Democracy, and, so far as the spirit and ethical faith of Socialism is concerned, this is true. In this sense it fulfils Democracy, for it declares not only the equal human worth of all the individuals naturally forming a community, but also the natural co-relation of those individuals as members, each and all, of an organic society. All the people of a natural local area form a local brotherhood; of a country, a national brotherhood; of the world, a human brotherhood; and these are organic, the life of one supplementing the life of another in a whole that is more than its parts. Social development, as we have it, is more or less a blind struggle (enforced by nature) to arrive at that right ethical relationship. In our industrial society, Capitalism—the vested interest of a rich class in the means of life—is blocking progress. Socialism would, therefore, have society abolish or buy out this interest, itself become the capitalist, make the organiser of industry its servant like any other, and secure that the elementary needs of every human life born into the world shall be a first charge upon the social estate.

In this view it is society which is opposed to Capitalism. It is society, and not labour pure and simple, which should own the means of production, for these are necessary to all—men, women, and children—and not merely to those who, as servants, actually use economic machinery. It is society (embracing the countless social forces that have brought a measure of social security, stability, peace, goodwill, economic character, and social morality) which is the prime creator of wealth, and not "the workers" any more than the capitalist. This is obvious. Yet, if we consider the conflict as purely between capital and labour we fail to recognise this fact, and society does not get its due.

The democratic interest is to have a co-operation of all democratic forces in attaining this more highly developed social existence. For Democracy also teaches that none can give to a man what he will not seek for himself. If B has not come forward he cannot, after all, complain that A has an unfair share of the advantages of being in the field. Unless B does advance, no unselfish social action on the part of A can entirely make up his deficiency. The moral is, not to attack A, but to urge forward B, C, D, and E, that each may equally have his part in a social organisation healthy and fair for all. Hence, the true democrat, convinced that the conflict with Capitalism is a social conflict, preceding and accompanying a wide social reconstruction, must heartily desire the advance, not only of labour, but of every backward human interest. He will want to see the consumer take his place. He will encourage women—one-half of adult humanity, and natural custodians of the children, who are a majority of all humanity—to become alert concerning their own and the children's interests in social politics. He will know that religion, science, literature, art must be active in social life if it is to be wholesome. Indeed, unless religion, with art for a handmaid, so influences the minds and hearts of the citizens as to keep them reverent of some deep and true realities, the spirit which has carried us so far is likely to die out of the most highly organised state, for society, no more than the individual, can live to itself.

Would not society, so developed, become, as a bureaucracy, equally as tyrannous as Capitalism? From Tolstoy to Lord Rosebery, there are those of many different motives who are ready to prophesy it. And if social reconstruction be left either to doctrinaires—men of one idea—or to officials, experts, and specialists, there is likely to be that danger. Yet the way to avoid it is not to block progress toward an intelligent social system, but to rouse and educate the whole people. If this, the essential part of democratic reform, is not done we may indeed exchange one tyranny for another probably not so bad. In the pressure of the problem of poverty there is driving force sufficient to effect that. Meanwhile let us remember that, despite fearful references to "huge centralised monopolies," there is nothing necessarily tyrannous in a well-organised society. Our very earth itself is a unit in a solar system—exclusive, huge, centralised! Centralisation as an end in itself, pursued by central authorities for their own sakes, is another matter. Social power concentrated in a few hands would simply mean, under another form, a perpetuation of the present state. This grave danger already threatens. It will probably dog every step in social change. Yet, again, the remedy for it is not less Socialism but more Democracy. Let us have a whole people healthily alive to their human rights, and, granted an equal constructive spirit, there will arise a social order—flexible, richly complex—just to majorities, giving room to minorities, providing for men's bodies, yet yielding space for their souls.

The problem of social justice is sufficiently difficult to-day, but seventy years ago it was bewildering. Then the mariners saw ahead of them a confusion of currents, but no land; now the shores of a new world begin to exhibit some trustworthy outlines. In these years Democracy has found a plan of action; social legislation has more than begun; and the great municipalities—those true States within the State—have commenced their object-lesson.

There were strong men in those days; it may easily be doubted if the present generation has the same robust independence. But the strength was for repealing old laws, for freeing the press, for defying bad taxes, for breaking idols, for getting breathing space rather than for building. In constructive effort men seemed to go no further than the first lesson in unity and solidarity—association. Hence, experiments in associated effort were legion. The action might be of any kind, in any direction, provided that it involved association. A thousand such movements ended in nothing; but one success, recompensing for all failures, has come down to us in Co-operation.

Yet this very success has had an obscuring effect. It has perpetuated this habit of seventy years ago, of respecting the means regardless of its end. We need, therefore, boldly to question the word.

Taking it as commonly used in England, it covers, mainly, three different ideas. One is of co-operation by workers in the production of wealth for their own profit.

A second idea is of a community aiming at being economically sufficient to itself, a "State within the State," growing until it is the State. The third is of consumers, especially working-class consumers, reserving to themselves, against Capitalism, the economic value of associated buying. The man with money to spend has a power in his hands, and (in this conception) that power is to be used democratically, for the collective good, indefinitely. Inspiring all three ideas there are similar feelings of social injustice, the same moral faith in mutual effort, similar hopes of a better era. Hence, Co-operation stands for a certain community of character and desire, differences notwithstanding. But, in relation to the conflict before us, these variations in conception are of such unequal value that ultimately they must lead to wide divergences.

The first idea of Co-operative production by workers for workers has gained strength from the same causes as those which have given to the labour movement its prominence. It appeals to the special interest of the most advanced in Democracy. Even the Co-operative Store member, though he may hunger for dividend, is more occupied in mind with the cause of the worker. Moreover, the dominance of the capitalist notion that the royal road to wealth is through production for profit, first and last, has affected others than capitalists. Even Carlyle taught that work (though the product thereof were "but the pitifullest infinitesimal fraction of a product") was the first virtue. It is easy to understand the faith of the Christian Socialists of 1850 in self-governing workshops, and all the further efforts resulting in the modified movement of Labour Copartnership.

Yet this is surely the wrong way forward. We work to live, not live to work. We dig to eat, and think to know; and these are wholesome processes; but, could we have infinite food and all knowledge, none of us would make that continuous concentrated effort which is labour, whether of thinking or digging. Only under the artificial conditions of Capitalism does it seem good merely to "find employment." In a natural society it would be clearly wrong to set men working unnecessarily. These, of course, are truisms; but they lead to a less well-perceived truism, that production is naturally secondary to consumption. Capitalism has reversed this order. It has produced, and, relatively, overproduced. If we are to oppose Capitalism upon its own competitive ground we must begin with the consumer.

The proof of the theory is in the practice. What, therefore, is the actual case in regard to workers' independent productive societies? In the first place, they show no uniform development. In England, as in America, bootmaking is a favourite industry for small capitalists, and the same may be said of printing. Hence, in each of these trades a dozen societies spring up, while in other domestic industries, even more important, not one appears. Competition naturally results. Each society seeks to draw strength from the organised consumers; but, with the best of will, it is in the nature of the case impossible for any one or all of them, in return, either to widen and deepen, or unify and consolidate the consumers' national movement. The very dividends paid to consumers, if one varies from another, become competitive. On the other hand, such societies are powerless to advance Democracy one step toward controlling the great industries—steel smelting, machine making, producing leather or other raw materials. They become, therefore, so many separate agents for the great capitalists—the masters of land, minerals, transport, finance, and so on. Hence, while they may have real virtues of a local kind, especially in comparison with private firms possibly supplanted, in regard to any march against Capitalism each forms a *cul-de-sac*.

It is similar with profit-sharing. To the individual capitalist, who considers profit as wholly the reward of ability, profit-sharing is a possible idea. Copartnership (with labour as a strictly junior partner) may have money in it. A shilling or so extra reward may lure to his service more efficient workers (enabling him to discharge others less valuable), and create a general keenness most advantageous to himself. But, from the point of view of social justice, profit-sharing appears in a different light. How apply the principle justly to the profits of railways, varying not according to any difference in the efficiency of their respective servants, but with the natural advantages which each either misses or enjoys? How distribute a fair percentage of "profit" to navvies making roads, waterworks, docks, canals? What belongs properly to postmen of the large gain that comes to the Post Office through its conservative charges? If it is unfair that the insurance companies should reap the whole advantage of a death-rate reduced by common civilisation, would it be a remedy to give a bonus to insurance clerks? Would justice be done by giving in part the monopoly value of liquor licences to barmaids? What share of what special profits is to reward soldiers, policemen, firemen, civil servants, teachers? If a duke gave a rebate on ground-rent to business men tenanting his land it would act as a grant-in-aid, enabling them to compete more keenly. But, on the other hand, would it help matters if ducal gains were shared with gamekeepers? No, there is only one just and democratic appropriation of profits, which is neither by the capitalist, as at present, nor by individual workers, but by democratic society, on behalf of every man and woman and child born thereunto. So far from approximating to that, individualist profit-sharing leads directly away from it.

With the second of the three conceptions of Co-operation we must deal all too briefly. Let us merely notice, therefore, that, although it has the honour of being the ideal of the Pioneers, it was, again, a special product of the special conditions of their time. The people, unenfranchised, bewildered by the individualist philosophers whom Capitalism encouraged, hardly could have any synthetic idea of society as a whole. Hence the Owenite communities—attempts to form artificial societies against the big and (temporarily) capitalistic society. But of all tyrannies that of small communities of self-righteous sects is the worst. The communities dissolved. Their mantle fell upon the early Co-operators. But it was now re-fashioned. The community was to grow unostentatiously within the common human society, yet was to have its own aims, habits, and practices.

There are still prominent Co-operators who, while seeing it to be flattery to call the present movement a "State," still think that to become so distinct a body is the true ideal. The common Co-operative experience, however, is that the ideal remains hopelessly unrealised. Yet that may not be wholly the fault of much-abused performance. It is possible that the latter is more in line with truth than is the theory.

Where can we find a distinct line of cleavage between Co-operators and all other people? What is there to create the close bond required for a community? Maurice, Mazzini, Ruskin, Tolstoy and many another has sought to recall Christian religion to the common people and to its social aims, and the movement is of vital interest to Co-operators; but that interest is shared by all Democracy the world over. The economic and social education of the people goes on outside the Co-operative movement as within it. Neither the idea, the ethic, nor the method of co-operation is peculiar to the special movement. As with Socialism, there is no private property—it all belongs to the world.

These co-operative developments in society around, outside, and above the Co-operative movement are leading to Collectivism. A special claim is therefore made for Co-operation that it is voluntary Socialism. In the sense that consumers' Co-operation is a pioneer Socialism, this distinction certainly holds. But it gives no ground for an isolated movement in practical rivalry with public action. Instead it places Co-operators in the position of volunteers undertaking a special effort, yet belonging to, and being supported by, a regular army. Underlying the free movement are the compulsory restraints imposed by national law. Not only would it fare ill without them, but, were Co-operation to become universal, it would, in the nature of the case, itself become a "monopoly," and compulsory. Again, this prejudice in favour of Co-operative separateness is too highly coloured. As a citizen, in relation to municipal undertakings, a man is only theoretically less free than as a Co-operator. Though he be a municipal employee he is not compelled to ride on the municipal cars, as he is not compelled to buy at a Co-operative Store. A municipal service may, indeed, preclude capitalistic tramways, but that is in the nature of the case. A municipal milk supply does not exclude private dealers. Further, if any municipal undertaking steadily involves public loss the ratepayers soon vote its cessation. In short, whatever one may think of philosophical anarchism, that creed is not so embodied in Co-operation as to make it an entirely unique and independent movement.

On the other hand, if municipal trading were to be forced into that unnatural position, it would prove an awkward rival. In all activities, according to the "Municipal Year Book" for 1909, the cities and county boroughs of these islands (exclusive of parish, district, and county councils) employ, presumably under good conditions, a quarter of a million people, against the Co-operative hundred thousand. Again, the official return of the total productions of the Co-operative movement for the year 1908 gave the figures at nearly £19,000,000. For revenues from municipal trading during the same period the figures, with Ireland excluded, are nearly £32,000,000. The one department of municipal tramways is employing capital to the amount of £45,000,000, with £9,000,000 gross receipts yearly. Moreover, municipalities extend their activities almost daily. There is no reason to object to this. Municipal trading, albeit the control of it is allowed to lapse into the hands of capitalists who happen to be more public spirited than Capitalism, is simply Co-operation writ large.

Reasons from facts, however, as well as from principles ought to prevent any rivalry between municipalisation and Co-operation. The ground that both have occupied is much too small to quarrel over. Pending the results of the present census of production, the total home trade, as apart from export trade, of the United Kingdom has been estimated at well over four thousand millions. Beside this huge sum either Co-operative or civic millions dwindle to odd figures. This fact, made more formidable by reflection in the streets of any large city, creates a difficult question for the advocate of Co-operative self-sufficiency. At what date, by single-handed combat with Capitalism, may it expect to gain the whole field? But we will leave this riddle and pass on to glance at a matter of detail which is a special problem in the movement. Congresses, acting according to the ideal of a movement complete in itself, declare the undeniable elementary justice of a minimum wage. Immediately the workaday realities create a dilemma. No member of a Co-operative Society is bound to purchase at the Store. So, in face of a huge well-directed Capitalism, paying low wages to what it would call "low-grade labour," and afterwards taking advantage of those low wages to tempt the consumer with unnaturally cheap goods, for serious productive works to pay an uncompromising minimum wage to all their workers would be something like a luxury. Again, Co-operation stands in precisely the same position in regard to the crucial problem of unemployment. Either the stores and factories must discharge workers at the special time when distress is most keen or risk their profits and dividends and, therefore, their custom just at this same season of common need. So the very voluntaryism of Co-operation thus declares itself inadequate, requiring State and municipal action to supplement it. To avoid this conclusion, sometimes it is suggested that there ought to be a Co-operative test—a kind of moral and intellectual tariff—imposed on candidates for membership, and that would be the logical outcome of the idea of a special community. But to raise such a barrier to the movement would at once destroy its real glory of democratic openness.

The alternative is to cease to be a people apart. It is to take a far greater place as a very necessary army of the one democratic host. For that would be the true place, than which there can be none better. Go in succession to a dozen Co-operative meetings, Trades Council meetings, popular Socialist meetings, workers' educational or similar classes, adult schools, brotherhood or other popular religious gatherings, and the reality will become manifest. These are varying sections—this one is in temper conservative, that one radical; but it is one people at heart, having one social cause. Nor is Co-operation a rival to the Socialist, the labour or any democratically religious, ethical, or educational movement. Its work is more truly co-operative—to supplement, to add to the instruments in the hands of the people. Let it, therefore, itself co-operate, and it will find in association a glorious work, in doing within its limits what no other movement can so well do; in teaching the people what no other movement can so well teach.

The previous pages will have been written in vain if they have not simplified the remaining task, and made it more easy to see in the third idea of Co-operation—that of a combination of consumers—a true line of democratic advance.

With the Rochdale Pioneers the returning of profits to the purchaser was something of a detail—a chance discovery in the pursuit of an ideal. A concentration upon that point would have seemed sordid. Certainly, it would be ignoble to make the manner of distributing profit the supreme question. Nowadays, the very word belongs, economically, to Capitalism. The huge value of the Pioneers' discovery lay in its gradually leading (by an open road of which the dullest could not fail to see the use) entirely out of the capitalistic circle of ideas.

In praise of the ordered march that so many have made along that highway there is no need to speak here. Workers for the people, all the world over, have combined to do it honour. It has gained admiration even from those whose vested interests have stood to lose by the migration. When appreciation is so wide and so sincere, it stands as a testimony not to be bettered. The present task is to review in regard to the issue the national organisation of consumers thus brought about.

The Labour movement took root as an instinctive rather than a logical challenge to Capitalism. It disregarded the platitudes of commercial success because of immediate needs, regardless of all distant goals. The complementary movement of Co-operation was not dissimilar. The people needed no telling that they received too little for their labour; and equally they knew themselves as unable to buy enough with their wages. Tools had been reft from the people; so, too, they had lost their barns and storechests. They organised according to the method of the Pioneers just to widen the vent through which, under Capitalism, the stream of necessaries trickled down to them. Only along the way has it been at all perceived that the united action of consumers leads directly to a larger future than the Pioneers themselves dreamt of.

For the movement to become large was an extraordinarily simple matter. Everybody buys. The more who buy in common the more economical it is, and the greater the saving. So the movement naturally widened. At the same time, equally naturally, it deepened. Whatever the attraction, the people had begun to control their own spending power, their own "effective demand," instead of handing it over to Capitalism as an Eskimo woman barters costly furs for a single sewing needle. Retail Societies became plainly a mere first step. Clearly, the next was for the retailers to constitute themselves a Wholesale Society. Plainly, this led to following the united stream of purchasing power back to the factory and the workshop. Yet, in modern industry, immediate productive works are not the ultimate sources. Hence this path of organised Democracy still leads direct to the further goal. For whether under Capitalism or Co-operation, demand, backed by money, does make its way to ultimate supply, and naturally carries with it a power of control.

The tendency of Capitalism is always toward reducing human affairs to a cut-and-dried business, severely subordinate to the one idea of profit. The contrary tendency of Democracy is to educate and humanise. Hence the consumers' movement could not be restricted to collective buying. The whole nature of the situation into which it entered and the needs of the class from whom it sprang demanded more. The many are subject to the few, not only through poverty, but by reason also of ignorance and mutual ill-will. So this consumers' movement, therefore, must organise some mutual education for its members, to introduce them to a larger and more social life. The economic gains naturally accruing to it provide the material means which, properly used, are invested rather than spent.

The State has, as yet, no women citizens. Greatly as the workers' wives are interested in their husbands' earnings, the business of the Trade Union, of the Trades Council, or of the Labour Party, is not directly theirs. Yet, notwithstanding the increasing number of women employed in factories and shops, the working housewives of the country are, and will be, legion. As consumers and buyers for yet more consumers they are not to be ignored. Thus arises a direct appeal to this huge neglected reserve of Democracy. The consumers' movement, however, cannot afford simply to reward with dividend the woman with the basket. It must educate her, also, as a buyer, a democrat, and a citizen. It must take part in one of the most urgent and beneficent of possible revolutions—the extension of that great name "the people," until the noun stands, as it ought to stand in all public affairs, for the women just as much as for the men.

Thus has consumers' Co-operation grown. It is limited by the spending power of the people; but even these comparatively narrow borders have not yet been reached. Again to quote the figures of "Riches and Poverty," though only half the total national income goes to the thirty-eight million people below the income tax level, that half does represent a sum of £885,000,000. Another £550,000,000 goes to a middle class. The great bulk of the first sum and a fair part of the second form the practical purchasing power of Democracy. As an instrument to its ends each sovereign is as real as a vote, as real as a trades unionist card of membership. Some of those whom money enfranchises are difficult to organise. The very poor, while in the slums their spending power is bought and sold over their heads as "goodwill," remain outside nearly all existing societies. Many individuals in other classes may have interested reasons for standing apart. On the other hand, the poor ought to be enlisted and the middle class might be far more largely won over. At present £107,000,000 represents the spending power organised. It is no more than a respectable nucleus. Yet, even so, consumers' Co-operation is an indispensable democratic movement. But the Socialist is usually grossly ignorant of it; the average trades unionist has hardly heard of it; the increasing number of middle-class enthusiasts for a social art, drama, and literature pass it by as a kind of shopkeeping. From the Church Socialist League to the Salvation Army a dozen religious bodies eager for the common good either give it only spasmodic attention or fail entirely to recognise its import. Whatever they do with their voices, their pens, or their votes, all these democrats give the great bulk of their earnings, involving all the personal influence that goes, or might go, with them, to the building up of oligarchy.

A democratic force in the world of undemocratic Capitalism, thus exists consumers' Co-operation. If a true outline of it has been given, then many conclusions easily and logically follow. First, it is not itself the Labour movement; its first duty is not to its employees. The true case is that the trades unionist and general labour movement and itself are both, so to speak, departments of a common Democracy existing for the people's whole welfare. The prime business of the one is with wages and conditions; of the other with prices and qualities. The two "departments" should naturally work together, each giving the other a different point of view. In the factories and workshops of Democracy as consumers, their rule for the unity of the movement must be supreme. That ensured, there is nothing to prevent a certain desirable amount of home rule. While unable to lift its workers far above the surrounding level, the consumers may be expected to improve sensibly upon the *average* wages of Capitalism, without insisting upon the driving that frequently goes with boated high wages. And though unable to abolish the monstrous evil of unemployment, they have, at any rate, the power in a dozen ways to moderate the ill and lessen its hardships; and the more loyally, intelligently, and unselfishly they co-operate the more this power will increase.

The movement is not a complete human society in itself. But the principles suggested lead directly to the more real part of the old ideals—a keen sense of national unity in what is practically one organisation, from the smallest retail Society to the remotest department of the Wholesale Society. They lead also to understanding the movement as a pioneer collectivism. The land, the railways, and other huge single economic forces, may reasonably be acquired by the people through the State. But for a long time to come neither the State nor the municipalities will have the freedom of a voluntary movement to acquire shops, factories, and so forth. It may finally prove that such partial action, on the present democratic basis, best serves the whole people. In either case both are instruments of the one public; the consumers' movement needing to play its part in the State in opposing tariffs, in securing sound laws against fraud and adulteration, in hastening, say, the State ownership of railways, and generally in furthering all collective action that is clearly along the lines of its own principles, while gaining from the connection the salutary play upon itself of the full force of public opinion.

The movement has grown through its material benefit to its members; it has also claimed always to be a defensive movement. But defence and offence are relative words. Which we use depends on the point of view. In every conflict each side believes itself to be the party attacked. So, while the movement should enlarge its activities for the defence of those who have too little for their well-being (capitalists are "not in business for health," but Co-operators are), it need not fear the word "aggression." Whether by State, municipal, or trades unionist action, every increase of real spending power, through old age or other just pensions, through higher wages, or relief to rates (if it involves actually setting closer limits to the rich, and is not lost through increased rents or prices), is a special gain to Democracy as consumers. Yet, as Professor Chapman has reminded us (C.W.S. "Annual," 1909), there is an ideal consumption. "By learning to avoid thriftlessness and thoughtlessness and the acquisition of worthless things, a society may really gain as much as from new inventions." The luxury of the rich is the poverty of the poor. Unwholesome expenditure of all classes is equally waste. It is right to win from Capitalism all the profit possible; but to put such gains always first is to pervert the movement. Consumers' Co-operation ought to stand as a democratic union against the waste of war, of tariffs, of competition, and, not less, of ignorant, technically uneducated consumption.

Finally, it would be failure if the movement were to remain limited to the present minority of available consumers. If ten million men, women, and children are in some degree served by the movement, thirty million remain untouched. Does it mean that Capitalism is better for consumers than their own organisation? This majority must be won over permanently; and that can only be done through a revival in the movement of the spirit of service. The lowest Capitalism seeks to bribe and trick the consumer with a thousand false gifts and cheap devices. But, "you cannot fool all the people all the time." Our methods will need to be as many—but different. At the least, we must emulate the serviceableness of Capitalism in its best and most public-spirited representatives.

Stand in front of any big cheap-jack shop, pass through the streets of any great town, go into the homes of the people, pick up any newspaper, and the fact must be borne home that the many need not only a larger power over materials but also knowledge and wisdom to use even the powers they have to more wholesome purposes. Workers to-day are unemployed, but other workers are mal-employed. There is a pathos in the common spectacle of wonderfully perfect machines running at high speed, of human beings carefully tending them year in year out, of business men seriously and strenuously active—simply to produce things which no well-informed person, healthily trained, would ever dream of demanding. Of what avail to better conditions if the object of the labour is of less consequence than the making of those images which created a vested interest in Ephesus? On the other side, in how many cases would not the worker himself gladly be quit of producing, often at the price of his health, things which he knows to be without real value? So we return to our starting point, that a first step toward a new social order is the organisation and education of the people by and for themselves, specially and definitely as consumers.

The long upward struggle of the people, led from age to age by the wisest, best, and frequently least-known, has brought us to a situation of apparent defeat. The rich and few appear more than ever strongly secure of power. But this is an illusion. That power is qualified by Christian civilisation as before it was not. Where its scope has increased since the Middle Ages, the increase is temporary. Already on all sides new forces of a Democracy never so well equipped are at the gate. We need an enthusiasm for bringing the separate hosts into that sane unity which gives one purpose to different armies with different methods. For modern conflicts are not terminated by single combats or spasmodic battles. Those forces win which maintain a well-related action, of high individual quality, through the months, and years if need be, of an ordered advance.

Moreover, modern soldiers cannot fight for their own personal ends. They are not freebooters. Conflict is always a duty that a man of good spirit is glad to conclude; and if it is selfish it ceases to be a duty. Capitalism is the result of a society undeniably larger and richer than of old. There will be no triumph for all unless victory over it brings a new social order still larger and richer than the present, as well as more equal, social, fraternal—a society to which men of all types and classes may honourably be loyal.

The future is and must be uncertain—

> It may be we shall touch the happy isles,
> It may be that the gulfs will wash us down.

With public opinion pliable as it is to-day, a great European war, involving this country, may arise in any year and throw back all our hopes. A more subtle foe—a progressive degeneration of character or physique—may yet undermine our best-founded structures. But whether this empire stands or falls, whether this race flourishes or decays, humanity will go on, and history is the witness that what is done for humanity is not done in vain.

24

JUSTICE, 10 MAY 1913, 7.

John Maclean

[John Maclean (1879–1923) was one of the leading revolutionary socialists of his time. Born in Glasgow to working-class parents, he trained as a schoolteacher, read Blatchford's *Merrie England* as a young man and joined the Social Democratic Federation, helping to form a branch of the SDF in Pollokshaws in 1906. Maclean was also a keen supporter of the local co-operative society there, campaigning to pressure school boards to establish adult classes in political economy, among other things.[Henry Bell, *John Maclean: Hero of Red Clydeside* (London: Pluto Press, 2018)] This letter from Maclean to the SDF's newspaper *Justice* demonstrates his hopes for co-operation as a vehicle for revolutionary change. Noting that "it used to be sacrilege not long ago to mention Socialism and Co-operation in the same breath", Maclean argues that the situation is rapidly changing and points to the impressive support recently given by Belgium co-operators to striking workers, which has also occurred in this country.[On the Belgium movement see Carl Strikwerda, "'Alternative Visions' and Working-Class Culture: The Political Economy of Consumer Cooperation in Belgium, 1860-1980", in Ellen Furlough and Carl Strikwerda (eds), *Consumers against capitalism?: Consumer cooperation in Europe, North America, and Japan, 1840–1990* (Lanham, Md.: Rowman & Littlefield, 1999)] He refers to the failed attempt to forge a formal political alliance between the co-operative movement and the Labour Representation Committee made at the Paisley Congress in 1905 which Maclean attended and looks forward to debating the same issue at the upcoming Aberdeen Congress. He is hopeful of success this time, as the Independent Labour Party according to Maclean has "systematically saturated all committees and associations inside the co-operative movement", and have successfully pushed a resolution regarding affiliation onto the congress agenda. He sees this part of a wider struggle between Liberalism and Socialism and he does not underestimate opposition, as "the Liberal caucus will not be pleased to see the co-operative movement depart from its old moorings". As it turned out, Maclean's assessment was over-optimistic – the resolution was defeated, though it garnered significantly more support than it had in 1905 – and the old moorings held for some years at least, until total war rendered them obsolete.[G.W. Rhodes, *Co-operative-Labour Relations 1900–1962* (Loughborough: Co-operative College, 1962)] The movement finally entered the formal political arena in 1917, though it preferred to retain its independence, refusing to affiliate to the Labour Party and establishing a separate Co-operative Party instead.]

THE CO-OPERATIVE UNION AND THE LABOUR PARTY.

Dear Comrade,—I am glad to see a correspondence on the above, as it used to be sacrilege not so long ago to mention Co-operation and Socialism in the same breath. The recent Belgian strike has certainly emphasised one side of co-operation that has not loomed very large in our discussions this side of the North Sea. Yet it is a fact that in recent years the co-operative movement has granted fair sums to strikes in our country. Had trade unionists and Socialists been more keenly alive to the real value of co-operation in the fight even greater aid would have been forthcoming. The co-operative organisation in the past has very largely been left to the religious and the Liberal elements amongst the workers. Let our men devote a tenth of the energy they have spent in modernising the trade unions and they will be surprised at the results. The I.L.P. have systematically saturated all committees and associations inside the co-operative movement, with the result that the leaders are invited to speak all over the country; and as a result of their work we have political resolutions such as will be discussed this year again in Scotland at the Aberdeen Congress. The I.L.P. have been at the business since their inception, and they will achieve their end sooner or later. I do admire their persistence and insistence.

Now, it is their resolution that comes up at Aberdeen.

I well remember the fight on a similar resolution at the Paisley Congress in 1905, just before the existence of the Parliamentary Labour Party. It was a great fight between Liberalism and Socialism, Socialism as the great vital principle. Never before did I hear such a fine debate on Socialism; never before did I see such intense excitement over any great issue. Brownlie was there from Woolwich, and can back me up. Because I expect the main issue at Aberdeen will be Socialism versus things as they are drifting. I suggested voting for the resolution to join the Labour Party. Should our men get a chance they could easily emphasise their Socialism and place the Labour Party in its proper place. What we have meantime to remember is that a definite resolution is up for discussion. Are we to take one side or the other? Had we been alert enough we might have had a resolution up asking the co-operative movement to join with the B.S.P. That, in my estimation, would have been a joke, as the B.S.P. at present hardly knows where it is, what with Militarism, Suffragettism, and Syndicalism. Until we settle affairs inside our ranks we can hardly have the face to ask such a body as the co-operative movement to join in with us, can we really?

I think there is a difference between the Labour Party as a national body and the Parliamentary Labour Party, the group in Parliament. The active element outside

Parliament is the rank and file I.L.P. one, as bent on Socialism as we are; the dominant element inside is the Liberal miner section, as bent on retaining their seats and Liberal support as any Liberal can be. The Aberdeen fight will be largely an I.L.P. rank and file one, so, therefore, we may with as fair grace as we can summon up stand by them, especially as I am convinced that the Liberal caucus will not be pleased to see the co-operative movement depart from its old moorings. If we vote against the new departure we help Liberalism and Anarchism combined, together with the illusion that co-operation alone can solve the social problem. For us the situation is a delicate one. I well appreciate the abhorrence most of us feel at the thought of strengthening the existing Parliamentary Labour Party with its policy of stand-pat, and am prepared for a howling opposition. Yet, in my present frame of mind, I see greater danger from a policy of co-operative stand-pat. Let a frank discussion arise. I have had an excellent show, and therefore request leave to withdraw in favour of others for and against.

In reply to comrade Leiper, I think it sound Marxism to deprecate direct political action by the co-operative movement. We do not wish the workers to seek representation in Parliament because they are producers and distributors of a few articles, but we wish them to capture Parliament because they are the producers and distributors of all commodities, though only consumers of a fraction thereof.

As Marxists we fight on a class basis, not on a trade one. It would be better if disputants would keep to the other, the more vital issue.

J. MACLEAN.

Part 4

UTOPIANISM AND THE RELIGION OF CO-OPERATION

25

J.T.W. MITCHELL'S PRESIDENTIAL ADDRESS, *THE 24TH ANNUAL CO-OPERATIVE CONGRESS, 1892* (MANCHESTER: CO-OP UNION, 1892), 6–8.

J.T.W. Mitchell

[J.T.W. Mitchell (1828–1895) was born in Rochdale, the illegitimate son of a beerhouse keeper. He started work in a cotton mill at the age of ten, learnt to read and write at Sunday school and joined the Rochdale Temperance Society, a connection he retained until his death. Working his way up from wool sorter to manager in a private firm, he eventually became a flannel dealer on his own account. Mitchell's connection with the co-operative movement began in 1853 when he joined the Rochdale Equitable Pioneers' Society, which elected him to the board of the Co-operative Wholesale Society in 1869. He took over as chairman in 1874 and helped turn the organisation into the largest and most successful of its kind in the world, with an annual turnover of over £10 million in the mid-1890s. [Percy Redfern, *The Story of the C.W.S. The Jubilee History of the Co-operative Wholesale Society Limited, 1863–1913* (Manchester: CWS, 1913)] Reproduced here is the speech he gave as president of the Rochdale Congress three years before he died in office. Fittingly, given the religiosity of his speech, it was delivered from the pulpit of the Methodist chapel in Ballie Street; Mitchell himself was an active Congregationalist and Sunday school teacher. Explicitly forging links between his own conception of co-operation and the earlier Owenite heritage, Mitchell refers to the Huddersfield co-operator Thomas Hirst, who proselytised the "community idea" on missionary tours around northern England sixty years before. He quotes the clause from the Pioneers' original rules referring to their aim of establishing a "home colony of united interests" in order to suggest that the wider vision was sustained, despite the success of storekeeping and dividend. Like the Owenites, Mitchell's ambitions knew no bounds. By organising and harnessing the consumption of the majority he believed co-operators would eventually be able to take over the entire economy: "My desire is that the profits of all trade, all industry, all distribution, all commerce, all importation, all banking and money dealing, should fall back again into the hands of the whole people". The young Beatrice Potter – who Mitchell had helped with her research – was impressed by the ambition though was sceptical about popular control, as was noted in Part 3.]

Mr. J. T. W. MITCHELL, on ascending to the pulpit, was loudly cheered. He said: Ladies and gentlemen,—You who compose this audience are met in a sacred place to consider a sacred question. In the name of the Equitable Pioneers and all other co-operators in Rochdale I give you a hearty welcome, and I trust that the cause under whose auspices we are met to-day, will take a new stride forward towards the completion of that great work, the successful part of which was begun in 1844 in Rochdale.

Co-operation did not begin in 1844, it began many years before. The struggle of the industrious classes of this country is not one of a score of years, but of centuries; and in its growth it has had to overcome selfishness which controlled the legislative and other forces of the nation, and which used the under classes to sustain and strengthen that selfishness. You had a Bill of Rights, and you had before that the appropriation of what I call the property of the nation, which ought to have been kept in the nation's hands, but it was appropriated for services rendered; it retained the property, but the charges of the services were thrown upon the nation. ("No, no.") There may be a difference of opinion about that. I know I shall say many things to which people will say "No, no" this morning, but I intend to say them none the less. It is time that namby-pambyism was crushed in these Congresses. We have had selfishness in centuries past, there is selfishness in our own day, and there is selfishness even amongst us. Pure as we profess ourselves to be, there are manifestations of that most unholy quality even amongst ourselves: and it will take co-operation all its time to prevent the growth of selfishness, and of selfishness controlling its financial forces. But I trust that there will be in this movement of ours that measure of unselfishness which will control its forces.

In 1692, there were established the Bank of England and the Stock Exchange. I give you these facts at the beginning, and I shall apply them presently. Those institutions were established 200 years ago; Rochdale to-day is worth 200 times as much as it was in 1692; but where has the increment of value gone? Has it gone to the multitude of the population? (No.) No, it has gone to a limited section. The township of Manchester, in which our Wholesale Society is situated, has increased nearly ten times in value. Where is that value gone? To a section of the community. The early co-operators made up their minds that there should be a change in that direction. At the beginning of the reign of George III. the struggle began, and it continued until his death. The National Debt was increased many hundreds of millions, the mass of the people were without employment, living in starvation, while the others lived in luxury. In 1815 the war was closed, but the struggle kept on. In 1828 Sir R. Peel (who was then Home Secretary of the Duke of Wellington's administration) said, "I wish the working classes would take their own affairs into their own hands." They took him at his word. In 1832 we had the Reform Bill.

Between 1828 and 1832 there had been a great struggle going on by co-operators, and some of the co-operators said of the trading classes of that day that they were corrupt, dishonourable, and practically dishonest. A person named Thomas Hirst spoke to thousands of his countrymen in as good speeches and as earnest words as any I ever heard, and he laid the foundation of this struggle for co-operation. The first Co-operative Congress was held in 1831, not 1832, as some have stated. There was a Congress held in Birmingham in 1831. The last of that series was held in Liverpool in October, 1832, at which a Wholesale Society was represented. There is an honourable name connected with those days—Robert Owen—but, so far as I can gather, he did not believe so much in co-operation; he thought the tribe of merchants could do business for them as well as they could do it for themselves. The rank and file did not believe in co-operation as we understand and practise it.

In 1844, when the Rochdale Pioneers began, there were great struggles both in Parliament and out. There have been many misconceptions about our society, therefore I want to show what were the real intentions of the Pioneers at the commencement. Their intentions were not altogether what some people have said, and I want to correct the error. This book I hold in my hand is one of the first copies of the rules. The name on the book is Samuel Ogden, No. 1, but I do not know whether he was the first member. At that time the committee worked for nothing. There was no bother in those days about fees and fares. At the end of the rules it says:—"If the auditor does not attend to his duties he is to be fined 2s. 6d." And the cashier was to pay 1s. Now, you committeemen, remember this, if the president was late, he was fined threepence, and if he did not come at all he had to pay sixpence. And so with the other committeemen. Some people have said that we co-operators have forsaken our first faith, and that we are nothing now but dividend hunters. The trade journals charge us with this; others say that the charm of dividend has passed away. Has it? You know it has not. I may say many things you have heard before, but it is necessary to repeat them over and over again. The old truth cannot be told too often.

I should not have made these remarks but for the sermon I heard last night from my own spiritual adviser, who is a capital adviser on spiritual matters, but not altogether reliable on co-operation. He was disparaging the store. Now, the very first thing the Pioneers did was to arrange for the establishment of a store. They saw that wealth was made by keeping a store, and they knew by bitter experience that the wealth thus created was used by its possessors to tyrannise over working people. A vast number of the wealthy people in Rochdale and other places have arisen from families who were very poor sixty or seventy years ago. They can run their carriages to-day, but they started from the poorest of the poor. Some of their ancestors baked bread in cellars. It is no discredit to earn a livelihood by honest industry. They rose from the slums of poverty, and we also want to use our powers to attain a competency for the time allotted to us in this vale of tears. Let us gather as much honey as we can, and leave some little for those who are left behind. The store was the beginning of money making, and I say to all, never despise the store.

Make as much dividend as you can make honestly, but don't make it for the sake of making it; appropriate it when you have made it.

When the Pioneers had made money they proposed to deal with it in this way—first in building houses. Among co-operators the idea largely prevails that they would like to build their own houses and live in them. I prefer the Pioneers' plan. I gather from the rules that the houses were to be built by the society, and that the members were to live in them. Then they were to commence manufacturing. They were to produce, distribute, and educate. Now another principle comes in. It was adopted in 1832. I will read the clause:—"That as soon as practicable the society shall proceed to arrange the powers of production, distribution, education, and government, or in other words to establish a self-supporting home colony of united interests for the common good of all." Remember that, not one interest, not individual, but united interests. The clause proceeds:—"That the cause of the difficulties and embarrassments under which society is now labouring in commercial affairs is attributable to individuals interested in the production of and distribution of wealth, and that in order to remove these difficulties it is necessary for society to be based on the principle of united interests." The Pioneers of 1844 adopted the principle laid down in 1832 of a common interest. Now, you teetotalers, look out for the next clause. The last work the Pioneers put down in their programme was—"That for the promotion of sobriety a temperance hotel be opened in one of the society's houses as soon as convenient." Thus, we find that the early co-operators were in the forefront of all good causes. If there are any co-operators here who have not signed the temperance pledge, I hope after hearing this they will do so. These were the principles laid down by the early co-operators. Their method of co-operation did not start with either capital or labour, but with consumption. Mark that. According to my conviction consumption ought to be the basis of the growth of wealth in this country. (Hear, hear, and "No.") So far as I am concerned all my labour and my efforts and the power of my voice will be in favour of making consumption the basis of the growth of all co-operative organisation. If you do not do that I know what will be the result. In a hundred years' time there will be, I trust, a still more intelligent population, the ages will move on, and all good causes will move on with the ages, so that the generations to come will have greater opportunities of enjoying life than those of the past or the present.

Now, why do I say that consumption ought to be the basis of all the accumulation of wealth? For this reason—that consumption bears all the charges. That is true from the highest to the lowest, from the richest man to the poorest peasant; and the humblest contribute most largely in proportion to their means to the luxury of the rich. All the charges come from consumption. If co-operators will take that principle as their standpoint every working man will be better off. If you do not establish that principle what will be the result? The plan of some capitalists is to get labour united in order to crush the poor consumer. I want as much as any one to see the elevation of labour. I think labour ought to be elevated. But how? That is the question. How? Simply by making the interests of our common humanity equal all round. I don't believe in the selection of a few to receive the contributions of the many, and watch them enjoy the luxuries I ought to have a share of. Ministers have got power, if they would use it, in this direction; and they know a text in the Old Testament which is very applicable to the case. The people wanted a god, and they brought their trinkets and made them into a god and fell down and worshipped it. It is very much like that in the present day. Poor people subscribe to make others rich, and then they fall down and worship them.

I don't believe in the present distribution of wealth. It is said that the United Kingdom has a capital of something like ten thousand millions sterling, equal to about £300 per head of the population. Now I say, that instead of one man having £200,000 or £300,000 and others having nothing, it would be better if they had £300 apiece. I am not opposed to capital; I am not opposed to wealth; I like it, and I want to accumulate it, but I don't want wealth to stand to the credit of the "upper ten," but of those who are sometimes called the "lower five." I want wealth to stand to the credit of the whole population. The joint-stock companies of this country own a thousand millions of money. The National Debt is about nine hundred millions, and the capital of railways as much. Between two and three thousand millions of money are engaged in those three enterprises. Now, what I would like would be for co-operators to allow their profits to be so massed together, that instead of a few persons owning this money, it would belong to the whole people of the United Kingdom. That is the burden of my remarks. My desire is that the profits of all trade, all industry, all distribution, all commerce, all importation, all banking and money dealing, should fall back again into the hands of the whole people. If co-operators will manage their enterprises in such a way as to concentrate all their trade in one channel, I am certain that this can be accomplished. I made a calculation the other day, that if the world would conduct its business on co-operative lines, the population of the world could have amongst them between three and four hundred thousand millions of money; and if the fifteen hundred millions of population divided it amongst them at so much each, it would be much better for the world at large. I am not one of those who would divide other people's property. I am nothing of the kind. I want no laws to be passed to divide anybody's property. What I want is for co-operators, trade unionists, and all the industrious classes of this and every other country to combine in keeping their own shop, making a good dividend, producing, distributing, and financing, and let all the profits come to those who consume the goods, because they have made them.

Another great power in the country is the newspaper press. It is said that there are about 5,000 periodicals and newspapers in the United Kingdom, and something like 40,000 in all the world. I have made an estimate which gives this rather curious conclusion, that all the advertisements in those papers were equal to about five hundred millions a year, or about equal to a lawyer's fee for each person. The power of the press is great in this and every country, but I do not think it is wisely used so far as co-operators are concerned. Why? Because a great political gathering has a five or six columns report in the newspapers, but for a great gathering of co-operators—except at Congress time, when we are better treated—we get only a three or four-inch paragraph. Co-operators and trade unionists have very few papers, and have very little influence upon the press. The trade unionists started a paper the other day, and I am told it has already collapsed. If co-operators are to have greater influence in the nation and in the world they will have to control the press more largely, and it must be of our own colour. The writers in newspapers fill many columns about how desirable it is that the working classes should have their condition improved; and then there is a line at the bottom to say that they cannot tell how to do it. That is the very thing we want the people to know. If any plan can be devised to renovate and bless mankind, by all means let us know it. But we don't get the information.

The three great forces for the improvement of mankind, are religion, temperance, and co-operation; and as a commercial force, supported and sustained by the other two, co-operation is the grandest, the noblest, and the most likely to be successful in the redemption of the industrious classes. Some are for Positivism, and others want an industrial republic; why don't they come into co-operation, which will do everything they want? What do I find? If people want to start a new organisation they desire to get associated with existing organisations in order to give them character and position. Now we, as co-operators, have been sought in that direction many times, but what I tell them is this—if you want the benefit of our organisation you must come and be one of us. We have spent our thousands and thousands of pounds in getting up an organisation of this magnitude, and we cannot appropriate its benefits to some struggling person who has some particular fad of his own. If you want your plan to succeed, come with us and we will do you good. I want co-operators to be all for co-operation. If others will help you, you can help them; but if you do not get them to help you, they will weaken your own forces.

I referred to the Stock Exchange and the Bank of England. In 1694 the national debt was about £684,000. In the days of William and Mary the rulers of the nation wanted some money, and they went to the merchants of London, and borrowed twelve or thirteen hundred thousand pounds. The merchants of London were wise in their day and generation, as I want you co-operators to be, and they were quite willing to lend this money if they got 8 per cent. for it. In the second place the rulers were to grant the merchants a privilege, and they did grant it, and so far as I know that privilege lasts till to-day, and it is a great financial force in this country, but not always used for the benefit of the people. At that time there grew up in connection with that privilege persons who were disposed to deal in securities, of course, private persons are always ready with their kind consideration to confer a benefit on those who have a privilege, and they dealt in those securities; they bought and sold them, and I do not say that they always exercised that due regard to integrity of dealing which is desirable in all financial transactions. If history tells true, there was a good deal of stock-jobbing in those days; and I don't think, from what I am told outside, that it is altogether abolished to-day. Those privileges given in the past are possessed now. The Bank of England has the privilege which was given to those rich merchants of London who lent money to the State.

It is said that a very considerable portion of the national debt was lent in those days by people who paid down £60 sterling for £100 of stock. That was the way our national debt has accumulated. When we find that there has been so much privilege and evil in the past, does it not prove, ladies and gentlemen, that you have undertaken a most arduous task? But you can accomplish it. The task is no greater than your power. Provided you bring all your trade within yourselves you will very soon shut up some of the other people's shops. Those privileged persons who have been fed and fattened at the public expense don't want to give up their privileges. We will let them alone if they are content with what they have got; but from this time henceforth let us make up our minds that all our trade shall come within our own channels, and let these men of privilege fight their own battle amongst themselves.

My time is gone, but there is another thing I must mention. I want to speak to you about the Wholesale Society and its productive departments. Some people write in the papers that co-operative production has been a failure. It has been nothing of the kind. It has been a grand success, and will be more so in the future than it has been in the past. Our Wholesale friends in Scotland and ourselves are doing a grand and noble work. Some of you will say, "Yes, they are doing better than you are." Well, about that we are not going to fall out this morning, but I think we are the best. My friend Mr. Maxwell is here, and he can speak for himself. So far as we are concerned, there is nobody in the world pays better wages than we do. The two Wholesale Societies have something like £500,000 invested in co-operative production. Sometimes we have profits and sometimes we have losses. We are like matrimony—it is for better or worse. Everything in this world is for better or worse. The profits of both Wholesale Societies far exceed any losses we have sustained. We have made about £80,000 in addition to interest, depreciation, and wiping out losses; therefore let no man say that Wholesale co-operation has not been a success. It has been, and will be, an eminent success. Some people think we shall injure others. Neither Wholesale Society will ever take any steps whatever to cause unnecessary injury to any existing society. We shall have to take steps forward. I have tried to show you, from the history of the Stock Exchange and the Bank of England, that when privileges were granted 200 years ago, individuals sought to gain an advantage from the State; and wherever there is a corporate institution the monied classes will cluster round it, and try to suck its honey. Therefore, if you want your great work to proceed it will have to proceed on corporate and not on individual lines, it will have to proceed in the interest of the entire body politic and not in the interest of a section of the community. While I live I shall work for these principles and try to persuade others to adopt them and work for them with all the force and energy of will I can; because if individual forces grow up and cluster around this movement of ours you may depend upon it the cause of co-operation will be weakened.

Now, friends, I have done. There are other things I should like to say, but I have been persuaded not to say them. ("Go on.") They are things that relate to persons outside. There is one thing I will tell you, the Pioneers started on honourable lines to do themselves good, not advertising themselves to do other people an injury. They never put misleading tickets in their window like the shopkeepers do to-day in towns where they are trying to hunt down a few working men who have joined together for their own benefit. This is done by many persons who ought to know better, and the trade journals gloat over their success in putting out the Wholesale Society. When you find the trade journals nearly every week publishing scandalous things about co-operation, ought you not to rise *en masse* and determine to bind yourselves together as one united force in order to do your own business in your own way, and let the outside people look after themselves?

I am bound to tell you another thing. In these trade journals you have read something about bribing managers. I was at a store not long ago, and the manager told me that some time previously he had received from a private firm two halves of a £5 note in separate letters. Let me remark parenthetically that these private firms tempt not only managers but committeemen. But this manager in question submitted the matter to his committee, and the committee told him to keep the money. Shortly after the representative of the firm visited the store, and very politely requested to know whether the manager had received the £5 note, at the same time placing another in his hands. The manager submitted this also to the committee, and again they told him to keep the note. And I am told that even the branch shopkeepers receive visits from the same firm, and the shopmen have half-sovereigns placed in their hands. But, as I said, this applies not only to the servants but to the committee themselves. I know a committee that was taken some miles into the country and entertained to a good dinner at a public house by a tea dealer. That I know because one of those who were going told the gentleman who told me—(laughter)—he couldn't go to a co-operative meeting because he was going to that dinner. Don't imagine that private firms are free themselves. I have known in my time as much—if not more—bribery with private firms as ever I have known with co-operative societies, and therefore if the trade journal to which I have referred replies to my remarks, let the writer find out those who have been guilty of bribery with private firms in times past. There is a gentleman in this room who for several years has received a cheque and has passed it through his cash account. Seeing that this is my one opportunity of speaking to the largest and most representative assembly possible within the limits of a year, I would urge you all to be true and faithful to the great cause with which you are associated, and tell those people who want to throw £5 notes or half-sovereigns into your midst to keep them to themselves, and their business to themselves.

If you will rally round the Wholesale Societies of England and Scotland you will find these two great organisations, with all their forces of distribution, production, banking, importing, and exporting—you will find they will do the best for you. The two Wholesale Societies have received money, and have also paid it away. I wanted to tell you that because the facts of to-day show that these societies themselves have in their funds nearly £200,000 more than the societies ever put into them. That is to say the societies in connection with the Wholesale Societies have drawn out every penny they ever put into them, and yet there is now nearly £200,000 more than they ever put in. These two great institutions are therefore creating their own capital, which capital will be useful for the redemption of the industrial classes.

I trust that this Congress in Rochdale will mark a new era of progress in the great cause which bands us together, and I also hope that Britain, yea, the United Kingdom of England, Ireland, and Scotland, bound together in one common bond, will raise itself higher than it has ever before been thought capable of being raised.

26

CO-OPERATIVE PRODUCTION (OXFORD: OXFORD UNIVERSITY PRESS, 1894), 730–732, 809–815.

Ben Jones

[Although Ben Jones was a staunch believer in the power of the CWS to change economy and society, his monumental study of 1894 is marked by an inquisitiveness and openness towards co-operative forms of all kinds, in the past and the present. The first extract below demonstrates this well, as it discusses the Bolton Co-operative Commonwealth Society and the visit made by the secretary of the Co-operative Union, J.C. Gray. This settlement was one of a number of experiments in community life that sprang up during the fin de siècle, inspired particularly by the writings of the Russian anarchists Leo Tolstoy and Peter Kropotkin. Others included Clousden Hill Free Communist and Co-operative Colony just outside Newcastle. [Matthew Thomas, *Anarchist ideas and counter-cultures in Britain, 1880–1914: revolutions in everyday life* (Aldershot: Ashgate, 2005); Nigel Todd, *Roses and revolutionists: the story of the Clousden Hill free communist and co-operative colony, 1894–1909* (Nottingham: Five Leaves, 2015)] Although generally short-lived, many co-operators were fascinated by these developments even as they regarded them as supplementary rather than alternative projects. The second extract is from the conclusion to Jones's work, which places the movement within the context of a wider transition. He reproduces the revealing exchange between J.T.W. Mitchell and Professor Alfred Marshall before the Royal Commission on Labour in 1892, where Mitchell coolly acknowledged that the movement's goal was citizen control of the entire economy – "and the sooner the better". Citing also Tom Mann's question to Mitchell about diversity, Jones underlines how democratic ownership of industries and services by municipalities and state are part of a more general co-operative tide, one that will eventually replace competitive capitalism. Although admitting that "we are some distance yet from this desirable state of things", Jones makes it all sound entirely feasible: it is for him a concrete utopia.]

The last society I have to notice brings one back to the old Owenite days, so far as the society's aims and methods are concerned. Writing to me in June, 1890, Mr. J. C. Gray said:

'Last evening I visited a novelty—a communistic society actually existing in a busy town like Bolton. The men are all socialists, followers of Gronlund and Bellamy. They have for two or three years worked in the evenings, without any pay, for the common good of the society. Starting with a subscription amounting in the whole to 10*s.*, they bought a few tools. Some of the members are mechanics and blacksmiths. They made more tools and machines. All labour is done between seven and ten at night, and after their ordinary day's work. They look upon it as a recreation, and certainly it is a splendid technical school for the men concerned. Last night we saw blacksmiths working at the forge, hand-loom weavers making quilts, power-loom weavers making cotton twills; mechanics making portions of looms for their own use; cabinet making, wood turning, brass and iron turning, drilling, clogging, boot making and repairing, &c., and all looking enthusiastic over the work. One man told me he had never missed an evening during the last eighteen months. They never think of the work as drudgery. I never saw working men with such confidence in each other. There are no trade jealousies. A man comes there and works at whatever trade he likes best. If he does not understand it, the others who are proficient are always willing and glad to teach. The wood turner was an engineer during the day, but at night he could excel as a wood turner. A man working at night as a mechanic, and doing his work well, was a cotton carder by day. The boot repairer and clogger worked in a mill for his livelihood, and so on, variety giving zest to their duties.

'They find a ready sale for everything they make. At present all the work and all the profits go to build up a fund to establish a "Commonwealth" on a large scale. When they have sufficient to do this, the members will be paid wages and take profits according to their work; but two-thirds of their wages will be paid in labour notes to be exchanged for the produce of their own community. They have asked my assistance in drafting rules to meet their case.'

This enterprise was registered in October, 1890, as the Bolton Co-operative Commonwealth Society, of North Bridge Mill, White Lion Brow[1]. A letter signed on behalf of the committee, by Joseph Ogden (secretary), and which appeared in *The Nationalization News,* of April, 1891, gave additional information.

'The society is intended to be worked on the following principles:—The present members and all who join within six months are called founder members; all who join after will be called contributing members, and must purchase £50 worth of goods from the society before they are transferred to the founder class of members. The benefit to be derived from being a founder member, is not dividend upon purchase, but constant and remunerative employment for all who are of a workable age;

and a part of the profits on labour will be kept in reserve for sickness, infirmity, and old age; also fatherless children, and widows of deceased members.

'The profits of the society, after paying interest upon capital, will be divided among the workers according to wages earned by each, subject to the following conditions:—It is calculated that it will require £100 for every worker to find him in capital for his employment; therefore no worker will receive any dividend upon his labour until such dividend exceeds £100; for which he will hold transferable shares bearing 4% interest. Thus the society will gradually develop its number of workers, and from the profits on labour the workers will gradually own their share of the capital of the society.

'At present the members are not reaping any benefit whatever, but are making sacrifices of money and labour.'...

The Future.

In the last three chapters I have endeavoured to show, that what co-operators have been aiming at, in all their various efforts, has been justice; and that they have settled down to the belief that justice can only be universally secured by means of democratic associations, the members of which are well-informed on the necessity for, and the best means of, obtaining it. Also, that the best form of democratic organization is, where the people are combined together on the basis of consumption; where, for their services as capitalists, or as workers, the members are remunerated by the payment of such fixed interest and wages, as the majority of the members of these organizations consider to be just; and, where all the members receive the goods produced, or the services rendered, at the exact cost of producing the goods, or supplying the services. But, where there are people who will not, or cannot, join in these co-operative efforts, although they are willing to have transactions with co-operators, and co-operators are desirous of transacting business with them, then, in such cases, the best form of co-operation is for the people with capital to join with the people who wish to be employed, in forming democratic associations for mutual benefit, to carry on business with those people who are unable, or unwilling, to become co-operators. Again, as in these last-mentioned cases each of the four contributors to the business, viz. the seller, the capitalist, the worker, and the buyer, helps to build up the fund commonly known as profit, each is entitled to a share of it; but there can be no harm, either as a matter of principle, or as a matter of practice, in any one of the four contracting to let any of the others have the profit, so long as the contract is made voluntarily, and with full knowledge of what is being done, as well as of what the results of the action will be. I now want to ascertain where the above-named conclusions will lead us.

I have already referred to W. Maxwell's evidence before the Labour Commission, in which he expressed himself as being favourable to municipalities and the nation each producing the goods, or organizing the services, required by the people, without the intervention of what is usually termed private enterprise[2]. Professor Marshall, as a member of the commission, was so impressed by the inevitable conclusion to which the system of co-operation by the consumer logically landed him, that he minutely questioned J. T. W. Mitchell on the point. The following questions by Professor Marshall, and answers by Mr. Mitchell, will explain themselves:

Q. 287. 'Should the co-operative system, on the lines advocated recently by you, Mr. Mitchell, be fully secured, and every Englishman become a co-operator, the result would be simply a new form of management of certain industries by government for the people?'
Ans. 'Every citizen (and I wish that could be brought about to-morrow) would have the power to vote for the Committee of the Wholesale Society.'

Q. 290. 'Then I will put it in this way, that if the co-operative system on the lines on which the English Wholesale is at present working were carried out according to your idea, the result would be the same as if the industries of the country were carried on by persons appointed by the individual citizens through the government, some slight changes in the constitution being made?'
Ans. 'To a large extent it would tend in that direction, and the sooner the better.'

Tom Mann, as a member of the Labour Commission, wanted to be certain that he accurately understood the above questions and answers; so he put several questions, which I give below, together with Mr. Mitchell's replies thereto.

Q. 387. 'I presume as you are trying to get control of the production of ordinary commodities on what we may term a democratic basis, your town council undertaking on behalf of the citizens of that town the control of your gas or waterworks, they too through the agency of the council are then controlling the production and distribution to that extent, are they not, of that commodity?'
Ans. 'Yes.'

Q. 388. 'That is to be approved of, is not it?'
Ans. 'Yes.'

Q. 389. 'As thoroughly as your own work?'
Ans. 'Yes.'

Q. 390. 'And if experience should show that there are other directions in which the town councils should enlarge their sphere of operations so that they could do it more effectively than you through your voluntary agency, you would still approve of it, would not you?'
Ans. 'Yes. It would depend upon the circumstances of the case.'

It may therefore, I think, be considered that the conclusion to which the theory of co-operation on the basis of the consumer leads us, is that the nation, being itself the consumer or user, should undertake to perform for itself, as part of the ordinary functions of government, everything that is required to be done, if the thing required is wanted in sufficiently large quantities to justify the formation of an establishment for doing it. By way of illustration, the application of the principle would cause the production of vessels of war, guns, rifles, ammunition, &c., for the use of the nation, to be carried on exclusively in government establishments, except perhaps in times of war, when the government establishments could not produce sufficient for the necessities of the special occasion; and it would then be, probably, inadvisable to lay down additional plant for temporary purposes. It would also ensure that the Post Office should provide its own horses and vans, instead of contracting, except where the services required were too small to maintain an establishment for the purpose. It would cause the railways to become the property of the state; and the ports and docks either to become the property of the state also, or the property of the county councils, or municipalities, in whose districts they may be situated.

The county councils and municipalities would organize their own services, instead of employing private firms, wherever the work to be done was sufficiently important to warrant them doing so; and, in cases where each had similar wants, which, in themselves, are too small to be supplied by a local establishment, the local authorities should combine in establishing a joint department; or the imperial government should do the work for them. For instance, uniforms for the county and municipal police, would probably not keep a factory in each locality continuously at work; but imperial workshops for the manufacture of army, navy, and postal uniforms, might very well also produce police uniforms, and supply them to the local authorities at the cost of production. Factories for the production of the cloth, &c., required, could also with advantage be established and worked by the imperial government. Printing and paper-making could likewise be undertaken.

The supply of gas and water is at present almost universally recognized as falling within the range of duties to be undertaken by local government bodies. The ownership of tram-lines is also allowed, but in a more grudging spirit; while the working of the tram-lines by the local authorities is only rarely permitted by law, or by the imperial government. These, being services universally required by the inhabitants, should be undertaken by the several local governments, if the citizens desire them to do so. There are many other services that could be advantageously rendered by county councils and municipalities. I will name one by way of suggestion. Fire brigades are mainly kept up at the expense of the citizens of each locality. If the local government authorities in each locality were to take into their own hands the insurance of the buildings in their respective districts, the profits which now go to the private Insurance Companies would far more than cover all the expenses of the fire brigades; and would thus relieve the citizens of the cost of their maintenance out of the rates.

What would the people save by this system of co-operation? First, private enterprise demands remuneration on capital at rates varying from 4, 5, to 10 % in Railway Companies, and up to 25 % or more in Insurance Companies. The nation and the local authorities can borrow as much capital as they require, at 3 % per ann. or less. Secondly, economists are never tired of telling us what tremendous salaries are paid by private firms to their superior employés. A large proportion of these amounts are excessive, and are in the nature of monopolies. If the situations were thrown open for competition, the remuneration would go down considerably, and would descend to the amount necessary to secure talent, energy, and trustworthiness. It is generally conceded that public bodies already get such services from their employés at a less price than is paid by private firms; the reason being that there is more competition for them, even although we have not yet got purely democratic government. Thirdly, the better treatment of the rank and file of the people can be secured without expense to the nation, by appropriating part of the above-mentioned savings to paying them better wages than they have received hitherto, or working them less hours than they have been previously worked, by private employers. Fourthly, the equitable treatment of all the citizens is ensured with more certainty, since there is far less chance of favouritism under government, than there is (say) in a Railway Company. It is almost an unheard-of thing to have the Post Office accused of treating one customer better than it treats all: but this is a common practice of Railway Companies: and the practice has sometimes ruined the individuals who have had to submit to their unjust treatment. The Railway Commissioners would never have been required, if the Railway Companies had administered their affairs with anything like the justice of a government department.

After the nation and the local authorities have co-operated for the performance of all the services that the citizens have deemed it desirable for them to undertake, the voluntary co-operative associations of consumers, both individualistic and federal, come into use to fill up the gaps and vacancies that have been left. And finally, after them, should come the associations of people with capital, and people without capital but willing to work, who should co-operate to supply or exchange services with those people who do not wish to co-operate, or who are in a position, which will occur while society is in a state of transition, where they cannot co-operate. But this imperfect form must be prepared to give way to the more perfect form of co-operation by the consumer, as soon as the people left outside the co-operative ranks are willing to be enrolled in them.

Already, the main lines of these co-operative systems are laid. But, to ensure more rapid progress, the national government requires to be purified of the parasites and hangers-on, whose interests lie in securing contracts for private firms; and the local authorities require to be released from the imperial restraint which prevents them rendering to the citizens the services these citizens may wish their own local bodies to perform for them. If, when they have freedom of choice, they choose to rely upon private enterprise, and so make fortunes for some few individuals at the expense of the public, let them do so: but the freedom to choose for themselves should be accorded to the citizens in each locality, and all autocratic control, whether it be in the imperial or in the local governments, should be abolished. Pure democracy, as being the best means of securing justice, should reign supreme.

As we are some distance yet from this desirable state of things, it behoves co-operators to consider what is the best method of accelerating progress. I think that we ought, as citizens, to actively engage ourselves in the conduct of both the local and imperial governments, with the object of gradually brushing away, as an obsolete piece of machinery, the method of governing the people by means of political partizanship. 'Justice to all,' and not loyalty to a party, should be the maxim, and the cry for 'Bread and Butter Politics' is really the popular rendering of the view that all government should be a system of co-operation for mutual benefit. The same principle, carried to its logical conclusion in our treatment of other nations, will have a tendency to abolish wars, by leading to the practical adoption of Tennyson's dream:—

'The Parliament of Man, the Federation of the World.'

Notes

1 Congress Report, 1891, p. 29.
2 See Chapter xxvii. p. 773.

27

CO-OPERATION AS A DEMOCRATIC FORCE: BEING A SERMON PREACHED BEFORE THE DELEGATES AT THE CO-OPERATIVE CONGRESS, HUDDERSFIELD ON JUNE 9TH, 1895, IN FITZWILLIAM STREET UNITARIAN CHURCH (LONDON: THE LABOUR ASSOCIATION, 1895), 1–7.

Ramsden Balmforth

[Born in Huddersfield, Ramsden Balmforth (1861–1941) was the son of a mechanic. Biographical information is thin, though he must have started working for the local co-operative society at a very young age, quitting in 1893 after twenty-one years of service to take up a scholarship he had won at Oxford to train for the Unitarian ministry. At a presentation organised by the society to mark the departure of their colleague (Balmforth received a copy of Ruskin's *Stones of Venice*, among other leaving gifts), he remarked on "the feeling of fellowship that had existed, and believed did exist to a great degree amongst the employees of the society". (*Huddersfield Chronicle*, 11 October 1893) He returned to take up his ministry at Fitzwilliam Street Church the following year, eventually emigrating to South Africa in 1897, where he became a peace activist. In a study published in 1900, Balmforth looked forward to a future when industry and society would be organised along municipal, socialist or communist lines, observing that the contemporary co-operative movement was helping "to prepare the way for the realisation of this higher order of society". [Ramsden Balmforth, *Some Social and Political Pioneers of the Nineteenth Century* (London : Swan Sonnenschein & Co., 1900), 216] The sermon reproduced here, published by the Labour Association, illustrates the strong connection that existed in many places between local cultures of nonconformity and co-operative culture. Consumer co-operation is helping to bring about "a true social life", according to Balmforth, because it is "substituting the application of the collective moral will for the anarchy of conflicting desires and interests". He argues that change must come from within as well as without, however, and urges consumers to boycott goods made by sweated labour. Quoting William Morris's dictum, he reminds co-operators to listen more attentively to "the voice of the producer", whose wellbeing must be a vital consideration in the fully democratic society of the future.]

> "I came that they may have life, and may have it abundantly."
> —John x. 10.

THESE words, which John puts into the mouth of Jesus, admirably express the aim and purpose of Christ's life. At a time when the life of humanity was at a low ebb Jesus came to renew it, to make it more abundant. The words express also the aim and purpose underlying that many-sided and elastic term—Co-operation. A generation has passed away since Mr. Ruskin gave utterance to his famous aphorism, "There is no Wealth but Life." Since that time a quiet revolution has been going on in the minds of all classes as to what should be the end and aim of human endeavour. And the change has taken place, not solely as a result of definite teaching, but rather through the slow evolution of what we vaguely call the "Time-Spirit." Ideals change; human activities seek to express themselves in different and ever-varying ways. Then, as these ideals and activities shape themselves anew, the economist or the philosopher comes along and frames new theories to fit the new manifestations of life and thought. There is, of course, a process of re-action as well. The theories themselves become "pious opinions," and the pious opinions develop into "articles of faith," and thus their influence slowly percolates into the conscious life of the mass.

And so, during the last thirty years, the professional chambers of the dismal science itself have been warmed and lit by gleams of affection, and sympathy, and conscience—perhaps thrilled, also, by fitful tremors of remorse! The end and aim of right-minded human endeavour is no longer the accumulation of riches, it is the living a more abundant life, or, as Socrates would say, the perfection of the nobler activities of the soul. This identification of Wealth with Life has widened, immeasurably, the spiritual out-look of man, and has widened also the scope for the application of scientific methods. All human effort and desire is now admittedly affected by a complexity of motives, instincts, and interests, not merely by the desire for material wealth. Character, rather than commodities, is recognised as the goal of human activity. Unrestricted competition is seen to be inadequate to the formation of a true social order. Economic science is now being slowly built afresh on new foundations. We are groping after a Science of Society.

This, you will say, was the A B C of the prophets and pioneers of Co-operation, and, in so far as this was the case, those prophets and pioneers may be said to have converted, or at least to have foreshadowed, a large body of the thought which now inspires the world. But great ideas and great principles require, from the very nature of the human mind, time, and education, and discipline, for their full comprehension and application. What the prophets see and proclaim as from the mountain tops, we poor mortals can only attain by years, sometimes ages, of strenuous thought and endeavour. And, as Cardinal Newman points out in his Essay on *Development,* the more fruitful, the more vital an idea is, the more complicated will be its development, the more difficult its full and varied realisation. And so Co-operation itself, a living and a fruitful idea, has been subject, and will be subject, to changes and complications in its development. It must ever be borne in mind that the co-operative movement is but the small concrete expression of a wider life around it. The aims and ideals which animate that wider life will, in their turn, re-act upon us, and so induce that aspiration and expansion which are the conditions of health and progress.

The desires, interests, aspirations, and activities, which this new outlook—this identification of Wealth with Life—foreshadows, are many. But I wish to confine myself this morning to one—the diffusion of the democratic spirit, and the consequent enlargement of our ideals and responsibilities. For this claim for more abundant life is really a claim for greater freedom, and this, likewise, though not so apparently, is a claim for increased responsibility. At the beginning of the century a similar claim for freedom was made, but there was then no corresponding sense of the sacred responsibilities which freedom involved. And so a breach was made in that organic unity of life which we call "society" or "humanity," and which theologians prefer to call "the corporate life of Christ." A yawning gulf was fixed between the sections which should have been as head, and heart, and members of the whole, a gulf across which Carlyle's Plugson shouted: "Noble spinners, this is the Hundred Thousand we have gained, wherein I mean to dwell and plant vineyards; the hundred thousand is mine, the three-and-sixpence daily was yours: adieu, noble spinners; drink my health with this groat each, which I give you over and above!" But the "noble spinners" have now for some time been pondering the question as to whether that kind of liberty is compatible with justice. And thus, as in all the incipient strivings of life, the higher ideal has first to be struggled for through the gross mesh of material things. Good and pious folk give people tracts and tell them to cultivate spiritual life on those. Co-operation, however, recognising the essential nature of things, demands a living wage, a reasonable working day, and the refinements of a comfortable home, as a basis without which the higher life is impossible. That question, however—as to the rightful distribution of wealth—Co-operation is slowly solving for itself by substituting the application of the collective moral will for the anarchy of conflicting desires and interests. Slowly solving, I say, and with gradual *approximation* towards the ideal, for have we not been told by Mr. Maxwell of certain societies—co-operative in name—which sink below the standard of common honesty in matters of wages and hours of labour? A fact, surely, which points to the necessity for the establishment of a given standard in our "State within a State"—a standard which, unless they rose to it, would place such societies outside the pale of the movement, as being like unto those ravening wolves which plunder the sheep, not of their wealth only, but of their Life itself. Every penny by which you underpay your servants, and every minute of overtime which you exact from them, is a robbery of that wealth called Life. Excessive labour binds men to the drudgery of mechanical toil, and so prevents the expansion and development of their higher faculties.

But there are other and equally vital issues with which the democratic idea is bound up. For if the highest form of wealth is Life, how important is the Labour which is the expression, the outward manifestation, of the principle of Life! The moment we have settled the just claims of each member of the Commonwealth, the moment we have apportioned to him his fair share of the produce—an exceedingly complex and difficult problem, I say, an ideal to which we can only slowly approximate—the moment we have done that, the question of surplus, bonus, dividend, becomes comparatively unimportant. Profit may be due to a variety of causes—inventive genius, a sudden demand for a special commodity, the value of a particular site, the congregating of large numbers of people at a given place, the increased efficiency of the worker—and therefore, its distribution is a matter of pure expediency to be determined by the strength of the contributing cause, and the furtherance of individual and collective welfare. But the unfolding of the spirit of Life, the outward expression of the vital principle, the Labour which should be part of the joy of Living—this unfolding, I say, is irrevocably bound up with the principle of religion itself. It is the very Life of the soul. That principle violated, the expansion checked, then the spirit itself is dwarfed and blighted by a cramping environment, and the soul of man is smothered within him. Just as a flower, given air, and light, and sunshine, and nourishment, unfolds and expands by its own inherent vitality, so does the human soul reach the perfection of its highest faculties and the goal of its noblest activities by the strenuous play of all its powers and aspirations. And it is the worth and beauty of the democratic idea that it claims for each individual soul the satisfaction of these high aspirations, limited only by the claims and welfare of the whole. Hence labour, production, service, life in expression—which makes up one-half or one-third our whole life—while submitting itself to discipline for the benefit of the whole, claims also, on *its* side, opportunity for the full development of all its capacities and powers.

The question may be asked—Shall that opportunity be allowed inside as well as outside the normal working day? And I answer, it must be allowed and encouraged in both. Freedom and responsibility, the powers and aspirations of the soul, cannot be bottled up and let out again at any given moment. They are an indestructible part of life itself, necessary, in due degree, at every varying stage, to its full and complete evolution. We are sometimes told that this labour, this service, this productive power, should be controlled by the voice of the consumer. And the question which industrial England will ere long have to set itself to solve will be this: Shall our industrial life be guided and controlled by the voice of the consumer or by the voice of the producer? And my answer to that would be that it must be controlled by neither exclusively, but by both in co-operation and co-partnership. It must never be forgotten that the consuming and the producing powers represent two diverse principles of human activity, two conflicting interests, which must be reconciled and harmonised ere life can be lived at its highest and best. Dante, in his *Inferno,* takes as the type of the consuming power in excess—Swine; and, on the other hand, I think we may take as a type of false or misdirected labour those Daughters of Danaus, who were eternally condemned to pour water through a sieve. And thus both powers may be abused. Neither can be considered apart from the other. The consumer is responsible for the way in which he feeds and promotes the activities of his life. The producer is responsible for the way in which he expresses and embodies the activities of his life. Where both sets of activities are wholly bound up in one individual, then their reconciliation becomes a problem for himself alone. But in our complex human society this isolation of the individual is not now possible. "We are members one of another." "No man liveth to himself, and no man dieth to himself." Both the consuming and the producing power are indissoluble parts or phases of the principle of Life—one, the energising, the other, the creative power. And the *creative* is surely the higher as furnishing us with the material and spiritual means by which we rise to nobler and more fruitful effort. Whereever then, this creative, this productive power—the life of the worker—is unduly dominated and controlled, even by the will of a majority, then is the democratic idea betrayed, and the aspirations of the soul stifled by the want of a free and bracing atmosphere. What, indeed, has produced those horrors of sweating and misery which are paralleled only by the slave plantations of the West, but the shortsighted morality and thoughtless whims of the consumer? What, indeed—to view the question from a higher standpoint—would become of our Art if we were to tell our painters and sculptors to body forth, not their own ideals, but the ideals and desires of their consuming patrons? What would become of our Poetry if we were to bid our poets attune their song, not to the strains and melodies of "the city that is within them," but to the ears of their consuming listeners? What would become of our vision of the Truth if our prophets and preachers were to mould their utterances, not according to the Divine voice within, but to please the ears and nurse the prejudices of their respective congregations? The ethical principle starts from within. And it is a principle which applies to every human relationship, that the discipline by which the soul attains its highest creative life, though it may often be necessary to impose it externally, is always best and most effective where it is *self*-imposed. That is the very essence of the democratic idea. "It is a low benefit to give me something," says Emerson: "It is a high benefit to enable me to do somewhat of myself." Development, though it may be aided from without, must always proceed from within.

How, then, does this affect our co-operative and industrial constitution? In this way—that the opportunity for this development from within must not merely be granted as a right, it must be welcomed as the expression of the inward voice of duty. Labour will not be content, ought not to be content, to come, cap in hand,

"Letting 'I dare not' wait upon 'I would,'
Like the poor cat i' the adage,"

either before a Board of capitalists, or even before a representative Board of consumers. It will claim to take its place on the same Board, bringing its contribution of service, of knowledge, of wisdom, to the common stock, so helping, by development from within the individual, the development of the organic life of the whole. "Fellowship is Life, and lack of Fellowship is Death," says the most melodious singer we have now left amongst us. And the noblest fellowship is that which reconciles conflicting interests, and resolves our individual discords into the higher harmonies of a true social life. The various parts of the body politic must work *with*, not *against* each other, and so produce that unity and mutual interdependence without which the highest form of fellowship and co-operation are impossible.

But the implications of the democratic idea are still more numerous. Just as a true creative power will produce nothing mean or low, so a true energising power will consume nothing vile or base. Unlike those modern Pharisees—whose religion is the true expression of their commercial life—of whose temple it was written:

> "They built the front, upon my word,
> As fine as any Abbey,
> But thinking they could cheat the Lord,
> They built the back part shabby,"

unlike these, I say, the temple of *our* faith, the expression of *our* life, from the smallest to the greatest part, must contain no sham, no semblance, no make-believe. I well remember the sub-manager of a department in a Lancashire cotton-mill telling me some years ago that he had once received instructions from his superior to put an increased amount of size into the fabric in order to give it a false appearance of strength and weight. At the risk of losing his situation the man refused, on the ground that the stuff contained sufficient size, and that any further addition would be dishonest to the purchaser, because it was intended to cheat him into buying something which seemed to be different to what it really was. That, I think, is the spirit we wish to see in our workmen. Character, expressing itself, embodying itself, in the things which it creates—the duty of truthful, faithful service, thus helping the satisfaction of grateful enjoyments.

This, you may say, is all very fine in a sermon, but it will not do in business. To which I must reply—then, for the sake of common manliness, let us clear our minds of cant. If we cannot strive to carry out in our work-a-day life the things we profess to believe in Church and advocate on the platform, let us close our Churches and Chapels, let us burn our Bibles, and let us call ourselves, not by the high-sounding title of "children of God," but rather, "children of the Devil." Falsehood, deceit, impurity, secrecy, and shams—these are the portion of the lower kingdom, in which, if we descend, we stain for ever the purity of our ideal, and make part of our spiritual life that unconscious "lie in the soul," than which there can be no more terrible retribution—loving the things we should hate, and hating the things we should love.

I know, indeed, how difficult, how seemingly endless, is our task. Principles, however fine and true, depend, for their application, upon persons, and if the persons fail, the principles have to wait for better men. There is a process of natural selection in ideals, in morals, in methods, as well as in nature and in life.

And so long as Co-operation falls below the best that can be done outside it, so long will there be room, and need, for private effort and enterprise to show it the example. How necessary, then, to level up, by education, the average ability, and capacity, and appreciation, on which the collective will and effort depend! Every domineering director, every uncivil official, every slovenly servant, retards, by the imperfection of his character and his work, the progress of the cause. Plato, in his *Republic,* in speaking of the Ideal State, tells us that it is guided by men of gold, who, having the divine metal within them, have no need of other earthly dross. But there are also in the State, he says, men of less divine and baser metal—men of silver, and men of brass and iron. Surely you have met these men of brass and iron in your general and business meetings! Think of it. Go back, some of you, to your stores, or even to our own local store, and make the simple proposition that the educational fund be increased from one to two per cent. of the profits, and see with what a loud clamour of dissent that needful proposition will be received. There you have democracy—in the raw. There you have the baser metal waiting to be transmuted into the divine. And it is that transmutation, first, within ourselves—for none of us are pure gold—then, by imperceptible degrees around us, it is that transmutation which must first be made, I say, ere the democratic idea can attain its full fruition, ere Life can become more noble and more abundant.

Let us, then, gird ourselves together for the high tasks awaiting us. Let us bind ourselves in a stronger and a holier fellowship. For ours is not the work and the struggle which is the inheritance of the beasts in their blind and tragic fight for existence. It is the combat, as of men and of angels, gifted with far-seeing vision and controlling powers, with the realm of darkness, of selfishness, and of sin, striving after the possession of the higher treasures of character, and the nobler harmonies of Being. Let us take care that none of the powers of that lower realm invade, in other guise, the citadel of the soul; that empty pride, and foolish popularity, and vaunting ambition, and vain-glory, do not usurp the place of other loves and other ideals. The call to labour is imperious; the field, wide as the confines of humanity; the purpose, guided by divine aspirations; the achievement, limited only by our courage and our will.

> "Languor is not in our hearts,
> Weakness is not in our word,
> Weariness not on our brow."

Inspired by the memory of the teachers and the workers who are gone, may our minds attain the sweep of an ampler vision, and our lives breathe forth a nobler passion, that thus our deeds may "wring a human music from the indifferent air," and so go sounding on to after ages and in other lives.

> "We fall to rise, are baffled to fight better,
> Sleep to wake."

RAMSDEN BALMFORTH

28

"THE 'COMMUNITY IDEA'", *MILLGATE MONTHLY*, NOVEMBER 1908, 87–91.

Catherine Webb

[Catherine Webb (1859–1947) was the daughter of a journeyman coppersmith from London, who had worked his way up to become manager of the Battersea and Wandsworth Co-operative Society and a director of the Co-operative Wholesale Society. An indefatigable worker for the cause, she founded the Battersea branch of the Women's Co-operative Guild, served on the central board of the Co-operative Union from 1895–1902, spoke and published widely on women's issues and edited the "Women's Corner" of the *Co-operative News* for a time. [Margaret Llewelyn Davies, *The Women's Co-operative Guild. 1883–1904* (Kirkby: WCG, 1904), 33–34] She had the highest aspirations for the movement, reminding her listeners to lay "firm hold of the central idea of 'community'", even when discussing the most mundane topics, such as organisation. [Catherine Webb, *The Machinery of the Co-operative Movement* (Manchester: Co-operative Union, 1896), 15] The article reproduced below is from the movement's illustrated monthly magazine. It demonstrates both an awareness of the legacy of Owenism and determined belief in the continuing relevance of utopianism. Against a contemporary background of renewed interest in "the community idea", Webb discusses the work of the Owenite feminist Mary Hennell, especially Hennell's *Social Systems and Communities* that was published separately in 1844. She summarises Hennell's overview of the history of common ownership since earliest times, attempting to pull out the connecting thread between earlier experiments and present practice. This historical recovery is vital, Webb argues, if co-operation is to develop "from a 'movement' to a 'commonwealth'". Although common ownership of the land and the establishment of communities like Queenwood have been central to this history, Webb maintains that there is now no other option but to build an alternative in the world as it is. "It seems to me that today, in the building up of a co-operative community", she writes, "we are not called upon to separate ourselves wholly from the social common life of the people. Indeed we cannot if we would".]

NOW, however humbly co-operation may begin, it must go on to manufacturing, and so to the possession of the land," wrote John Holmes in the *Co-operator* some half-a-century ago.

THE 'COMMUNITY IDEA'

It is impossible to glance along the shelves of an economist's library without coming to realise, that "possession of the land" runs like a dream thread through all the aspirations of all the reformers of all times. Whenever the dream takes definite shape, and finds expression in a tangible idea, the form it generally assumes is that of a "community" having equal rights in the common possession of land.

The co-operative movement has never wilfully freed itself from this dream, although, since the failure of Robert Owen's community schemes it has made few strenuous efforts to translate the dream into practice. To-day, however, we find the "community idea" gathering fresh force and momentum in the minds of active co-operators, and definite expression in the desire for a "Co-operative Garden City." Leaflets and pamphlets, setting forth in round figures and glowing phrases the practicability of the scheme, may be had for the asking;[1] and a strong team of co-operators—men and women—have been got together to lay hold of the dream thread and make it into a taut guiding line along the path of co-operative development.

The community idea thus being, as it were, in the air, I was delighted to receive one day a note from my friend Miss Clementina Black, saying:

> I wonder whether you would like to see two books—both a little out of the way—about which you might possibly care to write. One is a life of Stephens, the Factory Agitator, and the other is "Social Systems," by Mary Hennell, a friend of George Eliot. You will, I know, take care of them—as it happens dear Dr. Garnett gave me both of them. . . . On hearing that you would like to see them, I will at once send them.

Naturally, I did care to see them; and in Mary Hennell's forbidding looking little volume I have been enabled to trace the dream thread of the community idea through the long ages of the past, down to the moment when, in 1843, her gentle hand loosed its hold on life itself.

"Social Systems" was published in the drab days of printing; when dull green cloth boards, close-packed type, and no margins to speak of, were considered suitable medium for an economic treatise. So, to make up for its lack of typographical fascination, I must needs try to weave round Mary Hennell's work a little atmosphere of interest drawn from the literary surroundings of its author, interests which have woven themselves also into the life story of our greatest woman writer, George Eliot.

Nowhere can I gather a portrait of Mary Hennell; but we learn from the preface to her book, written by her brother-in-law, Mr. Charles Bray, that the essay was published first in 1841 as an appendix to "The Philosophy of Necessity," written by himself. It was re-issued in 1844 as a separate volume by her brother-in-law, as "a just tribute to her memory by him for whom she compiled it, and who for years had been a witness to her untiring zeal and energy in the cause of truth, and in the promotion of every object which appeared to her strong intellect to lead to the advancement and happiness of mankind."

Miss Marian Evans, who was afterwards to become so famous as "George Eliot," began her acquaintance with Charles Bray, his wife Caroline, and her sister Sara Hennell, in 1841, and they were destined to become her closest friends during the whole of her after life. In the life of George Eliot, written by Mathilde Blind, we learn that "Mr. Bray, his wife, and sister-in-law, were a trio more like some delightful characters in a first-rate novel than the sober inhabitants of a Warwickshire county town"; and from her husband's biography of her, we glean that her intercourse with the Brays at their charming house, Rosehill, Coventry, "is connected with some of George Eliot's happiest experiences, and with the period of her most rapid intellectual development."

It was in 1843 that the future novelist met Robert Owen at Rosehill. Queenwood, the last of the Owenite Communities, was then at the turning point of its brief career, and Owen himself was full of his schemes for the creation of "The New Moral World" and "The Rational System of Society."

One can imagine the talk that flowed round the hospitable table, and can see in fancy the strong intellectual face of Marian Evans shining with interest in the talk.

One imagines, also, that Robert Owen paid little special attention to the young lady friend of his host, and as little realised the keen criticism with which she would next day sum up the characteristics of the chief guest of the party. "I saw Robert Owen yesterday," she writes to her friend Sara Hennell, under date of September 16th, 1843: "Mr. and Mrs. Bray asked me to dine with him, and I think if his system prosper it will be in spite of its founder, and not because of his advocacy."

Mary Hennell, the elder sister of Mrs. Bray and Sara, died too soon after the acquaintance began to be included in this company of gifted friends, but we find tender references to her illness and death in letters written by Miss Evans to Miss Sara Hennell, in January and April, 1843. Mary, who was born at Manchester on May 23rd, 1802, died at Hackney of consumption on March 16th, 1843.

Both her father and brother-in-law were ribbon manufacturers of some standing. (If anyone wants to know how ribbons are made, let them consult Mary Hennell's long, exact, and most interesting account of the industry in "Knight's Penny Cyclopædia." It can be seen in any good reference library.)

The accumulation of wealth, however, by no means absorbed the full attention of Charles Bray. He was a prolific writer upon the educational and socialistic theories current in his day, and was an enthusiastic follower of Owen. He was present, we learn, at the opening of the Millennium at Queenwood, and helped to establish the Coventry Labourers' and Artisans' Society in 1843.

This society, by the way, made a flourishing start, it seems, with a general store, a bakehouse, a flour mill, and twenty-nine acres of allotment land. Its fortunes dwindled in course of years, owing, it is said, to mismanagement; but a new organisation took over the allotments under the name of the Earlsdon Garden Association. It has yielded now to the pressure of the new motive force which has turned Coventry (if one may be forgiven the pun) into the hub of the cycle world.

Mr. John Lower, the last secretary of the Association, tells me in a letter dated September 16th, 1908:—

"The Earlsdon Garden Association, as such, has ceased to exist, the land having been used for a building estate. Part of the land (five acres) had to be given up about seven years ago, and four years ago nearly all the remaining eleven acres. A few of the allotments not required were held till three years ago, when all of it had to be given up. This is much to be regretted, for it was a very successful Association. Another piece of land has been obtained and some of the old tenants have pieces of the new allotment, but the old association has ended."

Charles Bray was also the intimate friend of George Combe, and was active in promoting the Mechanics' Institute and the Provident dispensary of Coventry.

We can glean from all these details that the authoress of "Social Systems" moved quite in the heart of things co-operative as they had developed themselves in her day. It was the time of "enthusiastic experiment," and although the writer allows very little of her own opinion to appear in her essay, the reader cannot fail to realise that she brought more than common knowledge and interest to her task. What a task it was, and how well performed! With infinite research the principle of co-operation is traced in the social relationships of human society from the ancient histories of Crete and Sparta, down to the experimental communities of Owen, and the "Poor Colonies of Holland" founded as a result of Owen's teaching. It is enriched with interesting descriptions of the doctrines of St. Simon, Owen, Fourier, and by references to an innumerable number of more or less fugitive attempts at the establishment of "Social Systems" in many lands.

Besides the title page—in which, it will be noticed that some unknown hand has written in the names of the author and the editor of the little book—I have been unable to make an interesting picture of its pages. The pictures of Amana community, in America, and of the Assembly Hall of the Harmony Society at Economy, the headquarters of the Rappite community, are from a work by Mr. Charles Nordhoff, in which he describes the community societies of the United States as they existed in 1875. The pictures are interesting examples of the Garden City-like plans on which these communists built their colonies.

I find it astonishingly difficult to make selection from the rich field of information packed into Mary Hennell's 252 pages of interesting matter, leaving alone Mr. Bray's long and learned introduction of 114 pages! But seeing that we are in pursuit of a dream thread, and an idea, rather than precise facts, I must be content with gleaning here and there a sentence or two which will serve to carry us along.

Opening with a description of the Cretan commonwealth, when, some 1,500 years before the Christian Era, Minos laid down his famous laws of common equality—which held in force for nearly 1,000 years—we find there was no definite division of the land in Crete, but no one was allowed to lead an indolent life, whatever might be their rank; each was obliged to serve in the army or till the soil. "Rich and poor, men, women, and children, were fed at common tables, on the same diet, and at the public expense." All children were educated in common, in the same maxims, exercises, and arts. While these laws were in full vigour, our authoress notes: "Crete was held to be the peculiar abode of justice and virtue."

An equitable use of the land seems to have been the root principle of the people's happiness, however, for when, with the coming in of the iron age, and later the conquest of the Romans followed by the opening of the Christian Era, the laws of Minos were but obsolete relics of a far off past, the Cretans had become a sadly degenerate race—according to Saint Paul's account of them! For he writes, as we know, to Titus, that "The Cretans are always liars, evil hearts, slow bellies."

Tycurgus, too, whose unwritten laws ruled the ancient Spartan peoples for upwards of 400 years, made the land the basis of social equality, dividing it amongst his subjects, "who were not permitted to alienate, sell, or divide their respective portions." 9,000 lots were apportioned to Sparta, and 30,000 lots for the rest of Laconia. "He discouraged the arts, trade, and commerce, and all intercourse with foreigners, as sources of factitious wants, of corruption, and vice." Meals were in common, simple dwelling, clothing, and food were the portion of all. Moderation, temperance, rectitude, "obedience to the law and the dread of living to himself were the earliest lessons imprinted on the mind of a Lacedemonian."

The fame of the mothers and sons of Sparta have come down the ages to us as models of self-restraining citizenship. Land was the only wealth of Sparta, and her chief troubles came when, in following the trade of war, her citizens left the cultivation of the soil to an alien and a subject race.

Advancing from a description of the ancient Germans, who divided their arable lands afresh every year in order to preserve communal equality; and the barbaric warlike tribes of the North American Indians, who held the forest hunting grounds of their several tribes as common lands, to be defended in common against the enemy, Miss Hennell quotes a charming description of the "gentle Peruvians" who "had adopted the principle of common property," and divided their lands into equal shares. "One share was consecrated to the Sun, and the product was applied to the public rights of religion. The second belonged to the Inca, and was set apart as the provision made by the community for the support of government. The third and largest share was reserved for the maintenance of the people, among whom it was parcelled out."

In the ancient village "republics" of India, the fabulous communities of Ceylon where, as Diodorus reports, the people were allowed by law to live to 150 years and then to put themselves quietly to death: In the history of olden Egypt, and the story of the tribal life of the Israelites, the community idea expressed itself in the common use or possession of the land as the strongest bond of union. When the Christian era entered, the first Christian community held, we know, "all things in common," "but as Christianity spread and numbered among its converts persons of different nations, and of the most opposite modes of life, the bond of union was relaxed into simple affinity of doctrine and feeling."

Later on in the centuries we see this affinity drawing men and women into monasteries and nunneries, where, again, all things are held in common. But the dream thread is dropped, for, as Miss Hennell points out, in these monastic communities, "the foundation of co-operative union has been the belief of certain religious doctrine, and an enthusiastic zeal in support of them, not the conviction that this community of labour and property is the best means of securing the comfort and well-being of all."

A recital of all the curious sects that have from time to time broken away from conventional religious doctrines and established themselves in communities, would fill a far bigger space than I can claim. Even to mention all of those that come under Mary Hennell's notice is out of the question.

The Anabaptists, the militant sect that rose in the sixteenth century and seized the town of Munster in 1534; The Moravians, with their "common fund"; the Shakers, with their numerous societies scattered over the United States of America; the Dunkers, the Rappites, and the "Company of Zoar," are some of them. Miss Hennell quotes some remarks of Miss Martineau on these communities, which I cannot refrain from repeating, however, because they point a moral which seems to me highly important.

> The most remarkable order of landowners that I saw in the United States was that of the Shakers and Rappites; both holding all their property in common, and both enforcing celibacy. The interest which would be felt in watching the results of a community of property is utterly destroyed by the presence of the other distinction; or rather of the ignorance and superstition of which it is the sign. The moral and economical principles of these societies ought to be most carefully distinguished. . . . I believe it will be found that whatever they have peculiarly good among them is owing to the soundness of their economical principles; whatever they have that excites compassion is owing to the badness of their moral arrangements.

The special interest of the Rappites for us is that in 1825 Robert Owen had purchased of Mr. Rapp, the leader of the sect, the settlement of Harmony, in Indiana. Here he essayed to work out his scheme for a model community, "in which the principles of union, common property, and co-operation should be carried out."

With the advent of Owen in England, St. Simon and Fourier in France, as the apostles of the "Community Idea," we plunge into the turbulent times of economic controversy, out of which "Socialism" has evolved—or rather, had I not better say, is in process of evolution as the regenerating force in the coming social systems of the world.

Since 1844 much water has flowed over the mill in which social systems are ground into the stuff which feeds the daily needs of the peoples. We are a long, long way from the simplest ideals of social equality and social happiness of which men have dreamed throughout the ages!

But I find myself in the same danger that Mary Hennell did in winding up her essay—the danger of making "a melancholy, dispiriting conclusion." Like her, I would rather quote Fourier, and say that the dream thread of the Community Idea, and of its root foundation in the common possession of the land, is "too beautiful not to be possible."

As I have already said, there are indications that the Community Idea is stirring in men's minds afresh. The value of this glimpse over the hopes and failures of the past is, to my mind, that we go forward with renewed hope; building our new city in the light of experience; avoiding where possible the weaknesses that the failures of former builders have made plain.

It seems to me that to-day, in the building up of a co-operative community, we are not called upon to separate ourselves wholly from the social common life of the people. Indeed, we cannot if we would. But I see no reason why the dream of co-operative possession of the land should not be the next step to national possession of the land, and national enjoyment of its produce in perfect equality.

We have to-day the right to organise, the power to control vast sums of money—the accumulations of co-operative effort in distribution and production. We have facilities for intercourse unthought of in Owen's day, and we have what was so sadly lacking in the organisation of his schemes, a great body of men and women trained in the art of associated action, and educated in the management of affairs.

These are driving forces of the greatest strength, and it needs but the fire of a new-kindled enthusiasm to make them carry co-operation forward from a "movement" to a "commonwealth."

Note

1 From the joint secretaries of Co-operative Garden City Committee, 22, Red Lion Square, London, W.C.

29

CO-OPERATION FOR ALL (MANCHESTER: CO-OP UNION, 1914), 115–124.

Percy Redfern

[Redfern produced this short textbook as an introduction to the history and principles of co-operation. His was a prominent voice within the movement by this time, and he had recently published *The Story of the CWS* (1913), a dense, well-researched text produced to mark the wholesale's fiftieth anniversary. The extract reproduced below is from the final chapter in *Co-operation for All*, which was entitled "Ideas and Ideals". An autodidact in the classic mould, Redfern's love of reading comes across strongly, with references to Henry Thoreau, Arnold Bennett, Pascal, Matthew Arnold and St Francis of Assisi. As these names suggest, there is also the concern with the spiritual dimensions of co-operation here, more specifically an attempt to raise the consumerist strategy onto a higher plane. Redfern had been struggling with this problem for some years; his first book had been a study of Tolstoy's philosophical outlook. [Redfern discussed his personal quest in his autobiography, *Journey to Understanding* (London: Allen & Unwin, 1946)] Though committed to J.T.W. Mitchell's vision (later becoming Mitchell's biographer) and defining co-operation in his jubilee history of the CWS as "voluntary collectivism", Redfern was also sensitive to the fact that prioritising consumers through the CWS had definite shortcomings, particularly the organisation's bureaucratic tendencies and often ungenerous treatment of labour. We see him grappling or rather circling round these issues in this extract. Proud of what has been achieved, Redfern advises co-operators to be more ambitious and outward looking, "to live in the movement, but not bury ourselves in it". Moreover, there is no going back to the dream of a "self-contained community", for "we cannot shut ourselves up inside a world of our own". Near the end of the chapter, Redfern refers obliquely to the occurrence of strikes in CWS factories but quickly shies away from the subject with rhetoric about the "co-operative commonwealth", towards which all are striving. Understandably, Redfern finds it impossible to resolve the contradictions, which fully played out in the movement's subsequent history.]

IDEAS AND IDEALS.

IT was Thoreau who said that books should be read as deliberately as they were composed, and Arnold Bennett who spoke of newspapers being written in a hurry to be read in a hurry. For my part, I hope these pages will neither be skimmed and put aside like a newspaper, nor pondered upon as if to read them were a duty; for they are no more than an index to the co-operative movement itself. St. Francis of Assisi, more drastic than Thoreau, permitted no books to his immediate followers. The living-day of God and man was to be their illuminated page. Nevertheless, the morning and the evening may waste themselves upon us unless by means of a book their meaning is thrust upon our inert minds, and we are roused to see our day and generation anew.

So, too, with the industrial co-operative movement. It also requires that we view it afresh. At present it is curiously misunderstood. Journalists, professors, clergymen, labour members, and even men and women who have joined its own household look upon it through preconceived and distorting ideas. They praise its dross as gold and despise its gold as dross, and never suspect their assay. Capitalists are commercially successful at the expense of ideals; co-operation, too, is commercially successful; co-operators, therefore, depart from their ideals—in such a groove of bad logic their minds appear to run. But every act that leads to bankruptcy is not virtuous; and the popular choice is not in all things degraded. Therefore, let us honour the successes of the co-operative movement and stand up for what the millions of its rank and file have proved to be good in co-operation, against all the superior persons in the world.

Certain valuable features of the movement have been focussed in this little book. There are others besides; for it is a movement rich in local initiative, and some good new thing is always appearing here and there. Only a large and continually growing book could present it all. At the lowest reckoning there is food for enthusiasm. Nevertheless, having first valued our assets, we must not neglect the co-operative rule of depreciation. Capitalist companies sometimes show high profits by omitting to "write down;" but co-operative societies do not. They are not all for the present; they care for the future also. In the same manner we must have our stocktakings of ideas and ideals. We must guard against inflated views and pretensions by a sound and careful writing down. We must not risk future disillusionments and consequent reactions.

There is no corruption in the co-operative movement that compares with scandals of the past in Church and State; and the national and municipal life of to-day is not more clean. On the other hand, co-operation has a public standard to maintain. A private trader may give orders influenced by personal favours, or offer shares in his private company at a high interest to buyers of his goods, or dismiss an old worker to make room for a relative or friend. In the public trade of co-operation such things are wrong—absolutely and entirely wrong. Aided on one side by a glorious wealth of sterling and enduring qualities, while beset upon the other by competitive tides fretting against the dykes of average human nature, this standard we have to maintain.

The greater danger is less from positive wrong-doing than from easy-going, servile content with small aims and comfortable routine ways. A great Belgian co-operator once wrote of it being possible under certain circumstances for co-operative officials and servants to live like "mites in a cheese." "After us the deluge," said the aristocrats who brought France to revolution. Since ancient Rome until to-day pioneers have laboured to build up institutions, and their successors have eaten up the inheritance. The larger a movement grows the more easy it becomes to give up effort and be carried along by the active. But when each abandons initiative and enterprise to others a movement at last ceases to move at all. . . . The salt against such decay is in the pioneer spirit. It is in a spirit so alive and fearless and public, so eager to grasp new opportunities, so earnest for the future, that none can escape the force of its health. It is in the spirit of youth, of supple energy and joyous life. This spirit of beginnings is needed in the co-operative movement.

We have learned that co-operation has become great and wealthy. It has its fortune of £41,000,000 saved for its members in share capital, and its total annual purchases (wholesale, retail, and productive) of £130,000,000. But if we measure these figures by the population of the United Kingdom, reduced to households of five, we find they average for each household only £4. 10s. and £14. 10s. respectively. Yet the private capital of the four countries in 1911 has been reckoned at from eight to fourteen thousand million sterling, or an average of from £890 to £1,550 for each household. And, with an annual national income of £2,000,000,000, the annual private purchases can hardly total less than £900,000,000, or an average for each household of £100. This difference is great on paper, and when we look about us it is still plainer to our eyes. The private shops of London, great and small, stretch together in line for miles on miles, with never a co-operative store between them. The vast multiple shop companies have opened their seventy thousand shops since co-operation began, and even in those towns where co-operative stores are big and strong.

Pascal wished that men should realise both their greatness and their littleness. We, too, as co-operators, must look on both sides, and learn that we are still in the early days. We are not yet rich and prosperous. Not in our time can co-operators afford to take it easy. We are poor. We are feeble. Millions know little or nothing of us. Look down the list of Government contractors in the *Labour Gazette*. There are scores and hundreds of private firms, but none co-operative.[1] Or look through any directory. The multitudes of the names of shopkeepers overwhelm the references to co-operative stores. . . . We are not in the least discouraged by these odds. All that has been done, hitherto, has been accomplished in the face of them. But we must look onward to the work before us rather than backward on things accomplished, so that we may keep the missionary, pioneer spirit, and devote our best to the commonweal.

He who reads only one book, said Matthew Arnold, will cease to understand even that one. The co-operator who has no outlook beyond the co-operative movement is likely to share the same fate. We need to live in the movement, but not to bury ourselves in it. Welcoming the spirit of the pioneers we need not, therefore, accept the mistakes and limitations of past generations. "The world is wider to us than it was to our mothers in times bygone." The Home Colony of the pioneers was to be a self-contained community, a real state within a state. To-day the realisation of that ideal on any minor scale is clearly impossible; and if it were not impossible the attainment would be a misfortune. A limited community, self-sufficient and self-centred, with its offices and positions of trust frequently descending from fathers to sons, or passing on from one to another of an enlarged family, would suffer dry-rot. From the Pitcairn Islands to the Celestial Empire a universal law has declared against men or communities living to themselves. We can take a larger place amidst the democratic forces of the nation and the world; but we cannot shut ourselves up inside a world of our own.

The dream of self-sufficiency is denied, indeed, by the nearest facts. Seeking to employ our own members, we do actually enlist 145,000 persons in our service. But, excluding the Army and the Navy, there cannot be less than a million people on the pay rolls of the national and local government authorities. The Post Office, alone, employs 250,000. Yet even these figures and the co-operative are lost in the huge total for the United Kingdom of 20 million workers for wages and salaries. Again, proud of our progress in membership, we need to remember that the host of the trade unionists already exceeds our own; moreover, apart from its political side, the labour movement has surpassed the co-operative in attracting and training coming leaders, in creating newspapers, influencing the press, effecting researches, and moulding public opinion. Indeed, while we dream of the state within a state, many writers are classing co-operation not even as a distinct and complementary power, but simply as a kind of side-show within the labour movement. . . . "Lift up your heads," cried a Congress President; and we need to lift our eyes from our own lesser world that we may take our proper place in the greater sphere.

The deepest truth is often in paradox, as when we say that self-realisation comes through self-forgetfulness. And the simple truth about the co-operative movement is that living to itself it will lose its life, but in living to the great world it will gain all. Let us realise the want and hunger of mankind, and devote all the powers of the movement to human service; then, born of a new spirit, fresh, bold, and masterful conceptions will arise and triumph over little thoughts and ways. For example, the strength and the weakness of co-operation is in its local organisation. The big society lives to itself, while the weak society, a few miles away, starves for want of capital and local force. But the great multiple shop firms prosper by each shop being a branch from the parent stem, and all working together in one organisation, and by one command. Now, co-operation is capable of so combining its forces in one national society that the local interest will be left uninjured, while the benefit is added of one national control. There are, however, so many obstacles in the way that nothing can overcome them—except a great national enthusiasm to see co-operation mightier for good in the starved and thwarted lives of the people.

So with our service to the consumer. It is only by looking out on the life of the nation, and realising the weakness and poverty of the purchasing poor, that we can increase to the full the possible efficiency of the movement for service. Except co-operation there is nothing to stand for the consumer. Trade unionists organise as producers; manufacturers federate as employers and sellers; each and every trade and profession organises to protect its interests, and increase the return for its services. The consumer remains, with charges maintained against him, with technical skill employed against his ignorance, with the press muzzled against enlightening him, with opportunities restricted, with everything to leave him isolated, helpless, and poor. Even the Government is quite languid about him, and if it moves at all moves only in a casual and arbitrary way to protect some fragment of his interests when some particular abuse has become flagrant.

The consumers' interests are everybody's affair, and yet that is nobody's business, unless it is the business of the only direct organisation of the consuming poor, the linked co-operative stores of Great Britain. And if millions of consumers still prefer the service of shopkeepers, merchants, and manufacturers, with all the faults of competitive methods, it can only mean one of two things—either the consumers need some simple facts to be put plainly before them; or our own service, as their professed champions, is wanting in skill, in enterprise, and in earnest, honest devotion. Therefore we must never rest until, by study and knowledge, by public campaigns, and by concerted national efforts, we have won over not a minority only, but a majority of the people. For this is the only way to keep our movement alive and vigorous within, and to maintain and increase its efficiency.

Some will say, "Ah, but that only means more trade, and co-operation has an ideal beyond the shop counter." In reality it means a war against poverty. The census of production has shown that, in a number of trades, employing in all 3,685,000 persons, the average production is only £76 per head; and the conclusion has been drawn that a national minimum wage of 30s. a week is impossible. And it will be impossible for each adult amidst these millions to receive the value which 30s. represents to-day, if they are to be paid on the basis of manufacturers' prices while they themselves must needs buy back the stuff of life at retail figures. Why are the many poor? Primarily not because of receiving only 20s. or 30s. a week, for the wage that would spell poverty in America would mean affluence in India or Japan. They are poor because of the little that the wage will buy. They are poor because food and warmth and shelter, and a patch of land, and a few hours of sunny leisure are so much more costly to the Englishman than to the negro in Africa. . . . Let us admit that poverty is a complex and not a simple problem; nevertheless, very much of its solution is in enabling the consumers to buy and possess the materials of life, and use them to the most vital effect with the least friction and waste.

And what of the claims of labour and the employee? Again, progress is by looking out and beyond. A zeal for considering the hundred and fifty thousand workers within the employment of the movement is generous and right; yet there is a tendency to forget that the wage-earners in capitalist employment number seventeen or eighteen millions. Granted that we have not reached our limits. Even on the present distributive sales we could double the total of sixty thousand workers engaged in co-operative production. But without a great forward movement in distribution we could not do much more. Even with distribution extended to the utmost, there will remain the millions in the export trades, working indirectly for the consumers of South America, Africa, Asia, and the Colonies; and, besides these, the shipbuilders, the railwaymen, and the rest. It follows that we can help the people as a union of consumers to a far wider extent than we can touch their lives as employers. And it is an enthusiasm for the larger mission which will enable us to meet the second claim without either the weakness or the secret hostility which now sometimes exist.

If we are keen for an extended service, and eager for the knowledge that will better equip us, welcoming all allies, we shall have a living standard by which to judge the value of intelligence and devotion in others. Capitalism continually is trying to sift the man especially able to "make money" from the routine and less-interested worker. It creates an aristocracy of economic power, for whom the prizes of high salaries, directorships, and special investments are reserved. Co-operation also has recipients of wages and of salaries, but its tendency is to increase the one and restrain the other. And consistently with co-operation, again, there can be no special privileges of investment and ownership; all is for the commonwealth. Nevertheless, we, too, are in business, and we learn that capitalism may be inhuman, but that capitalists from their point of view are not exactly foolish. We discover that the quality of the management will go a very long way toward making or marring a department or a society, and that (although it does not end with him) good management certainly begins (or fails to begin) with the chief in command. We find that labour is not only to be measured by time but by intensity; that quality may outweigh quantity; and that there is all the difference in the world between the worker who tries and thinks, and has ideas, and puts in moral effort, and the one who "slacks." Now, if co-operation is to fulfil its mission it cannot afford to encourage slackness and indifference, nor to let ability feel that its only chance is on the other side; and neither must it be a taskmaster or a slave driver How may we reconcile these things?

Sometimes they go unreconciled. There is discouragement and waste, and possibilities of service are neglected or uncultivated; or there is ill-will, culminating now and then in strikes. And, although no strike of co-operative workers ever has compared in length or bitterness with disputes under capitalism, such a strike is always a symptom of disease. The health of co-operation is not in civil war; it is in unity and common effort. Rich people frequently imagine themselves to be the pillars of society. Working people too often are ready to accept the view, almost as absurd, that labour (construed in practice as limited to weekly-wage earning) is the sole fountain of wealth. Poets and artists, again, traditionally despise the men of business, and ignore commercial affairs. The captains and lords of industry despise everybody who fails to "make money." These conceits of class or calling are those which invade the co-operative movement whenever it slackens in its mission. The unity then is broken, and we have the idealist who is indifferent to the lessons of business failure or success—whose ideas become one-sided and mischievous in consequence. And we get the business head who is inwardly contemptuous of everything apparently beyond the counter and the cash box—whose very business becomes narrow and inefficient as a result. There can be no co-operation without mutual respect. There can be none without mutual interest. Co-operation means that all manner of people, if they serve the commonwealth, are useful to the commonwealth. But that service cannot easily be imposed from above, as under some great autocratic trust. It must spring for the most part from a common willingness to organise and be organised; and that willingness will be in proportion to the vigour of our mission.

There is no patent medicine for co-operative health, no ideal or idea which, swallowed in faith, will make us whole. But this may be said: Just so far as the great mission dominates us, so far can we do justice and more than justice to all and each, as each and all serve and strive for the commonwealth. Ours is no narrow test of service. It is economic and technical, and social and human. It demands the respect and sympathy which can see both sides and understand, and the will and purpose that can act. It needs an enlisting of personal will (even a machine may be tended, dull as the work is, with a greater or less degree of personal goodwill), and a requiting of personal service in return. It is a service in which, as members and customers, members of committees and of guilds, organisers and helpers—all participate. And it is a service that will become richer for all as co-operation is made a living movement in the nation's life, a power to call thousands together and move them to song, a spirit of life and joy communicating itself from each to each. . . . Let us have leaders whose hearts are with the people, but who will stand alone rather than be turned from a right course; let our banners blazon out the message of our mission against poverty and meanness of life—then, with a common faith in the power which men derive from unselfish fellowship, the hosts of our army and the people around shall have a new spirit in their midst of hope and joy.

Note

1 Through canteen scandals and the war this state of affairs is changing.

Part 5

GENDER AND CONSUMER ORGANISING

30

"VICE PRESIDENT'S ADDRESS", MISS GREENWOOD ON WOMEN'S POSITION, *REPORT OF THE 17TH ANNUAL CONGRESS OF DELEGATES FROM CO-OPERATIVE SOCIETIES...1885* (MANCHESTER: CO-OP UNION, 1885), 71–72

[Miss Greenwood's father, Abraham Greenwood, an early Rochdale activist and promoter of wholesaling, remarked during a discussion on education at the first annual Co-operative Congress in 1869: "The intellectual education of women was all very well – but the most pressing want now was the education of their daughters in the kitchen management, the economy of food, and the right kind of food. This would be of the greatest advantage to the comforts of home, and the promotion of good temper". [*Proceedings of the Co-operative Congress...1869* (1869), 73] Clearly, Greenwood's daughter did not take her father's advice, as this speech reproduced from the 1885 Congress demonstrates. Unfortunately, we know fairly little about Miss Greenwood, who was a keen supporter of the Women's Co-operative Guild and is in fact credited with first suggesting its name (it had initially been called the "Women's League for the Spread of Co-operation"). She was active locally, helping to form in November 1883 one of the earliest branches in Rochdale and serving as its secretary, and nationally from the following spring when she became vice-president of the WCG. [G.D.H. Cole, *A Century of Co-operation* (Manchester: Co-operative Union, 1945), 215, 217] In her address to the Co-operative Congress in 1885, Miss Greenwood looks back over what had been achieved during the past two years. She admits that after an initial period of enthusiasm, progress has been slow. Indeed, the Guild had a total membership of only 416 at this point, as the general secretary, Mrs Laurenson, revealed in the report which followed this address. Urging co-operative women to overcome their apathy and timidity, Miss Greenwood also points to male hostility as an explanation for the Guild's faltering growth, "'so called co-operators' who tell them 'we should do more good staying at home and educating our children.'" As the extract from William Marcroft which follows Greenwood's suggests, patriarchal attitudes were a serious obstacle to women's participation and gender conflict was to remain a key feature of the movement throughout its subsequent history, to damaging effect.]

VICE-PRESIDENT'S ADDRESS.

It has fallen to my lot, as vice-president of the "Woman's Co-operative Guild," to take the chair, in the unavoidable absence of Mrs. Acland, whose indifferent health will not permit her to be present on this occasion. In Edinburgh, two years ago, when our Guild was formed, everybody present seemed in a state of high excitement and enthusiasm; the prospect looked bright and glowing, and all felt there was a glorious future before us. We had tried no work at that time; we have been working two years now; let us look at the results. We find ten branches have been started in different parts of the country; these branches have not been begun without difficulties—with some of them it is still uphill work, I have no doubt; in places where we expected the best results, there have been no results at all. A great deal of the enthusiasm we had at Edinburgh seems to have passed away, or died out; some who pressed forward at first have fallen from the ranks, others have found that it meant working, not talking. But had we no work to do, our undertaking would be worth nothing; if we have only succeeded these last two years in rousing a few of our fellow-women to take a greater interest in their society, we have done some little good; we prove by the work we find for ourselves that there is work for the Guild to do. Guild work means giving of your leisure and your thought to the women you have drawn around you; preparing yourselves for little thanks, wrong constructions, unjust criticism. Some of the most unjust criticism comes from co-operators, or so-called co-operators. We are told by some of them "we should do more good staying at home and educating our children." My answer is, a woman who has no feelings of humanity, or does nothing to help her fellow-women, cannot educate her children, for children are educated by your words and deeds. Some of us have no children to educate; we have taken upon ourselves a higher education, that of humanity. Tennyson says:—

> Go teach the orphan boy to read,
> Or teach the orphan girl to sew,
> And pray heaven for a human heart!

Ruskin says (in 71 of "Frondes Agrestes") "God appoints to every one of his creatures a separate mission, and if they discharge it honourably, if they quit themselves like men, and faithfully follow the light which is in them, withdrawing from it all cold and quenching influence, there will assuredly come of it such burning as, in its appointed mode and measure, shall shine before men, and be of service constant and holy." Degrees infinite of lustre there must always be, but the weakest amongst us has a gift, however seemingly trivial, which is peculiar to her, and which, worthily used, will be a gift also to the race for ever. There is no member present here but can do something to help on a good cause, if it is only to give the leader of their Guild their support with a cheering word when things look dark. I value an encouraging word from the women I work amongst more than I would a newspaper full of praise. Nothing was ever begun but croakers arise and say it will never do; and it never *will* do if we sit still with our hands folded We must work both with our hands and hearts, for if our hearts are not in our work, we shall do little good. There is plenty of work still waiting to be done; the scheme of associated homes for country and seaside residence is yet to be tried; and in the near future I hope to see a school founded where the sons and daughters of co-operators may be taught the principles of co-operation, and that as they grow into men and women, literature may be found for them in our stores and workshops. This little Guild of ours, that now looks so little and puny, may be the grain of mustard seed that will grow into a mighty tree; and as the Guild grows in years, we hope to see it grow in usefulness.

31

THE MARCROFT FAMILY AND THE INNER CIRCLE OF HUMAN LIFE (ROCHDALE: E. WRIGLEY & SONS LTD., 1888), 50–52.

William Marcroft

[William Marcroft (1822–1894), was born in Middleton, Lancashire, the illegitimate son of a farm servant. Marcroft's early life was hard; he began work at the age of six collecting dung, then was taken on as a piecer a year and a half later. Gaining employment at a machine-making works in Heywood he eventually became a grinder, married Jane Smith the daughter of a local brewer at the age of twenty two, then worked his way up to foreman at a works in Oldham. As a young man, Marcroft was active in the Oddfellows, the Machine Grinders' Society and the temperance movement, though the co-operative movement became his chief passion, especially after the defeat of the Amalgamated Society of Engineers in the 1852 lock-out. He became a leading figure in the Oldham Industrial Co-operative Society and a keen promoter of co-operative production, serving as a director of one of the most famous of the so-called working-class limiteds, the Sun Mill Company. His wealth at death amounted to nearly £15,000, a remarkable sum for an individual from such humble origins. [R.E. Tyson, "William Marcroft (1822–94) and the limited liability movement in Oldham", *Transactions of the Lancashire and Cheshire Antiquarian Society*, 80 (1979); Donna Loftus, "Capital and community: limited liability and attempts to democratize the market in mid-Nineteenth Century England", *Victorian Studies*, 45/1 (2002)] Marcroft was fanatically thrifty, saving most of his wages and insisting that his family live on a frugal diet and wear homemade clothing. His wife Jane must have had a sorry time, managing on the meagre weekly allowance Marcroft provided, a practice which subverted the normal custom in the region whereby the husband gave up his wage to his wife who then made him an allowance. Neighbours disapproved of Marcroft's stingy ways, taunting Jane that "If my husband could not trust me with his wage, he should spend it hisself". [*The Marcroft Family...*, 63] Marcroft's sanctification of the home as woman's natural sphere, reproduced below, is an excellent albeit extreme example of the patriarchal obstacles within the movement that so infuriated women like Miss Greenwood and Catherine Webb.]

It is said, "If you would know the character of a would be reformer, you must follow him home to see if he has put his own house in order." The home is said to be the Englishman's castle. Is it to be a castle of order, peace and cleanliness, or a castle of confusion, disturbance, and filth? Young men, make your choice. Each can be had at the same price. In the homes of the poor, where intelligence, industry, and carefulness are ever in action, happiness and cheerfulness are intertwined in mutual hope and resignation, to make the best of the circumstances, in which the family are placed. The home of the great wage earner is too often one of negligence, the husband of hard toil merely thinking to supply an abundance. The sight of the home of dirt and disorder troubles him; he seeks a second home the house at which intoxicating liquors are sold, where in general there is cheerfulness, cleanliness, civility, and friendship—such places act as nets laid, to catch wandering husbands.

Beauty commands attention everywhere, and is appreciated by men as well as women. A clean and tidy woman, is the prettiest sight on earth; but a dirty, slovenly woman, is the most offensive thing in creation.

An hour earlier rising in the morning, would enable the wife and mother to light the fire with patience, prepare breakfast, clean the hearth, and put each article in the house in its proper place—to wash her face and hands, comb her hair, and make tidy her clothing. Thus, on the husband coming to breakfast, order and cleanliness would welcome him to comfort—the table covered with a white cloth, the pots clean and placed in nice order, the food all ready for the keen appetite, the wife speaking inviting words of kindness, telling the husband of some happy event.

The morning well started makes the household duties throughout the day an amusing, pleasant recreation. What unpleasant circumstances have arisen, because of the expected meal not being ready in time, or not cooked in a proper manner. When a woman is married, she is not to think of herself as a person to dress in fine clothes, flirting, skipping and gossipping from house to house, with neighbour women, but to become a sedate wife, or mother, ever anxious for the comfort of her husband. Wives should ever have it present in their mind, that other people are interested, and make it a part of their business to make their houses more agreeable to the husband, than does his wife. Life should ever be one of courtship, constantly trying to make dullness into brightness, sorrow into gladness, and making themselves acceptable in the sight of one another.

To enable the wife to perform the many obligations of family life in a cheerful manner, the husband should be at home as much as possible. The wife has need of the husband's advice and companionship. It requires the husband and wife to act in union to make home a place of love, joy, and contentment. Husbands, sons, and daughters, should, when at home, ever be doing little acts of assistance. Every such help makes the whole so much less for mother, whose anxiety ever is to make the home a place of happy resort. United efforts make a union of family comforts. The natural tendency of a woman in her varied duties and obligations of life, is to be clean, tidy, and modest, and, as a mother, sociable and affable in conversation; and as in her house, so are the bed-chambers kept in nice order, clean and healthy.

Home is the heaven gained in female life. There she makes a world as she wills it; order, cleanliness, regularity, and comfort are the four points of her compass. The husband is the altar of her worship, and to guide her children to do right is the pleasure of her life.

32

THE RELATIONS BETWEEN CO-OPERATION AND SOCIALISTIC ASPIRATIONS (MANCHESTER: CO-OP UNION, 1890), 12–13.

Margaret Llewelyn Davies

[Margaret Llewelyn Davies (1861-1944) devoted her life to the Women's Co-operative Guild. She grew up in a Christian Socialist environment; her father John, a rector in Marylebone, London and later in Kirkby Lonsdale, was a friend of Maurice, Ludlow and other leaders of Christian Socialism. Llewelyn Davies studied at Queen's College, London and Girton College, Cambridge, then moved into the developing field of social work and tried to establish profit-sharing workshops, with no success. She joined the Marylebone Co-operative Society in 1886 after reading William Thornton's *On Labour*, which described co-operation as the "child of Socialism…destined to beget, at however remote a date, a healthy Socialism as superior to itself in all its best attributes as itself is to its parent". [Gillian Scott, *Feminism and the politics of working women. The Women's Co-operative Guild, 1880s to the Second World War* (London: UCL Press, 1998), 38] Llewelyn Davies became convinced that harnessing the "basket power" of working-class women would provide a key lever with which to effect a socialist transformation of economy and society. She was a member of the Marylebone branch of the WCG before becoming the organisation's general secretary in 1889, a post she held until 1922. Under her leadership, the guild went from strength to strength, building a reputation as the co-operative movement's radical moral conscience. In this pamphlet, first delivered as a paper at the Co-operative Congress held in Glasgow in 1890, Llewelyn Davies attempts to collapse together co-operation and socialism, by which she means Fabian collectivism. Both can be traced back to Owen she argues and both sought "to substitute a system of association for one of competition". Referring to the need for political representation, and in keeping with her Christian Socialist background, she put a great deal of faith in enlightened individuals rather than the organised working-class, though belief in the ability of the latter increased thereafter. Llewelyn Davies was also sensitive to the problems of statist social reform, attempting to strike a delicate balance in the paper, though co-operators' suspicions towards the state were not easily overcome.]

The Relations Between Co-operation and Socialistic Aspirations.

"Ex Tenebris Lux."

In treating of the relation that Co-operation bears to Socialism, I shall endeavour first to show that the aims of both systems are similar, then to describe and compare the methods that each is employing or would employ, and finally to judge how the common ideal may be best obtained, considering the state of things in the industrial world at the present time.

AIM OF SOCIALISM AND CO-OPERATION.

Both systems may be said to owe their origin to the anarchy produced by the Industrial Revolution, which inaugurated a reign of free competition, or a state of things as near to free competition as human nature would allow, resulting in the realisation of enormous fortunes on the one hand, and of poverty and degradation on the other. Capital was all-triumphant, and labour was crushed under a remorseless tyranny. Co-operative and socialistic schemes had as their object the delivery of labour from this slavery.

The ideals of Co-operation and Socialism are so much in harmony that they may practically be considered identical. Mr. Neale has said that Co-operation only differs from Socialism in this, that Co-operators employ a slower process in realising their ends than the prophets of modern Socialism are willing to adopt. Robert Owen was the father of both movements; Lassalle's Socialism consisted in organising co-operative productive workshops similar to our own, except that the capital was supplied by the State, and not by individuals or societies; and one of the leaders of the Catholic Socialists desired "all good Christians to adopt this idea of co-operative associations of production upon the basis of Christianity." Both Co-operators and Socialists desire to see a more equitable distribution of wealth, to bring within the reach of all the advantages enjoyed at present only by a few; to give as equal opportunities as possible to all, so as to secure the highest development of each; and to make the conditions of life such that our sense of justice is not violated, and such that it may be possible to realise that society is a "brotherhood, and not a collection of warring atoms." Briefly, the common object is to substitute a system of association for one of competition. It is believed that (1) economic and (2) moral benefits would result from such a change.

(1) I shall not attempt here to weigh the advantages and disadvantages arising from competition. I merely recognise that it is freely condemned by both Socialists and Co-operators. It is impossible to speak with certainty as to what the result, economically, of abolishing competition would be, yet—supposing a system were substituted by which, instead of land-owners holding back land out of the market, and charging exorbitant rents; instead of capitalists trying to keep down wages,

and labourers trying to force wages up—if, instead of this antagonism between the owners of the three instruments of production, they were to work in harmony together, it is thought possible that not only would better men, but more wealth, be produced. We might liken our present industrial system to a cart being pulled by three horses, each straining in its own different direction. The horse called "Capital" is the strongest, and is pulling the cart mostly in its direction; but its course is impeded by the sideway pullings of the other two horses, "Land" and "Labour." The cart advances, and in the direction which "Capital" wishes, but its progress would be much greater if the horses were pulling together, each abreast of the other.

In distribution the waste in our present system is well known, and has been ascertained in some detail. In production, under an associative system, where the workers would have an authoritative voice, a reduction in the hours of labour would probably take place, and either wages would go up, or the equivalents of higher wages would be brought within the reach of all. The result would probably be that better work would be produced, owing to the improved condition of the workers; and as much work might be done with shorter hours, for the same reason; and unproductive labour and consumption would probably be largely replaced by productive labour and consumption.

(2) But it is not only because such a change might produce economic advantages that it would be welcome, but because it seems not unreasonable to suppose that a great intellectual and moral development would be the result. Tendencies to competition must always exist; but the instinct of self-preservation is not to be left unrestrained. We recognise that there are higher objects than the wish to live, or even than the noble ambition of "getting on" by means of other people's shoulders. Certain qualities, no doubt, are produced by the struggle for existence and the struggle for wealth, but hardly those that we admire most. It is surely the duty of society to see that its conditions are such as to create and stimulate an altruistic spirit. Altruism is the only finally satisfying course of conduct; but if the first necessaries to existence—food, comforts, leisure—can only be procured through competition, the lower satisfaction is gained at the expense of the higher. Co-operators and Socialists desire to see society so organised that all who are willing to work should be able to obtain, by working, the necessaries of life, and to obtain them in such a way that others may not be made to suffer in the process.

METHODS.

(1) *Socialistic.*—The method by which Socialism seeks to secure the fullest development of each individual, and thus of society, is by replacing "the system of private and competing capitals by one of united collective capitals." It proposes, by a collective method of production, the instruments of production being owned by all, to apply the profits for the good of all. Socialism has been thus described: "In the first place every socialistic doctrine aims at introducing greater equality in social conditions, and secondly, at realising these reforms by the law of the state."

There is much misconception about the measures that Socialists would adopt. Socialism does not necessarily imply a hard and fast industrial system; it does not imply community of goods; it does not imply "an equal division of unequal earnings," nor a periodical redistribution of wealth; nor is it necessarily concerned with religion. What it wishes to do is, by placing the ownership of the instruments of production beyond the power of private individuals, to prevent monopolies, and to make it impossible for individuals to amass huge fortunes, and to live luxuriously, as drones, on the interest arising from the possession of land and capital, and supported by the labour of others. The instruments of production will be owned by the whole community—either "nationalised" or "municipalised"; the public departments will be maintained by the returns to collective labour instead of by taxation; and individuals will receive their share in proportion to their work, to be utilised at will in private consumption, but not for further production.

(2) *Co-operative.*—Co-operators think that the aims above stated may and would be best attained by *voluntary association,* and they thus form a sort of half-way house between the Socialist and Individualist schools. They believe that by using the accumulated capital of the working-class for production on a collective method, and dividing the profits either between labour and capital, or labour, capital, and consumption, that distribution and production may be so organised as to do away ultimately with competition, and so as to procure a more equitable distribution of wealth. They trust that gradual education and development will make men perceive that this associative system is a higher one than the competitive system, and that a man's truest satisfaction will be found in sacrificing his individual material gains, or a part of them, for the sake of the community. They believe that under their system the development of the individual progresses at the same time as, and by means of, the gradual change in outward conditions, so that as opportunities open out men are worthy to take advantage of them.

COMPARISON OF METHODS.

In looking forward and trying to ascertain how far the co-operative methods seem as if they were likely to gain the end in view, there are two chief points that suggest themselves as difficulties to be overcome, and for which adequate solutions have yet to be found and adopted.

1. First, does there seem any reasonable hope, near or remote, of our being able, on our present lines, effectively to restrain competition? I think I may say that genuine Co-operators anticipate the time when all industry will be carried on on a co-operative basis. If we were content, as some friends of the movement seem to be, with the prospect of seeing co-operative and individualist enterprises running on happily side by side, we should feel that Co-operation was not so much a system, as a practical scheme for mitigating our present competitive system, rather than superseding it.

While trade and industry are as at present only partially co-operative, the existence of co-operative societies only increases competition. Even in our own co-operative world, competition has not yet been checked—we see productive societies competing with each other, and productive societies with the Wholesale societies. There is no central institution whose decisions are recognised as final on such questions as the number and position of societies. The Co-operative Union has no binding authority invested in it. The hope is that some scheme of federation may be devised, which would be so obviously beneficial to the whole movement, that Co-operators would feel constrained to adopt it. It is urgently necessary that still more attention should be given to this question, more efforts made at conciliation, and better constructive schemes thought out. But if the voluntary system is so difficult to work, and so slow in producing an effect, even amongst professed co-operators, there will be still greater delay in checking competition in the outside world, and in absorbing all trade into the co-operative system. It will probably be centuries before individual enterprise will not appear more attractive to most minds than associative. The strength of self-interest is fairly obvious at the present day by the existence of the notoriously large class of "dividend-hunters." Are we sufficiently sure that our voluntary system alone will produce the best results in the long run, as to feel justified in waiting to reduce the present chaos and suffering, till, through education, we see the lower instincts yielding more universally to the higher?

2. Then, again, it seems to me that we have not as yet shown sufficiently clearly any effective method by which the present force of capitalism and landlordism may be met and overcome. The power of capital is at the present day enormously greater than the power of labour, remarkable as are the results achieved by the latter. The starvation point with labour is much nearer than with capital, and the combination of capitalists is much easier and demands much fewer sacrifices than the combination of workers.

In America, where greater enterprise is displayed, and larger openings occur, we can trace most clearly the working and development of capitalism. Small capitalists are being entirely driven out of the field; joint-stock companies are taking the place of large individual capitalists; and "rings," "trusts," and "syndicates" have now almost absolute control in the labour market. In the United States, joint-stock companies are reckoned to hold a quarter of the total value of all property.[1] A few companies control the whole of the anthracite coal produce of Pennsylvania, where the " 'coal barons' agree to fix absolutely the wholesale price of coal, always securing an immense rise before winter sets in." The great "Copper Syndicate" and "Standard Oil Trust" show the expansion capitalism is capable of; and similar results are to be found in other businesses. In England, every kind of business is rapidly being converted into a joint-stock company. Co-operators are pursuing the same road as capitalists, in so far as joint ownership and management are superseding individual ownership and management—but does it seem probable that co-operative production under its present conditions will overtake and outstrip capitalist enterprise? It is most difficult to foresee in what way a more hopeful system will be introduced, and what form production will take in the future—whether the Wholesale Societies will undertake the whole of production;

whether the individualist productive societies will federate; whether a federation of stores will produce locally for themselves; or whether it will be with trades unions that the future of production will lie. The latter course appeals to me as perhaps the one from which the best results might be obtained. If co-operators and unionists joined hands, then there would be capital, skill, and a market. One of the many difficulties that beset co-operative enterprise is, that co-operators and co-operative societies are unwilling to apply their money to any large extent to production. And it is easy to see that there is much excuse for the unwillingness of individuals—if not of societies—to invest savings in ventures which must necessarily involve considerable risk. The Wholesale Societies possess capital, and are willing to utilise it for production; but while the difficulty of want of capital does not exist in cases where production is carried on by them, there are other difficulties—*e.g.,* the inevitable centralisation, which makes this system not altogether satisfactory.

With regard to the land question, which bears directly upon all other economic questions, we must face the fact that individual ownership would be out of place if society were founded on a co-operative basis, and we must show how it may be replaced either by state or municipal ownership, or by some other form of associative holding.

The question I wish to put is—can we reasonably expect that the monster of self-interest, with its many heads of competition, capitalism, landlordism, &c., will be slain by the co-operative sword alone? Are there not many cases in which legislative interference would give chances of success which co-operative enterprise could not otherwise attain?

It is here that Co-operators and Socialists join issue, and the difference on this point explains the lofty contempt that each party often expresses for the other. I cannot here enter into the immense practical difficulties there are in the way of the attainment of Socialism, but I think we may allow that Socialists have a comprehensive, though not a rigidly defined system, and that they show themselves practical in demanding support for measures which evidently tend towards Socialism, *e.g.,* measures for reducing the hours of labour, and other acts interfering with the liberty of the individual, for the taxation of the land and for extending state and municipal control.

Co-operators have always shown distrust of parliamentary interference, and a certain pride in their independence of legislation. But, however much there is to disgust in party politics, we cannot afford to despise parliamentary action, considering the good that has already resulted from it. There need be no exaggerated belief in the efficacy of Acts of Parliament; but we should all, I think, be inclined to believe in the good results that might be obtained from Acts passed by an educated labour majority. It is on the common ground of education that Co-operators and Socialists would do well to meet. I have indicated what Co-operators have to learn from Socialism, namely, education in the direction of parliamentary action; and we may well hope that Socialists will recognise the usefulness of the practical training for an associative system that is gained through co-operative enterprises, and also the value of the results already obtained. The voluntary and compulsory methods are not exclusive of each other; both are valuable, and there need be no antagonism between the advocates of the two systems.

And it would be well, not only for Co-operators and Socialists to draw more closely together, but for all the various labour organisations to be brought more in contact with each other, so that they could realise that the separate problems are only parts of one great question.

But along whatever lines progress will make its way in the future, there seems a prospect of a fairer world for our descendants. Reformers are numerous; and with none are aspirations purely material. All seek a change in outward circumstances, in order that the best life may be led by all. It seems impossible to doubt that there is a unity of purpose—an order to which the whole creation moves—that will satisfy our ideas of justice, and gradually become clearer as time moves on. We now recognise that slavery was a system under which an individual was deprived by society of his due, and the day will come when an order of society will have been evolved, so that the "white slavery" that still mars our civilisation will in like manner no longer exist, and the brotherhood of men will be realised. Meantime, to procure this progress, we shall need courage and perseverance, and the faith of

"One who never turned his back, but marched breast forward;
Never doubted clouds would break;
Never dreamt, though right were worsted, wrong would triumph;
Held, we fall to rise; are baffled to fight better;
Sleep to wake."

Note

1 See "Fabian Essays," ch. iii.

33

THE WOMEN'S GUILD AND STORE LIFE (LONDON: 1892), 1–8.

Catherine Webb

[A talented propagandist, Catherine Webb edited a popular early textbook, *Industrial Co-operation: the story of a peaceful revolution* (Manchester: Co-operative Union, 1904), and later published a widely read history of the Women's Co-operative Guild entitled *The Woman with the Basket* (Manchester: CWS, 1927). Like activists such as Miss Greenwood, Webb had to struggle from the start against male hostility within the movement, blaming the organisation's slow initial growth on "'so-called co-operators' who tell women that 'we should do more good staying at home and educating our children'". Webb's response to such criticism, voiced at the Co-operative Congress in 1885, was that theirs was "a higher education, that of humanity". [Gillian Scott, *Feminism and the politics of working women. The Women's Co-operative Guild, 1880s to the Second World War* (London: UCL Press, 1998), 70] Growing up in fairly comfortable circumstances herself thanks to the movement's growth in South London which enabled her father's rise, Webb was nevertheless keenly aware of the importance of reaching out to working-class women in their daily lives, educating them as consumers and citizens but learning from them too. [Barbara J. Blaszak, *The Matriarchs of England's Cooperative Movement: A Study in Gender Politics and Female Leadership, 1883–1921* (Westport, Conn.: Greenwood Press, 2000), 105] As we have already seen, she also had the highest aspirations for the movement. Webb's pamphlet reproduced here demonstrates her understanding of the store as a cultural form with enormous potential to empower female working-class consumers. Webb believed that what she termed "store life" might generate a completely new way of life or culture, which crucially depended on the participation and meaningful involvement of both women in their various roles and also children. The stated intention might be to knit members together into one big family, but Webb's text points once more to divisions within the movement, this time in relation to female agricultural workers employed by a co-operative society whom she describes as "Poor, rough, faces tanned, and hands hardened by out-door toil, uneducated, uncouth…".]

IT seems to me that the object of the festival we are holding here to-day is not so much the triumphant celebration of the establishment of the 100th branch of the

Guild, as the determination of the exact position and relation of the Guild to the Co-operative movement as a whole; the opportunity, as it were, for drawing up a Charter of rights, privileges, and duties; of giving forth some definite idea of policy, and, if possible, inaugurating some benefit scheme for women which shall give an objective meaning to the Guild, and make it not only a recognised power in the movement itself, but a distinct motor in the movements of the day which have for their object the advancement of true civilisation.

My part in this laudable ambition is but a small one, and scarcely touches either charter, policy, or scheme, but perhaps forms some of the groundwork upon which all three may be built up.

First let us try to define

WHAT IS MEANT BY STORE LIFE.

Does it consist of the figures on the balance sheet? so much trade done, so much dividend paid?

These things may indicate a living or dying society, but they do not constitute the "life" of a store in the sense in which we wish to consider it. This is surely made up of the *persons* whose sympathies, interests, and destinies even, centre round the success or failure of the store.

Who are these persons? I answer, the members, committees, committee's wives, employés, employés' wives, and all the children and young people connected with them. These should, to carry out the true ideal of our movement, be so closely knit together that the good or ill of each should be the good or ill of all, as in one huge family, and to each and all of these, I feel, that a Guild member who would earnestly carry out the first object only of the Guild, viz., "To draw co-operators together in a friendly spirit," owes duties and obligations it would be well for us to clearly recognise. Lest our ideas should get in a serious muddle, perhaps it would be well to take these persons in the order I have named them, and consider our relations with each in turn.

MEMBERS FIRST.

I am presuming, of course, that the great majority of Guild women are members of the store in their own name, if not, I think they ought to be, and I am also presuming that they are among the best of members, the most loyal, the most consistent, the least fault-finding, and the best propagandists. If not, again, they ought to be. They owe this, at least, as a matter of example to their fellow-members. Of what use is it to take upon oneself a name and badge, intended to mark one as being more deeply interested in Co-operation than an ordinary member, if we have no proof to offer the members of our sincerity?

Can we not also show an example of really intelligent interest in the business of our various societies by careful study of the balance sheet, preparatory discussion on any important matter requiring decision at quarterly meetings, and attendance at those meetings?

The Co-operative world itself would be considerably astonished, I fancy, to know in what a large number of stores women are in the majority as members, and I cannot help thinking, by the way, that if we could draw all these women into the ranks of the Guild, Co-operation would move along at a speed never before dreamt of.

Our annual report shows that at present there are only 6 women on management and 73 on educational committees.

Is this a sufficient representation for the large majorities of women members?

Should we not endeavour to train ourselves into sufficiently business-like habits and knowledge to take our share in the management of businesses so largely devoted to women's interests?

It seems to me that in plain duty to the women members, the Guild should devote considerable attention to this end, forming classes for systematic study of business detail, so that should the opportunity arise a really suitable candidate may be forthcoming to represent them.

These are some of the duties we owe to our fellow-members, others there are which will readily suggest themselves to you, and upon which I need not enlarge, such as ever willing help in propagandist work, social gatherings, etc.

COMMITTEES.

How much the "Life" of a store is regulated by these persons.

Everybody has heard of sleepy committees, muddling committees, go-a-head committees, and knows that generally speaking store life is sleepy, muddling, or go-a-head accordingly.

Now what are the duties of the Guild to the committees? First let us never lose sight of the fact that as a rule their work is voluntary and honorary, and that the least return they can expect from members who *place them in their ofttimes difficult position,* is confidence and sympathy.

As far as our vote and influence goes, let us help to elect men and women worthy of respect, then render them their due, and refrain from carping criticism and interfering with their policy or actions.

If, as sometimes happens, they prove unworthy or, with the best of intentions and heart, utterly incapable, surely our strongest remedy is in the ballot-box rather than agitation, recrimination, or heckling, which stirs up nothing but ill-feeling and an unco-operative spirit.

I will not deny that criticism is sometimes necessary, and a little gentle prodding now and then—especially of sleepy committees—extremely salutary, but when necessary, let your criticism and prodding be administered in a perfectly constitutional manner. That is, as an unanimous expression from the Guild, tendered in proper accordance with the rules of your society.

Then and then only will your criticism have its due weight.

I think also we should teach committees that they may place confidence in the Guild, by never taking any concerted action (outside our internal Guild plans I mean) without duly consulting or acquainting them with our proposals.

A house divided cannot stand, and none know like those who have been behind the scenes, how dreadfully the progress of co-operation is hindered by want of harmony and mutual confidence between those who make up the inner life of the store. Personally I wouldn't give twopence for the moral backbone of a committeeman, who, dear, courteous, kind-hearted man, accedes to every practical or unpractical suggestion of the Guild, simply to please the ladies; but, some of the most practical business-like committeemen in the movement have yet to be taught, that women *do* possess sufficient common sense and intelligence to be listened to with consideration at least, when they make well-thought-out proposals or suggestions as to the management of store life.

The foregoing remarks refer to the managing committees, but many of them apply with equal force to educational committees, with whose work the objects of the Guild are so nearly akin that it is a sad state of affairs indeed when they cannot act together in harmony.

COMMITTEEMEN'S WIVES.

I don't know that I have ever seen these persons specified as a class before, but they do seem to me to form a distinct and important element in store life. I believe it is very frequently the case that committeemen's wives are among the best and most enthusiastic of Guild members, but not invariably.

However it may be in the north, in the south every spare hour of a committeeman's life is spent at the store, and ofttimes many hours that can ill be spared from home and family, and the only help his wife can give to the cause her husband is so deeply interested in, is to patiently and cheerfully endure the long hours of loneliness, and bear a double share of the burden of home cares. This she frequently does without even being able to participate in the things which interest her husband, for, as she will pathetically tell you, "He comes home too late and too weary at night to tell me anything, and there's no time in the morning." How much these wives have to do with true progress who can say? It's quite certain that a committeeman is not likely to prove a success whose wife is opposed to or indifferent to Co-operation. What then is the Guild's attitude towards the wife of a committeeman? Certainly try, and keep on trying, to induce her to join the Guild, but if by reason of her home ties she is unable to attend the meetings, is not that a stronger reason for never leaving her out of our calculations? Should we lose anything of our hoped-for influence on the "Life of the Store," by keeping her posted up with all the plans and proposals of the Guild? By counting her as one with her husband on all matters on which we wish to gain his interest? By inviting her as a guest with her husband to all social gatherings or other meetings, where the presence of a committeeman is desirable? Some such method as this would, I feel sure, have a distinctly educational effect, and go far to promote that unity of action so desirable for rapid progress.

EMPLOYEES.

If one were asked "What is an ideal Co-operator?" we should be apt glibly and unhesitatingly to answer, "The Co-operative productive worker, to be sure." I fancy, however, if all the world were making boots, say, in a productive workshop we should still want somebody to distribute them out to us, even if we had to find a supernatural being to do it.

Perhaps it's personal jealousy because I can't make boots and can only keep accounts, but I fail to see, and always have failed to see, that an employé in a distributive store, whose whole living is derived from serving Co-operators, who can, if he choose, take shares in the society he serves, is any less ideal than the bootmaker. And yet to this day he is comparatively ignored as a class representative of the highest form of Co-operation.

On the other hand, to hear the way in which some Co-operators address their employés one would think there was positive degredation in the work. Cannot the Guild do something at least to help reconstruct public opinion on this point? I hold that the higher the estimate in which a man holds his daily work the better servant he is likely to prove, and the less need there is for check systems.

The employés are, of course, entirely under the control of the managing committee, and no outside body can attempt to interfere with that control; but the Guild can do much to improve the life of the employés by helping to shorten the hours of work, by arranging their shopping hours during the times of least pressure of business, by interesting themselves in their physical and mental welfare. In societies where several women and girls are employed surely there is scope for influence. I remember once meeting some women farm hands whose appearance interested and somewhat distressed me. Making inquiries I learnt that they were regularly employed on the farm of a flourishing society, working in the fields from morn to night, but no one knew whether they were members of the society or understood from what cause they were working. Neither had it occurred to anyone to invite them to become members of the Guild branch.

Poor, rough, faces tanned, and hands hardened by out-door toil, uneducated, uncouth they might be, but I *cannot help thinking* that their lives might be considerably brightened and elevated by the sympathy and help of the Guild. We, who yearn to brighten the lives and elevate the minds of all working women, are surely throwing away our opportunities when we neglect such natural material as the women and girls in our own employ.

Many societies employ also a large number of women in shops as drapers, milliners, and dressmakers, and it is to act as guardians of their well-being I see the greatest need for the presence of women on the committee of management. Then, too, many of these young women look forward to one day becoming housewives. Are they to be allowed to slip from your service with no better knowledge or higher aims than they could gain in a competitive house of business?

It would not do to promise you that however hard you may try you will draw many of them into active work in the Guild. Indeed, their hours of leisure are so few that I do not think it is reasonable to expect them to give up much time to Guild work, but I would say as of the committeemen's wives, never leave them out of your calculations in any project of pleasure or scheme for the fuller development of store life.

EMPLOYEES' WIVES.

Happening to visit a branch of the Guild last winter where the meetings were held over the store, I remarked how cosy and comfortable the room looked, and asked, "Who gets it ready for the meetings?" "Oh! the manager's wife." "Is she a member of the Guild?" "I don't know," was the reply, "but should hardly think so. You see she has six children!" Now the special attraction of that evening's meeting was to be a discussion on "Need women always be household drudges?" so it was suggested that this possibly overburdened manager's wife should be invited to attend. This was done, but without a little preparation it is not always possible to leave six children in a room by themselves if it is only two or three steps away; and our friend had to decline the pleasure of an hour or two's rest and change of thought, because it had not occurred to anyone to provide a relief guard for her army of young co-operators. I do not think the moral of this little incident needs much pointing.

Sometimes we get a new manager or storekeeper who comes from country to town or *vice versâ,* bringing his wife with him to live, sometimes over the store and sometimes not; but almost invariably bringing her away from familiar associates and friends to a strange place and unknown people.

Very few women can live entirely without some friend of her own sex to whom she can speak personally; but among whom is our manager's wife supposed to find her friends? Who is to make the first advances toward acquaintance?

Is it usual for the man's fellow employés' wives to call on her, or should the committeemen's wives be the first to offer her friendship? It would be well for store-life, I think, if there was more kindly feeling among the wives of employés and committees; but would it not be a graceful action on the part of the Guild to be the first to hold out a welcoming hand to the new-comer, whose heart is very often sore at leaving accustomed scenes and faces.

Is the man any less likely to try his hardest to please his new masters or to fit into his new surroundings if his wife is made to feel at home?

Or, again, one of our young men takes to himself a wife, perhaps the daughter of a co-operator—if so, well and good; she will find her place amongst us without much trouble—but more probably he marries a stranger from another town, to whom the stores is but the name of the shop where her husband works, and nothing more.

Who is going to teach her that it *is* something more and that she herself may form no insignificant factor in its prosperity, by encouraging her husband to render it his best service, by herself loyally supporting it? Here is Guild work undoubtedly.

CHILDREN AND YOUNG PEOPLE.

Now we come to a field of influence of such practically unlimited extent that I fear I shall get lost upon it, if I try to say too much. You hardly need me to tell you that the world may count our labour lost, if the principles our fathers, and we have striven so hard to formulate, do not become the natural inherent guiding principles of the next generation.

This can only be accomplished by training the young children. Each individual member of the Guild, who has children of her own, has work to do in this direction, but much more may be done by united action. I hold that juvenile penny banks are absolutely necessary in every society, as giving training in habits of thrift, and I would suggest that wherever possible children's classes, singing classes, girls' and boys' clubs, recreative clubs, and any effort which will give a conscious or even unconscious sense of *association,* should be used to build up in the minds of our young people the principles of true co-operation.

Then, too, I hope the Guild will not lose sight of the proposed Orphanage Scheme, and will never let an opportunity slip of advocating the introduction of co-operative chapters in school text books.

IN CONCLUSION.

Knowing so well the thorough thoughtful and practical attention any suggestion made in earnestness is likely to receive at the hands of the Guild, I have done no more than indicate the direction in which I feel some of our plain duties and best opportunities for usefulness lie, leaving with each branch the working out of details. I trust no one will think that I speak without a full knowledge of the difficulties in the way, of the discouragements, disappointments, prejudices, jealousies, misunderstandings, back bitings, apathy, and distrust, we are likely to meet with. No life made up of complex human nature is free from these things, and sometimes I fancy store life is fuller of them than any other. But shall they hold us back?

There was once a good lady, a laundress, whose collars were so beautifully polished that they were the pride and glory of all the young men fortunate enough to be counted among her customers. So great was her fame that at last it was agreed that she must possess some secret patent unknown to other laundresses. She was approached on the matter, and confessed that she had a patent, and being pressed hard consented to divulge it. My patent, said she, consists of clear starch, hot irons, and brains evenly applied.

Now then, is it not the ambition of the Guild to so polish and brighten co-operative life, that it shall shine in the world, as a beacon of hope to all working men and women? I firmly believe we have in our hands the patent with which to accomplish this end, if, for clear starch, we use clear principles, for hot irons, warm zeal and enthusiasm, and with the aid of what brains we may possess, apply it evenly to all the component parts of our store life.

CATHERINE WEBB.

June 17th, 1892.

34

THE WOMEN'S CO-OPERATIVE GUILD, 1883–1904 (KIRKBY LONSDALE: WCG, 1904), 141–147, 161–163.

Margaret Llewelyn Davies

[This extract is from the first history of the WCG, published to mark the organisation's "coming of age" or twenty-first anniversary. Under Llewelyn Davies' leadership, the guild became more overtly feminist, launching various campaigns on specific women's issues such as equal pay within co-operative enterprises, "open membership", maternity rights, divorce law reform and female suffrage. Poverty was an abiding concern. Llewelyn Davies called for a "People's Store" in 1899, with low prices and dividends and provision for a "settlement" with resident workers, which was taken up by the Sunderland society in 1902, with some initial success though the venture collapsed two years later. [G.D.H. Cole *A Century of Co-operation* (Manchester: Co-operative Union, 1945), 221–223] From one angle this activity appears in line with traditions of middle-class philanthropic endeavour and forms of "social motherhood", but this was also a genuine attempt to make the movement more socially inclusive which directly challenged the complacent attitude of some leading male co-operators, forcing them to confront an issue that was becoming centre stage in socialist propaganda. A chapter on "Citizenship" in Llewelyn Davies' history documented the activities of guildswomen as elected Poor Law Guardians, numbers of which had steadily increased in the late 1890s, as well as their protests against the abolition of vestries and School Boards, on which women sat, and their replacement by Borough Councils, from which women were barred. The extract from this chapter reproduced below illustrates the major role played by the guild in the politicisation of consumption before World War One, educating ordinary consumers about prices and waging a staunch defence of free trade, a policy recently challenged by Joseph Chamberlain and the Tariff Reform League. Understandable given the guild's concern for working-class housewives, this tactic reinforced links between the Liberal Party and co-operation, while further alienating socialists such as Harry Quelch who once described free trade as "one of the most impudent humbugs that was ever foisted on long-suffering humanity". [Peter Gurney, *Co-operative Culture and the Politics of Consumption in England, 1870–1930* (1996), 189; Frank Trentmann, *Free trade nation: commerce, consumption, and civil society in modern Britain* (2009)]]

Other occurrences have also contributed to produce this awakening among women, especially among Co-operative women. Questions of taxation, leading to rises in the price of food, affect Co-operators and working women very closely indeed. The Guild began to take action in 1894, when, joining with Co-operative Societies, it forwarded a memorial to the Chancellor of the Exchequer in favour of what is known as a "Free Breakfast Table," urging the removal of taxes from tea, coffee, cocoa, chicory, and dried fruits. The policy laid down was subsequently followed up by vigorous petitions to Chancellors, resolutions to M.P.'s, and speeches by women on the proposed sugar[1] and corn duties, and culminated in the great protest that has been made by our members in favour of free trade, when the fiscal campaign of last year (1903), was sprung upon the country.

"In the campaign against the proposed fiscal changes the Women's Co-operative Guild, which has done more, perhaps, than any other organisation to educate the wives and daughters of industrial toilers of the country on social and economic questions, will play no mean part." So speaks a leading article in the *Co-operative News*. There was no doubt of the line which the Guild would take on this matter. The Congress at Lincoln last year (1903) gave the lead in no uncertain way. It expressed its "emphatic disapproval of any proposal for interfering with the policy of free trade by a system of preferential tariffs, which it believed would enrich monopolists, impoverish the people, corrupt public life, and embitter international relations." A few branches reported disagreement, but, taking it as a whole, the Guild has stood firm to the free trade policy, and has not been misled by specious arguments. A special paper, "The Necessity for Free Trade," was issued by the Guild, and discussed at conferences, while many branches arranged lectures from prominent free trade champions, among whom Mrs. Bury came to be included.

But it was felt that more than one of the ordinary Guild campaigns was needed at this crucial moment, and that something special was demanded from Co-operative women. So on October 10th, 1903, there appeared the following notice at the head of the "Woman's Corner":—"The Guild is organising a great Free Trade Demonstration on November 11th, in the Free Trade Hall, Manchester." Then came an appeal to our members in the following words:—

> "There has never been a national crisis when our members had more right to speak out or more claim to be heard. As Co-operators, women will see that the prosperity of the country depends on the spending power of the people, which would be decreased by high prices, consequent on taxation of food. And as chancellors of the family exchequers, women know best the importance of being able to make the money go as far as possible. A Co-operative mother is not likely to believe in taxing food, nor be duped by the suggestion that if taxes were taken off tea and tobacco, it would not signify if bread and meat were dear. In order that women may come in their thousands and uphold the Free Trade policy, we have engaged the Free Trade Hall, in Manchester, which is capable

of holding 4,000 persons. . . . Let us show that Co-operative women can be roused, and make our voice heard throughout the length and breadth of the land."

Help was sought from Manchester women's associations, and with their cooperation a remarkable demonstration of women took place. The hall was decorated with Guild banners and free trade mottoes. Long before the beginning of the meeting, Guilds-women and others began to arrive, coming in large numbers from the surrounding towns. Labour and anti-Protection choruses, accompanied by the great organ, were sung, and excitement and expectancy were high when Mrs. Bury (the Chairman) led the way on to the platform, followed by a remarkable array of speakers and supporters representing nearly all shades of social and political opinion. The speakers were: Miss Garland (Women's Free Trade Union), Mrs. Cobden Unwin (daughter of Richard Cobden), Mrs. Booth (Co-operative Guild), Mrs. John Winbolt (weaver), Mrs. Byles (Salford), Mr. Ernest Beckett (Conservative, and Unionist Free Food League), Mr. Alfred Emmott (Liberal, and Free Trade Union), and Mr. Philip Snowden (Socialist). Very interesting letters of sympathy were read from prominent women—Lady Aberdeen, Lady Henry Somerset, Mrs. Henry Fawcett, Mrs. Bright Mc.Laren (John Bright's sister), Mrs. H. J. Tennant, &c. The speeches were excellent, and the audience alive to every point. The applause broke out again and again as speaker after speaker emphasised the need for the Parliamentary vote. The following resolution was carried unanimously:—

"That this meeting of women declares its steadfast adherence to the policy of Free Trade, and condemns all attempts to revive the system of Protection, which would impoverish the people, enrich monopolists, corrupt public life, and embitter colonial and international relations; and seeing that women, both as workers and housewives, are so deeply concerned in this question, deplores that they cannot make their protest effective through being debarred from the Parliamentary franchise."

What greater impetus could have been given to the question of Women's Suffrage, with which this chapter will fittingly close, than the present fiscal crisis? The agitation for the right of citizenship began and continued for many years almost entirely among middle-class women; but a very marked change has come in this respect within recent years, and working women have now come forward to claim the vote, not only from the point of view of justice, but also because they see how closely the actual needs in their lives are connected with it.

In 1893, the leaders of the Women's Suffrage movement decided to promote an appeal to Members of Parliament, from women of all classes and parties, to show that the vote was more widely desired than was thought. Books were issued for the collection of signatures. The Guild contributed 2,225 names, and the Appeal Secretary, in her letter of thanks, said that the Co-operative women had worked splendidly. Four years afterwards, in 1897, at the time when a Women's Suffrage Bill was before Parliament, the Guild took up the subject on its own account, and issued papers entitled, "Why Working Women Need the Vote," which were discussed at the Southern Sectional Conferences.

> "After this month let us hear no more of 'Working women do not want the vote.' The tone throughout the meeting was most practical and sensible. Working women want to make themselves felt in public life for definite purposes—to improve the social laws and administration, and particularly to watch over the lives of women and children. To reject from the electorate public-spirited workers like these is a folly which nothing but voluntary ignorance can account for."[2]

Resolutions in support of the Suffrage Bill were enthusiastically passed. A few months later a letter, signed "A Guild Member," appeared in the "Woman's Corner," strongly condemning the attitude Mr. Broadhurst, M.P., had taken on this Bill, at a meeting of the National Liberal Federation, at Derby. Twenty-three branches proceeded to pass resolutions of protest, and these were forwarded to Mr. Broadhurst, whose reply was as follows:—

> "MY DEAR MADAM,
> "I asked that those most fitted to vote, viz., married women and servant maids, should be included. I did not promise to vote for the Bill if they were included. I did not say I would vote against the Bill.
> "Yours, &c.,
> "H. BROADHURST."

This letter is rather mysterious, and the necessity for the importunate widow's policy is obvious. Mr. Maddison (then M.P.) was also written to, concerning his remark at the Women's Liberal Federation meeting, that the only women who wanted votes were idlers or Tory bigots, and we wished to know under which head to place the thousands of our Co-operative women who desired to be voters.

In 1900 began a remarkable new move among the trade unionist women of the North, in which Guild members have taken some part. A monster petition, organised by the North of England Suffrage Society, was signed by 29,359 women cotton operatives in Lancashire, and presented to certain Members of Parliament at the House of Commons. Miss Reddish (President of Bolton Branch of the Guild) introduced the deputation, among whom were several Guild members. The following year the Yorkshire and Cheshire textile workers followed suit, with a petition signed by 31,000 women. Miss Reddish and seventeen Guild members were among the deputation to the Members of Parliament. In the short space of eleven months Lancashire, Yorkshire, and Cheshire women textile operatives contributed 68,000 signatures.

This work led on to further very interesting developments. Branches of the Weavers' Unions were asked to make Women's Suffrage a trade union question, and a Women's Suffrage candidate for Parliament has now been selected for Wigan, whose candidature is promoted by a special Labour Representation Committee of women, including members of the North of England Suffrage Society and textile workers. Out of the 29 on the Committee 13 are members of the Guild.

Thus we see Co-operative and trade unionist women each approaching the question of the Parliamentary suffrage, from their own special standpoints of workers and consumers, seeing more clearly every day the fundamental importance of the enfranchisement of women...

FORMER chapters have shown the place which the Guild is taking in Co-operation, and how its Co-operative goal is full and real citizenship in the Co-operative State, so that women may serve as Co-operative citizens on terms of equality with men.

How, it may be asked, has the movement, as a whole, received the Guild and regarded its policy? It may be said with gratitude, that had it not been given generous recognition and sympathy, its position would not be what it is to-day.

But there has been, and still is, considerable prejudice to live down, and, though opposition is less openly expressed than it used to be, it is none the less strong in many quarters. It is especially roused when women see that there is something more for them to do than buy loyally at the Store, and proceed to demand open membership, to come forward for seats on Boards of Management, or stand for prominent positions in the movement. But opponents are gradually being won over, as they work side by side with women in the service of the movement; and Co-operative women need fear no set-back, if they remain united and resolute in their loyalty to the Stores, to the policy of justice in employment, of truth in business dealings, and of fellowship in a common Co-operative life.

The other goal which all working women's organisations are bound to seek, is that of national citizenship. As soon as women are in earnest as regards industrial and social reform, they are inevitably led to perceive how handicapped they are, by laws which prevent their election to town and county councils, and debar them from the parliamentary suffrage. It is not only because women's own particular interests suffer, that they demand that such indignities should cease. The nation cannot afford to sacrifice anything in the battle for a juster life. It must inevitably suffer if it leaves more than half the community on one side, undeveloped and unrepresented; it cannot afford to dispense with the help which women can bring.

Nor, as long as Guild members remain willing to learn, need they fear their own inexperience. The Guild is, their training ground—their own organisation, to use in the ways which will be of the greatest service to themselves and others.

It is not only the individual who has been made conscious, through the Guild, of latent power, but a new element is entering into public life. Working-women form the largest section of the community. Four million women and girls are actual wealth-producers, receiving payment for their work. Still larger in numbers are the married women, who, as home-makers, contribute by their unpaid labour just as directly as wage-earners to the support of family life. This class is now, through organisation, finding its voice, formulating its needs, and taking its part in administrative work as Co-operators and citizens.

Notes

1 An inquiry was made among certain Guild members as to the difference the proposed ½d. per lb. tax would make in their weekly expenditure. The amount of sugar used varied a good deal, according to the size of family, the ordinary amount being from 6lbs. to 10lbs. a week. The tax on this would mean an increased expenditure of from 3d. to 5d. a week. The Women's Trade Union League joined with the Guild in asking for a deputation (which was refused) to the Chancellor of the Exchequer.
2 "Woman's Corner," *Co-operative News,* March 27th, 1897.

35

"THE EFFORTS OF WOMEN IN THE CO-OPERATIVE MOVEMENT", *BOLTON CO-OPERATIVE RECORD*, JANUARY 1916, 8–9.

Sarah Reddish

[Sarah Reddish (1849–1928) was born into a family of textile workers in Westleigh, Lancashire. Her father was an active co-operator, serving as secretary and librarian to the Bolton Society. At the age of eleven, she began work as a silk-winder, later becoming forewoman in a cotton mill in Bolton. Reddish joined the Bolton Society in 1879 and was president of the local branch of the WCG from 1886 until 1901. Elected onto the guild's central committee in 1889, a grant funded by Mary Llewelyn Davies' mother allowed her to quit the factory and work as a full-time organiser for the guild between 1893–1895, a role she performed with great enthusiasm. She was also an active suffragist and helped get guild backing for the franchise bill at its annual conference in 1904. In her obituary, Llewelyn Davies warmly remembered Reddish talking about "the large Socialistic vision of a new life which filled her mind". She was not the only socialist feminist at this time with high hopes for organising consumption for women – so had Teresa Billington-Greig, though her book, *The Consumer in Revolt* (1912), disparaged co-operation – and Reddish saw the guild in this light, believing that it had the potential to bring great numbers of working-class women "into active life". [Gillian Scott, *Feminism and the politics of working women. The Women's Co-operative Guild, 1880s to the Second World War* (London: UCL Press, 1998), 50, 93; June Hannam and Karen Hunt, *Socialist Women: Britain 1880s to 1920s* (London: Routledge, 2001)] The extract below is a paper she delivered at a "ladies' concert" organised by the Bolton Society during the First World War. Drawing on Holyoake's history, Reddish chose to remind her listeners of the legacy of Owenite feminists, particularly Emma Martin, and underlined the success of the guild, which now had 600 branches and a membership of 32,000. Significantly, Reddish supports her argument for universal co-operation by quoting the words of an old Owenite, Dr Channing, who looked forward to the establishment of a "community" where "no class nor sex will seek a monopoly of honour or good".]

Miss Reddish, who was introduced by the Chairman as one who had done splendid work for women, took for her topic, "The Efforts of Women in the Co-operative Movement." In his book on the Co-operative movement, Mr. George J. Holyoake devoted a chapter to the early advocates of social reform and Co-operation, and especially referred to the lady advocates in the period 1829–1841. In one of Bernard Shaw's plays, in which Miss Ellen Terriss took the leading rôle, the character Miss Terriss sustained was always discovering the best quality in all she met; and Mr. Holyoake gave them commendatory references to the women in the social movement. There was, he said, a Mrs. Wheeler, "who attracted considerable attention by her well-reasoned lectures"; Miss Reynolds, who "excited great admiration for her effective speaking"; Mrs. Barnby's "written papers were always pleasant and sensible"; and Madame D'Arnemout's "lectures were popular both in England and America." But the most notable of his group of women writers and speakers was Mrs. Emma Martin, who had "the wit and courage of several men. She delivered lectures in the stormiest times and to the most dangerously-disposed audiences." This was before the advent of the modern Co-operative movement, and in a period of great poverty, and when the people were suffering great hardships. The women to whom she referred had their successors in the movement to-day, and she would name only three. There was Miss Potter, now Mrs. Sidney Webb, who, along with her husband, had written a history of trade unions, and had written much on the Poor Law and social questions. Then there was Miss Catherine Webb, who, like her father, had done notable service in spreading the principles of Co-operation; and the third was Miss Mary Ll. Davies, who became the Women's Guild Secretary 26 years ago. During those years she had, by pen and speech and the display of great organising ability, built up the Guild. The Women's Guild was originated in 1883. At the start it was a very small affair, but now it had 600 branches, with a membership of 32,000. The object of the Guild was to propagate and educate by teaching the history, principles, and practice of Co-operation. They should keep in mind that the Guild was a self-governed democratic body, and, whilst cultivating loyal effort in the various Societies, it urged the members to fit themselves to serve in representative capacities in the Co-operative movement, and also for citizen duties on public bodies. The Guild had a great work before it, and was capable of doing much, having a strong army of speakers throughout the country. The most important

HELP WOMEN COULD GIVE

to the Co-operative movement was by becoming active and intelligent members of the various Societies, understanding the principles of the movement. There were many thousands of members of Societies in their own right, for the movement did not recognise any sex distinction, and marriage was no disqualification in membership. Women, in the main, were the purchasers, and that was the foundation of the Co-operative structure. Let them be faithful in the exercise of their purchasing power, and the super-structure of human helpfulness, material and moral, would become finer as time went on. Women were helping by their savings to provide the share capital, and there were now 1,500 Co-operative Societies in the United Kingdom, with over three million members. Each Society was a distinct democracy, an organisation of consumers, and all were consumers. Women had been alert enough to perceive the advantages of membership, the getting of reliable goods at market prices, with the result that the dividend gave them an increased spending power of the weekly wage, with the additional advantage that they were partners in ownership and control. There were two emblems very commonly in evidence in Co-operative Societies, viz., the bee hive, with bees hovering about it, representing industry; and the other the figure of a woman, with eyes blindfolded, holding the scales in even balance, representing justice and equtiy. An emblem was a figure or design typifying an idea, and the emblems she had just named were finely typical of the principles on which Co-operation was based. Bees respected only those who contributed to the common store, and drove out the drones. In the Co-operative movement there was no room for idlers—all must contribute to the general well-being. The figure of justice was typical of the principle of equity which governed the use and division of profits. The profits capitalised, in whatever form, whether of land, buildings, live stock, equipment, stock in trade—even the collective possessions of the members. The profits, as dividends, were distributed equitably—that was, in proportion to the purchases made. If there were no purchases there was no dividend. Mr. Holyoake wrote of this method of distribution as "the discovery which created Co-operation." It certainly had been the means of its success, for the members profited by supplying their own needs instead of paying other people to supply them. But that was not all, for they had to recognise there was

AN ETHICAL SIDE

to the movement; they had to see that labour had an equitable reward. To do that they must control production. They could do that through the Co-operative Wholesale Society. The C.W.S. federated the Societies just as the individual Society federated its members. The Bolton Society had in stocks, shares, and loans, £142,000 invested in the C.W.S., and by their support of that Society the members of the Bolton Society were helping forward industrial Co-operation—the organising of industry to produce what the members required. The C.W.S. was both merchant and producer, and from it the various Societies made purchases. Through the C.W.S. the members had a share of control in determining the working conditions and wages of the employees. The English and Scottish Wholesale Societies had 34,000 employees. Therefore, already, the members had great power over industry, and they should increase that influence by only buying articles which were of Co-operative production. Their motto should be, "Buy our own goods from our own works." C.W.S. meant "Co-operation wisely self-governed" or they could put it another way: "Co-operators well served." To sum up: Co-operation was an organised effort to supply their needs, with a high ethical purpose of an equitable reward to all engaged in purchasing, providing, or producing. As they increased the demand the C.W.S. would increase the supply. Those who grasped the principles of Co-operation knew that they were working towards the attainment of conditions which would give the happiest community—"a community," to use the words of Dr. Channing, "in which the members will form one body; in which no class nor sex will seek a monoply of honour or good; in which no section is a prey to others; in which there is a general desire that every human being may have every opportunity to develop his powers." Might all of them strive for this ideal.

Part 6

INTERNATIONALISM, EMPIRE AND WAR

36

INTERNATIONAL CO-OPERATION AND THE CONSTITUTION OF THE INTERNATIONAL CO-OPERATIVE ALLIANCE (LONDON: CO-OP PRINTING SOCIETY, 1895), 1–8.

Edward Owen Greening

[E.O. Greening (1836–1923) was born in Warrington, into a middle-class family. From 1853 he took part in the Anti-Slavery Society and was a founder member of the Union and Emancipation Society established in the early 1860s to support the cause of the North in the American Civil War. This commitment to radical liberal politics led Greening to stand, unsuccessfully, in Halifax in the 1868 general election. From this time, he became an enthusiastic advocate for co-operation, particularly profit-sharing, which he regarded as a panacea for class conflict. Greening introduced co-partnership into his own wiredrawing firm and in the Agricultural and Horticultural Society he founded in 1868 with Christian Socialist support. International co-operation drew together Greening's concerns for peace at home and abroad. Pressure for co-ordination of national movements had been mounting for some years. At the 1889 annual Co-operative Congress, the old Owenite E.T. Craig had criticised Bismarck's foreign policy and asserted that international co-operation "would produce a higher state of civilisation and happiness…(and) render unnecessary the terrible engines of destructive war". [*21st Annual Co-operative Congress, 1889* (Manchester: Co-op Union, 1889), 97] But the practical work of establishing an international body was taken up most ardently in the early 1890s by profit-sharers like E.V. Neale and Greening, who regarded it as an alternative to and antidote for the Second International formed by socialists and Marxists in 1889 that preached the gospel of class war. [Johnston Birchall, *The International Co-operative Movement* (Manchester: Manchester University Press, 1997), 40–44] In this pamphlet, Greening discusses the recent congress in London at which the International Co-operative Alliance was formally established. Although delegates at the congress managed to widen the ICA to encompass other forms of co-operation besides profit-sharing, Greening gently steers his own course, emphasising "the Kingdom of Co-operation, like the 'kingdom of heaven', is within men" and that, "Great communistic ventures attempted through sudden political and social revolutions often fail because they leave the mass of the people unchanged".]

THE internationalisation of Co-operation is a natural development in the evolution of our movement. Although I have had the happiness to suggest and to assist in pioneering the recent Congress and the alliance which has come out of it, I am fully convinced that steps of the kind were inevitable, and probably so at an early date. I am proud that the co-operators of Britain should have the glory of leading the way. We owe something of that honour to our brothers of France, especially MM. de Boyve and Charles Robert, who, as representatives from the French co-operators to our annual British congresses, have steadily urged forward the accomplishment of the great idea whilst leaving to us the credit of initiation. So far back as 1886, M. de Boyve pressed the question at our Plymouth Congress, and when in 1892 our lamented leader, Edward Vansittart Neale, joined me in taking the first preliminary steps (at the time of the Rochdale Congress), both M. Robert and M. de Boyve went with us full of encouragement and help.

With these words of acknowledgment to the chief originators of the present international movement, I will now explain why I regard internationalisation as natural and necessary in Co-operation.

If we consider the rock basis of our movement, we see it is a basis of voluntary concord. Co-operation differs from merely political movements, which are based largely on enforced uniformity. The laws of a kingdom, although voted by a mere majority, are enforced upon all within the kingdom by coercion, which extends even to the taking away of life and liberty. So far as the laws of a kingdom extend, and can be enforced, there must be uniformity of action. All men must have their children vaccinated in a place where vaccination is compulsory, and no man could easily have his children vaccinated in a place where vaccination was legally prohibited.

But in Co-operation it is otherwise. Men and women come into our societies every day and go out of them without necessarily changing their place or their mode of living, their religious or social associations, their hobbies, their habits, or their tastes. Co-operation means free consent, and its growth means the growth of the idea of mutuality in the minds of men. The kingdom of Co-operation, like the kingdom of heaven, is within men. A man becomes a good co-operator in any country, under any kind of government, and under all kinds of laws, so soon as he sees the fallacy of the old selfish idea of getting on by isolation, and realises his true relations of mutuality with others.

The result of this basis of voluntary concord in Co-operation is two-fold. First, we have had Co-operation (since its birth 50 years ago) springing up simultaneously in every civilised country. Second, we have seen it developing itself in every variety of form, taking its shape from the local characteristics of each people, reflecting their local aims, satisfying their local needs, relieving their local wants, embodying even their local prepossessions. And when we take broad views of large groups of co-operators, the picture of diversity in unity becomes very striking. The British, a commercial people, have mainly developed commercial stores. The French, a people of creative genius, have mainly developed co-operative production. The Germans, who, with the Dutch, have hereditary financial instincts, have mainly developed co-operative banks. The Danes, an agricultural people, have originated co-operative creameries, and the Italians have taken the lead in artistic Co-operation.

And yet we find throughout all there is an identity of aim, a unity of views, an agreement, even as to methods, which is almost miraculous when we consider how little inter-communication has been possible between these masses of workers in every country, speaking different languages, professing different religions, and practising different pursuits.

Our great Festival Choir at the Crystal Palace will serve as a very good illustration of the co-operative movement of to-day in various lands. It is composed of thousands of singers from every part of the country. All ages and both sexes are represented. The voices differ in every case. But the singers group themselves voluntarily into masses of bass, tenor, soprano, and contralto, according to their natural gifts. . . . . The composers of the music do not call upon the 6,000 singers to sing in unison; bass and tenor, soprano and contralto, sing different notes. Yet the mighty host of voices blends in one harmonious strain of music which stirs the heart of the listener in all its depths, so complete and perfect and powerful is the conjoined effect.

I have endeavoured to take a summary census of Co-operation in all countries from the reports furnished to the International Co-operative Congress, but I have found it impossible at present to compile anything like a complete table of our movement as a whole. One of the most important of the future tasks of the Alliance must be to prepare such a table, and, perhaps, re-issue it annually.

At present we can see there are a million and a quarter co-operators in Great Britain, in 1,700 societies, with a capital of about £18,000,000; in Germany there are a million co-operators, in 10,000 societies, with about £30,000,000 of capital; in France over a million of co-operators; in Austria and Hungary nearly a million, with about £9,000,000 or £10,000,000 of capital; in Denmark, 100,000 co-operators, and immense numbers in Italy, Belgium, Holland, Switzerland, Russia, Servia, Roumania, the United States of America, in our Colonies, and in other countries. The lowest computation I can make places the total membership in Co-operation now at 6,000,000, representing probably a population of 25,000,000 souls, a number greater than the population of any nation on earth, if we except the few leading Empires like Britain, France, Germany, Austria, Italy, the United States, China, India, and Japan. I think we may also believe that the working capital now in the hands or under the control of the co-operators of all countries will not be far short of 100 millions sterling.

Such being the basis of the International Co-operative Movement, and such the present estimated position of Co-operation at home and abroad, I have now to state the outcome of the recent Congress of representatives from almost every country in which Co-operation exists.

The Alliance Committee having honoured me with a commission to state, at the outset of the Congress, our aims and views, I summarised them as follows in an opening paper:—

"Our constitution should be inclusive, so as to gather up all elements of strength and success. I do not mean by this to suggest any surrender of principle. By all means let this Congress and future ones clearly decide what is essential to the practice of true Co-operation, and use the immense moral power of a grand concensus of opinion to bring all our friends to accept agreed views, and to cause small local dissensions to cease. But wherever essentials in principle are accepted, let us tolerate every variety of organisation which can fairly be recognised as co-operative. Let us keep an open door for every co-operative organisation to come into the alliance, and for every willing individual to work in the cause. Let the conditions of membership be few and simple; the necessary payments light enough; the organisation sufficiently elastic in its character. Details had better be left to be arranged by a small committee chosen from the representatives of all countries interested in our project, and this committee should meet before the Congress separates. But we should, I think, agree upon these general characteristics of our alliance at the outset.

"Each country should pledge itself to establish a centre in which information should be available to all of what is doing by co-operators in other countries. These centres should recognise it as their duty to circulate widely the literature of International Co-operation, being careful to work as far as possible through existing organisations. The International Alliance should seek to establish new organisations for propagandist work where none already exists—to put new life into the old organisations—to keep records of everything relating to Co-operation at home and abroad—to spread a more comprehensive knowledge and conception of the full meaning of mutuality applied to every phase of human life.

"The International Alliance should, I think, abstain from any form of trading; but it should be the business of the International Committee to found suitable agencies which will bring existing co-operative business organisations into relations with those of other countries. A sample room, an office, and, above all, a competent agent, animated with the true Co-operative spirit, will be needed, and little more. Let each agency begin with small expenses and a moderate establishment. Let us be content to grow steadily into the larger developments worthy of our mighty movement. We have to learn by experience exactly what can be done in the new field of work, and how it can be best done. Such has been the policy which has brought us success in the past. And these methods have the advantage of educating and training our people to do their own work. Great communistic ventures attempted through sudden political and social revolutions often fail because they leave the mass of the people unchanged. We must ever bear in mind the examples of the wise co-operative leaders of the past, who have been content to carry out their most far-reaching plans gradually, whilst leading the people step by step along with them. So when those wise leaders passed away their work has stood firm, as we see, the people themselves understanding, appreciating, and upholding it."

Substantially these views were accepted by the Congress. We had some friendly differences on one or two points, we had much consideration of details, and at least one warm discussion. But, eventually, all the following resolutions were carried with an agreement almost amounting to unanimity.

The first four resolutions constituted an International Co-operative Alliance, and appointed committees to prepare a constitution and organise mutual trading relations. The fifth resolution called for an active policy in the development of productive co-operation. The sixth and seventh I quote entire, premising that they were agreed to by the co-operative representatives of all countries:—

"That this Congress, being strongly convinced that no permanent settlement of the relative position of Capital and Labour is practicable without the admission of the worker to a share in the profits over and beyond the ordinary wages, and that such admission is possible in a manner fair alike to employers and employed, urges upon all employers of labour the adoption of the practice indicated; and desires to put its opinion on record that fidelity to the co-operative principle requires all co-operative associations employing labour to assign to their workmen a fair share of the profits, and also a voice in the management."

"That, in the opinion of the Congress, it is desirable for the higher development of co-operative production that, where the principle of profit-sharing is applied, arrangements should be made for capitalising a fixed proportion in the name of each worker as a part of the capital by the aid of which he is employed."

Then a resolution was passed in favour of peoples' banks, and one advocating the federation in each country of all branches of Co-operation. The next resolution was a very warm acknowledgment of the greatness and value of our British store movement, accompanied by recommendations to develop educational, social, and recreative features, and to make our employés co-partners in profits, capital, and propagandist work. Finally, a resolution was passed recognising the gravity of the agricultural crisis throughout Europe, and advocating Co-operation in farming, in sale of produce, in supply of seeds, manures, etc., in cream and butter-making, and other well proved methods.

The outline constitution adopted for the Alliance embodies all these resolutions, but leaves an open door for all co-operators and co-operative societies to come in, although they may not be able at present to fully carry out in actual practice the high principles which the Alliance has accepted as its guide and aim and policy. Another Congress is to be held next year, probably at Paris, to complete the constitution of the Alliance. A central committee has been appointed, London being honoured with being made headquarters. The subscriptions for the present are fixed as low as £1 for societies, and 2s. per annum for individuals.

Since the International Congress last month, the United Board of the Co-operative Union at Manchester have passed a resolution of adhesion. The Federation of Productive Societies, the Council of the Co-operative Festival, the Labour Association, and the Women's Guild had previously adhered in principle. Almost all the great European organisations are affiliated.

I am hopeful that in this latest work of ours will be found the beginning of a power strong enough to advance the cause of peace between nations and prosperity amongst all peoples.

37

WHEATSHEAF, OCTOBER 1902, 52–53.

Édouard de Boyve

[Published in the monthly paper produced for local societies by the CWS, the article reproduced below is an account of the ICA congress that took place in Manchester in July 1902, written by Édouard de Boyve (1840–1923) and translated from *l'Emancipation*, a French co-operative journal that de Boyve had founded in 1887. Born in Paris into a solid bourgeois family, de Boyve's mother was English and his natural bilingualism aided international links. An advocate of the Rochdale model of co-operation, in 1883 de Boyve established a consumer co-operative at Nimes and three years later he struck up a close relationship with the political economist Charles Gide. De Boyve regarded co-operation as a solution to the antagonism between capital and labour, a healing balm that would render class conflict unnecessary. Other French co-operators took a different view and the socialists split in 1895, though they rejoined in 1912. [Ellen Furlough, *Consumer Co-operation in France: the Politics of Consumption, 1834–1930* (Ithaca: Cornell University Press, 1991)] As we have noted, middle-class leaders such as Greening, Neale and de Boyve provided much of the initial impetus behind the formal international organisation of co-operation, de Boyve regarding the ICA as a defence against socialist internationalism. [Peter Gurney, "'A Higher State of Civilisation and Happiness': Internationalism in the British Co-operative Movement between, c. 1869–1918", in Frits van Holthoon and Marcel van der Linden (eds), *Internationalism in the Labour Movement 1830–1940* (Leiden: Brill, 1988), 561] The article illustrates just how deeply embedded the practice of internationalism was within the culture of the British movement at this time. The CWS was clearly trying to prove its credentials in Manchester against the profit-sharers who had sought to corral internationalism for their own ends. However, de Boyve's report also reveals the limits to this wider view as he notes how at the celebratory dinner English delegates sang "God Save the King" after the first toast, and 100 guests "Socialists, Anarchists, or otherwise, felt bound to take part, by rising, in this manifestation of respect for the Sovereign who represents, to English eyes, that British power of which they are proud".]

The Congress of the International Co-operative Alliance, held at Manchester, was brought to a close on Saturday, July 26th, at 1-15 p.m., by a vote of thanks to Mr. H. W. Wolff, who presided over all its sittings.

The Congress was composed of Co-operators from all countries; France and Belgium in particular being strongly represented.

These representatives of various nationalities, speaking different languages, had some difficulty at first in making out the sense of the proposals of the speakers.

Those delegates who spoke French were hardly able to understand the official interpreter of the Congress, who had to turn the English speeches into French.

Under these circumstances, the votes of the first two sittings can hardly be taken as an exact expression of the *wishes of the majority.*

The resolution proposed by M. Goedhart, a Dutch delegate, in favour of profit-sharing among employees was not understood; if it had been the minority would have been the majority.

Two of our French friends wished to raise the point next day, but they were told that the vote was over and done with. This was perhaps pushing respect for parliamentary rules a little too far.

The confusion ceased on the morning when the English Co-operators wired to London for Mr. Smith, a well-known interpreter, and highly esteemed by all who have frequented the International Congresses.

Mr. Smith has the power of conferring eloquence on speakers who have it not, and what is still more difficult, that of rendering in English the shades of meaning, the French spirit, the very manner of our friend Gide. Mr. Smith almost did that.

Leaving aside this criticism of the first translator, we must say that the Organising Committee, at the head of which were Mr. Mc.Innes, as Chairman, and Mr. Gray, as Secretary, did wonders.

The Manchester International Congress was superior from every point of view to all those that have taken place up to the present.

The Exhibition, where the productions of the English Wholesale figured prominently, was most successful. Military bands (music has a great attraction for the English) drew large crowds, who were able to judge with their own eyes of the power of the Co-operative movement in England. During the seven days of the Exhibition, 50,000 visitors were counted.

The Wholesale's factories were not the only ones to show their productions, there were also those of the independent Productive Societies who are joined together in the Labour Association. Some French Agricultural Syndicates showed their butters; and the Danish Agricultural Association showed their eggs, which have on the shell a stamp with letters indicating the place of origin and date of despatch, which enables the Association, in case of a claim, to know what member is in fault.

. . . .

The Wholesale gave a garden party on the first evening of the Congress at the Botanical Gardens, Manchester; refreshments were served in the Palm House, where a number of tables for four persons were laid. The Police Band played in succession the national airs of all the countries represented; the "Marseillaise" was followed by the "Russian Hymn" (Russia was represented at the Congress by a broad-minded Pole, M. de Weydlich, a delegate from the Agricultural Syndicates of Poland).

The garden party concluded with a vocal concert, preceded by a speech of welcome addressed by Mr. Shillito, Chairman of the Board of Directors of the Wholesale, to the foreign Co-operators. The principal delegate from each country said a few words. Count de Rocquigny spoke on behalf of France.

Every day after the sitting of Congress, which began at nine in the morning and ended at one, the delegates visited one or two factories of the Wholesale.

When there was any distance to go, the Reception Committee provided railway tickets for each of the delegates, which enabled them to travel by a train specially provided to convey them to their destination. The generosity of the English Co-operators did not end even here, for the Wholesale Society distributed, to each visitor who had a delegate's card, samples of their productions: a box of soap, pots of jam, a box of biscuits, a case of cigars—one would have had to buy a portmanteau in the warehouse of the Wholesale if one wanted to bring all these gifts home to France.

On the Thursday the delegates made a pilgrimage to the cradle of Co-operation, at Rochdale. The descendants of the 28 Pioneers offered the visitors a cold repast in their great lecture hall; it was six o'clock in the evening. Before inviting their guests to sit down, the Rochdale Co-operators sang a hymn asking God to bless the meal. I remark the fact as a study in customs. This habit of saying a prayer before meals is, it seems, widespread among Co-operators. There are even a number of Co-operative Societies connected with the Temperance Societies, and whose members abstain from beer or spirits.

Such customs are scarcely ours!

I am forgetting to mention that M. Charles Gide delivered at Rochdale a splendid speech in honour of the Pioneers, which met with great applause.

In mentioning all the kindnesses shown to us by the English Co-operators, I must specially speak of the great dinner given to the members of the Congress by the Organising Committee. Mr. Mc.Innes, the Chairman, and Mr. Gray, the Secretary, signed the invitations.

Mr. Mc.Innes had arranged beforehand who were to speak and what toasts they were to propose, after the English fashion. He raised his glass first in honour of "the King," and the English, standing up, sang "God Save the King."

The 100 guests, Socialists, Anarchists, or otherwise, felt bound to take part, by rising, in this manifestation of respect for the Sovereign who represents, to English eyes, that British Power of which they are proud.

"A country that has such love and respect for its Government, of whatever kind, and that has so deep a religious feeling, is very strong!" said some of the foreign delegates around me.

I leave my readers to furnish their own comments on English patriotism.

The odd moments of time left to the delegates were used in visiting the warehouses of the Wholesale, which are situated in the centre of Manchester. Some of the foreign Co-operative Associations entered into business negotiations with the Wholesale.

. . . .

The fraternal relations between English and French Co-operators began in 1885 through the presence of Vansittart Neale, Holyoake, and Johnston at our first French Co-operative Congress. How far we have advanced since then!

The whole credit for it belongs to the Central Board of the French Co-operative Union, which has never since 1885 ceased to keep in friendly touch with the apostles of English Co-operation, and which from the earliest days urged the formation of an International Co-operative Alliance.

It is necessary to point out the results of the work done by the French Central Board in order that its usefulness may be recognised. It is too often forgotten that the French Central Board has done much for the development of Co-operation.

When knowledge becomes more widespread among French Co-operators, and when they cease to be led by politicians, they will at length do justice to our first French Co-operative institution, around which all Co-operative Societies will rally.

It now remains for us to thank for their cordial and brotherly hospitality Mr. Mc.Innes (Chairman of the Organising Committee), Mr. Gray (the Secretary), the Directors of the English Wholesale, those of the Manchester and Salford Co-operative Society, and last but not least the Co-operators of Rochdale and Hebden Bridge.

38

T.W. ALLEN'S SPEECH, *THE 40TH ANNUAL CO-OPERATIVE CONGRESS, 1908* (MANCHESTER: CO-OP UNION, 1908), 359–360.

T.W. Allen

[Thomas William Allen (1864–1943), the son of a minister, was born in Abertillery, South Wales. Employed by the Blaina Co-operative Society when he left school, Allen worked his way up in the movement to become manager of the society, then from 1910 a director of the CWS. During the First World War he was chairman of the Consumers' Council and acted as secretary to the Food Controller, for which service Allen was knighted in 1919. His career can be seen as evidence of the incorporation of co-operative leadership by the capitalist state, certainly, though he had the highest ambitions for co-operation as an alternative to capitalism. [Peter Gurney, *Co-operative Culture and the Politics of Consumption in England, 1870– 1930* (Manchester: Manchester University Press, 1996), 213-216] Reproduced below is the welcome address Allen gave to foreign delegates at the Newport Congress in 1908, where he was honoured with the presidency. Scores of overseas co-operators attended the annual congresses, and his speech underlines how important such displays of international solidarity were to British co-operators at this time. Allen differentiates between international conferences of "rulers" and gatherings of "the people" such as the congress, which were vital if war was to be avoided, and he goes on to blame armed conflict on elites as "most of the quarrels that have been were not the people's quarrel's at all". Allen's speech also illustrates how the ICA – which he regards as a crucial agency enabling a shift in democratic power across individual nation states – had by this time been wrested fully away from profit-sharers and anti-socialists such as E.O. Greening and Édouard de Boyve. Importantly, for Allen there is a religious dimension to co-operative internationalism: "Our day of Pentecost has come; we are of one accord in the place".]

The Congress reassembled at 7 p.m. on the evening of Monday, June 8th, for the purpose of receiving the deputations from the co-operative unions and organisations of other countries. The chair was taken by Councillor T. W. Allen (President of the Congress), supported by Mr. W. Lander (Deputy-Chairman), Mr. Aneurin Williams (Chairman of the Executive Committee of the International Co-operative Alliance), and Mr. J. C. Gray (General Secretary), along with the twenty-three gentlemen who had been duly appointed to represent their respective countries, a list of whom is given in the earlier portion of this report. The pleasure of the proceedings was enhanced by the presence of the Gloucester Co-operative Choir and Glee singers.

THE PRESIDENT'S WELCOME.

The PRESIDENT delivered an address of welcome to the foreign delegates, which was listened to with rapt attention. Mr. Allen said: Representatives of this great movement from many lands, once again, with downright heartiness we greet you, and extend to you, in the name of British co-operation, a right royal people's welcome to our country and to our Congress. Contemplating this splendid gathering, remembering the great thoughts and purposes which have induced you to cross the seas to confer with your fellow co-operators, our pulses quicken and our hearts glow with a radiant hope for the future of our cause. It was a happy thought on the part of Mr. Gray and the Co-operative Union to institute this special session of Congress; not only is it an expression of the growing significance of the international movement, but an indication of a desire on the part of British co-operation to show its gratitude for the many favours received and generous hospitality extended to our representatives when visitors upon your soil. You come on no ordinary business. Occasionally, our rulers meet each other in conference, and by so doing remove international misunderstandings and clear up misrepresentations. Interchanges between representatives of the people are equally necessary for the peace and commerce of nations. We think of other days, days of war and of bloodshed, days when men were taught to believe they did each other service by carrying fire and famine, destruction and death to each other's land. We remember that most of the quarrels that have been were not the people's quarrels at all, but those of our rulers for imaginary gain and supremacy, and we rejoice that, in some instances, in spite of monarchs and governments, we are learning to take our hands from each other's throats to clasp them as friends and brothers. Your visit will strengthen the bonds of mutuality existing between us and make it more difficult for those who thrive by discord to stay the democratic advance towards international sympathy, brotherhood, and peace. For years the International Co-operative Alliance has been working as a great co-operative Parliament for the interchange of exalted ideas and aspirations for the just government of the commercial world. It has not laboured in vain. We are debtors to all the great souls, living and dead, who have laboured to bring us together. Helpful ideas have been communicated; workers of different nationalities have been brought face to face, problems have been discussed and solved, and co-operative production in many lands has been brought into association with co-operative distribution in others. To-night, thanks mainly to the Alliance, we can look each other in the face as brethren; we gaze into each other's eyes and are not afraid, and this because we seek each other's good; desire, earnestly desire, each other's prosperity. Our day of Pentecost has come; we are of one accord in the place. We have tasted the new wine of love for all the human race. We speak in many tongues, but there is no confusion, the voice is one and united. We are moved by the same passionate fervour for humanity, we are impelled by the same ideals, we have the same problems to face, the same burdens to carry, the same goal to attain. We hear with joy of each other's successes and desire closer union in order that we may hand the cup of life more quickly to those who thirst for social justice. "Everywhere the old empty conception of the brotherhood of man translates itself into a sense of comradeship in a common cause and sympathy in common sufferings," and we rejoice that this great international movement of ours is a pioneer to a truer and more perfect system of social righteousness among the nations. Gentlemen, our hearts beat in unison in a great purpose. We stretch our hands, desiring to be joined with you in all things for the uplifting of humanity. We have a great message to deliver, a message of truth, reaching out to the uttermost parts of the earth and into the innermost needs of the heart. Teaching and being taught in the principles of our cause, exchanging ideas and exchanging our products, let us go forward, breast to breast, consolidating the bond of union between the nations, developing the great international ideal upon which we have set our heart—a co-operative brotherhood for the ennoblement of the nature and the healing of the people.

These eloquent and hopeful words were enthusiastically applauded.

39

"CO-OPERATION AND SOCIALISM", *CO-OPERATIVE NEWS*, 14 JANUARY 1911, 46–47.

Hans Müller

[Little is known about Dr Hans Müller (1866–1950), a prominent Swiss co-operator and frequent contributor to discussions about international co-operation in Britain. He served as general secretary of the International Co-operative Alliance between 1908 and 1913, dividing his time between London and Zurich. At the 1901 Congress held in Middlesbrough Müller explained that he had once agreed with those socialists and Marxists who condemned co-operation as destined to fail and campaigned instead for state intervention, but came to appreciate the potential power of the consumer after reading works by Ernest Busch, a German clerk, and Beatrice Webb. He also observed how delighted he had been to discover in Britain "a new type of co-operator, whose ideas were those of Robert Owen". [Peter Gurney, *Co-operative Culture and the Politics of Consumption in England, 1870–1930* (Manchester: Manchester University Press, 1996), 166-167] For Müller, greater international co-operative organisation was vital if co-operators were ever going to "depose the world-governing power of capital". [Hans Müller, *The International Co-operative Alliance and its Importance to the Co-operative Movement* (Manchester: Co-operative Union, 1909), 9] The extract below first appeared as a section in a longer essay he wrote for the *Year Book of International Co-operation* produced by the ICA; reproduction in the British movement's national press underlines the strong interest in its concerns before World War One. According to Müller, it had been the "socialist labour movement" which had paved the way for the ICA, and he calls for a "synthesis" of Marxism and "Nealeism" in the piece, between socialists committed to class struggle and revolution, and co-operators who argue for an evolutionary approach, pitching their appeal to all humanity. Despite undeniable differences of ideology and practice and the anxieties of moderate leaders such as E.V. Neale and Édouard de Boyve, socialists and co-operators, Müller maintains, share much common ground, not least a belief in the necessity for "revolutionary" change involving a complete transformation of social and economic life. Indeed, for Müller, it is co-operation that is bringing about economic change most successfully, and in the here and now, as it systematically "replaces capitalistic enterprise by the communal activity of co-operation".]

Co-operation and Socialism.

There is no question that the international labour movement has effectually prepared the way for the International Co-operative Alliance, for it first taught the masses of the people that their interests are identical and independent of national barriers, that their emancipation can only be effected by setting up a different economic order to the existing capitalistic one, and that they can only achieve freedom and competence by their own strength. If these three great ideas of the socialist labour movement had not been widely popularised amongst the people, the International Alliance would not have been able to attain to the position it now holds in fifteen years. It must associate itself with these truths in all its activities. It, too, preaches the solidarity of all working and co-operatively-organised men, without distinction of race or creed, and bases on it its raison d'être and its tasks; it also declares that it will work towards transforming the capitalistic economic order into a co-operative order by a systematic extension of co-operative institutions; it also takes its stand on the belief that this transformation is only possible when all workers organise their own economic forces and strive to develop co-operation on democratic lines.

The inner spiritual affinity between the international labour movement and the international co-operative movement, as it is embodied in our Alliance, is undeniable. There can, therefore, be no further question as to any opposition between the principle of the co-operative international and that of the international desired by socialist workers, as Neale and de Boyve originally intended there should be. Reference to the fact that the socialist international is revolutionary and political, while the co-operative international works by legal means and need not concern itself with politics, does not affect the inner spiritual relationship of the two. Just because the International Alliance cannot from its very nature concern itself with politics, i.e., with the conflicts for the establishment of equity between the communities of a State, it is of no concern to it, whether the socialist labour party (which must take part in the political contest in the interests of labour) use revolutionary or legal methods to attain their object. In addition, it is apparent to any unprejudiced observer of the revolutionary social democracy, that as a rule they do not behave differently from any other party, and use the same means as other parties do, in order to gain influence and power in the body politic. They are, in fact, only described as revolutionary, because the social and political order they are contending for rests on a new principle. But in this sense the co-operative movement, as represented by the Alliance, is also revolutionary, and that idea has been variously expressed in the English and Scottish co-operative press. In a certain sense, it can be said that the co-operative movement is more revolutionary in its methods than the most radical political revolutionists, for the latter can, at best, only consign superannuated institutions of justice and administration to the rubbish heap, but never change the economic basis of society, because this cannot be subverted by political measures. But the co-operative movement promotes the transformation of the capitalistic into the co-operative method of production by means of the economic organisations which it creates, and thereby revolutionises the basis upon which existing social and political institutions rest. It replaces capitalistic enterprise by the communal activity of co-operation. Though this work is carried on silently and in a wholly legitimate way, it still tends to shift society from the capitalistic principle on to a different economic basis. In this sense the co-operative movement is doubtless "revolutionary"—indeed, it is that in a deeper sense than the most radical social legislation can be.

Nevertheless, Vansittart Neale and de Boyve were not altogether mistaken when they thought they perceived in the international labour movement an element which was foreign to the co-operative movement; they only sought it in the wrong direction, and therefore failed to discover it. The element which causes the labour movement and the co-operative movement to take different roads to arrive at what is fundamentally the same goal is the class character of the labour movement. It is a class movement, the co-operative movement is not. The labour movement appeals to the class consciousness of the working classes, but the co-operative movement to their human consciousness. The feeling of solidarity of the organised labourer only extends to his class mates; in the members of other classes he sees, if not exactly his enemies, at least beings with whom he has nothing in common. The true co-operator's feeling of solidarity, however, extends to all humanity, and is not confined to any class, nation, or creed.

This psychological difference between the "class-conscious" socialist and the co-operator—which cannot here be further dealt with, although much more might be said on the subject—has its basis in the different spheres of influence of the two types. The socialist stands and works in the existing social order, with its contradictions and violent political and social conflicts; it is inevitable that he should be dragged into the vortex of its turmoils and passions. The co-operator, on the other hand, has already placed his foot on the land of a new society in the making; he cultivates a portion of the land of the future. Inside co-operation there are no more class divisions and class wars; here we are already in the kingdom of freedom; here all exploitation, all oppression has ceased; here we are brothers—men. In the relations of the members of a society to each other absolute equality reigns, and therefore class consciousness and the tactics of class warfare have lost all significance. What is required to bring co-operation to perfection is a pure human consciousness of solidarity, trust in each other, faithfulness in the performance of our co-operative duties and obedience to self-imposed laws.

This expansion of the working man's personality into the free co-operative man, this elevation of the soul of the masses is after all the most difficult problem of our age. On it really depends whether our movement reaches our goal and whether we succeed in creating a new social order. If men are discovered who are capable of creating this order out of their inner consciousness—for all order which exists amongst mankind arises from the soul and not from external material factors—then the co-operative ideal will be realised; but if they fail, or if they do not appear in sufficiently large numbers, then our movement will fall to pieces. Every co-operator knows from a thousand daily experiences that we are only able to realise the co-operative ideal in so far as we find intelligent and capable helpers in our fellow-men.

This circumstance makes it necessary that the co-operative movement should, notwithstanding its mental affinity to the labour movement, maintain its independence of the latter. It may be recognised that the co-operative international owes much to the socialistic movement, that the latter indeed smooths the way for the advance of the former. It must further be conceded by all experts that the economic theories of the socialists were far superior to those of the co-operators Schlage, Vansittart Neale, Holyoake, and Charles Robert; that the reconciliation of capital and labour which the latter strove for is an illusion and Utopian; and that in the co-operative movement the only object aimed at can be to take from production and supply its capitalistic character and to bring it over into the co-operative domain. In brief, one may have the deepest appreciation for the socialist labour movement and its teaching, and yet as a co-operator, repudiate the tendency apparent in it, and so much in evidence at the Cremona Congress, which aims at making the co-operative movement into a weapon for the "class-conscious proletariat." A co-operative movement which enters into the service of a party, that uses political and social organisations as tools, must necessarily lose its significance as a factor in the social transformation, as pioneer of an economic order founded on the solidarity of the human race. A "class-conscious" co-operative movement is a nonentity. In so far as Neale and his friends resisted the demands of the socialist party to use the co-operative movement "as a third army corps in class warfare," they were undoubtedly right; but they erred on the other side, when they thought they must place the co-operative movement at the service of the reconciliation of capital and labour. On this point Marx and his school saw much more clearly. If the system of competition, if the merciless conflict of all against all is to cease in economic life, capitalistic methods of production must be supplanted and labour must be organised and regulated for the common good. That will never be brought about by giving the worker a capitalistic share in the profits of the firm which employs him, but by putting co-operative industry in the place of the firm, and especially that form of co-operation which aims at the organisation of consumption.

Thus the problem which confronts the Alliance appears now to be to bring about a synthesis between Marxism and Nealeism, between the doctrines of the revolutionary working man's socialism and the teaching of the Christian co-operative socialists.

Just as surely as the numerous societies formed by working men with socialist tendencies that have joined the co-operative international have changed the being of the latter, it cannot be gainsaid that so surely will their activity in the Alliance and their co-operative work transform the former—must indeed transform them. Regarded from this standpoint, the International Alliance gains an importance for the whole social movement, the extent of which can now hardly be estimated, but which may certainly claim the attention of all those who care for the progress and improvement of our social conditions.

40

"MR W. LANDER'S VISIT TO WEST AFRICA", *BOLTON CO-OPERATIVE RECORD*, NOVEMBER 1914, 3–4.

William Lander

[According to the jubilee historian of the Bolton Co-operative Society, William Lander (1860–1924) was "without doubt, the most prominent local Co-operator in the movement" before the First World War. Born in Manchester, Lander's father was a blacksmith and his own working life commenced at the age of seven, first with a railway company, then later in a cotton mill. He joined the Bolton Society in 1879, was elected on to the educational committee and subsequently held every office in the society, including that of President. He became a director of the Co-operative Wholesale Society in 1894 and was a stalwart champion for the production side of the movement thereafter. [F.W. Peaples, *History of the Great and Little Bolton Co-operative Society: showing fifty years of progress, 1859–1909* (Manchester: 1909), 471–473; Percy Redfern, *The New History of the C.W.S.* (London: J. M. Dent & Sons Ltd., 1938), 581] Lander had utopian ambitions for the movement. "Co-operation was the highest form of Socialism" – he declared in a speech in 1910 – "it aimed not at making its main men rich, but in making the masses feel that the movement was theirs, and that they each had a share in the millions the Co-operative Wholesale and other kindred Societies were handling each year". [Joseph Bennett and John Baldwin, *City of Bradford Co-operative Society Limited. Jubilee History 1860–1910* (Bradford: Wm. Byles & Sons Ltd., 1911) 224–225] This extract from the monthly newspaper published by the Bolton society is a report of an illustrated lecture Lander gave about a recent trip to Sierra Leone, where the CWS had secured a concession for palm oil to use in its soap making factory on the banks of the Manchester Ship Canal at Irlam. Demands for co-operators to control directly sources of raw materials grew louder in the early twentieth century and Lander's visit was part of initiatives aimed at cutting out capitalist producers. He prefaced his talk with an attack on the "system" that had allowed a "despot" like the Kaiser to plunge Europe into war that summer and which must be defeated. Lander's account is fascinating, for it combines heartfelt criticism of how "the white man" continued to assert "a superiority over the black", with a deep-seated cultural racism that takes for granted the justness of the co-operative movement's particular version of the civilising mission.]

Mr. W. LANDER, a Director of the C.W.S., made a successful appearance on Wednesday, September 30th. at the Victoria Hall as a lecturer, and thoroughly interested his audience in Sierra Leone, where the Co-operative Wholesale Society has secured a concession in the palm oil district. There was a good audience, who followed Mr. Lander most appreciatively, especially when he described the views thrown upon the screen. Mr. Clegg occupied the chair, and, without any speech, introduced Mr. Lander to give his lecture on "A Short Description of my Visit to West Africa."

Mr. Lander first made reference to a visit he paid to Germany about twelve months ago with respect to machinery required in the production of palm oil. At that time, he said, there was no indication of the wide-world warfare we were witnessing to-day. German commercialism was then developing the resources of the country and increasing the business of the country, and many conceived that forces were operating which would bind the nations together. It was especially thought that the Co-operative movement would be a bond of alliance between the nations. But the system which permitted a despot to attempt to overthrow modern civilisation, culture, education, and Christianity had thrown Europe into the throes of the greatest war the world had yet seen. Such a system must be put down at whatever cost, so that liberty and freedom could be established amongst the nations, and that the barbarities and cruelties which disgraced the nation that committed them should never recur. They had each to do their duty. He believed that Providence rules, and he would say, without a desire to rouse bitterness either between individuals or nations, that "right is right, and God is God, and right the day must win," and therefore he would pray, "God defend the right and give righteousness success."

ORIGIN OF SIERRA LEONE COLONY.

Mr. Lander then turned to his subject, and described Africa as an exceedingly interesting country, and with it was associated the name of David Livingstone, one of the greatest of Englishmen. So far back as 348 years before the Christian era there were traces of its commerce, but Europe knew little of the country up to the 15th century. In that century the Portuguese carried on trade with it, and Drake brought England in touch with the country. It was, however, the slave trade which brought England in close touch with West Africa. The labours of Wilberforce and the noble band associated with him abolished slavery under the British flag. This was in 1838, but previously there had been the American War of Independence, and many American slaves had become free men. The idea came of the repatriation of these coloured men, and a colony was founded at Sierra Leone, the capital of which was named Freetown, as its inhabitants were freed slaves. This was in 1790, and in 1791 a charter was granted to a trading company, financed by British capital, to develop the country. Like other countries in a backward state of civilisation, the colony had been exploited by capitalists. Why had the Co-operative Wholesale Society gone to the country? The answer was that they needed its products. As they knew, the Society had gone into many productive enterprises, and in some of them they had been faced by bodies of men who desired to prevent Co-operators having free access to raw materials in the markets of the world. The individualistic class did not believe in Co-operation, and their efforts were directed to stemming the tide of its success. But those at the head of the Wholesale Society believed that there were no difficulties too great for Co-operators to overcome. They had conquered in the fields of distribution and production, and they were determined to control the raw material and avoid it passing through the hands of those who "toil not, neither do they spin," but made great fortunes out of the consumers. It had, therefore, been decided that in connection with the soap-making business they should get palm oil nut direct from the cultivator. It was to make arrangements for this that a party, of which he was one, visited West Africa.

WHAT THE PARTY SAW.

The party obtained 40 slides of incidents connected with the visit, and also places visited, and by the aid of these Mr. Lander, in a pithy and instructive commentary, imparted much information. His breezy speech and humorous allusions to adventures kept the audience fully interested. He first exhibited a map of Africa, and then of the little portion of it comprised in Sierra Leone, a country about the size of Ireland. Freetown had 77,000 of a population, 40,000 of whom were said to be Christians. The colony had been described as "the white man's grave," but from what he saw the white man would die in England as soon if he lived the same life here as he did out there. The white man, he regretted to say, asserted a superiority over the black which often led in life to what was a bad example, and was not always justified. He was ashamed to see a whip in the Customs House, with which an official would belabour a native who displeased. And yet he (Mr. Lander) came into contact with natives who were cultured scholars. One of them, who held a University degree, he heard preach a most magnificent sermon. There was a High School at Freetown, the motto of which was, "Learn to labour and to wait" (the Co-operative motto), and there students were trained for the University. Amongst the uneducated people the language spoken was a sort of pidgin-English, and on market days it sounded a perfect babel. Freetown did not possess either a gasworks or an electricity works, and the streets were lit with oil lamps. In fact, the dwellings and surroundings were most primitive, but the Corporation was wakening up to its duties and opportunities. Fortunately, it had a good water supply. Matters would soon be better if the educated black men had an equal chance with the white men to fill the civil offices, but the black man was held back. The Civil Service ought to be open to merit, irrespective of colour. To Europeans the climate was very trying, as the temperature was high, and the rainfall heavy, giving a humidity of 79 degrees. When the party left the narrow-gauge railway, on which there were two train services a week, they got right into the country, and had to depend upon native accommodation, sleeping on the floor in the native huts, which had no doors. They were able to have a choice of English food, which they carried with them, as the party had 240 carriers, "boys" who could bear a burden of 70lbs. These carriers' wages were usually 3d. a day, but the party paid them 1s. 6d. each, which delighted them. A picture of meeting with the chief of the land, where a concession was fixed up, led ultimately to Mr. Lander describing the obtaining of what was the chief object of this concession. In it were 320 square miles. There was growing upon the land dense tropical vegetation and trees, principally palm trees. All the party sought was permission to erect mills in which to crush the palm nut and extract the oil. After the chief and others had been propitiated with gifts of clothing, &c., the party made it clear that they wished to help the natives. They wanted to encourage them to cultivate the palm trees and to bring the produce to the mills which the Society would erect, where they would be paid a fair price. Satisfactory arrangements were made, and the mills will in due time be run for the benefit of the producers, and also of the Wholesale Society, the consumer. Incidentally he humorously showed the desire of the natives to wear clothing if they could get it. They were naked not from choice but from necessity, and the trade they did with the Society in palm produce would no doubt lead to the Wholesale Society's goods being bought by them. One of the first things the Society proposed for the benefit of the natives was the opening of a Co-operative Store near the oil mill, where the natives would be able to get goods.

41

W.J. DOUSE'S PRESIDENTIAL ADDRESS, *THE 47TH ANNUAL CO-OPERATIVE CONGRESS, 1915* (MANCHESTER: CO-OP UNION, 1915), 54–55.

W.J. Douse

[Originally from Windsor, William John Douse (1842? –1927) worked in a bakery from the age of nine and was apprenticed to a confectioners at thirteen. He moved to Nottingham in 1873 where he was employed in the private retail trade and a few years later became active in the Nottingham Co-operative Society. His Baptist background helped facilitate Douse's development as a public speaker and he soon rose to prominence within the co-operative movement both locally and nationally; he was elected on to the management committee of the local society from 1878 and served on the Central Board from 1890. [Joyce Bellamy and John Saville (eds), *Dictionary of Labour Biography*, Vol. VII (London: Macmillan, 1972)] A keen exponent of neo-Malthusianism and critic of women's rights, Douse was hardly the most left-wing co-operator and the fact that he was honoured with the presidency of the first annual congress held after the outbreak of war was significant. [Peter Gurney, "The Making of Co-operative Culture in England, 1870–1914", DPhil thesis, University of Sussex (1989), 247–248]. In his inaugural address – an extract from which is reproduced here – Douse followed some other leading co-operators such as William Lander in apportioning blame for the outbreak of war on the German monarch, though he raised the temperature considerably in a thoroughly jingoistic diatribe against "the fiendish ferocity of the Kaiser and his murderous Huns", "the modern Attila" that desired nothing less than "to enslave the world". Although delegates qualified and questioned Douse's xenophobic tub-thumping during the congress, total war understandably heightened the credibility of such views and brought them more to the fore within the movement.]

I dare not hope that in so large a gathering as this but that many of you have had your hearts lacerated by the terrible and solemn fact of the death of loved ones, whose lives have been sacrificed in the heroic defence of human right and justice; or it may be they have been wounded and will carry to their graves the evidence of the fiendish ferocity of the Kaiser and his murderous Huns. Friends, be comforted. The loved ones have heroically suffered martyrdom and are now wearing the martyr's crown. We represent some 3,000,000 of Britain's most loyal subjects, and are convinced that our Government was bound in honour to take up arms when the modern Attila tore into shreds the parchment he had signed to assure for ever the inalienable rights of brave little Belgium. We hate war, but our hatred of treason, chicanery, and blasphemy, yes, and the cold, callous, calculating murder of men, women, and children, incites the solemn declaration that it would have been moral cowardice on our part, and brand us as a nation with infamy, if we did not make every needed sacrifice with our Allies to crush once and for ever the monstrous attempt of Germany to enslave the world. Attila has recklessly departed from all the canons of civilised warfare, and his methods of terrorising would put to the blush the most bloodthirsty cannibal. History will immortalise the verdict of the jury of a few weeks ago in regard to the loathsome tragedy of the "Lusitania," when it was placed on record that it was a case of a murder against the Kaiser and his military clique, and I make bold to say here and now that the drowned victims of his lust for power and world dominance, with the use of death-dealing gases and poisoned water springs, find their apt delineation in the play of "Hamlet," who says—

"Murder, most foul, as in the best it is;
But this most foul, strange, and unnatural."

Well may Robbie Burns pathetically sing in his dirge—

"Man's inhumanity to man
Makes countless thousands mourn."

I leave this painful subject, but duty demands that our sacred cause should declare its detestation of the foul deeds done under the name of German "Kultur," and that we express our solemn conviction that God is seated on the throne of inexorable justice and that ere long the victory for national honour, freedom, progress, and altruism will be won, assured that—

The Kaiser's heart will feel the avenging rod;
"Vengeance is mine. I will repay," saith God.

Part 7

THE SENSE OF THE PAST

42

"HISTORY OF THE ROCHDALE PIONEERS", *DAILY NEWS*, 6 JULY 1857.

G.J. Holyoake

[Holyoake's influential early history of the Rochdale Society of Equitable Pioneers began life as an article in the *Daily News*. A decade earlier, the editor had patronised him as an autodidact with necessarily limited views, so Holyoake was no doubt pleased to place his work in a paper read by many middle-class liberals, with whom he was eager to forge connections. [Lee Grugel, *George Jacob Holyoake. A Study in the Evolution of a Victorian Radical* (Philadelphia: Porcupine Press, 1976), 48] The articles were pushed out by reports of the Indian Mutiny, Holyoake later explained, though it is clear from the editor's comments that prefaced the initial contribution that there was distance between them: Holyoake's "incorporation" by the intelligentsia was never easily or finally achieved. Entitled *Self-Help by the People: History of Co-operation in Rochdale*, the complete work was published in 1858 (a year before Samuel Smiles published his manual of bourgeois self-improvement) and it established a myth that credited the Pioneers with the invention of successful co-operative practice and cast Rochdale as the birthplace of a developing movement, a myth that has proved remarkably resilient, continuing to the present day. Significantly, Holyoake dedicated the book to Lord Brougham for his promotion of "Social Science", although Owenites would have winced at this, as would Chartists who reviled Brougham's anti-democratic politics. [Eileen Yeo, *The contest for social science: relations and representations of gender and class* (London: Rivers Oram Press, 1996)] *Self-Help* was hugely successful, helping to establish scores of local societies both in Britain and on the continent; the book went through at least thirteen editions between 1858 and 1907 and was translated into many languages. According to Holyoake's early biographer, *Self-Help* took "co-operative inspiration all over the civilised world". [Joseph McCabe, *Life and Letters of George Jacob Holyoake* (London: Watts & Co., 1908), Vol. 1, 292] Thereafter Holyoake established himself as the chief historian of co-operation, publishing a history of the Halifax Society in 1867 that pushed the communist millennium far into the future. His major opus, *The History of Co-operation*, was published in two volumes in 1875 and 1879. The second volume was dedicated to John Bright and was an especially tendentious work for by this time Holyoake had become a fervent advocate of profit-sharing – a potential antidote for class conflict for some prominent businessmen and intellectuals – and he shaped the history to serve this cause as well as distorting Owen's thought, prompting Henry Travis to accuse Holyoake of completely misrepresenting the earlier phase. [Peter Gurney, *Co-operative Culture and the Politics of Consumption in England, 1870–1930* (Manchester: Manchester University Press, 1996), 119-120; Grugel, *George Jacob Holyoake*, 141] Holyoake is best regarded as a "propagandist", then, rather than a historian, a description that he himself preferred.]

HISTORY OF THE ROCHDALE CO-OPERATIVE PIONEERS.

[We have much pleasure in giving a place in our columns to a series of papers containing a history of a remarkable social experiment. Deeming it most expedient to allow the intelligent author to tell his story his own way, we have allowed his parenthetical comments to remain, even when they may chance to express opinions dissimilar from our own.]

I. THE FIRST EFFORTS, AND THE KIND OF PEOPLE WHO MADE THEM.

Human nature must be different in Rochdale from what it is elsewhere. There must have been a special creation of mechanics in this inexplicable district of Lancashire—in no other way can you account for the fact that they have mastered the art of acting together and holding together as no other set of workmen in Great Britain have done. They have acted upon Sir Robert Peel's memorable advice; they have "taken their own affairs into their own hands;" and what is more to the purpose, they have kept them in their own hands.

The working class are not considered to be very rich in the quality of self-trust, or mutual trust. The business habit is not thought to be their forte. The art of creating a large concern, and governing all its complications, is not usually supposed to belong to them. The problem of association has many times been tried among the people, and as many times it has virtually ailed. Mr. Robert Owen has not accomplished half he intended. The "Christian Socialists," inspired by eloquent rectors, end directed by transcendent professors, aided by the lawyer mind and the merchant mind, and what was of no small importance, the very purse of Fortunatus himself,* have made but poor work of association. They have hardly drawn

---

* Here we must express our dissent. They failed precisely because they were aided by the purse of Fortunatus. In France, we are assured all those "Associations Ouvrières" which refused to accept money from government in 1848 are prospering, while those which accepted it have either ceased to exist or are on the eve of ceasing to exist. Sacrifice and self-reliance are the secret of success in these as in all other enterprises.—ED. D.N.

a single tooth from the dragon of competition. So far from having scotched that ponderous snake, they appear to have added to its vitality, and to have convinced parliamentary political economists that competitive strife is the eternal and only self-acting principle of society. True, reports come to us ever and anon that in America something has been accomplished in the way of association. Far away in the backwoods a tribe of bipeds—some mysterious cross between the German and the Yankee, have been heard of, known to men as Shakers, who are supposed to have killed the fatted calf of co-operation, and to be rich in corn, and oil, and wine, and—to their honour be it said, in foundlings and orphans, whom their sympathy collects, and their benevolence rears, But then the Shakers have a narrow creed and no wives. They abhor matrimony and free inquiry. But in the constituency till lately represented by Mr. Edward Miall there is liberality of opinion—Susannahs who might tempt the elders again—and rosy-cheeked children, wild as heather and plentiful as buttercups. Under all the (agreeable) disadvantages of matrimony and independent thought, certain working men in Rochdale have practised the art of self-help, and of keeping the "wolf from the door." That animal, supposed to have been extirpated in the days of Ethelbert, is still found showing himself in our crowded towns, and may be seen any day prowling on the outskirts of civilisation.

At the close of the year 1843, on one of those damp, dark, dense, dismal, disagreeable days, which no Frenchman can be got to admire—such days as occur towards November, when the daylight is all used up, and the sun has given up all attempt at shining, either in disgust or despair—a few poor weavers out of employ, and nearly out of food, and quite out of heart with the social state, met together to discover what they could do to better their industrial condition. Manufacturers had capital, and shopkeepers the advantage of stock: how could they succeed without either? Should they avail themselves of the poor law? that were dependence; of emigration? that looks like transportation for the crime of having been born poor. What should they do? They would commence the battle of life on their own account. They would, as far as they were concerned, supersede tradesmen, millowners, and capitalists: without experience, or knowledge, or funds; they would turn merchants and manufacturers. The subscription list was handed round, the Stock Exchange would not think much of the result. A dozen of these Lilliputian capitalists put down a weekly subscription of two-pence each—a sum which these Rochdale Rothschilds did not know how to pay. After 52 "calls" had been made upon these magnificent shareholders, they would not have enough in their bank to buy a sack of oatmeal with; yet these poor men now own mills, and warehouses, and keep a grocer's shop, where they take 70,000*l*. a year over the counter in ready money. Their "cash sales" in their last quarterly report, which we subjoin, show their ready money receipts to reach 1,400*l*. a week.

The origin of the Rochdale Store, which has transcended all co-operative stores ever established in Great Britain, is to be traced to the unsuccessful efforts of certain weavers to improve their wages. Near the close of the year 1843, the flannel trade—one of the principal manufactures of Rochdale—was brisk. At this auspicious juncture the weavers, who were, and are still, a badly paid class of labourers, took it into their heads to ask for an advance of wages. If their masters could afford it at all, they could probably afford it then. Their workpeople thought so, and the employers of Rochdale, who are certainly among the best of their class, seemed to be of the same opinion. Nearly each employer, to whom the important question was put, at once expressed his willingness to concede an advance, provided his neighbour employers did the same. But how was the consent of the others to be induced—and the collective agreement of all to be guaranteed to each? The thing seemed simple in theory, but was anything but simple in practice. Masters are not always courteous, and workpeople are not proverbially tacticians. Weavers do not negotiate with their superiors by letter; a personal interview is commonly the warlike expedient hit upon—an interview which the servant obtrudes and the master suffers. An employer has no *a priori* fondness for these kind of deputations, as a demand for an advance of wages he cannot afford may ruin him as quickly and completely as a fall may distress the workmen. However, to set the thing going in a practical and a kind way, one or two firms, with a generosity the men still remember with gratitude, offered an advance of wages to their own workpeople, upon trial, to see whether example would induce the employers generally to imitate it. In case general compliance could not be obtained, this special and experimental advance was to be taken off again. Hereupon the Trades Union Committee, who had asked the advance on behalf of the flannel weavers, held, in their humble way, a grand consultation of "ways and means." English mechanics are not conspirators, and the working class have never been distinguished for their diplomatic successes. The plan of action adopted by our committee in this case did not involve many subtleties. After speech-making enough to save the nation, it was agreed that one employer at a time should be asked for the advance of wages, and if he did not comply, the weavers in his employ were "to strike" or "turn out," and the said "strikers" and "turn-outs" were to be supported by a subscription of 2d. a week from each weaver who had the good fortune to remain at work. This plan, if it lacked grace, had the merit of being a neat and summary way of proceeding: and if it presented no great attraction to the masters it certainly presented fewer to the men. At least Mrs. Jones with six children, and Mrs. Smith with ten, could not be much in love with the two-penny prospect held out to them, especially as they had experienced something of the kind before, and had never been heard to very much commend it.

The next thing was to carry out the plan. Of course, a deputation of the masters waiting upon their colleagues would be the courteous and proper thing, but obviously quite out of the question. A deputation of employers could accomplish more in one day with employers than a deputation of all the men could accomplish in a month. This, however, was not to be expected; and a deputation of workmen on this embassy was a rather interesting affair.

A trades deputation, in the old time, was a sort of forlorn hope of industry—worse than the forlorn hope of war—for if the volunteers of war succeeded they commonly won renown, or saved themselves; but the men who volunteered on trades deputations were often sacrificed in the act, or were marked men ever after. In war both armies respect the "forlorn hope," but in industrial conflicts the pioneer deputy was exposed to subsequent retaliation on the part of millowners, who did not admire him; and—let it be said in impartiality—sad as the fact is—the said deputy was exposed often to the wanton distrust of those who employed him. A trades deputation was commonly composed of intelligent and active workmen—or as employers naturally thought them "dissatisfied, troublesome fellows." While on deputation duty, of course they must be absent from work. During this time they must be supported by their fellow-workmen. They were then open to the reproach of living on the wages of their fellows, of loving deputation employment better than their own proper work, which indeed is sometimes the case. Alas! poor trade deputy, he had a hard lot. He had for a time gave up the service of one master for the service of a thousand. He was now in the employ of his fellows, half of whom criticised his conduct quite as severely as his employer, and begrudged him his wages more. And when he returned to his work he often found there was no work for him. In his absence his overlooker had contrived (by orders) to supply his place, and betrayed no anxiety to accommodate him with a new one. He then tried other mills, but he found no one in want of *his* services. The poor devil set off to surrounding districts, but his character had gone before him. He might get an old fellow-workman (now an overlooker) to set him on, at a distance from his residence, and he had perhaps to walk five or six miles home to his supper, and be back at his mill by six o'clock next morning. At last he removed his family near his new employ. By this time it had reached his new employer's ears that he had a "leader of the Trades Union" in his mill. His employer calculated that the new advance of wages had cost him altogether a thousand pounds last year. He considered the weaver, smuggled into his mill, the cause of that. He walked round and "took stock" of him. The next week the man was on the move again. After a while he would fall into the state of being "always out of work." No wonder if his wife, who generally has the worst of it, with her increasing family and decreasing means, began to reproach her husband with having ruined himself and beggared his family by his "trade unioning." As he was daily out looking for work he would be sometimes "treated" by old comrades, and he naturally fell in with the only sympathy he got. A "row" perhaps occurred at the public-house, and somehow or other he would be mixed up with it. In ordinary circumstances the case would be dismissed—but the bench was partly composed of employers. The unlucky prisoner at the bar had been known to at least one of the magistrates before as a "troublesome" fellow, under other circumstances. It is not quite clear that he was the guilty person in this case; but as in the opinion of the master-magistrate he was quite likely to have been guilty, he gave him the benefit of the doubt, and the poor fellow stood "remanded" or "committed." The chief shareholder of the *Milldam Chronicle* was commonly a mill-owner. The reporter had a cue in that direction, and next day a significant paragraph, with a heading to this effect, "The notorious Tom Spindle in trouble," carried consternation through the ranks of his old associates. The next week the editor had a short article upon the kind of leadership to which misguided working men submit themselves. The case was dead against poor Spindle. Tom's character was gone. And if he were detained long in prison his family was gone too. Mrs. Spindle had been turned out of her house, no rent being forthcoming. She would apply to the parish for support for her children, where she soon found that the relieving officers had no very exalted opinion of the virtues of her husband. Tom at length returned, and now he would be looked upon by all who had the power to help him as a "worthless character," as well as a "troublesome fellow." His fate was for the future precarious. By odd helps and occasional employment when hands were short, he eked out his existence. The present writer has shared the humble hospitality of many such, and has listened half the night away with them as they have recounted the old story. Beaten, consumptive, and poor, they had lost none of their old courage, though all their strength was over, and a dull despair of better days drew them nearer and nearer to the grave. Some of these ruined deputationists have emigrated, and these lines will recall in distant lands, in the swamps of the Mississippi, in the huts of a Bendigo digging, and in the "claims" of California, old times and fruitless struggles which sent them penniless and heart-broken from the mills and mines of the old country. In the new land where they now dwell—a strange dreamland to them—their thoughts turn from pine forests, night fires, and revolvers, to the old villages, the smoke-choked towns and soot-begrimed monotony in which their early life was spent. Others of the abolished deputationists of whom we speak turned newsvendors or small shopkeepers. Assisted with a few shillings by their neighbours—in some cases self-helped by their own previous thrift—they have set up for themselves, have been fortunate and grown independent, and trace all their good fortune to that day which cost them their loss of employment.

G. J. HOLYOAKE.

43

OUR STORY: THE CO-OPERATIVE MOVEMENT (MANCHESTER: CO-OP UNION, 1903), 7–28.

Isa Nicholson

[Little is known about the author of this textbook for young co-operators, apart from the fact that she died before it was published. *Our Story* was written for use in weekly classes for juniors organised by educational committees of local co-operative societies and provided a basic account of the history and structure of the movement. Such classes were very popular and so was Nicholson's book, which had sold 61,000 copies by 1911 when it was republished for the ninth time in a penny-illustrated edition that ran to 250,000 copies. Fred Abbotts, who went on to play a national role as a co-operative journalist and educationalist, attended these classes in Walsall before the First World War. He later recalled how he had learnt "the childish version of the Rochdale Pioneers" from Nicholson's history and had read it until he knew "the thing off by heart almost, and I became very interested in the educational side". Around 17,000 children were attending these classes by 1914. [Peter Gurney, *Co-operative Culture and the Politics of Consumption in England, 1870–1930* (Manchester: Manchester University Press, 1996), 127–128] Although most of these children did not go on to become activists, it seems likely that a significant number internalised this heroic account of the rise of co-operation as a working-class defence against capitalist exploitation. One of these was Muriel Jordan from Leeds, who attended junior classes in the 1920s and who remembered that they had a social as well as an educational function. Muriel came first in the examination held at the end of the course and to her great delight was awarded a prize of five shillings in book tokens. [Peter Gurney, *Co-operation and consumerism in interwar Britain: transcripts of interviews with Co-operative Society members from Lancashire and Yorkshire* (UK Data Archive: University of Essex, 2012), 205] The chapters from Nicholson's work reproduced here give a pessimistic account of early industrial development and portray Robert Owen as a saviour of the common people.]

CHAPTER I.

The Darkest Hour.

OUR Story opens very sadly. I am sorry that it should be so; I should like to make it a bright one from the first chapter to the last. But it is necessary that you should know something about those dark days, just before the sun of Co-operation arose, and pushed aside the heaviest clouds that hung over England and its people. I think those dreadful times, of which I must tell you a little, were the very saddest our country has ever known, and certainly they were the hardest for the poor little children.

Those of my young readers who live in Lancashire or Yorkshire may have had pointed out to them some very old cottages, where the handloom weavers lived and worked, before the invention of steam-driven machinery. Very dark, gloomy little places these cottages must have been, even in their best days. One wonders how the spinners and weavers managed to turn out such beautiful fine work. Some had little sheds attached to their houses, but others had to live and work in the same room, and that must have been very unhealthy and disagreeable. The dust and fluff must have covered even the food that was cooked and eaten.

Yes! it is certainly better to have factories and workshops apart from the dwelling-houses, as we have them at the present time; and now there are stricter laws for their regulation, and inspectors appointed by the State to see that these laws are put into force, and that the mills are kept clean and airy. It must be pleasanter and more healthy working in them than at home in the old-fashioned way, as not only spinners and weavers but nearly all artisans did in the olden days.

But it was not always so. When first machinery worked by steam power came into general use the change pressed very, very heavily upon the poor people. Whilst they worked for themselves at home, or for some employer who had just a few workmen and boys under him, they were at least free, and felt themselves of some importance, and even my very young readers know what a difference that makes. When is a child who loves its mother so happy as when helping her to clean or tidy up, and being praised for its work and called "Mother's little helper?" Besides, the margin between master and servant was so fine that each workman felt that a little extra care and frugality might enable him to become employer in his turn. Another advantage of this home work was that many were able to get a little change of occupation. Towns were not so large or so thickly populated, nor was land so valuable, as at the present time, and most of these little cottages had good-sized gardens attached to them; so when trade was bad the artisans could turn to gardening, and so make ends meet, and get a little fresh air and healthy exercise at the same time.

But the freedom and importance were both at an end when the machinery invented by Watt, Hargreaves, Arkwright, and Crompton displaced the old handlooms some hundred and thirty years ago. Large factories were built, and into these the workers must go or starve. And now, alas! their brains were of little account—for the future they were only "hands."

But this was not the worst! The heaviest part of the work was done by the machinery, so the men's superior strength was no longer of consequence to their new masters; women could manage the looms equally as well, and they could be hired for less wages, so hundreds of good, skilful workmen were thrown out of employment.

Soon it was found that, as these new looms were quite low, even children could be taught to work them, and child labour was still cheaper than that of women. Very unwillingly, at first, did the parents consent to let their children enter these factories; it was like giving them up altogether, for mills were then built outside the towns on the banks of the rivers, so that the water power could be made use of more readily. But soon the dread of starvation compelled them to bring their little ones to be apprenticed to the new trade, and imprisoned within those great stone walls.

Up to this time the English people had simply worked and manufactured goods to supply their own and each others' needs; there was comparatively very little foreign trade. But the invention of this new machinery changed all this. Only in England was it used, and soon there was a great demand abroad for English-woven goods, and the weaving industry prospered greatly.

The millowners became possessed with a craving for wealth, and were determined to make the very best of these years of plenty, no matter what befel those who worked for them; and, alas! there were no laws worth speaking of to stop them. So in their haste to get rich they thought of another cruel, heartless means of obtaining possession of more little white slaves.

I often wonder, when I read of those horrible times, how those wealthy manufacturers could bear to enter their own children's warm, snug nurseries, and feel their soft arms round their necks and their sweet kisses on their cheeks, knowing that they had *other little children* shut up fast in their mills and miserable sleeping hovels—children who were constantly beaten, starved, and neglected.

But I must tell you about this new plan. They sent agents to the workhouses in London, Birmingham, Edinburgh, and other large towns to bargain for pauper children to apprentice to the weaving trade. They *called* it apprenticeship, but these little ones were really bought like slaves. Poor-law Guardians, in these days, are obliged to be very careful to whom they give up the children in their charge, and their officials have to visit their homes to see that they are properly treated. But there were no such restrictions a hundred years ago, and pauper children were often most cruelly treated. But we will charitably hope these Guardians did not quite understand what they were doing, for, you see, there were few newspapers, and no trains or telegraph wires to take the tidings from one town to another of how English children were being done to death in the cotton mills of Lancashire, Nottingham, and Derbyshire. So these poor little creatures, some little more than babies, were carried away by road in wagons, and by sea and canals in barges, and once at their destination and shut in behind those high walls they were actually in prison, and seldom, if ever, were permitted to come outside. Night and day the dull thud, thud, drone, drone of the machinery sounded in their ears, for, except maybe on Sundays, the wheels flew round and round and never stopped their clamour.

The workers, both grown-up and children, worked in sets, the former sixteen and even eighteen hours a day. The very tiny children were made to pick up the raw material from the floors; cannot you *feel* how their little backs and ankles must have ached, and how sore those tender baby fingers would be scraping continually against the rough floors? Six hours without a break the children worked, and then had only half an hour allowed for dinner, and only black bread and porridge to eat. I will not tell you more, for it is too sad a tale, especially for the ears of my very little scholars.

Well, the masters became richer and richer, and used more and more child labour, and the workers got poorer and poorer, and became so desperate that they were ready, if a chance came, for riot and rebellion. But there is an old proverb which tells us that "The darkest hour is just before the dawn," which means the same as the more homely saying that "When things are at their worst they begin to mend." Those of you who have to leave your warm beds and turn out to your work on a cold winter's morning know how dismally dark it is before that first faint glimmer in the sky gives the promise of dawn.

CHAPTER II.

Before the Dawn.

NO one knew it till long years afterwards, but the promise of brighter days for *all* the workers of England had already been given in the birth of one of the two boys who, each in their own time and way, set themselves in their manhood to the task of making their native land a happier one for the poor and oppressed.

They were widely separated in age, position, and opinions, yet, with a few noble comrades, they became known throughout England, and indeed all the civilised world, as great social reformers—the friends of the poor and helpless—the saviours of the children—and both lived to be old men and see some good results of their labour and sacrifice.

The boy with whom our Story is most concerned—who, indeed, began the Story—was born on the 14th of May, in the year 1771, and when I tell you that he opened his little eyes and set up his first cry in a little village among the Welsh hills, you will be able, I daresay, to tell me that boy's name and the name of the village also.

Newtown (now so famous as the birthplace and last long home of Robert Owen) is a long, straggling place with only one main street, but surrounded with beautiful scenery, "rippling brooks, rugged waterfalls, and shady glens." On the preceding page is an illustration of Mr. Owen's house. "Which is it?" I know you will say, as

I did when it was first shown to me. Well, it is the one with the signboard "Ford" over the window and on the wall, for it is now a stationer's shop.

They knew how to build houses in those old days; they were not run up anyhow, and such poor materials used that they fell to pieces again within one generation. It is one hundred and thirty-six years ago since that May day when the neighbours in the village went about telling each other that Mrs. Owen had got another baby, yet the late Mr. Holyoake (Robert Owen's friend) has said that he believed the house would last another century yet.

Little Robert's parents were poor people, but were highly respected in the village. His father was a saddler by trade, and filled the position of local postmaster also. He was a well-read man for his time, and wishful that his seven children (of whom our hero was the youngest but one) should be taught as much as possible. Robert must have been a wonderfully sharp, clever boy, for we read that his master promoted him to be monitor in the school when he was only seven years old, and that he was so fond of his studies that he was first at school in the morning and the last to leave it at night. Naturally, in a little village everyone knew the sort of child he was, and, moreover, he was "a nice boy," good humoured, and obliging, and so all those who had books lent them to him—the clergyman, the doctor, the lawyer, and others—and by the time he left his home in Wales he had read quite a number of what you would probably call very dry books. But his school life was a very short one, for he began to earn his own living when he was only nine years old, for you see in those days there were no school attendance officers—indeed, parents were not obliged to send their children to school at all; they just pleased themselves about it, and could and did put them to work in the fields, mines, or factories, almost as soon as they could toddle about.

Robert's first place was with a retail shopkeeper, but he only stayed with him for one year, and then came a sad parting from parents, brothers, sisters, and home; for it was decided that he should go to a brother who had settled in London.

Think of a little boy of ten, however sharp and old for his years, having to set off alone on a journey like that, with no hope of seeing those he loved again for a long, long time; because, you see, there were no trains to whirl him up to London and back in a few hours. The only way of travelling was by the stage coach, over rough, jolting roads. The owner of the coach wanted to put the little boy inside, but there was a cross, unfeeling man among those more favoured passengers, who objected, and would not make room for him, so there was nothing for it but to scramble up on to the top for the long, cold night ride. But I know the coachman would be pitiful, and wrap the poor child up as snugly as he could in the horse rugs, and would speak cheerily to him now and then. All the same, it was a cold, sore, and sorrowful little boy that was met at the coach office and welcomed to the London home of his married brother.

He did not stay long there. In six weeks' time he was off to Stamford in Lincolnshire, as a draper's assistant. From this position he worked himself up till, when only nineteen years of age, he became partner, then sole master of a small machine-making business in Manchester. He did very well, but he was quick enough to see that the day of small manufacturers was drawing fast to a close, as the day of small shopkeepers is doing at the present time.

So he gave this up to become manager of a mill, and later we find him managing partner of a spinning mill at New Lanark, in Scotland. There his real life work began, and there we will follow him in our next chapter.

CHAPTER III.

The Dawn.

ROBERT Owen was about twenty-eight years of age when he became managing partner of the spinning mill at New Lanark, a village on the banks of the Clyde, with beautiful surroundings of hill, wood, and water.

But though living in the midst of such lovely scenery, Mr. Owen found the workers in New Lanark in the same pitiful plight as those he had left behind in Lancashire. The houses were in a tumble-down condition, there was a fearful amount of drunkenness in the village, and many of the mill hands were very dishonest. Most men finding such a sad state of disorder would have dismissed the worst offenders, and tried to get a steadier set of workers; but Mr. Owen believed it was their circumstances that made them inclined to be wicked, and he nobly set about to improve their lives and make them happier, and, therefore, better men and women.

One of the first things was to teach them cleanliness—no easy task, when their homes were so poor and they were so ignorant. Then he saw how they were cheated by the shopkeepers, to whom they were always in debt, what poor, inferior food was sold to them, and how heavily they had to pay for it. Presently the idea occurred to him to establish stores for them in connection with the mills. He bought everything with ready-money from the best markets, and contracted for fuel, milk, and other articles, to be taken to the people's doors and sold to them at cost price, at a saving of 25 per cent in the spending of their wages. Good and plentiful food and cleanliness in their persons and homes, added greatly to their comfort, and good conduct in due course followed.

Then there were the children to be thought of and cared for. Among these were four or five hundred pauper children between the ages of five and ten, procured from the surrounding parishes. These were fairly well housed and fed as times went, and some little teaching had even been attempted before the new master's reign, but, poor little mites, how could they be expected to learn lessons, tired and worn out as they were with a long day's work—yes, longer than your fathers have now! As for the infants, there were no schools for them, and in their small, uncomfortable homes they seemed sadly in their mothers' way, and always crying and in trouble.

When Robert Owen thought of his home and happy school life his heart was filled with pity for the wee Scotch bairns, and, as soon as he could manage it, he did a thing for which tired, over-burthened mothers have reason to bless him to-day. He built and opened at New Lanark the first infant school ever known in the kingdom.

Ah! you know all about infant schools—you have been taught in them, and proudly taken your little brothers and sisters there to the baby class, as soon as they were three years of age—and this infant school established on the banks of the Clyde a century ago, must have been even nicer than yours to-day. Babies were admitted as soon as they could walk, and they had good times, I can tell you. Mr. Owen forbade the teachers ever to speak crossly to the little ones, but they were to show them how to make each other happy. Books were very little used— the teaching was given by word of mouth—but pictures and coloured maps were great features in the school. There was a splendid playground and a playroom for wet weather; indeed, it was all like playtime to these happy little ones.

At twelve years of age they were admitted into the works, if their parents wished it, and there was a good choice of trades for them without going outside Mr. Owen's establishment. He had a great idea of communities supplying their own needs as far as possible, and so in connection with the various branches of cotton manufacture, he had mechanics, iron and brass founders, forgers, and turners in wood and iron and all sections of the building trade employed. All his workers were well cared for—new cottages were built, their wages were increased, and hours of labour reduced. To assist those who wished to improve their education, and to give pleasure to all, a lecture hall was erected and a library of books collected. Under these happy conditions of life and labour, New Lanark became a model village, and an object-lesson for the civilised world. When Mr. Owen had thus practically shown that human beings, like machinery, worked best when properly cared for, and that instead of being reduced to beggary, as his partners had feared, his wealth and theirs was increasing year by year, he tried to prevail upon other manufacturers to copy his example.

Our dear old country used to be called "Merrie England" in olden days. Robert Owen dreamt, not only at night, but all day long, of making it merrie England again, if only he could lead the people to co-operate one with another, instead of fighting against each other. So he drew up a circular, and had it printed and distributed among the millowners, telling them what he had done, and how much fresher and healthier his people were, and how much more work they could do now that they had better food, and more rest.

Did the masters listen to this grand appeal, do you think? No, indeed; they simply laughed at it. "If Mr. Owen wants to beggar himself, he can do so," they said; "but he must not think he can dictate to us, or persuade us to ruin ourselves and the country, too, by following his mad notions. What would become of the country's trade if we all began to raise wages, shorten hours, and do away with child labour?"

But Robert Owen and a few staunch friends went on agitating for better laws for the protection of labour, and stirring up the working people to try to help themselves and each other. But, you see, they were so poor and so ignorant and crushed down that they could not do much to raise themselves. Still, a beginning was made. A few among the poorer classes here and there collected together a little share capital and started what they called union shops, and there were a few Co-operative papers printed in different parts of the country. But you know, in doing your lessons, how you have often to "try, try again," *and* again, before you get them correct. So it was with these first attempts at Co-operation. The people had to learn the right way to go about it, and they failed so often that they got discouraged (just as you do with a difficult sum), and most of those who tried gave it up, and the Co-operative papers ceased to be printed. But other help was at hand. The dark clouds of misery were slowly lifting, and the first glimmer of dawn could now be seen.

44

"THE GREAT MINERS' LOCK-OUT. £67,000 WITHDRAWN FROM THE SOCIETY, 1893", IN *THE CORONATION HISTORY OF THE BARNSLEY BRITISH CO-OPERATIVE SOCIETY LIMITED. 1862–1902* (MANCHESTER: CO-OPERATIVE WHOLESALE SOCIETY, 1903), 93–99.

[Scores of local co-operative societies celebrated their fiftieth anniversary or "jubilee" in the late nineteenth and early twentieth century. Commemorative histories were usually published to mark these events and were distributed to all members of the society for free. This extract is from the text produced by the Barnsley Society that had over 20,000 members at this time, which was brought forward to celebrate the society's fortieth anniversary in order to coincide with the coronation of Edward VII and Alexandra. The frontispiece to the volume featured photographs of the new king and queen, surrounded by royal insignia, underscoring just how deeply embedded respect for monarchy was within the membership. However, the historical consciousness communicated by the anonymous author was also suffused with working-class pride. The extract details the aid rendered by the society to striking miners during the 1893 lock-out, the most serious wave of industrial unrest since the general strike half a century earlier. The author had to tread carefully here. Many members of the society were miners and the Yorkshire Miners' Association was a bastion of Lib-Labism. The constituency was also staunchly Liberal; when Pete Curran stood for the Independent Labour Party in Barnsley in 1897 he polled less than 10% and there was no breakthrough for Labour until the franchise was expanded after the First World War. However, the text does suggest a more radical trajectory for co-operation. "So keen a struggle between capital and labour was probably never known in the history of this country", the writer observes and they go on to demonstrate how the dispute served as a great advertisement for the cause of co-operation despite the riots in the locality, which included the shooting by troops of two onlookers – the

Featherstone Massacre – tactfully overlooked in the account. [Quentin Outram, "The Featherstone Massacre and Its Forgotten Martyrs", in Quentin Outram and Keith Laybourn (eds), *Secular Martyrdom in Britain and Ireland* (Cham, Switzerland: Palgrave Macmillan, 2018)] Moreover, in the preface to the volume, the author emphasised how co-operation is inevitably being drawn into the political field, because of economic attacks from private capital that is increasingly organised along monopoly lines: "today Co-operation has to cross swords with the weapon of boycott used by private traders. This is an age of Trusts, and if the term be applied to Co-operative Societies, then is has proved a Trust for the benefit of many, and is as widely different as the Poles as others which seek to enrich but a few capitalists".]

NO history of the Society would be complete without an extended notice of the never-to-be-forgotten four months' miners' dispute in 1893. So keen a struggle between capital and labour was probably never known in the history of this country, and perhaps no Society rendered more momentous assistance or was so thoroughly prepared to meet the large demands upon its funds. In all probability no test as to the status of the Society could have been, on the whole, more beneficially applied; no amount of advertising or of speechmaking could have provided such an object lesson to the district as that presented by the ready way in which all claims on the Society were met. The sad events of the struggle, coupled with the way the Society met the extraordinary demands made upon it, will be handed down from one generation to another. On the 29th of July, 1893, the pulley wheels not only of South Yorkshire, but throughout the Federation area, ceased to move, and most of the miners stopped work. The duration of the struggle was in all probability never dreamt of, but the members of the Yorkshire Miners' Association agreed to draw no strike pay for the first fortnight, no doubt anticipating by that time the lock-out would be on the wane; unfortunately, this was not so, and after five weeks' duration the struggle became keener. Some five or six million tons of coal which would have been raised in the Federation area remained in the pits; prices increased rapidly, and Durham and Northumberland worked their pits to the fullest extent. The strike had a most disastrous effect on the South Yorkshire coke trade, as many of the Derbyshire and North Lincolnshire furnaces, so largely fed by local fuel, were damped down.

The men, during the first five or six weeks of the struggle, behaved well, but afterwards proceedings of a regrettable character took place, despite the appeals of their officials not to break the law. On the evening of September 4th a disturbance broke out in Barnsley, several men suspected of filling coal at Barrow Colliery being hooted, and the same night and next day windows were broken, with the result that tradesmen's places of business were partly boarded up. On September 5th and 6th the Wombwell district was in a state of great excitement, a mass meeting being held and resolutions passed in favour of all men being drawn out of the pits and the filling of coal stacked at the collieries discontinued. The same day the Hoyland Silkstone and Rockingham Collieries were attacked, and a good deal of damage was done. The Barrow, Wharncliffe Silkstone, Tankersley and Thorncliffe, as well as Earl Fitzwilliam's pits, were threatened, and contingents of police were drafted into the district. The Wath Main Colliery was the scene of sad devastation. A detachment of the 6th Dragoons from York were stationed in Barnsley, and extra police were drafted into the town. During the tenth week of the struggle a number of pits were thrown open for men who chose to resume work at the old rate of wages, and several small collieries were re-started and supplied local coal. As the sad struggle wore on various attempts were made to settle the dispute, but without effect, until the sixteenth week, when the action of the Government, with Lord Rosebery as mediator, brought the sad struggle to a close, and a Board of Conciliation was appointed. The men resumed work at the old rate of wages, and since that period coal wars on a gigantic scale have happily been unknown. It may be questioned by some whether the above *résumé* of the struggle was needed, but it should be remembered that the Society is so largely dependent upon the mining community that the descendants of the present generation will all the better realise what their forefathers fought for. When it is stated that the Miners' Federation funds, amounting to £167,000, were exhausted in the struggle, that the members of the Society withdrew over £67,000 of their savings—they were never sent empty away—in order to fight the battle, no apology is needed for a lengthy reference.

Looking back, it can now be seen how the miners fought heroically a four months' battle for what they termed a "living wage." The coal trade after a period of activity was, as the owners said, again at its ebb, and they sought to secure from the miners a large reduction in wages, but the men stood on a new principle, and to many it seemed an impossible one. They demanded that their livelihood must not be the victim of the manipulation of the markets, that they were entitled to a reasonable day's wage, and below a *certain limit* it was not possible to go. The recollection of this weary struggle will awaken many painful thoughts; and the endurance of families can never be forgotten. But what has this to do with the Society? The proportion of mining workers to the membership must be a great one, and, thanks to the existence of the Society, the suffering and sacrifice endured was mitigated in thousands of cases. The miner is not as black as he is painted, though often spoken of as a class of men as "improvident and thriftless." Thousands of men had learnt the value of saving money for emergency, and, even with little in the way of subscriptions, their "nest egg" had nicely accumulated. The men, it will be remembered, evidently knew the enormity of the struggle, having decided that for the first fortnight they would live on their own resources. The Co-operators could do so with complacency, and in hundreds of cases the period was spent at the seaside, thanks to the "divi."

To what extent the Society was able to render help, of course, cannot be accurately ascertained, but the balance sheet and minute book for that period reveal some striking figures. The struggle practically commenced in August, and, as stated, the Yorkshire miners decided to forego strike pay for a fortnight. The distress grew more acute, and on the 25th September, 1893, a special meeting of the members was held in the Co-operative Hall to consider the desirability of making a special grant from the Reserve Fund to alleviate the distress. The suggestion of the Committee to grant £150 per week for four weeks was considered by the meeting to be insufficient, and £250 per week for four weeks was voted, to include the grant of the Wholesale Society. The distress became so keen that on the 20th of October the Committee recommended another grant of £250 per week for four weeks, which was endorsed. Thus £2,000 or thereabouts was paid, and the Society also assisted local soup funds and other agencies for alleviating the distress.

During the half year July to December, which included the four months' stoppage, there was £7,500 less money paid into the share capital account, and over £21,000 more withdrawn than in the preceding half year, the sum of £67,456. 8s. which was paid out that half year being equal to one quarter of the Society's share capital. There are few bodies which could stand such a test, but it was got through without the slightest difficulty, and stamped the hall mark on the Society's security for all time. It is equally remarkable how comparatively little the Society's business suffered during such a trial, which proved so great a test to others. The decreased business done was only £35,000 in round figures, and barely 350 members had, no doubt through the force of circumstances, to sever their connection with the Society. But a few months after the strike had ceased the lost ground was recovered, and another era of progress still unbroken was entered upon.

The state of trade prior to the strike was depressed, and, as pointed out by the President (Mr. Fairclough) at the half-yearly meeting held in June, there was a turnover of £5,000 less compared with the previous half year, and £9,000 less than in the corresponding half year, whilst the withdrawals were larger than in any previous half year, which the Chairman explained was greatly due to the negotiating of mortgages. Referring to the threatened strike, the Chairman said 15,000 members held on the average £16. 10s. each in the Society, and the members had saved £141,000 in four years, which would be a grand back set to the men if they had to come out on strike. Dealing with the point as to what effect the strike was likely to have on the Society, he predicted that it would be the same as in Lancashire during the cotton famine in 1874, when they came out of it better than they went into it, because everybody had seen the value of Co-operation. They had 10,000 miners amongst their members, or about two-thirds of their membership, and every facility would be given for the withdrawal of any amount. As is shown in the early part of the chapter, all withdrawals were readily granted and promptly paid, and therefore the unrest or panic predicted subsided, and throughout South Yorkshire the Co-operative movement seemed to spread more rapidly. After the struggle money soon flowed into the coffers of the Society; and in 1896, three years after the struggle, the capital of the Society had reached £327,864, against £253,287 in 1893, or an increase of over £74,500.

45

"INDUSTRIAL ACCRINGTON: HISTORICAL SKETCH OF ITS DEVELOPMENT", IN *A HISTORY OF FIFTY YEARS OF PROGRESS OF ACCRINGTON AND CHURCH INDUSTRIAL CO-OPERATIVE SOCIETY LTD., 1860–1910* (MANCHESTER: CO-OP NEWSPAPER SOCIETY, 1910), 194–205, 208.

James Haslam

[James Haslam (1869–1937) was born into a family of handloom weavers in Bolton. Starting work as a half-timer in a cotton mill at the age of eight, he later attended evening classes, converted to "new life" socialism and joined the Independent Labour Party. Haslam was victimised for trying to unionise piecers along with Allen Clarke, who later found him employment on the *Labour Light*. Henceforth he worked as a full-time journalist, writing for the local and co-operative press and publishing a novel, *The Handloom Weaver's Daughter*, in 1904. He joined the staff of the *Co-operative News* in 1915 and a year later helped found the CWS journal, *The Producer*. Haslam was commissioned to write two jubilee histories for co-operative societies in Lancashire, the Eccles Provident and the Accrington and Church, from which the extract below is taken. A cluster of these works were published around this time (upwards of twenty), coinciding with a spurt in co-operative growth fifty years or so earlier. [John K. Walton, "Co-operation in Lancashire, 1844–1914", *North West Labour History*, 19 (1994)] Haslam's text closed with a chapter which placed co-operative development within the context of related industrial and social events. His was not the only jubilee history to provide a wider canvas – many others did likewise, drawing on the emerging field of industrial or economic and social history and citing works by Arnold Toynbee, Thorold Rogers, J.R. Green and H. de B. Gibbins – but his account is one of the more interesting.

[Peter Gurney, *Co-operative Culture and the Politics of Consumption in England, 1870–1930* (Manchester: Manchester University Press, 1996), 128-136] History from below was part of the democratic struggle for Haslam, a way of educating the "working classes...how long and in what unblushing ways they have been imposed upon by those who have presumed to rule them". Leaning on the work of an earlier local historian, Charles Williams, Haslam suggests how workers were "brought under the whip of organised capital" during the industrial revolution, causing them to resist as consumers as well as producers. However, this is also a highly progressive and at times class conciliatory narrative, which condemns machine breaking "mobs" as backward-looking and recommends the writings of Benjamin Hargreaves, son of the owner of a local calico printing works, as "an inspiration to young men desirous of achievements in industry".]

INDUSTRIAL ACCRINGTON.

Historical Sketch of Its Development.

CO-OPERATORS, no doubt, are as interested in the growth of the town in which they live, as they are in the development of the society which they control. In the latter half of the nineteenth century, at any rate, few forces, if any, among the working classes did so much towards the elevation of citizenship as may be attributed to co-operation. It is quite true that in most of our northern manufacturing towns, working people had perceived the advantages of collective bargaining concerning wages, hours of labour, and other conditions of industrial life, before they fully recognised the value of collective purchasing of the commodities by which they lived from day to day. But for the greater part of their history the two movements have grown side by side. In Accrington, they may be said to have begun at one and the same time. The Accrington Weavers' Association, which was formed in 1858, was started by men who were mainly interested in the commencement of the co-operative society in 1860. Hence, it is probable that the members of these two democratic agencies will have some interest in the history of the town in which they have played such an important and ennobling part, especially on behalf of the labouring and artisan classes.

But it is not the intention here to review any of the ancient history of Accrington, little of which is known, and much of that little is doubtful. Still one may go back a long way—to early mediæval times—and discover the foundations of some of the institutions now existing in modern shape among the factories and forges that stamp the town with its manufacturing characteristics. It is the intention here, however, only to take a cursory review of some of the leading incidents which left their mark upon the town and the people during the nineteenth century. Distance in time gives a charm and something of a sacredness to early history which much of it, perhaps, does not merit. One thing to be said for early records of the doings of men is, that the working classes by reading of them, learn how long and in what unblushing ways

They Have Been Imposed

upon by those who have presumed to rule them. But although there appears to have been a gap in the records of performances of men and women in Accrington for many, many years during the earlier part of modern times, we may begin to see how the town began to shape itself towards the size and importance which it commands to-day. Like most of our large spinning and manufacturing centres, it is chiefly a product of the materialistic nineteenth century. At the beginning of the great Industrial Revolution, Accrington was a village of handloom weavers. It was touched by the new industrial spirit out of which the modern factory system was developed, at the same time that most other towns and villages were re-awakened in the latter half of the eighteenth century. Mr. Charles Williams, who in 1872 wrote a sketch of the history of Accrington, and a review of its institutions, gives us an interesting glimpse of what the town was like in about 1780. Within the thirteen years that preceded this date, Hargreaves had made known the invention of his spinning jenny, Arkwright had come forward with his water-frame, Crompton had eclipsed both patents by his wonderful spinning "mule." A few years prior to the completion of Hargreaves' machine in 1767, James Watt had announced his patent "for the method of lessening the consumption of steam and fuel in fire-engines." Seven years after 1780, Cartwright, the Kent clergyman, invented the power-loom. Fourteen years before 1780, Adam Smith published his "Wealth of Nations." Thirteen years after 1780, the Whitney cotton gin was perfected. Six years before 1780, it had been treated as an offence against the law to weave a fabric consisting wholly of cotton. But by 1780, the industrial world of England was opening its eyes to the possibilities that lay before it. The working classes, having been deceived and oppressed so much previously, were alarmed with the wonders that were about them. Later on they rose in rebellion against the trend of industrial changes.

But in 1780 Accrington was being affected, like other surrounding habitations, by the transformation of manufacturing and economic life, from the wooden machinery in the cellar and the back kitchen to the iron wheels under the roofs of factories. The limpid streams from the hills were to be polluted. The cottage workshop was to be superseded by the factory. Men, women, and children were to be brought under the

Whip of Organised Capital,

and were still to be the victims of social, political, and industrial injustice. And at this time—in 1780—we are told that cows browsed in green fields where now stands Blackburn Road, Union Street, Warner Street, Abbey Street, Whalley Road, and Burnley Road. There was an old factory in Grange Lane; near the Seven Stars were three other small factories, one being on a spot now covered by Duke Street, behind Church Street. There were St. James' Chapel and the Bay Horse Inn, as well as the Black Bull, a hostelry that sometimes provided a meeting-place for the original committee of the co-operative society. The Black Bull in 1780 was the chief house of entertainment in the district for man and beast. Mr. Williams tells us that by the time the traveller could have viewed the things that were then to be seen in Accrington, he would be hungry, and would desire to retrace his steps from Woodnook Factory, "as quickly as possible to the Black Bull to order his dinner. While the landlady was spreading the cloth, he would have a look at the mill, which has been grinding wheat into flour for eight hundred years, and peep into the Baptist meeting house, which was opened in 1765, and was the only chapel in the town." In 1780 Accrington had five factories, giving employment to only about forty spinners, "whilst hand-loom weaving made every house a hive of industry."

In 1782 came the establishment of the Broad Oak Print Works, of which Mr. Thomas Hargreaves, the son of a jersey-weaver, was the first manager, bookkeeper, and general factotum. Subsequently Mr. Hargreaves became a partner. A dissolution of the concern took place in 1811, and in 1812 calico printing was recommenced there in the name of Messrs. Hargreaves and Dugdale. In that year the manufactory consisted of about half-a-dozen small buildings, covering an acre of ground. It was described as being situated near a village (Accrington) containing three or four thousand inhabitants. Up to 1816, the machinery was driven by water, and the cloth printed was such as had been woven on handlooms.

Calico Printing,

which has been an important feature in the industrial activities of Accrington and district, was first introduced into Lancashire in 1764, at Bamber Bridge. It was founded in North-East Lancashire by a member of the Peel family. He first established works at Brookside; subsequently he removed to Church. Afterwards, places were started at Sawley, Burnley, and at Foxhill, near Church. The print works started at Sabden, Primrose, Sunnyside, and Broad Oak, were early offshoots of the extensive properties of the Peel family, one or another of the founders of these concerns having acquired their knowledge at Peel's works at Church. But of the development of the industry, technical and general, an entertaining and instructive account appears in a publication issued in 1884, being recollections of Broad Oak, and a description of Messrs. Hargreaves' Print Works at Accrington, written by Benjamin Hargreaves, the son of the founder of the firm. The work is an inspiration to young men desirous of achievements in industry. About 1880, there were employed in the spinning and weaving department at Broad Oak 810 persons, receiving £400 a week; about 810 persons were also employed in the printing department, being 300 less than formerly; the reduction was due to the increase in machine work and the diminution of hands employed in block-printing. The wages were about £500 a week, and the production from 1,000 to 1,200 pieces a day...

In the latter part of the period from 1821 to 1831, a conflict arose between the adherents to the old forms of industrial work and those who were pressing forward the innovations of the machine age. The hand-loom weavers were being crushed to starvation and the workhouse. The price of their products had been brought down from 10s. to 1s. 3d. per piece. They hated the new conditions and the machinery which had been the cause of them; they looked upon the promoters as the enemies of working-class society. And they rebelled against them. They joined in a

Machine-breaking Campaign,

led by a popular agitator, nick-named Wheel Rim. Monster meetings were held. At Clitheroe they were disturbed by a troop of cavalry that rode among them. In 1826, the "loom smashers" marched into Accrington and paid a visit to the Old Factory (in Grange Lane) and the one at Woodnook. They compelled shopkeepers to give them food and money; indeed, they created a panic of fear in the town that was talked of for over forty years after. But in spite of this and other outbreaks that followed, Accrington continued to flourish. One cannot read of these days of the beginning of the new industrial life, without thinking that it was a pity that the working classes did not exert the same energy and make the same sacrifice to secure the control of the new forces for the common good, rather than in struggling hopelessly against inevitable changes.

Probably the first strike that affected Accrington was about 1815. At that time the masters had to pay an excise duty of threepence for every yard of cloth printed for home trade. They claimed that they could not meet the charge and pay the "high rate" of wages then prevailing. The men, however, a self-reliant and independent race, swore that they would fight to the last against any reduction. A struggle ensued. It extended all over North-East Lancashire. Threats were resorted to; indeed, one dark night a blunderbuss was fired at Edmund Walsh, foreman of the block-printers at Broad Oak. He escaped, however, unhurt. A reward of £50 pounds was offered for the arrest of the man who discharged the weapon, but he was never discovered. About three years before this there had been local disturbances in connection with the riots of the Luddites. These formed a body of discontented workmen in 1811 and 1812 and 1813, who in their protests against dear bread, broke up machinery, set fire to factories, and shot at employers. Driven half mad by poverty and hunger, they could think of no better way of expressing their intense feelings. Many of them were afterwards hanged at Lancaster Castle.

Of the mobilisations of the hand-loom weavers, already alluded to, in 1826, Benjamin Hargreaves, in writing of the time, has a vivid description of the entry of the infuriated mob into Accrington. It was in May—he thinks—of the year. He says:—

> A huge mob of some three or four thousand men, women, and lads, armed with cudgels, sledge-hammers, crowbars, and scythes were seen coming into Accrington. They marched direct to Messrs. Sykes' mill,

at the Grange. My brother Robert, hearing that a mob was coming, and having an intimation what it was after, hastened to the mill and hid himself behind the chimney of a house near at hand, and saw all that passed. The first thing was that of a woman smashing a clock that hung in a passage. The next was an onslaught on the looms with crowbars and sledgehammers. These disappeared like pottery ware, and all was finished in the way of destruction. A consultation was held, at which the question was put, "Shall we go to Broad Oak?" It was decided not to go, for Mrs. Hargreaves, they said, had always been kind.

As a matter of fact, Mrs. Hargreaves met the mob when they were entering the town and gave them sixpences, oatmeal, and bacon, and in other ways tried to allay their temporary wants. Of course, one must not speak of the outlawry of these poor men and women too harshly. Bitter things were said against them at the time, and have been since repeated. But they were families who were desperate with starvation! Victorious at Accrington, however, the inflamed weavers carried their work of destruction elsewhere. They kept at it for over a week, visiting White Ash, Blackburn, and Haslingden, then to Bury, Oldham, and Manchester. They

Destroyed Every Power-Loom

they could find. But at Chadderton the poor fellows were met by twenty riflemen, who used their weapons and killed five or six of the old weavers. Public meetings followed. As far as Accrington was concerned, much of the distress was allayed—with the help of the Government—by a decision to construct a new road to Blackburn. Mr. Macadam, the noted road constructor, was consulted in the matter, and the making of the road provided the unemployed with work. A few years after that the Burnley road was made.

These early years of the nineteenth century had not been too easy for the working classes. Time rarely weighs too lightly with them. Periods of hardship have occurred frequently since then; they are still in evidence. Unfortunately, the working classes do not quickly learn the lessons they should convey in respect to their relations with privately organised capital...

But we have space only to pass hurriedly to other notable events in the history of the town. A brief glance at dates shows how Accrington advanced, through her desire not to be behind other manufacturing towns. In 1831, the population numbered 6,283, and it had 1,206 houses. In 1841, population was 8,719, and houses 1,666; 1851, population 10,374; and in 1861, a year after the commencement of the co-operative society, it had increased to 17,688—an increase at the rate of 70·5 per cent., the highest percentage of the century; the number of houses was 3,404. Rateable value for the same period grew from £24,829 to £35,782. But for the first years of the century, working-class life was punctuated by many dramatic incidents. In addition to those already given, poverty and oppression were their lot in 1829. Distress again goaded them into fighting that which they thought oppressed them. But they fought against machinery, instead of waging persistent war against the system of economics, custom, and legislation that held them in bondage. However, in 1829, a wave of depression distorted their feelings once more, and to swell their ravings—ravings arising out of the sheer necessity of food—a detachment of infantry was stationed at Accrington, the old workhouse having been turned into a barracks; there would have been less necessity for either, if there had been a greater display of justice and equity in the things of life.

Nevertheless, the development of the town continued. Power-loom mills were increased. Churches and chapels were erected year after year, and with them the Haslingden Union was formed in 1837. Private enterprise took the place of public ownership. In 1841, the Accrington Gas and Water Company was formed; and it was in that year that the township was first lighted by gas. The working classes of Accrington, as elsewhere, had suffered most of the results of the inequalities and inefficient administration of the Factory Acts. The housing conditions were not much to boast of. In 1846, "a working man would have been looked upon as an aristocrat if he possessed a house of his own." This pregnant phrase was written by a co-operator of the town in his recollections of the time. The meaning of it will be best understood by those who are acquainted with living accommodation in Lancashire at that period, as indicated by Engels in his "Housing Conditions of the Working Classes in 1844." The Chartists were busy in North-East Lancashire. In 1842, a great demonstration of these far-seeing democrats was held on Whinney Hill. The plug-drawing riots affected the neighbourhood. These were connected with the bread riots of the early forties. Bread was dear, and the people could not buy it; they had to resort to meal and water; so they protested and went about

Drawing the Plugs

of steam boilers, to let off the water at the mills and bring the machinery to a standstill. They still thought that machinery was responsible for all the ills and knocks they had to bear; but the wrongs they suffered were due, no doubt, to the monopoly exercised over machinery. In a real co-operative state of industry, the thing they cursed would have been their greatest blessing. Another expedient to which they resorted was that of "shuttle-gathering." They were evidently getting less violent; they conceived the idea of gathering shuttles from looms to save the machinery; as these could not be replaced by the owners for several weeks, business had to be suspended. Yes, they were getting less violent. They were moving towards the more peaceful methods of collective bargaining. By the time that the Cotton Panic had come in the early sixties, they were prepared to bear their tears and privation with a patience and heroism that form one of the most impressive features of the history of the Lancashire working classes...

The co-operative society has not been by any means the least of the great undertakings that have helped to change the aspect of the town. To what extent it has played its effective part may be seen from the pages of its history. Citizens may also learn from this volume to what an extent the society has rendered financial aid to industrial development, apart from its never-ending influence in having increased the sobriety, intelligence, dignity, and reliability of the working classes. This, no doubt, has made them into a greater asset to the industrial activities and social endeavours with which the town now vibrates.

46

THE MEN WHO FOUGHT FOR US IN THE "HUNGRY FORTIES": A TALE OF PIONEERS AND BEGINNINGS (MANCHESTER: CO-OPERATIVE NEWSPAPER SOCIETY, 1914), 58–74, 167–172.

Allen Clarke

[Charles Allen Clarke (1863-1935) was one of the most talented working-class journalists and writers of his generation. Born in Bolton, he left school at thirteen to work in a mill. Politicised by a lock-out of engineers in the locality in 1887, Clarke joined the SDF the year after and established a short-lived periodical, the *Labour Light*. Along with J.R. Clynes and James Haslam, he also helped form a union amongst piecers in the cotton mills, a move resented by male spinners jealous of their skilled status which led Clarke to regard trade unions as essentially selfish. Although he stood, unsuccessfully, for parliament as a joint ILP/SDF candidate in the general election of 1900, Clarke disliked socialism from above, expressing his preference for Owenite, self-governing communities in his popular work, *The Effects of the Factory System* (1899) and later establishing a short-lived settlement just north of Blackpool that drew support from Tolstoy. [Paul Salveson, *Lancashire's Romantic Radical: The Life and Writings of Allen Clarke/Teddy Ashton* (Huddersfield: Little Northern Books, 2009)] Clarke wrote a novel to commemorate the seventieth anniversary of the foundation of the Rochdale Society of Equitable Pioneers in 1844, two chapters (or "pictures") from which are reproduced below. The story focusses on Charles Howarth, one of the twenty-eight workers who established a store that paid a dividend on purchases. Romantic melodrama adds spice to this imaginative retelling, in the form of a sub-plot concerning a calculating, selfish shopkeeper named Saddleback who has designs on Howarth's younger sister Emily, but whom she eventually casts aside in favour of a brave radical suitor, Mark Stafford, on the run from the police during the "insurrection" of 1842 at the beginning of the novel. Importantly, although Howarth describes himself as "not exactly a Chartist, but an Owenite Socialist, a

Communist, a Co-operator" (p. 44), Clarke emphasises Chartist involvement and the radical roots of the contemporary co-operative movement throughout the text, in order to reshape the myth of the Rochdale Pioneers and help politicise present day practice. Like some modern historians, Clarke shows how the Pioneers were not apolitical but were instead deeply immersed in the popular political movements of their time. [John K. Walton, "Revisiting the Rochdale Pioneers", *Labour History Review*, 80/3 (2015), 215–247]]

Picture VI.

THE CHARTIST AND SOCIALIST MEETING.

CHARLES HOWARTH and the young man who had asked the way to the Chartist meeting place, made their way to the little room in Yorkshire-street, where the Chartists and other agitators met every Sunday afternoon and on certain evenings during the week.

At the door stood a buxom, healthy-faced young woman, talking to a young man.

"Coming in, Ann?" said Charles Howarth, as he passed her.

"Of course," said Ann. "I'm tryin' to get a lost sheep back to the fold." And the young woman glanced at the young man and laughed; but the young man did not seem pleased.

"That's Ann Tweedale," said Charles Howarth to his companion. "She's wonderfully interested in reform work. Ready to work for any scheme to benefit the workers. Stands her corner and does her share like a man."

While Charles was eulogising her, Ann Tweedale was saying to the young man, whose name was Benjamin Standring: "Thou can either come in here wi' me or go for a walk by thysel'."

"But look what a nice day it is!" said Ben. "It's a shame to go sittin' indoors."

"Fine day or no fine day," said Ann, "it's a shame an' a disgrace for any young fellow that reckons to be aught of a man to stay away from a meetin' where men are tryin' to plan how to help poor folk out o' their misery."

"I'd sooner take thee a-walkin'," said Ben.

"I daresay tha would," said Ann. "But, as I've said afore, tha either comes in here wi' me, or tha can go an' do what tha likes aw on thy own. Th' chap that won't fight against poverty is no chap for me."

"Very well," said the young man, seeing that there was no other way of enjoying the young woman's company only by following her, "I'll come in to th' meetin' "; and he looked as if he was facing a serious surgical operation.

"Tha'll put a different face on, or I shan't have thee with me," said Ann Tweedale. "Look a bit more cheerful, or tha'll stop outside whether or no. This is neither thy funeral nor mine, tha knows. Come on!" and she turned to enter the Chartist room. "But remember," she said, with a droll glance back at the swain behind her,

"I haven't asked thee to come. I've not begged thee to come here. Tha'rt pleasin' thysel', tha knows. I don't ask thee to run after me—I don't ask thee to trail all over th' town after me; in fact, to tell thee the truth. I'd as lief be left alone. But if thou will persist in runnin' after me, then tha'll ha' to look at things as I do, or else look somewhere else for a lass, that's all. Come on—an' look joyful"; and Ann Tweedale marched into the room where Charles Howarth and the young man he had shown the way there were already seated amongst forty or fifty other men and a few women.

The subject under discussion was the "sacred week"—the week all the workers everywhere were to cease work—a proceeding in more recent times termed "the general strike"—and which had already broken out spasmodically and sectionally, in some parts of the country, and notably in the Potteries, as we have seen.

The Rochdale Chartist branch was standing aloof from this "sacred week" movement. Amongst the Chartists—as probably amongst all reformers—there were two classes—those who sought to achieve their end by violent means, even by insurrection and arms, and those who adhered to the peaceful methods of education and legislation. The Rochdale contingent of the army of agitation marched under the latter standard; indeed, a considerable section of it had grown altogether tired of looking towards Parliament and political action for any help; and were advocating co-operation as the best thing the workers could take up. The Chartist leaders, and their followers in the main, however, were for political action, and denounced and derided the Owenite Socialists and Co-operators, who believed that the best way to reform was by doing something themselves, by helping themselves, instead of wasting time by striving to get delegates into the House of Commons. The Chartist chiefs looked on Robert Owen's appeals to humanity and justice as silly lures drawing the democracy aside from the true line of march. Bronterre O'Brien wrote in the *Poor Men's Guardian* and other Chartist papers, that the only way the workmen could effectively deal with the masters was by conquering them, not wasting time in trying to conciliate them. He said that from the beginnings of history there had been a conspiracy of the rich to fleece the poor and keep them in subjection. He pointed out, in straight, stirring language, that as the poverty of the poor was essential to the riches of the rich, there could be no compromise; there could only be class-war till such a state of things was ended. He ridiculed the idea that the masters would ever legislate in the interests of the men, except when scared by impending revolution, and even then they would only tinker and trick, taking away with one hand what they gave with the other.

The majority of the Rochdale Chartists, as already said, were of a quieter and less drastic school; they did not believe that all capitalists and masters were heartless and shameless; they had hopes that reform could be won by reasonable agitation. Some few, however, were as vehement as Bronterre O'Brien, and inclined to physical violence, which he was not. His aim was not to smash looms and spinning-frames, but to capture Parliament; not to break the machinery of manufacture, but to run the machinery of the State.

Though all the persons assembled in the Rochdale Chartist Room were of one opinion about the sorry state of the country, there were differing opinions as to the best way to set about remedying it—there were Chartist views, Owenist views, Teetotalist views, Co-operative views, Trade Union views, with the Ten Hours Bill to the fore, Anti-Corn Law League views, and sundry other views—all seeking utterance and pointing the only way to the Millennium.

A fine, handsome young man named Tom Livsey, aged about twenty-seven, yet, young as he was, a member of the Board of Guardians and beloved by the poor for his kind ways; a young man, round-faced, with honest merry eyes, high and wide forehead, and slightly curly hair over the ears, great upper lip, showing dogged resolution, straight nose, firm mouth (yet with curves of fun and lines of poetry about it), and strong chin, arose and said: "We hear, comrades, that during the last week there has been rioting in the Potteries, and at Leeds in Yorkshire, and at Blackburn, Chorley, Wigan, Bolton, Stockport, Ashton, Oldham, Accrington, Clitheroe, Manchester, and other places, including Preston, where the 72nd Highlanders charged the crowd and shot two weavers dead, besides wounding several others. There was a cavalry charge at Bolton, and several persons severely injured."

"Well, and what are we going to do in Rochdale?" asked a grim, white-faced young man named Bob Butterworth, whose father had been transported for taking part in a Chartist rising a few years before. "Let us stop all the works here." Bob Butterworth, who was a little, dark man, with keen protruding eyes, spoke fiercely.

"There's a lot already ceased work here," said Charles Howarth, "you know the flannel-weavers are out on strike, and I think it's a foolish game."

"Pozzi, the shopkeeper in Yorkshire-street, says all the men on strike are rogues and vagabonds, and ought to be locked up," said Bob Butterworth. "But we'll burn his shop about his ears if he's not careful. I say let everybody come on strike all at once. Let's get every workman to come out, and march to the factories, draw the plugs, and empty all the boilers."

"And what good will that do?" said Livsey. "The only result will be that some of us will get shot, killed or crippled, and others of us sent to gaol or transported to that hell of the convict hulks on the other side of the world——"

"Where my father is!" said Bob Butterworth, bitterly.

"We sympathise with thee, Bob," said Tom Livsey; "but running our necks into that noose won't help thy father. If it would I'd be one of the first to do it. Our plan is to stick to our peaceful programme. You know that the magistrates have already got the 11th Hussars in the town to be ready for any disturbance. They're only wanting the least excuse to shoot and slay some of us. There's a few of us—and I'm one" (and here the speaker smiled), "they would be glad to put a bullet into, if they only get the chance. But they're not going to get shut o' me just yet. I mean to keep alive to plague 'em for a good many years yet. I'm going to disappoint 'em. They'd rejoice if we'd only no more gumption than kick up a bit of a bother, and give 'em the opportunity they're waiting for. We're hurtin' em' far more by doin' nowt than by doin' summat just now." (Livsey sometimes shuttled dialect words and phrases into his orations.) "Even as it is, I'm not sure whether there'll not be warrants out for some of us."

"Then let's not be arrested for nothin'," said Butterworth. "We might as well be hanged for sheep as lambs."

Tom Livsey looked at Butterworth in his bright, droll way. "I don't mind bein' hanged for a sheep, Bob, nor for a ram" (this was a jocular allusion to the Ram Inn, owned by Mr. Lord, whose daughter Sarah Livsey was courting, and it caused smiles). "Nor," went on Livsey, "do I even object to being strung up as a lamb, but I've made up my mind that I'll never be hung for a goose!"

"Hear, hear!" cried big John Bent—a tailor—and Miles Ashworth—a flannel weaver.

"Seeing that I was born when th' Battle of Waterloo was being fought," said Livsey, "happen me an' my mother thought we'd had enoof o' feightin' for a while; yet I'm as fond of a tussle as anybody, though I'd sooner battle wi' brains an' reason than wi' guns an' bayonets, for we get nowt but ghastly corpses an' famine an' national debt fro' th' latter, while by th' former we can get schools an' education, an' better houses, an' streets lit up wi' gas, an' better conditions of labour, an' better wages, an' happier times for everybody. It's because I want to do my share in bringin' those better days about that I don't want to go to the gallows just yet; though my owd skoolmester—that rank old Tory an' uphouder o' that unholy Trinity—Church, State, and Aristocracy—I mean owd Hugh Oldham, did once say to me, when I were axin' him a two-three questions about taxes, an' tellin' him that in my opinion—though I were nobbut a lad then I had my een open—th' privileged classes plundered th' poor o' their bit o' brass, an' that if ever I lived to be a mon I'd see if I couldn't help to get an alteration—Owd Hugh put th' prophet on in his paddy, an' said to me: 'You'll be hanged or transported for your damnable radicalism—you will, sir. Get back to your seat, and get the Catechism by heart, an' learn to revere your pastors and masters—stop in all dinner-time an' learn the Catechism!' Eh, how I remember that jolly day! I stopped in th' school, an' stood on a desk, an' was havin' a mock catechism with some o' th' lads, axin' 'em why Owd Hugh's head was not a possessive verb but an irregular one, because it was hollow an' had nowt in it, when in stalked Owd Hugh hissel, an' yelled: 'So, Master Livsey, this is your way of learnin' the Catechism, is it? Come down from that desk, sir, an' I'll parse your verb with this cane till you're in regular subjunctive mood!' But I didn't give him th' chance, I jumped off that desk an' bolted out o' that school i' quicksticks! Well, I didn't believe in force then, and I don't now! As you know, I was one of those who formed the Chartist Society in Rochdale; one that got Jack Taylor, our Town Clerk, who owns this room, to let us have it for meetings; and I shall be the last to leave it—and that will never be till the people get justice. But I am sure we shall never get it by mad rioting."

As he said, Livsey, along with John Taylor (a hat-maker of Spotland), William Simpson, and a few others, was one of the founders of the Chartist Club in Rochdale. An enthusiastic youth, only twenty-two years of age at the time, he made his first speech at a meeting held to commemorate the birthday of the great Chartist orator, Henry Hunt (just released from prison, whither he had been sent for advocating the political rights of the people). There was a torchlight procession, headed by a band, and Feargus O'Connor, with lungs like a blacksmith's bellows and a terrible trumpet voice; the Rev. Joseph Raynor Stephens, a Wesleyan minister, who declared "the principle of the People's Charter is the right of every man to have his home, his hearth, and his happiness—the question of universal suffrage is, after all, a knife-and-fork question"; and John Taylor and Tom Livsey addressed the great meeting, numbering 3,000, and held on some spare land. "Why should we succumb to our oppressors?" said Livsey, in the full grandiloquent platform style, "after placing in their hands the power which our forefathers rent from the Sovereign? and which he sought to maintain with despotic sway, until our then distracted nation was deluged with the people's blood? That was in 1649," he said: "but are things any better now? We have let things drift back into their old original state of aristocratic intolerance, till we find George the Third dismissing Pitt because he would not ask Parliament for more money to maintain that wastrel who was afterwards George the Fourth. Whereupon the King called upon Mr. Addington to become Prime Minister. Yes, the old chap—George III.—ought to have been put into a lunatic asylum, for none but a madman would have given the reins of government into the hands of such a monster as Addington—one of the class always oppressing and fleecing the people." Somebody in the crowd called out: "Reet owd mon, but what can us poor folks do?" "What can you do?" said Livsey, "why, organise and demonstrate and agitate for the six points of the Charter. That's what we can do—that's what we must do if we would be free!"

After a few others had aired their views—and in those days, as in our time, there were in every reform association men who talked simply because they liked to be talking and not because they had anything to say—the young man who had entered the Chartist room with Charles Howarth got up, and said: "I am a stranger here—if I may be allowed to say a few words—"

"Go on, my lad!" said Livsey, "I like thy looks. Thou'rt no spy nor traitor, I'll warrant."

"You shall judge for yourselves what I am!" said the young man. "First of all, my name is Mark Stafford, and I come from Burslem———"

"In the Potteries, where the rioting's been?" cried Livsey.

"Yes; from the Potteries where the rioting's been," said Mark Stafford. "I was in the fight. My teacher, guide, and friend, George Capper———"

The Rochdale Chartists knew and honoured the name, and cheered.

"George Capper did all he could to keep the mob quiet, but in vain; and I think he was arrested in the fight."

Then Mark Stafford described the riot, the cruel charge of the soldiery, and his own escape and flight and tramp to Rochdale.

"Well, thou'rt among friends now," said Livsey; "an' thou'll be safe here, unless some of our wilder spirits go in for making useless ructions here and bringing the soldiers and police down upon us. But I think there's not much fear o' that in Rochdale. We've not much faith in these 'holy weeks.' We saw how the first attempt at one fizzled out three years since."

"But if we are not to fight, or strike, what then are we to do?" asked Bob Butterworth. "Don't forget Pozzi, and remember what he's called us."

Charles Howarth stood up and said: "Let me give you my idea. While agitation means education, and is all right in its place, we want to be doing something more than spouting and shouting. When are we going to do anything substantial? Can we feed the hungry with gusts of eloquence, or clothe the naked with flights of oratory? For years and years we have been talking and parading, yet our cupboards are still empty and our backs still bare? While we are beating the air with words, while we are trying to blow down the barriers to Parliament with our breath, poverty, ignorance, disease, and crime still prevail and seem not to lessen. For thirty, forty, fifty, sixty years this clamour for reform has been going on, and little done as yet that is of any help to the workers. The generations dream and die, and go to the grave in the chains in which they were born. Instead of seeking freedom and prosperity through Parliament and the laws, why not begin to make our deliverance with our own hands? If we want anything doing, we must do it ourselves. We must not delegate it to others. Suppose we get a score—fifty—a hundred men into Parliament, what then? How many years will it be before anything is done? You know how slow is legislation; you know how every Bill—especially if it is for the relief of the people, is discussed, delayed, blocked, and then, in most cases, rejected; and it seems to me we shall all be dead and gone to dust before we get anything through Parliament. Not that I am against Parliamentary action. Get as much of that as you can, but let it be a minor part of our programme. Let us go direct, not roundabout. I don't believe in trailing over Blackstone Edge to get into the next street. I want us to be practical. Let us start doing something ourselves, and we needn't worry much about Parliament. If I want to get from Rochdale to Bacup, and somebody tells me to agitate till Parliament makes a carriage for me, I think I should be wise to set off immediately on Shanks' pony."

"Goo' lad, Charlie!" cried Tom Livsey. "That's the sort!"

"Now what is it we want?" said Charles Howarth. "There has come to our house, this last week, one of those little things that set a chap thinking greatly. I mean a baby. From the baby I have learned this—that we want, first of all, food and clothes for every child; after that, education and opportunity to become a good citizen. Now, that's clear; it's food we want; it's clothes we want. But we haven't enough wage to buy 'em. If we wait till Parliament passes laws to give the workers more money, we may wait till the moon gives us cheese and the stars drop bread. We all know that the middleman—the shopkeeper—charges us much more for provisions than he pays. Let us then, for a start, save something—and thus increase our income—by doing without the middleman. Let us join together, start our own shop, buy our own provisions, and sell them to ourselves."

"That's been tried," said Livsey. "That's the co-operation started by Robert Owen. Well, where are all those co-operative societies now? Gone—and all their papers too! Same with the Communist colonies. All gone down the nick!"

Charles Howarth smiled. "I know all that tale," he said. "I've read all about the co-operative and communist ventures, from Fourier's efforts in France to Robert Owen's in this country. I know how that movement began with a fine flourish, and any amount of organs to push it. I have read how, in 1827, that noble and pure Irishman, William Thompson, who abjured flesh food and drank nothing but water, published a book giving wise directions for the establishment of co-operative colonies. I've read how such a colony was formed on Thompson's and Owen's lines at Ralahine, and was successful, only coming to an end when, on the death of Vandeleur, the landlord, who held the estate in his name, the unjust British laws would not recognise a co-operative community as tenants, nor permit the society to become owners. I've read how these, and many more, have all failed and passed away. What's more, I was a member of the society started in Rochdale ten years ago—I see other members here, too, to-day—and I think I have found out why they all failed."

"Well, what's to prevent others failing?" asked Butterworth.

"It came to me like a flash of inspiration to-day. For a long time I've been pondering whether co-operation couldn't be put on a successful basis. There was no reason why it shouldn't. But the little thing necessary evaded me till to-day. But I've got it now. Ay, I've got it."

"Well, an' what is it?" said Tom Livsey.

"Ay, let's be havin' it," said Ann Tweedale.

"It is a plan that's never been tried before," said Charles Howarth. "The collapse of other co-operative stores was due to two things—first, people getting stuff on strap, or tick—that's on credit; and secondly, buying goods at other shops instead of their own. To take the last reason first—why did they buy at other shops? Because their own had not special inducements. Now, by my plan, I propose, after putting a small percentage of profits aside for emergencies, to divide the profit amongst the members—so much in the pound, according to what they have spent. That's the lever that will lift the world to co-operation. The more folks spend at our shop, and the more dividend they'll have. That will keep customers from going to other shops. It will also make everyone of them an interested shareholder—which wasn't the case with the co-operative stores that have gone down and dwindled out. The poor man, though he spent pounds there, never got any division of the profits—that went only to those who could afford to put more or less capital in the concern. By my plan every customer becomes a shareholder—and every man who eats food can become a customer; we make the whole public shareholders—and everyone gets a dividend on what he spends. As they've got to spend their money somewhere, there'll be every inducement to spend it with a society that will give them so much in the pound back. Then further, the credit system has been the ruin of the other co-operative stores. I propose a strict cash trade—no strap, money down. Run on these lines, I am sure a co-operative shop will pay, and pay well."

"By gow, but tha's got it, Charlie!" cried Ann Tweedale. "It's a gradely grand idea to give every customer a divi. on what he spends."

"Ay, there's summat in it," said Tom Livsey. "That's a brilliant bait, that the more folks spend and the more they'll get. They'll devour for divi. But won't this scheme spoil the shopkeepers? And my folks keep a grocer's shop. Hold on, Charlie. Don't ruin us all!" and Livsey laughed.

"Moreover," said Charles Howarth, "the people will have something to fall back upon in lean times, or when out of work, or on strike. The flannel weavers are on strike here, and it's a clammin' game. If we'd only had a store going like the one I have suggested, they would have had some money saved up. This profit-sharing according to amount spent will help working men to fight their battles. It will give them that without which no war can be waged—money. No longer will they be at the mercy of masters in labour disputes. What a good thing it would have been if only some of us had had a few pounds to face this present strike. However, that's only a side issue. The main thing is a cash trade and a dividend in proportion to purchases."

"The scheme's worth trying," said Miles Ashworth, a weaver with a big family. "There's eight of us at our house. That would mean a tidy bit o' profit for us—or 'divi.' as Tom Livsey calls it. I wish we only had some of it just now."

Others joined in the discussion, and asked questions, which Charles Howarth answered.

"I can't see much i' these co-operative schemes that always end in failure," said Bob Butterworth. "I'm o' th' same opinion as Bronterre O'Brien, in his articles in th' *Poor Man's Guardian*. Capture Parliament, he says; get men into th' House o' Commons, an' get hold o' th' reins, that's th' game. He's no faith in these little 'buyin' an' dividin' ' attempts. They only draw men aside fro' th' greit goal—they're nobbut red herrin's, that's what they are."

"It's politics that's the red herring," said Charles Howarth. "Men are wasting money and time in battering at the doors of Parliament, when they might be building up their own salvation. One co-operative society will accomplish more in a year than Parliament in a century."

"Well, thou's given us summat to think about, so's how," said Miles Ashworth. "I'll talk this thing o'er wi' th' missis."

"That's the thing," said Charles. "Talk the idea over with your wives—they'll see the beauty of it at once. Women are quicker to see the way to salvation than men."

"That's true," said Ann Tweedale. "I wish we could get more women to our meetings. I've not much faith i' men—their heads are too thick to feel where th' shoe pinches———"

Laughter interrupted Ann, but she went on: "Oh, it's reet. If ever th' workin' folks is to be saved, it's th' women that'll have to do it."

"Ann Tweedale is right," said Charles Howarth. "Get the women working with us, and we'll win the world."

Picture XVI.

PIONEERING.

THERE was another meeting called at "The Weavers' Arms," near Toad—or Todd—Lane, to hear Charles Howarth give a detailed paper on his co-operative scheme. The various trade unions of the town were each invited to send two delegates, and they all responded.

Howarth read his paper, and put forward his proposals; and the meeting started to discuss the matter. As at most meetings of this kind, there was a deal of talk—most of it off the subject, as several of the speakers—which is usually the case with orators—wanted rather to air their own pet views than discuss anybody else's. Some of the extreme Chartists were flatly opposed to co-operation.

"What we want is th' Charter—get men in Parliament to push th' Charter!" said one man. "We're only wastin' time an' money by chasin' co-operative red herrin's."

"And how long?" said Charles Howarth, with that resolute jaw of his and the decisive lips, and the firm face showing keen insight and organising ability; "how long shall we have to wait to get enough men into Parliament to do for us by legislation what we can very well do for ourselves if we'll only shape and set about it? We haven't one man in Parliament yet, and at the rate we're going on, it will take a few million years to get a dozen elected. And where shall you and I be then? Far out of the sphere of these bread-and-butter questions, I'm sure—wherever it be. I'm not against Parliamentary action—go in for it by all means—go in for any plan that will help to abolish injustice and starvation; but at the same time, when there's so obvious a remedy to hand, let us begin to help ourselves. We can't keep on clemming till we get men enough to vote for our programme. And you all know how bad things are just now. Our Member of Parliament, Mr. Crawford, has declared in the House of Commons——"

"That's where we should have representatives to speak up for us," cried a Chartist.

"I've granted that," said Charles Howarth; "but the chances are so remote of returning any that in the meantime we'd better be doing something else to help ourselves. As I was saying, Mr. Crawford, in a recent speech in the House of Commons, said that in Rochdale there were 136 persons living on sixpence a week! Just think of it—sixpence a week! 200 on tenpence per week; 508 on a shilling per week; 855 on one-and-six a week, and 1,500 on one-and-tenpence per week; that's a total of over 3,000 persons, out of an adult population of about 10,000, existing—Heaven knows how—on less than two shillings a week. And startling, disgraceful, and incredible as that statement seems, we here all know it to be true. Mr. Crawford also said that though these persons were living in a town where flannel was manufactured, five-sixths of them had scarcely any blankets, while a hundred had none at all; and many families were sleeping on chaff beds with no covering. We must help these people to get bedding, and we can do that by providing them with cheaper food by co-operation."

"Better to get 'em more wages!" cried a trade unionist.

"Go in for more wages, too," said Howarth, "as fast as you can; for the more wages you have and the more you'll be able to spend at the stores. I'm heart and soul with you for more wages. But I think they can be got without such a silly game as striking. You see where strikes land us. They leave us poorer than ever—and generally beaten in the bargain. It's a terrible slow job forcing wages up. But we can begin saving money at once by co-operation. There's nothing to stop us doing that. We don't need to agitate for votes to do it; we don't need to go on strike; we don't need spend years in fretting our souls out in weary waiting; all we need do is work together—and the thing's done. I'm sick of waiting—sick of talking; I want to be doing something. Let's get agate, as we say in Lancashire. And you may take it from me that as working men get a bit of money behind them, and are in a better position to fight for their interests, they'll have all the better chance of getting better wages, and, if need be, sending men into Parliament. For power always tells; power always compels respect; and whatever we may say about its abuses, money is power; and a pound in a co-operator's hand is worth a dozen Parliamentary representatives in the bush. With our co-operative money, used as I trust we shall use it, we could do wonders—build our own houses, schools, libraries, and in time possess our own factories. We could build this old world anew, and make it brighter, better, and bonnier than ever it has been before. Co-operation is salvation!"

James Smithies, by trade a woolsorter, who also did bookkeeping, a man of happy method and tact, stood up and supported, as an able and indefatigable lieutenant, the man who was destined to become the general and captain of co-operation. Like Howarth, Smithies was a Social Reformer or Owenite Socialist.

Miles Ashworth, once a marine, now a flannel-weaver and a Chartist; and his son Samuel, a young man of nineteen, also a flannel-weaver, enthusiastically declared that they were ready to start work straight away for co-operation.

William Cooper, a flannel weaver and a Socialist, and a clever man at figures and calculations, spoke to the same effect; as also did James Tweedale (brother of Ann Tweedale), a clogger and Socialist; John Bent, a tailor and Socialist—you find no reform movement or agitation without a tailor in the start of it; Ambrose Tomlinson, a Chartist; and several others, including Tom Livsey. Some criticised and opposed Howarth's project, while others asked questions regarding detail, which Howarth answered ably, showing clearly why previous co-operative ventures had gone down; "and they always would go down," he said, "so long as the rich in the character of shareholders ran away with all the profits." Under his scheme, he repeated, "every member would share in the profit—and the bigger his family, the bigger his dividend; profit being according to purchase."

Then up jumped John Kershaw, a collier of mystic religious tendencies, for he was a Swedenborgian, and said: "I propose we print Mester Howarth's paper on Co-operation, and distribute copies all over th' town amongst likely people." This was seconded and agreed to, and immediately three pounds was collected in small sums from those present, to pay for the printing. Kershaw undertook to give out the bulk of the pamphlets, though Ann Tweedale and Smithies, and Miles Ashworth also helped. Kershaw spent a couple of weeks on the job. He left the pamphlets at various houses, saying he would call for them in a fortnight; and Kershaw found his task instructive—sometimes entertaining, and sometimes disagreeable. At some places he was rudely received. When he called for the tract he always asked if it had been read, and followed this question by asking what they thought about it, which often led to a little debate. At the old Clegg Hall farm—which had long had the reputation of being haunted by a fearsome boggart—the occupant was a man of about fifty years of age. Kershaw said to him: "Well, have yo' read th' tract I left?" "Ay, I've read it," said the man, gruffly. "Well, what done yo' think about it?" said Kershaw. "Here it is," said the man, fetching the tract to the door; "tak' it an' brun it." "Oh, it rayther sounds as if yo' didn't like th' tract," said Kershaw. "I like it as weel as I like th' Clegg Hall boggart," said the man. "But this scheme is no boggart," said Kershaw, "it's a good fairy, an angel, to help men to help theirsels." "Tak' it away," said the man. "I want naught to do wi' it. There's far mooar Owd Nick about it, i' my opinion, than angel. An' if thou wants to know what I think about thee and this Socialist an' Chartist gang that's sent thee round, I con tell thee." "Oh, go on—tell me," said Kershaw. "Well," said the man, "I think yo' all ought to be hanged, an' th' sooner an' th' better for th' country. Such folks as yo' are noan fit to live. Yo' go about makin' men dissatisfied, an' yo' only mak' things wuss. Yo're th' cause of aw th' ills i' th' land." "Nay, nay," began Kershaw, but the man turned away, saying: "Be off wi' yo', an' never show yore face here again!" and shut the door.

At another place where Kershaw called for the tract he had left, the woman said: "Ay, we've read it; but we don't quite understand it. And we're Church folk, an' durn't want to bother wi' no new religion." "But, this is co-operation," said Kershaw. "We durn't want noan," said the woman; "th' Church is good enough for us."

Thus Kershaw and the other pioneers got some fun as well as irritation and insult out of their canvassing. But they met with plenty of derision and discouragement; and that worst of all hindrances to progress, indifference. Yet they were not disheartened; they were full of faith in their vision, full of confidence that they could make a good start towards realising it; full of hope for the future.

And so they wrought valiantly.

47

"AN IRISH UTOPIA", IN *LABOUR IN IRELAND. LABOUR IN IRISH HISTORY. THE RE-CONQUEST OF IRELAND* (DUBLIN: MAUNSEL & CO., 1917), 129–144.

James Connolly

[James Connolly (1868-1916), Irish revolutionary and socialist, was born in Edinburgh to poor Irish immigrant parents. His father was a manure carter and Connolly left school at the age of ten, working in a variety of low paid jobs until he enlisted in the army in 1882. Deserting seven years later, Connolly converted to socialism and joined the Socialist League initially, then other organisations including the Independent Labour Party after its foundation in 1893. Moving to Dublin in 1896 to become a paid organiser for the Socialist Club in the city, he was increasingly drawn to nationalist politics, attempting to fuse these concerns with socialism in his writings and speeches and through the Irish Socialist Republican Party, which he formed. After a stint in the United States, Connolly returned to Ireland where he plunged into trade union and political agitation. He helped establish the Independent Labour Party of Ireland in 1910 and took over from James Larkin as general secretary of the Irish Transport and General Workers' Union after the Dublin lock-out of 1913, which garnered a great deal of material and moral support from the Co-operative Wholesale Society. Connolly's place as a patriotic martyr was secured after he was executed by the British state in May 1916 for his part in the Easter Rising. [Ruth Dudley Edwards, *James Connolly* (Dublin: Gill & Macmillan, 1981)] Connolly disagreed with Horace Plunkett and the Irish Agricultural Organisation Society that regarded producer co-operatives, especially creamery societies, as the best means to improve rural life and he argued instead that prioritising the consumer was necessary in order to create the "Co-operative Commonwealth" of the future. [Patrick Doyle, *Civilising Rural Ireland. The Co-operative movement, development and the nation-state, 1889–1939* (Manchester: Manchester University Press, 2019), 133-134] The extract reproduced below is from his ground-breaking *Labour in Irish History*, which was first published in

1910. Here, Connolly provides an account of the Owenite experiment in co-operative living and working at Ralahine, County Clare, drawing on the history written by E.T. Craig, who had overseen the venture. [Vincent Geoghegan, "Ralahine: an Irish Owenite Community, 1831–1933", *International Review of Social History*, 36/3 (1991), 377–411] For Connolly, Ralahine provided a blueprint for socialist transformation and by returning to this "Irish Utopia" he hoped to remind readers of the revolutionary potential of co-operation. As he acutely observed, Ralahine was "an Irish point of interrogation erected amidst the wildernesses of capitalist thought and feudal practice, challenging both in vain for an answer".]

In 1823 the great English socialist, Robert Owen, visited Ireland and held a number of meetings in the Rotunda, Dublin, for the purpose of explaining the principles of Socialism to the people of that city. His audiences were mainly composed of the well-to-do inhabitants, as was, indeed, the case universally at that period when Socialism was the fad of the rich instead of the faith of the poor. The Duke of Leinster, the Catholic Archbishop Murray, Lord Meath, Lord Cloncurry, and others occupied the platform, and as a result of the picture drawn by Owen of the misery then existing, and the attendant insecurity of life and property amongst all classes, and his outline of the possibilities which a system of Socialist co-operation could produce, an association styling itself the "Hibernian Philanthropic Society" was formed to carry out his ideas. A sum of money was subscribed to aid the prospects of the society, a General Brown giving £1,000, Lord Cloncurry £500, Mr. Owen himself subscribing £1,000, and £100 being raised from other sources. The society was short lived and ineffectual, but one of the members, Mr. Arthur Vandeleur, an Irish landlord, was so deeply impressed with all he had seen and heard of the possibilities of Owenite Socialism, that in 1831, when crime and outrage in the country had reached its zenith, and the insecurity of life in his own class had been brought home to him by the assassination of the steward of his estate for unfeeling conduct towards the labourers, he resolved to make an effort to establish a Socialist colony upon his property at Ralahine, County Clare. For that purpose he invited to Ireland a Mr. Craig, of Manchester, a follower of Owen, and entrusted him with the task of carrying the project into execution.

Though Mr. Craig knew no Irish, and the people of Ralahine, as a rule, knew no English—a state of matters which greatly complicated the work of explanation—an understanding was finally arrived at, and the estate was turned over to an association of the people organised under the title of "The Ralahine Agricultural and Manufacturing Co-Operative Association."

In the preamble of the Laws of the Association, its objects were defined as follows:—

"The acquisition of a common capital.

"The mutual assurance of its members against the evils of poverty, sickness, infirmity, and old age.

"The attainment of a greater share of the comforts of life than the working classes now possess.

"The mental and moral improvement of its adult members.

"The education of their children."

The following paragraphs selected from the Rules of the Association will give a pretty clear idea of its most important features:—

"BASIS OF THE SOCIETY.

"That all the stock, implements of husbandry, and other property belong to and are the property of Mr. Vandeleur, until the Society accumulates sufficient to pay for them; they then become the joint property of the Society.

"PRODUCTION.

"We engage that whatever talents we may individually possess, whether mental or muscular, agricultural, manufacturing, or scientific, shall be directed to the benefit of all, as well by their immediate exercise in all necessary occupations as by communicating our knowledge to each other, and particularly to the young.

"That, as far as can be reduced to practice, each individual shall assist in agricultural operations, particularly in harvest, it being fully understood that no individual is to act as steward, but all are to work.

"That all the youth, male or female, do engage to learn some useful trade, together with agriculture and gardening, between the ages of nine and seventeen years.

"That the committee meet every evening to arrange the business for the following day.

"That the hours of labour be from six in the morning till six in the evening, in summer, and from daybreak till dusk in winter, with the intermission of one hour for dinner.

"That each agricultural labouring man shall receive eightpence, and every woman fivepence per day for their labour (these were the ordinary wages of the country, the secretary, storekeeper, smiths, joiners, and a few others received something more; the excess being borne by the proprietor) which it is expected will be paid out at the store in provisions, or any other article the society may produce or keep there; any other articles may be purchased elsewhere.

"That no member be expected to perform any service or work but such as is agreeable to his or her feelings, or they are able to perform; but if any member thinks that any other member is not usefully employing his or her time, it is his or her duty to report it to the committee, whose duty it will be to bring that member's conduct before a general meeting, who shall have power, if necessary, to expel that useless member.

"DISTRIBUTION AND DOMESTIC ECONOMY.

"That all the services usually performed by servants be performed by the youth of both sexes under the age of seventeen years, either by rotation or choice.

"That the expenses of the children's food, clothing, washing, lodging, and education be paid out of the common funds of the society, from the time they are weaned till they arrive at the age of seventeen, when they shall be eligible to become members.

"That a charge be made for the food and clothing, &c., of those children trained by their parents, and residing in their dwellinghouses.

"That each person occupying a house, or cooking and consuming their victuals therein, must pay for the fuel used.

"That no charge be made for fuel used in the public room.

"That it shall be a special object for the sub-committee of domestic economy, or the superintendent of that department, to ascertain and put in practice the best and most economical methods of preparing and cooking the food.

"That all the washing be done together in the public wash-house; the expenses of soap, labour, fuel, &c., to be equally borne by all the adult members.

"That each member pay the sum of one half-penny out of every shilling received as wages to form a fund to be placed in the hands of the committee, who shall pay the wages out of this fund of any member who may fall sick or meet with an accident.

"Any damage done by a member to the stock, implements, or any other property belonging to the society to be made good out of the wages of the individual, unless the damage is satisfactorily accounted for to the committee.

"Education and Formation of Character.

"We guarantee each other that the young children of any person dying, whilst a member of this society, shall be equally protected, educated, and cherished with the children of the living members, and entitled, when they arrive at the age of seventeen, to all the privileges of members.

"That each individual shall enjoy perfect liberty of conscience, and freedom of expression of opinion, and in religious worship.

"That no spirituous liquors of any kind, tobacco, or snuff be kept in the store, or on the premises.

"That if any of us should unfortunately have a dispute with any other person, we agree to abide by a decision of the majority of the members, or any person to whom the matter in question may be by them referred.

"That any person wishing to marry another do sign a declaration to that effect one week previous to the marriage taking place, and that immediate preparations be made for the erection, or fitting up of a suitable dwellinghouse for their reception.

"That any person wishing to marry another person, not a member, shall sign a declaration according to the last rule; the person not a member shall then be balloted for, and, if rejected, both must leave the society.

"That if the conduct of any member be found injurious to the well-being of the society, the committee shall explain to him or her in what respect his or her conduct has been injurious, and if the said member shall continue to transgress the rules, such member shall be brought before a general meeting, called for the purpose, and if the complaint be substantiated, three-fourths of the members present shall have power to expel, by ballot, such refractory member.

"Government.

"The society to be governed, and its business transacted, by a committee of nine members, to be chosen half-yearly, by ballot, by all the adult male and female members, the ballot list to contain at least four of the last committee.

"The committee to meet every evening, and their transactions to be regularly entered into a minute book, the recapitulation of which is to be given at the society's general meeting by the secretary.

"That there be a general weekly meeting of the society; that the treasurer's accounts be audited by the committee, and read over to the society; that the 'Suggestion Book' be also read at this meeting."

The colony did not use the ordinary currency of the country, but instead adopted a "Labour Note" system of payment, all workers being paid in notes according to the number of hours worked, and being able to exchange the notes in the store for all the necessities of life. The notes were printed on stiff cardboard about the size of a visiting card, and represented the equivalent of a whole, a half, a quarter, an eighth, and a sixteenth of a day's labour. There were also special notes printed in red ink representing respectively the labours of a day and a half, and two days. In his account of the colony published under the title of "History of Ralahine," by Heywood & Sons, Manchester (a book we earnestly recommend to all our readers), Mr. Craig says:—"The labour was recorded daily on a 'Labour Sheet,' which was exposed to view during the following week. The members could work or not at their own discretion. If no work, no record, and, therefore, no pay. Practically the arrangement was of great use. There were no idlers." Further on he comments:—

"The advantages of the labour notes were soon evident in the saving of members. They had no anxiety as to employment, wages, or the price of provisions. Each could partake of as much vegetable food as he or she could desire. The expenses of the children from infancy, for food or education, were provided for out of the common fund.

"The object should be to obtain a rule of justice, if we seek the law of righteousness. This can only be fully realised in that equality arising out of a community of property where the labour of one member is valued at the same rate as that of another member, and labour is exchanged for labour. It was not possible to attain to this condition of equality at Ralahine, but we made such arrangements as would impart a feeling of security, fairness and justice to all. The prices of provisions were fixed and uniform. A labourer was charged one shilling a week for as many vegetables and as much fruit as he chose to consume; milk was a penny per quart; beef and mutton fourpence, and pork two and one-half pence per pound. The married members occupying separate quarters were charged sixpence per week for rent, and twopence for fuel."

In dealing with Ireland no one can afford to ignore the question of the attitude of the clergy; it is therefore interesting to quote the words of an English visitor to Ralahine, a Mr. Finch, who afterwards wrote a series of fourteen letters describing the community, and offered to lay a special report before a Select Committee of the House of Commons upon the subject. He says:—

"The only religion taught by the society was the unceasing practice of promoting the happiness of every man, woman, and child to the utmost extent in their power. Hence the Bible was not used as a school-book; no sectarian opinions were taught in the schools; no public dispute about religious dogmas or party political questions took place; nor were members allowed to ridicule each other's religion; nor were there any attempts at proselytism. Perfect freedom in the performance of religious duties and religious exercises was guaranteed to all. The teaching of religion was left to ministers of religion and to the parents; but no priest or minister received anything from the funds of the society. Nevertheless, both Protestant and Catholic priests were friendly to the system as soon as they understood it, and one reason was they found these sober, industrious persons had now a little to give them out of their earnings, whereas formerly they had been beggars."

Mr. Craig also states that the members of the community after it had been in operation for some time, were better Catholics than before they began. He had at first considerable difficulty in warding off the attacks of zealous Protestant proselytisers, and his firmness in doing so was one of the chief factors in winning the confidence of the people as well as their support in insisting upon the absolutely non-sectarian character of the teaching.

All disputes between the members were settled by appeals to a general meeting in which all adults of both sexes participated, and from which all judges, lawyers, and other members of the legal fraternity were rigorously excluded.

To those who fear that the institution of common property will be inimical to progress and invention, it must be reassuring to learn that this community of "ignorant" Irish peasants introduced into Ralahine the first reaping machine used in Ireland, and hailed it as a blessing at a time when the gentleman farmers of England were still gravely debating the practicability of the invention. From an address to the agricultural labourers of the County Clare, issued by the community on the occasion of the introduction of this machine, we take the following passages, illustrative of the difference of effect between invention under common ownership and under capitalist ownership:—

"This machine of ours is one of the first machines ever given to the working classes to lighten their labour, and at the same time increase their comforts. It does not benefit any one person among us exclusively, nor throw any individual out of employment. Any kind of machinery used for shortening labour—except used in a co-operative society like ours—must tend to lessen wages, and to deprive working men of employment, and finally either to starve them, force them into some other employment (and then reduce wages in that also) or compel them to emigrate. Now, if the working classes would cordially and peacefully unite to adopt our system, no power or party could prevent their success."

This was published by order of the committee, 21st August, 1833, and when we observe the date we cannot but wonder at the number of things Clare—and the rest of Ireland—has forgotten since.

It must not be supposed that the landlord of the estate on which Ralahine was situated had allowed his enthusiasm for Socialism to run away with his self-interest. On the contrary, when turning over his farms to the community he stipulated for the payment to himself of a very heavy rental in kind. We extract from "Brotherhood," a Christian Socialist Journal published in the north of Ireland in 1891, a statement of the rental, and a very luminous summing up of the lesson of Ralahine, by the editor, Mr. Bruce Wallace, long a hard and unselfish worker for the cause of Socialism in Ireland:—

"The Association was bound to deliver annually, either at Ralahine, Bunratty, Clare, or Limerick, as the landlord might require, free of expense—

Wheat	320 brls.
Barley	240 brls.
Oats	50 brls.
Butter	10 cwt.
Pork	30 cwt.
Beef	70 cwt.

"At the prices then prevailing, this amount of produce would be equivalent to about £900, £700 of rent for the use of natural forces and opportunities, and £200 of interest upon capital. It was thus a pretty stiff tribute that these poor Irish toilers had to pay for the privilege of making a little bit of their native soil fruitful. This tribute was, of course, so much to be deducted from the means of improving their sunken condition. In any future efforts that may be made to profit by the example of Ralahine and to apply again the principles of co-operation in farming, there ought to be the utmost care taken to reduce to a minimum the tribute payable to non-workers, and if possible to get rid of it altogether. If, despite this heavy burden of having to produce a luxurious maintenance for loungers, the condition of the toilers at Ralahine, as we shall see, was marvellously raised by the introduction of the co-operative principle amongst them, how much more satisfactorily would it have been raised had they been free of that depressing dead weight?"

Such is the lesson of Ralahine. Had all the land and buildings belonged to the people, had all other estates in Ireland been conducted on the same principles, and the industries of the country also so organised, had each of them appointed delegates to confer on the business of the country at some common centre as Dublin, the framework and basis of a free Ireland would have been realised. And when Ireland does emerge into complete control of her own destinies she must seek the happiness of her people in the extension on a national basis of the social arrangements of Ralahine, or else be but another social purgatory for her poor—a purgatory where the pangs of the sufferers will be heightened by remembering the delusive promises of political reformers.

In the most crime-ridden county in Ireland this partial experiment in Socialism abolished crime; where the fiercest fight for religious domination had been fought it brought the mildest tolerance; where drunkenness had fed fuel to the darkest passions it established sobriety and gentleness; where poverty and destitution had engendered brutality, midnight marauding, and a contempt for all social bonds, it enthroned security, peace and reverence for justice, and it did this solely by virtue of the influence of the new social conception attendant upon the institution of common property bringing a common interest to all. Where such changes came in the bud, what might we not expect from the flower? If a partial experiment in Socialism, with all the drawbacks of an experiment, will achieve such magnificent results what could we not rightfully look for were all Ireland, all the world, so organised on the basis of common property, and exploitation and mastership forever abolished?

The downfall of the Association came as a result of the iniquitous land laws of Great Britain refusing to recognise the right of such a community to hold a lease or to act as tenants. The landlord, Mr. Vandeleur, lost his fortune in a gambling transaction in Dublin, and fled in disgrace unable to pay his debts. The persons who took over the estate under bankruptcy proceedings refused to recognise the community, insisted upon treating its members as common labourers on the estate, seized upon the buildings and grounds and broke up the Association.

So Ralahine ended. But in the rejuvenated Ireland of the future the achievement of those simple peasants will be dwelt upon with admiration as a great and important landmark in the march of the human race towards its complete social emancipation. Ralahine was an Irish point of interrogation erected amidst the wildernesses of capitalist thought and feudal practice, challenging both in vain for an answer. Other smaller communities were also established in Ireland during the same period. A Lord Wallscourt established a somewhat similar community on his estate in County Galway; *The Quarterly Review* of November, 1819, states that there was then a small community existent nine miles outside Dublin, which held thirty acres, supported a priest and a school of 300 children, had erected buildings, made and sold jaunting cars, and comprised butchers, carpenters and wheelwrights; the Quakers of Dublin established a Co-Operative Woollen Factory, which flourished until it was destroyed by litigation set on foot by dissatisfied members who had been won over to the side of rival capitalists, and a communal home was established and long maintained in Dublin by members of the same religious sect, but without any other motive than that of helping forward the march of social amelioration. We understand that the extensive store of Messrs. Ganly & Sons on Usher's Quay in Dublin was the home of this community, who lived, worked and enjoyed themselves in the spacious halls, and slept in the smaller rooms of what is now the property of a capitalist auctioneer.

BIBLIOGRAPHY

Adams, T. 1987. "The Formation of the Co-operative Party Re-Considered". *International Review of Social History* 32 (1): 48–68.
Backstrom, P.N. 1974. *Christian Socialism and Co-operation in Victorian England*. London: Croom Helm.
Bestor, A.E. 1948. "The Evolution of the Socialist Vocabulary". *Journal of the History of Ideas* 9 (3): 259–302.
Bevir, M. 2011. *The Making of British Socialism*. Princeton: Princeton University Press.
Black, L., and N. Robertson eds. 2009. *Consumerism and the Co-operative Movement in Modern British History: Taking Stock*. Manchester: Manchester University Press.
Christensen, T. 1962. *Origin and History of Christian Socialism, 1848–54*. Aarhus: Brill.
Church, R.A. 1971. "Profit-Sharing and Labour Relations in England in the Nineteenth Century". *International Review of Social History* 16 (1): 2–16.
Cole, G.D.H. 1945. *A Century of Co-operation*. Manchester: Co-operative Union.
———. 1951. *The British Co-operative Movement in a Socialist Society*. London: Allen & Unwin.
d'Alroy Jones, P. 1968. *The Christian Socialist Revival, 1877–1914. Religion, Class, and Social Conscience in Late-Victorian England*. Princeton: Princeton University Press.
Doyle, P. 2019. *Civilising Rural Ireland. The Co-operative Movement, Development and the Nation-State, 1889–1939*. Manchester: Manchester University Press.
Furlough, E. 1991. *Consumer Co-operation in France: The Politics of Consumption, 1834–1930*. Ithaca: Cornell University Press.
Gide, C. 1921. *Consumers' Co-operative Societies*. Manchester: Co-operative Union.
Gurney, P. 1994. "The Middle Class Embrace: Language, Representation and the Contest over Co-operative Forms in Britain, 1860–1914". *Victorian Studies* 37 (2): 253–286.
———. 1996. *Co-operative Culture and the Politics of Consumption in England, 1870–1930*. Manchester: Manchester University Press.
———. 2005. "The Battle of the Consumer in Postwar Britain". *Journal of Modern History* 77 (4): 956–987.
———. 2015. *Wanting and Having: Popular Politics and Liberal Consumerism in England, 1830–70*. Manchester: Manchester University Press.
———. 2015. "'The Curse of the Co-ops': Co-operation, the Mass Press and the Market in Interwar Britain". *English Historical Review* 130 (547): 1479–1512.
———. 2017. *The Making of Co-operative Culture in England*. London: Bloomsbury Academic.

———. 2019. "'Co-operation and Communism Cannot Work Side by Side': Organised Consumers and the Early Cold War in Britain". *Twentieth Century British History* 30 (3): 347–374.

———. 2020. "Redefining 'the woman with the basket': the Women's Co-operative Guild and the Politics of Consumption in Britain during World War Two". *Gender & History* 32 (1): 189–207.

Harding, K. 1988. "'The Co-operative Commonwealth': Ireland, Larkin, and the *Daily Herald*". In *New Views of Co-operation*, edited by Stephen Yeo. London: Routledge.

Harrison, J.F.C. 1969. *Quest for the New Moral World. Robert Owen and the Owenites in Britain and America*. New York: Charles Scribner's Sons.

Hilson, M. 2002. "Consumers and Politics: The Co-operative Movement in Plymouth, 1890–1920". *Labour History Review* 67 (1): 7–27.

———. 2006. *Political Change and the Rise of Labour in Comparative Perspective: Britain and Sweden 1890–1920*. Oslo: Nordic Academic Press.

———. 2018. *The International Co-operative Alliance and the Consumer Co-operative Movement in Northern Europe, c. 1860–1939*. Manchester: Manchester University Press.

Hunt, K. 2000. "Negotiating the Boundaries of the Domestic: British Socialist Women and the Politics of Consumption". *Women's History Review* 9 (2): 389–410.

———. 2010. "The Politics of Food and Women's Neighbourhood Activism in First World War Britain". *International Labor and Working-Class History* 77 (1): 8–26.

Jones, B. 1894. *Co-operative Production*. Oxford: Oxford University Press, 1894.

Kinloch J. & Butt, J. 1981. *History of the Scottish Co-operative Wholesale Society Limited*. Glasgow: Co-operative Wholesale Society.

Lancaster, B. 1987. *Radicalism, Co-operation, and Socialism: Leicester Working-Class Politics, 1860–1906*. Leicester: Leicester University Press.

Llewelyn Davies, M. ed. 1931. *Life As We Have Known It by Co-operative Working Women*. London: Leonard and Virginia Woolf.

Masterman, N.C. 1963. *J. M. Ludlow: The Builder of Christian Socialism*. Cambridge: Cambridge University Press.

Menzani, T. 2007. *La Cooperazione in Emilia-Romagna: dalla Resistenza alla svolta degli anni Settant*. Bologna: Il mulino.

Norman, E. 1987. *The Victorian Christian Socialists*. Cambridge: Cambridge University Press.

Pollard, S. 1960. "Nineteenth-Century Co-operation: From Community Building to Shopkeeping". In *Essays in Labour History, 1886–1923*, edited by Asa Briggs and John Saville. London: Macmillan.

———. 1971. "The Foundation of the Co-operative Party". In *Essays in Labour History, 1886–1923*, edited by Asa Briggs and John Saville. London: Macmillan.

Purvis, M. 1998. "Stocking the Store: Co-operative Retailers in North-East England and Systems of Wholesale Supply, c. 1860–77". *Business History* 44 (4): 55–78.

Raven, C. 1920. *Christian Socialism, 1848–1854*. London: Macmillan.

Redfern, P. 1913. *The Story of the C.W.S. Being the Jubilee History of the Co-operative Wholesale Society Limited, 1863–1913*. Manchester: Co-operative Wholesale Society.

———. 1938. *The New History of the C.W.S.* London: J.M. Dent & Sons.

Rhodes, R. 1995. *The International Co-operative Alliance during War and Peace, 1910–1950*. Geneva: International Co-operative Alliance.

———. 2012. *Empire and Co-operation: How the British Empire used Co-operatives in its Development Strategies, 1900–1970*. Edinburgh: John Donald.

Robertson, N. 2010. *The Co-operative Movement and Communities in Britain, 1914–1960. Minding Their Own Business*. Farnham: Ashgate.

Saville, J. 1954. "The Christian Socialists of 1848". In *Democracy and the Labour Movement*, edited by John Saville. London: Lawrence & Wishart.

Scriven, T. 2017. *Popular Virtue. Continuity and Change in Radical Moral Politics, 1820–70*. Manchester: Manchester University Press.

Scott, G. 1998. *Feminism and the Politics of Working Women: The Women's Co-operative Guild, 1880s to the Second World War*. London: UCL Press.

Taylor, M. 2003. *Ernest Jones, Chartism, and the Romance of Politics, 1819–1869*. Oxford: Oxford University Press.

Thompson, E.P. 1994. "Homage to Tom Maguire". In *Persons and Polemics*. London: Merlin Press.

Thompson, N. 1984. *The People's Science: The Popular Political Economy of Exploitation and Crisis, 1816–34*. Cambridge: Cambridge University Press.

———. 2015. *Social Opulence and Private Restraint: The Consumer in British Socialist Thought since 1800*. Oxford: Oxford University Press.

Trentmann, F. 1997. "Wealth versus Welfare: the British Left between Free Trade and National Political Economy before the First World War". *Historical Research* 171: 70–98.

———. 2008. *Free Trade Nation. Commerce, Consumption, and Civil Society in Modern Britain*. Oxford: Oxford University Press.

Tsuzuki, C. 1991. *Tom Mann, 1856–1941: The Challenges of Labour*. Oxford: Oxford University Press.

Webb, B. 1895. *The Co-operative Movement in Great Britain*. London: Swan Sonnenschein.

Webb, B. & Webb, S. 1921. *The Consumers' Co-operative Movement*. London: Longmans.

Webster, A. 2019. *Co-operation and Globalisation. The British Co-operative Wholesales, the Co-operative Group and the World since 1863*. London: Routledge.

Wilson, J., A. Webster, and R. Vorberg-Rugh. 2013. *Building Co-operation. A Business History of the Co-operative Group, 1863–2013*. Oxford: Oxford University Press.

Yeo. S. 1977. *Religion and Voluntary Organisations in Crisis*. London: Croom Helm.

———. 1977. "A New Life: The Religion of Socialism in Britain, 1883–1896". *History Workshop Journal* 4 (1): 5–56.

Yeo, S. ed. 1998. *New Views of Co-operation*. London: Routledge, 1988.